Shipwreck!

SHIPWRECK!

A Chronicle of Marine Accidents & Disasters in British Columbia

JOHN MacFARLANE

Copyright © 2021 John MacFarlane
First edition, March 2021; second edition, April 2021

All rights reserved. No part of this publication may be reproduced, distributed, or transmitted in any form or by any means, including photocopying, recording, or other electronic or mechanical methods, without the prior written permission of the publisher, except in the case of brief quotations embodied in critical reviews and certain other noncommercial uses permitted by copyright law. For permission requests, contact the publisher at the address below.

admin@nauticapedia.ca

ISBN: 978-0-9936954-8-3 (second edition; softcover)
ISBN: 978-0-9936954-4-5 (first edition; softcover)
ISBN: 978-0-9936954-5-2 (eBook/epub)
ISBN: 978-0-9936954-6-9 (eBook/Kindle)

The information contained in this book is not suitable for any legal purpose. Additional information, such as details of construction or ownership records for these vessels, may be found online in The Nauticapedia at:
http://www.nauticapedia.ca/dbase/Query/dbsubmit_Vessel.php

THE NAUTICAPEDIA

The Nauticapedia project was originally started in 1973 to record data about British Columbia vessels. It can be accessed online at www.nauticapedia.ca. Detailed information on all the vessels mentioned in this book can be accessed through the searchable database. Readers with more information to add to these histories can reach the author through the web page.

Cover and page design and typesetting by Jan Westendorp:
katodesignandphoto.com

Ingram Spark

This book is dedicated to the many seafarers (as crew
or as passengers) who have perished over the years
on dangerous waters and to the men and women
who work tirelessly on behalf of the mariner
to ensure the safety of their lives while at sea.

No writing has ever been written which does justice to the indomitable courage, the reckless daring, the terrific dangers, the unspeakable hardships, the heartbreaking labors, the terrible privations and the sublime heroism which were all in the everyday work of the sailormen. The wealth, progress and civilization they helped to establish was their downfall and today the ships of sail have gradually faded in grim figures of the past to live only in the memory . . .

—Able-Seaman Thomas P MacKenzie
(of the Ship Thermopylae)[1]

Contents

Preface	ix
Introduction	1
A Chronicle of some Marine and Freshwater Wrecks and Disasters	9
Glossary	387
Bibliography	389
Acknowledgements	393
About The Author	395
References	397

PREFACE

It has been estimated that over the centuries there have been somewhere between one million and three million shipwrecks in the world. No one knows for sure and many say the true number will never be known.

Likewise, we will never know anything close to the true number of wrecks that have occurred in British Columbia. Many wrecks have gone unreported or occurred without witnesses to the details. Others have simply disappeared into the environment. Still others have been salvaged—sometimes illegally—removing all tangible evidence.

For the purposes of inclusion in this book, "**wreck**" means a vessel, or part of a vessel, that is sunk, partially sunk, adrift, stranded or grounded, including on the shore; or, equipment, stores, cargo or any other thing that is or was on board a vessel and that is sunk, partially sunk, adrift, stranded or grounded, including on the shore.

This book contains the stories of about 1,850 of the best documented wrecks and marine disasters in British Columbia.

The online database, The Nauticapedia, contains records of more than 4,000 vessels that have sunk, been scuttled, or have met with some disaster during their lifetime. Many of these incidents are poorly documented or involve small vessels which avoided public notice—for example, the many recorded sinkings of small boom tugs are not included in this volume. The constraints of recording the sheer volume of these records make publishing a more complete list impractical. But all the records are available to researchers online in the Nauticapedia Ship Database.

Readers seeking details of construction or ownership records for all these vessels can consult the searchable databases in The Nauticapedia (www.nauticapedia.ca).

INTRODUCTION

Shipwreck. The word immediately suggests images of a boiling sea, a malevolent witness to the desperate battle between iron ships and murky depths, of a battered crew vainly attempting to salvage their ship—and their very lives—from the clutches of Davy Jones' locker.

The Mariposa sinking. (Image from the collection of the Maritime Museum of British Columbia #000103)

Too commonly, however, shipwrecks occur due to human error, a miscalculation in navigation, a poorly stood watch, perhaps even shifting ballast or in the old days, an explosion below decks as the boilers blew a vessel sky-high. There is nothing romantic about the tragic results of a sea-going vessel meeting an untimely end, and in many cases, taking the crew with her and yet, we are fascinated by wrecks.

As a youngster, I was captivated by the sea stories told by my grandfather and great uncles, relating tales of their days serving in ships, going from port to port as routinely as a commuter on a bus, but on occasion, facing peril when their vessel experienced a sudden calamity. These were the bits that caught my ear; these were the moments that fuelled my imagination with scenes of heroism and heartbreak.

My own firsthand experience with a shipwreck was a tame one. In 1957, encountering the rusted bones of the SS Ohio, I eagerly clambered up the bow of the ship, the only portion still visible. It was a steep climb to the top using the remains of the railings as a handhold. Surely, I thought, there will be some tangible piece I could remove to take home as a prize! But after decades of assault from wind and wave, only the very largest fittings remained and even the wooden deck resisted my efforts to pry free a souvenir piece.

Of course, my impulse to take something from the wreck has been felt by countless people, resulting in a negative impact on numerous wrecks around the world. I'm glad now, years later, that there was nothing to take. Souvenir hunting at wreck sites degrades the qualities of the wreck and depletes the archaeological record. The display of recovered ships' wheels and cargoes do little more than inspire a brief flicker of interest and completely overlook that at times, these wreck sites are also graves.

The interest in my family sea stories has not diminished. My appreciation for the preservation of our nautical history has developed from hearing those stories, and it is my aim to blend the history of those ships that worked and played along our coastline with the facts of their fate so that they—and their stories—will not be forgotten.

The *Prince Rupert* ashore on Genn Island with the *Prince George* standing by (Image from the collection of the Maritime Museum of British Columbia #000107)

The term "wreck." collectively encompasses anything without an apparent owner found afloat on, sunk in, or cast ashore by the sea. It is one of those collective nouns which are useful in precisely labelling quantities of specific objects. Correctly used it has a peculiar ring when applied in grammar—as simply the term "wreck."

The British Columbia Heritage Conservation Act[2] states that a "Heritage Wreck" means the remains of a wrecked vessel or aircraft if:

(a) 2 or more years have passed from the date the vessel or aircraft sank, was washed ashore, or crashed,

(b) or the vessel or aircraft has been abandoned by its owner and the government has agreed to accept the abandonment for the purposes of this act.

A vessel can sink for a variety of reasons:
- Foundering caused by storms, strong currents, large waves, and strong winds.
- Destruction by fire and explosions.
- Hitting objects (floating or submerged)
- Running aground (on both charted and uncharted hazards).
- Collision with other vessels or objects.
- Negligence by crews.
- Deliberate scuttling and sinking.
- Malfeasance and criminal activity.
- Vandalism.
- Navigational errors; and,
- Equipment failure (pumps stop, steering gear jams, engines malfunction).

Historically in European countries, the right to wreck belonged to the sovereign of the land and represented a source of income for the crown. In those early days, if no living thing escaped from a wreck the owner was deprived of the interest in the remains of the wreck. Later, representatives were appointed to control wreck and in England−s coastal counties this was done by people appointed as Vice−Admirals of the coast. These Vice−Admirals could keep half the wreck if they turned the other half over to the Crown.

In 1846 the British law was changed preventing the vice-admirals from participating in ownership of wreck which was then to be turned over to receivers in the admiralty. They kept the wreck for twelve months awaiting claims of ownership after which time, if unclaimed, would sell the wreck and credit the income to the consolidated revenue fund of the government.

Many people think that anything washed up on the beach is there for the taking —we have all picked up something or other of interest while beachcombing but who really owns those things? Is it really 'finders keepers, losers weepers'? The simple answer is "no", but it also depends on many other circumstances.

All wreck initially comes under the jurisdiction of the Receiver of Wreck, who takes responsibility for its care and disposal. In some instances, wreck will be removed to a storage area by the Receiver while an attempt is made to locate the rightful owner. If, after one year, the owner does not come forward larger wreck is auctioned off to the highest bidder. The income is divided between the salvor (or finder) and the Consolidated Revenue Fund of the Federal Government. In practice this does not usually generate much income for the government coffers but has been the standard practice for at least a century.

Most wreck tends to be of low commercial value consisting mostly of lost boats, canoes, and kayaks. For an unknown reason British Columbia leads all other Canadian Wreck Districts in these lost and found incidents. The wreck most frequently salvaged is derelict craft followed by old commercial ships, pleasure boats, valuable wreck cargo and, interestingly—aircraft.

The Receiver spends time each week attempting to resolve these cases and to reunite owners with missing craft, usually liaising with local police. In each week this may represent several dozen craft lost and found on the coast. Although the Wreck District crosses the prairies, not surprisingly, few cases of wreck are reported in Alberta or Saskatchewan.

Are you dreaming of finding valuable wreck? The correct procedure after finding a wrecked vessel without an apparent owner is to notify the Receiver of Wreck. In many cases the finder may be invited to take temporary custody of the boat for the Receiver of

Wreck on their own premises. After a year has passed without a valid claim, the boat is often turned over to the finder in lieu of salvage or storage fees.

Large vessels are usually stored on Government property and sold at public auction with a salvage fee paid to the finder from the proceeds of the sale.

To lawfully remove wreck the salvor must first obtain the right of salvage from the lawful owner of the wreck. This may be the insurance company if a claim has been paid to the original owners. Insurance companies sometimes retain interests in wreck for many years but now that anti–pollution laws are taking note of toxic substances escaping from wreck there is also an incentive for owners to quit their claims.

When recovering a derelict vessel, the salvor needs to be sure that it really is derelict, and that the rightful owner is not temporarily absent. Larger vessels which must be licenced or registered may be ineligible for re–registration if the salvor has not ascertained that they are indeed the owners of the vessel or that there is not a lien or prior claim. It is useful to first receive affirmation of the intent to abandon the wreck by a former owner. The Receiver will sometimes sell wreck on condition of "bare power of sail" in case there is an unknown lien on the vessel.

Conservation and Protection of Shipwrecks

The Historic Sites and Monuments Board of Canada (HSMBC)[3] only recognizes shipwrecks which are determined to be of national historic significance. Only a few shipwrecks have been federally designated, all based on their association with major events in the history of Canada—not because they are shipwrecks. For example, the wreck of the Valencia is recognized—but only for its association with the resulting lifesaving trail and modern infrastructure for saving life at sea.

In British Columbia in the 1960s and 1970s typically divers would take away souvenirs from wrecks, denuding them of artifacts and slowly destroying much of the physical record. But a new consciousness grew among the fraternity. Dive Charter Operators began to realize that a looted wreck was not interesting for their clients—and concluded that the wrecks needed to be protected.

In response to the looting of wrecks the Underwater Archaeology Society of BC (UASBC) pressed for protection prior to 1990 and saw protection given protection given to 7 wrecks through Orders-in-Council. The 7 original OIC protected shipwrecks were:

1. *Hera* (designated January 7, 1975)
2. *Zephyr* (designated February 3, 1977)
3. *Iroquois* (designated January 27, 1978)
4. *Ericsson* (designated June 25, 1985)
5. *Capilano* (designated November 6, 1985)
6. *Lord Western* (designated March 16, 1988)
7. *City of Ainsworth* (designated May 2, 1990)

Greater protection was granted in 1996 when the Heritage Conservation Act was promulgated giving specific protection to wrecks and their cargo. Now conservation is taught as an element in dive courses as well as wreck etiquette concerning how to visit a wreck without causing impact. Each wreck has a 'spirit of place' and all divers have a vested interest in their protection.

The Underwater Archaeology Society of BC (UASBC) has deep local knowledge of wreck sites. Some wrecks are more vulnerable than others and the locations are kept confidential. Some are, for example, grave sites and others contain large accumulations of collectables. Others are well known and popular dives and many of these were previously looted.

The archaeological values in wrecks may not be obvious to casual visitors. Some wrecks have special heritage significance. The ships may have been technologically advanced in design at the time of their construction. Or they may have close associations with famous individuals or historic events. We should not forget that many wrecks are ocean grave sites and may contain human remains. This is an added impetus for paying due respect to the wreck remains.

Wreck formation in scuttled vessels has become a focus for research by scientists interested in the development of reefs and the ability of the natural environment to recover from human interference. These studies are enhanced by the monitoring of wrecks and scuttled vessels which form a baseline for marine life colonizing fresh surfaces.

Shipwrecks in British Columbia[4] are open to all divers for diving but are protected under the Heritage Conservation Act. The premise behind this heritage wreck protection is to leave heritage objects intact, so that they can be studied and analyzed in the context of their surroundings. A wreck becomes protected automatically in BC once two or more years have passed since the vessel sank or was washed ashore, or the vessel is abandoned by its owner.

Managing diver impacts is difficult. The wrecks are unattended and, in many cases, out of public view in remote locations. Recreational diving is both a wonderful activity and an economic tourism driver in coastal locations. All dive operators realize that these wrecks are their 'bread and butter'—if they allow looting of wrecks it diminishes the commercial potential for their guiding services. They are an important medium for communicating proper protocols and values to their customers.

Wrecks may cause a hazard to navigation, fishing, and undersea cables. These are frequently salvaged to eliminate the hazards posed.

Commercial salvage and commercial exploitation of wrecks is an ongoing issue. The value of pre-nuclear steel recovered from wrecks has emerged as a new cause of damage by salvors. Steel that has not been exposed to and contaminated by nuclear radiation from nuclear tests is valuable for creating scientific instruments. In some countries large ships are being recovered from the seabed as scrap.

It is often rumored that there are wrecks on the BC coast that hold valuable cargo—even gold. When I worked at the Maritime Museum of British Columbia, in Victoria, there were people who would return regularly to complain that they thought that we were keeping the maps of wrecks with treasure aboard secret. They were convinced that we had secret files that could make people rich.

There is the remote chance that a wreck contains treasure trove. Very few have this potential, and the ones that may still have 'treasure' on board are difficult to find and reach economically and safely.

The illegal scavenging by looters of artifacts from wrecks is an alarming and unfortunate occurrence. The cumulative effect of divers removing even small artifacts slowly results in the stripping away of all the evidence of the wreck. Out of the context of the wreck itself, these items often possess little interest or value and should remain in situ.

The temptation to conceal wreck which has been found by a salvor from legal authorities must be tempered with the knowledge that to do so is to commit acts punishable by fines and in some cases significant jail terms. This can bring the ire of the police, the Coast Guard, Customs, or the Provincial Archaeologist. When material removed from a site is not delivered to the Receiver the finder is plundering wreck rather than beachcombing or salvaging. This wreck material in turn may be seized by the Receiver using the powers available for this purpose.

It is important to remember that many wrecks are strongly associated with the loss of life. Many wrecks were scenes of human tragedy and may be the final resting places of crew members or passengers and it is essential to show proper respect for grave sites.

Through the Oceans Protection Plan, the Government of Canada has passed Bill C-64, the Wrecked, Abandoned or Hazardous Vessels Act[5]. The Act prohibits vessel abandonment, which poses environmental, economic, and safety hazards, and brings the Nairobi International Convention on the Removal of Wrecks, 2007[6] into Canadian Law.

The Act increases owner responsibility and liability for vessels, addresses irresponsible vessel management, and enables the Government of Canada to remove problem vessels.

Lack of compliance could lead to fines of up to $50,000 for individuals and $250,000 for companies or corporations, while regulatory offence prosecution could result in a maximum fine of $1M for individuals and $6M for companies or corporations. The threat of these penalties helps to deter casual damage to wrecks. The Act will enable Canada to be a signatory to the International Marine Organization's Nairobi International Convention on the Removal of Wrecks.

A CHRONICLE OF SOME MARINE AND FRESHWATER WRECKS AND DISASTERS

A.L. Bryant[7] In 1930 she collided with ferry *Sonrisa*. In 1950 she was rammed by a tug at Centre Bay, Gambier Island BC. On October 3, 1950 she was cut in half and sank from a collision with the SS *Lady Cynthia* halfway between Finnistere Island and Whytecliff Point in Queen Charlotte Channel (Howe Sound) BC. The *Lady Cynthia* was proceeding down Howe Sound from Britannia Beach to Snug Cove and the *A.L. Bryant* was crossing from Gambier Island to Whytecliff Point. The *Lady Cynthia* was overtaking the *A.L. Bryant* but failed to keep safely clear and the *A.L. Bryant* failed to keep a proper lookout resulting in the loss of three of the seven men aboard the *A.L. Bryant*. They were crewman FW Longstaff, and two passengers WM Ingram and AP Wrotnowski. The remaining crewmen were rescued by the *Lady Cynthia*. The ticket of the First Mate of the *Lady Cynthia* (Alan Strang) was suspended while the master of the *A.L. Bryant* (JA McDonald) was severely censured by Mr Justice Sidney Smith.

A.P. Knight[8] 153015 On December 22, 1947 this research vessel burned at the Pacific Biological Station wharf at Departure Bay BC. Dr John P Tully stated: "The ship was 59 feet 11 inches long—one inch short of the requirement for steam ship inspection. It had a hot surface stationary diesel engine taken out of an old power plant-1904 vintage-and was started up by lighting blow torches on the top. It had a coal furnace, a gasoline engine for generating electricity, and a gas stove. It lasted thirty years before it blew up and burned."

Abnoba 155093 This vessel, owned by British Pacific Log Transport Co., was once a freighter and then converted for use as a log barge. On April 2, 1929, while being towed by the tug *Lorne*, she foundered in Muchalat Arm, Nootka Sound BC. Later, in 1930, she was broken up.

Aceaway[a] 189275 On February 22, 1980 this fishboat, owned by John G. Flottvik, Fort Langley, BC had a fire in the engine room while in Granville Channel BC and sank near Port Edward BC.

Achates[b,9] 126078 On April 09, 1908 while owned by Greer & Coyle Towing, she suffered a fire at Parsley Island in Howe Sound BC. In 1925 she was converted to oil. On June 08, 1930 while under command of Captain Thorvald Aaroe, she caught fire while stationed next to her boom of logs. The fire started in the engine room and spread quickly to the rest of the vessel. Her crew of two escaped unhurt. The fire damage was so extensive, that she sank after two hours of burning in eight fathoms of water close to Steep Island near Gowland Harbour, Quadra Island. Her steam engine and condenser, originally from HMS *Algerine*, were later salvaged by diver John Pieters.

Active Pass[10] 153375 On August 18, 1939 this fishpacker, owned by Mrs Narutaro Okukawa, Vancouver BC and Yasojiro Nishibata, Steveston BC, was swamped and sank in heavy seas at the mouth of the Fraser River BC near the anchored lightship at Sand Heads. The crew of three were picked up by the passenger steamer *Princess Kathleen*.

Ada[c] 080045 On December 29, 1915 this sealing schooner, owned by Joseph Boscowitz, Victoria BC, sank in Esquimalt Harbour and was a total loss.

Ada L. 193527 On January 22, 1970 this fishboat, owned by Donald JW Palmerley, Ladysmith BC was destroyed by fire.

Ada No. II 156813 On November 6, 1955 this fishboat, owned by John Clausen, Prince Rupert BC burned in Prince Rupert Harbour BC.

---

a   Built as H.C. 310; then Y.C. 14; then Y.F.P. 14; then Aceaway;
b   Built as Steel Head; then Achates;
c   Built as Ariel; then Ada

Adam[11] 122332 On March 29, 1934 this fishboat, owned by Mike Sakich and Ivan Bobic, Vancouver BC caught fire and was severely damaged near Paisley Island just south of Bowen Island BC.

Addison 155091 Circa 1935 this former freighter, converted to use as a log barge, was incorporated into the breakwater at Powell River BC. She sank on site at Powell River in 1943.

Adele[12] The *Adele* was known as the "Flying Dutchman" for her reputation as a seal poacher. On March 8, 1891, this sealing schooner was stranded on North Island in the Queen Charlotte Islands Group. She had been on her way to the sealing grounds in the Bering Sea with a crew of five and a boy. They had been intending to engage First Nations sealers at North Island. After anchoring she was caught by a strong gale and began to drag. More anchors deployed failed to stop her drift and she came close to shore. The tides were some of the highest of the year and she was unable to get back to sea on the next high tide. At low water, her back was discovered to have broken, so the crew stripped the wreck of valuables and took it ashore. Captain Hanson travelled by canoe with area residents to Masset and obtained a sailing boat which he used to evacuate the crew and the valuable gear. He sailed to Port Simpson awaiting the arrival of the *Danube* to return to Victoria. The local First Nations people thinking the vessel was plated in copper burned her for salvage but were disappointed to find little of valuable after the fire.

Admiral Evans[13] 03904 (US) On March 9, 1918 this passenger vessel sank in Hawk Inlet Alaska and was recovered by the Pacific Salvage Co. steamer *Salvor*. On March 19, 1920, under Captain MM Jenson, she was transiting amidst heavy fog in Discovery Passage. The pilot, mistaking a burning stump for a navigational light, altered course and in the process, cut off the stern of the tug *City of Lund*, throwing Captain Henderson and the owner, Oscar Thulin, onto the log boom they were towing. After the incident, while trying to ascertain the damage, the tug ran aground in Duncan Bay. As for the *Admiral Evans*, the 117 passengers aboard were removed and the *Salvor* was called in to refloat the vessel. A hole in her bottom was patched before she could be pumped out. After removing cargo from her forward hold, she was finally refloated two days later and proceeded northward apparently undamaged. The *Admiral Evans* was scrapped in Japan in the 1930s.

Admiral Knight[14] 214059 (US) On July 27, 1919, while bound for Ketchikan from Seattle under Captain HJ Allen, she caught fire off Sand Heads at the mouth of the Fraser River. The fire started in the engine room and in noticeably short time the whole vessel was in flames. A marine fireman, B Neilson, was severely burned. The *Princess Victoria* managed to rescue her crew. Even after she was abandoned, the *Admiral Knight* continued steaming under her own power. Salvors towing the vessel were forced to abandon her near the Cowichan Gap. Eventually the boilers exploded. She later sank at Cable Bay, Galiano Island BC. An unanticipated consequence of the sinking was the fouling of swimming beaches in Vancouver with oil making them temporarily unusable.

Aegean Sea[15] (Liberia) On September 4, 1972 the freighter *Aegean Sea* collided with the freighter *C.E. Dant* (operated by the States Lines) in the Strait of Juan de Fuca. The two freighters remained stuck together with the bow of the *C.E. Dant* in the port side of the *Aegean Sea* that suffered serious damage to her forward holds. They were locked together for 67 hours while salvage operators awaited favourable tides for when the vessels would be in shallower water in case they had to be beached. The *Aegean Sea* had been travelling in ballast to Hong Kong and was afterwards towed to the Yarrows ship yard in Esquimalt BC by the *Sudbury II*.

Agnes C.[16] 152808 On November 16, 1943 this fishboat, owned by James Parsons, foundered 2.5 miles southwest of Price Island in Milbanke Sound BC after she sprang a plank. The crew of six evacuated the ship by dinghy, seeking refuge on Price Island. Three were left behind while the others rowed to Ivory Island in search of help.

The three marooned crewmen were later picked up by the mission boat *Thomas Crosby*.

Agnes W. Dods 134660 On August 08, 1928 this fishboat, owned by Sidney Canning Co., Victoria BC foundered at the southeast end of Aristazabal Island near Hecate Strait. BC.

Alakasla[17] 138297 On September 17, 1930 this cannery tender, owned by HC MacAulay, Vancouver BC burned one mile offshore from the Beechey Fish Trap (one mile east of Secretary Island) BC. She had been returning from the west coast to Vancouver when a fire broke out. To save the ship, Captain Russel ran her onto the beach at Beechey Bay, but she was destroyed. The Captain and the engineer/mate H Forsyth were unharmed.

Alaska[18] On August 30, 1967 this Alaska Steamship Line train ferry was struck broadside in Broughton Strait off Malcolm Island by the freighter *Northland Prince*, northbound from Vancouver to Prince Rupert. Three passengers and a crew member on the *Northland Prince* were injured in the collision. The *Alaska* was transporting railway cars and freight between Seattle and Alaska.

Alaska Prince[a,19] 141710 On January 11, 1960 this vessel, owned by British Columbia Steamships Co. Ltd., Vancouver BC, was hit by the *Princess Elaine*, in thick fog off Prospect Point. The *Alaska Prince* was severely damaged in the incident and was beached a little to the east of the Capilano River to prevent her from sinking.

Alaskan[b] 130445 This gas schooner, owned by British Columbia Coast Freight Co., Vancouver BC foundered in heavy weather on January 02, 1923 and was wrecked on the rocks 1.5 miles off Pachena Point at the end of Mabens Beach. She had been travelling from Barkley Sound to Victoria with a cargo of 'box shooks'. Eleven lives were lost.

---

a   Built as Border Prince; then Chilkoot; then Alaska Prince
b   Built as Mischief; then Alaskan

Albatross[20] 116929 She was built as a torpedo boat for the Royal Navy based at Esquimalt BC. After de-commissioning she was converted to a tug by Captain JA Cates. On August 16, 1908 she dragged her anchor under heavy winds at English Bay, Vancouver BC and was stranded with holes in her hull. Joe Fortes rowed out to the ship and carried the engineer ashore. The incoming tide filled her until only her funnel was left showing above the high water. She was eventually towed off for repairs.

Albatross[21] On September 17, 1937 this American fishboat, while under command of Captain John Satra, was stranded on Midge Reef in Seaforth Channel BC. During the stranding, nine members of the crew were removed by the passenger vessel *Northwestern* while the American halibut schooner *Electra* stood by. The *Albatross* had been herring fishing in southwestern Alaska waters.

Alberdyce[22] 126886 In May 1937 this tug sank in 75 feet of water near Cape Mudge BC. She was salvaged by the *Cherrypicker*, owned by West Coast Salvage & Construction Co. Ltd., and beached for temporary patching. She was towed to Vancouver for repairs.

Albern 328292 On May 24, 2016 this tug owned by Jones Marine Group Ltd., Chemainus BC sank off the Gabriola Bluffs BC.

Alberni 126072 On March 27, 1910 this tug was in a collision with the steamer *Canada* off Point Atkinson BC while under command of Captain W Best. On March 07, 1912 she collided with a rock in Pender Harbour BC under Captain A Lyttle. The crew and Captain AL Bissett were all saved. On March 14, 1915 she was owned by Vancouver Dredging & Salvage Co., Vancouver BC and while under command of Captain EM McMullen she was working with the salvage barge *Skookum II* at the western entrance to Active Pass to free the *Sea Lion* stranded on a reef with a cable to the shore. The *Alberni* was swept over the cable by the current and she capsized. She sank slowly and had floated into the center of the pass before she sank.

Albert K.[23] 156818 On September 7, 1936 this troller fishboat was destroyed by fire 200 yards past the Warrior Rocks, in Hecate Strait BC. Mr & Mrs John Salden were forced to evacuate in the boat's dinghy and spent twelve hours on the open sea. Mr Salden started to row to shore when a storm overtook them and forced Mrs Salden to lay on the bottom of the boat for safety. They reached Squadaree, nine miles from where they had lost their boat at midnight. They were brought to Prince Rupert in a fishboat operated by John Kildal.

Alberta[a] Following a grounding in 1893 at Ainsworth BC she was sold for salvage and rebuilt at Kaslo BC. She was renamed as the *Alberta* and registered in Canada #103296. She was laid up in 1902. She grounded in 1905 at the dock in Kaslo. She was laid up at Mirror Lake. Her hull was sold to Gus Matthew at Riondel and her machinery was sold to the Columbia & Okanagan Steamboat Co. for the American steamer *Columbia*. Her engines were built in 1888 for the steamer *Crescent* on Flathead Lake ID. She worked from Bonners Ferry to Kaslo and Nelson. The wreck was sold for $350 to George Alexander and rebuilt as the *Alberta*. In 1895 she worked on the Bonners Ferry to Kaslo and Nelson run. After the steamer *Kaslo* appeared she was relegated to relief steamer. She was laid up in Kaslo after 1901 and sank at the dock in Kaslo in 1895 was raised and dismantled on the ways her machinery going to the *Columbia* (202431). Her hull became a houseboat at Galena Bay where, as a derelict she was destroyed by fire in 1920.

Albion 107716 On September 9, 1910 this tug owned by The Pacific Towing & Lighterage Co. Ltd., Victoria BC was stranded at Black Point, Scow Bay in Malaspina Strait BC.

Alcatraz[24] (US) On June 21, 1858, while under command of Captain H Taylor, she capsized while rounding Macaulay Point, heading for Victoria harbour, with the loss of 14 lives all from California.

---

a Built as State of Idaho; then Alberta

Alco[25] 151180 On March 28, 1959 while chartered to the Burton Mining Co., she burned at Newquiat Inlet, 20 miles from Tofino, Vancouver Island BC. The fire broke out in the Crofton, berthed alongside, and spread to the *Alco*.

Aleli 133887 On September 17, 1924 this tug owned by the Department of Lands & Forests, Victoria BC for the British Columbia Forest Service burned in Howe Island BC.

Alena B.[26] On July 7, 1972 this fishboat owned by the Francis Millerd Co., Vancouver BC sank off Point Atkinson BC. Four crewmen were rescued before she sank by the yacht *Hayboy*. She had hit a submerged object en route from Rivers Inlet to Vancouver BC and went down with a cargo of fish.

Aleutian Island 154643 In 1941 this seiner was seized from her owner, Takutaro Tanaka, Vancouver BC, by the Canadian Government. In 1942 her ownership was transferred to His Majesty the King. On September 17, 1961 she foundered.

Aleutian Queen[27] 179090 On November 10, 1965 this fishboat owned by Aleutian Fish Co. Ltd., Vancouver BC was in a collision and sank in Queen Charlotte Sound BC near Scott Island, about 12 miles WNW of Frederiksen Point VI.

Alexa Sea[28] (US) Zachary Dunn stated that "she was an American troller that hit the beach around Denny Island while on its way north to Alaska, almost sank. She was refloated and towed to Shearwater and repaired. The owner abandoned it here about 7 or 8 years ago. I bought it as a scrap boat for parts."

Alexandra (Vancouver Island Registry) In 1864 this passenger freight vessel was in service between Victoria and the Fraser River. Zachary Dunn stated that "she was an American troller that hit the beach around Denny Island while on its way north to Alaska, almost sank. She was refloated and towed to Shearwater and repaired. The owner abandoned it here about 7 or 8 years ago. I bought it as a scrap boat for parts." She collided with and sank the *Fidelator* off Clover Point, Victoria BC.

Algerine 141145 In 1917 HMS *Algerine* was loaned to the Royal Canadian Navy to serve as a depot ship at Esquimalt. She was sold on April 11, 1919 for use as a salvage tug. She was wrecked on October 13, 1923 in Principe Channel, BC when she ran aground on Brodie Rock. She was salvaged and then towed to Victoria where she was sold for scrap in January 1924. Her mast still stands on Bastion Square in Victoria BC.

Algie 153350 This fishpacker is said to have been engaged in rum running 1929–1934. She formed part of the pre-war Fishermen's Reserve Fleet and was briefly mobilized in 1939. On October 15, 1942 she ran aground on a sandbar at the mouth of the Fraser River. She was refloated on the high tide after half her cargo of salmon was unloaded into scows. On January 19, 1943 while owned by British Columbia Packers Ltd., Vancouver BC she was rammed by the fishpacker *Koprino*, five miles from the Ballenas Islands with Captain Backwell in command. At first, the crew thought the collision was a glancing blow, but she began to fill with water. The *Koprino* took on the crew and the *Algie* sank.

Alice[29] 112244 On February 09, 1907 this tug was swamped and foundered in Knight Inlet BC. The crew of the little vessel had been timber cruising when an awfully bad storm came up. They sought Protection Point but could not approach the shore and anchored. They were so worried the made for the shore in a small dinghy and were thrown up on the beach. In the morning there was no sign of their vessel.

Alice C. 138122 In 1928 this tug owned by Gosse Packing Co. Ltd., Vancouver BC was reported to have been wrecked in Deer Pass and was a total loss.

Aliford[a,30] 130617 On September 26, 1917 about one-half mile from the NE point of Nelson Island this tug owned by JJ Holmes & Herb Harris, Vancouver BC. She caught fire and exploded. It was thought that it started with spontaneous combustion in the coal and an explosion started a fire. Captain Holmes and his four crew members escaped when she sank only because the lifeboat was on the rail at the time of the mishap. At the time she was towing logs from the Beaver Lumber Co. to Anacortes WA.

Alki[31] (US) On August 5, 1886 this US steamer ran on the rocks at Belle Chain Reef five miles east of Plumper Pass. Captain Blackburn and his crew evacuated in small boats and made for Victoria. They were intercepted by the steamer *Manzanita* which rescued them landing them as Cadboro Bay. The *Alki* was in the coal trade between the Nanaimo collieries of the Vancouver Coal Co. and San Francisco.

All Star 176243 On May 8, 1973 this halibut fishboat owned by John MW Haffenden, Vancouver BC was in a collision with the *Joan W. II* off Cape Roger Curtis BC.

Allaverdy[b] 171806 She formed part of the pre-war Fishermen's Reserve fleet. She was mobilized September 15, 1939 and was commissioned into the Royal Canadian Navy Fisherman's Reserve as HMCS *Allaverdy*. She was employed as an Examination Vessel based at York Island BC and at Vancouver BC. In 2013 she was owned by Ky Fan Phan and Phuong Thi Phan when she sank on February 6, 2013 off Point Grey near the mouth of the Fraser River. Both men onboard were rescued from the water.

Aloha In 1906 this B-class sloop was found drifting near Deep Cove and without a crew, her two owners (brothers) were presumed drowned. In 1909 she was destroyed by the fire which razed the Stanley Park yacht clubhouse in December of that year.

---

a   Built as Juneau; then F.H. Folsom; then Aliford
b   Built as Allaverdy; then HMCS Allaverdy; then Allaverdy

Alola[a,32] 157240 On April 20, 1966 this cabin cruiser, owned by Arthur E Simpson, exploded, and was destroyed by fire in Coal Harbour, Vancouver BC and was declared a total loss. The boat was approaching the Royal Vancouver Yacht Club when she exploded, apparently shortly after refueling.

Alpha (Vancouver Island Register) This colonial era schooner is said to have been the first vessel built at Nanaimo. On November 27, 1868 she was wrecked while sailing from Victoria to Honolulu Hawaii with a load of lumber when she was driven ashore on Flores Island.

Alpha[33] 045956 In 1898 this freighter was sent to Canada's west coast for the gold rush shipping service. On December 15, 1900, this freighter was wrecked on Yellow Island (later Chrome Island). Nine lives were lost. Her anchor was salvaged and displayed in 1973 at the Denman Island Ferry landing. Some of her wreck was salvaged by diver John Pieters.

Alpha[34] On September 23, 1891 this sidewheeler, owned by AW Thompson, New Westminster BC, was destroyed by fire in False Creek, Vancouver BC. In the morning, while under the command of Captain McLenean, she entered False Creek under full power while on fire. Her crew jumped overboard to save themselves and the vessel burned in the inlet. As the tide turned, she re-floated and drifted out to sea. Captain McLenean rowed after her and succeeded in getting a line on board, towing her to the beach between the English Bay logging camp and Jericho. She sank and broke in two, with her machinery scattered. She was reported as a re-built vessel from the hull of the Richmond, and her machinery, which had been burned in Victoria in 1887.

Alpha[35] 100500 On March 20, 1916 this fisheries tender under Captain SW Miller (and a crew of six others) was swamped and sank off Rachel Island and was a total loss. She was travelling enroute

---

a   Built as Madeline Vee; then Algoa; then Alola

from Bellingham to Alaska and between Lucy Island and Kennahan Island she was struck by a heavy sea and turned over, the ship going down in five minutes. Captain Miller and John Christianson caught hold of a small boat, but the others had already disappeared. The small boat overturned with only Christianson clinging to it. It took about 4 hours, but he made his way toward Metlakatla landing on a small island. He emptied the boat, found a piece of wood to act as an improvised paddle and made his way to Metlaktala.

Amaryllis[a] 153219 In 1918 she served as a sub-chaser in the US Navy. During the Second World War she served as a patrol vessel at Yorke Island 1942. On February 7, 1948 while owned by Armour Towing & Salvage Co., Vancouver BC she foundered 2.5 miles off Scarlett Point in Queen Charlotte Strait with the loss of three lives.

Amakusa Island[36] 9303900 (IMO) The Transportation Safety Board of Canada reports that "On 14 July 2014, at 2209 Pacific Daylight Time, the bulk carrier *Amakusa Island* ran aground on a charted shoal while approaching an anchorage located approximately 11 nautical miles southwest of Prince Rupert, British Columbia. The vessel was under the conduct of a pilot at the time. The vessel refloated on the rising tide approximately 4 hours after the grounding. There were no injuries or pollution, but the vessel sustained damage to its hull."

Amazon (The) 189964 On August 4, 1975 this fishboat owned by George Komoto (MO), Ucluelet BC left harbour and was reported as missing and presumed lost off Winter Harbour BC with the loss of one life.

American Girl[37] (US) In November 1899 this schooner was lost on the west coast of Vancouver Island. She had left San Francisco bound for Port Gamble on October 8th, 1889 but is thought to have been dismasted off Cape Flattery after losing all her sails in a series of southeast gales. She was sighted as a drifting derelict south of Graham Island.

---

a   Built as Amaryllis; then RCAF M.9 Amaryllis; then Amaryllis

Amethyst[38,39] (US) This San Francisco schooner was found floating upside down in Middle Channel Barkley Sound in April 1902. She was from San Francisco and was abandoned in waterlogged condition after being wrecked off the California coast. On February 18th, the schooner *Gem* reported wreckage—the after house, a companionway, and a mast. She had been in the lumber trade to California and Oregon ports. She drifted hundreds of miles north until her discovery. Her hull had been entered from the bottom through a hole chopped by unknown persons after her arrival in BC waters. It was presumed that her crew were all lost. After being looted she was salvaged and later put back into service.

HMS Amphion in the naval dry dock at H.M. Dockyard Esquimalt for repairs (Image from the collection of the Maritime Museum of British Columbia #000096)

Amphion (HMS) In Victoria's Beacon Hill Park there is an odd marine relic which causes puzzlement when people see it. The commemorative plaque tells a bit of the story. "Crumpled Iron Has A History: On November 6, 1889, Lord Stanley, Governor General of Canada, embarked for Vancouver following a visit to Victoria. HMS Amphion carried the Vice–Regal party and while travelling in fog, struck a sunken reef off Killett (sic) Bluff, Henry Island. The ship was extremely damaged but returned safely to Esquimalt. The bilge keel or rolling chock was crumpled like a concertina as exhibited here." Lord Stanley is better known to Canadians as the original donor of the Stanley Cup. Curiously, there is a typographical error in the spelling of Kellett Bluff. Captain E Gray Hulton RN was in command at the time and no pilot was embarked. There was a very dense fog over the entire Strait. Just past Plumper Pass Light in Haro Strait, hidden in the fog, was Kellet Bluff where the rocks lay underwater extending out from the shore. When the ship struck them both the inner and outer hulls were pierced causing water to flow into the ship, flooding four compartments. She came to anchor in Constance Cove and was drydocked in Esquimalt. Lord Stanley was driven to the Driard Hotel in Victoria. Despite heavy pumping the ship developed a 22° list to starboard. She entered the dry dock the next day and repairs were undertaken. The crumpled bilge keel was recovered and eventually found its way to Beacon Hill Park.

The remains of the crumpled iron keel of **HMS Amphion** in Beacon Hill Park, Victoria BC (Photograph from the Robert Hanna collection.)

Anchorite[a] 138299 In June 1930 she was owned by Clarke Gibson as a seiner and fishpacker in the summer and as a logging tug in the winter. She was stranded and broke up at the southeast end of Flores Island (VI) BC.

Anderina 130879 On February 25, 1930 this tug owned by Michael Pappas, Vancouver BC foundered and was stranded off Texada Island BC.

Andrada[40] (UK) This four-masted schooner sailed November 12th from Santa Rosalia CA for Portland OR. In December 1900 she took on an American pilot (Captain Cordiner) at the Columbia River bar and then disappeared. She had foundered while bound from the

---

a Built as Evelyn; then Anchorite

Fraser River canneries to Liverpool England with a cargo of salmon. The tug went out in search of the overturned hull reported by the Chilean bark *Temuco*. Last seen off the entrance to the Columbia River, the wreckage turned up on the west coast of Vancouver Island. She was found on her beam ends several miles offshore, her name board and wreckage found on shore in Clayoquot Sound. It was reported that 30 lives lost. One theory advanced at the time was that she was in a collision with the *Ardnamurchan* which disappeared about the same time after sailing from the Fraser River with a cargo of salmon.

Angerona 096993 In 1895–1901 she was owned by Charles W. Busk, Balfour BC for service on Kootenay Lake. In 1901 she was owned by the Balfour Steam Navigation Co., Balfour BC. After the White Grouse boom ended in 1897, she sat at the wharf in Nelson, became waterlogged and foundered in 1900.

Anglo-Canadian II[41] 176499 The tug *Anglo-Canadian II*, owned by Nootka Marine Construction Ltd., Gold River BC, sank close to Canal Island at the convergence of Eliza Passage and Tlupana Inlet in Nootka Sound on January 02, 1984 as she was towing a Nootka Marine Construction Ltd. wooden pile-driver heading for Tahsis.

Ankle Deep[a] 121755 On June 19, 1929 this tug owned by John S & George H Shannon, Vancouver BC burned in English Bay, Burrard Inlet.

Ann Bernard (US) On February 26, 1862 while en route from San Francisco to Sooke she was wrecked on the coast of Vancouver Island with the loss of two lives.

Anna B[b] 193790 A 1960 court decision held the vessel's master liable for the 1957 sinking of a Marwell Equipment Ltd dredge because of a collision in the Fraser River. This vessel was purchased by Oran

---

a Built as Ethola; then Ankle Deep
b Built as USS APc-22; then Stormbird; then La Dene; then Anna B

Diamond of California in 1962 for a cruise to Alaska and renamed as the *Anna B*. She foundered on June 6, 1963 at False Pass AK USA.

Anna J.[42] 215226 (US) On September 4, 1935 this Seattle-based halibut schooner was in collision with the passenger ship *Prince Rupert* in Seymour Narrows BC. The *Prince Rupert* hit the stern of the schooner in early morning darkness and did not stop. The *Anna J.* was southbound to Seattle at the time of the incident. Captain Edward Lawler ran the vessel ashore where she sank with 17,000 pounds of halibut in her hold.

Anna O.[43] 141829 On August 27, 1937 this fishboat, under command of Captain James Fiddler Jr, was in collision with the *Bonilla* 14 miles east southeast from Point Upwood, Texada Island, Georgia Strait. The incident occurred at midnight, while carrying a cargo of salmon. After she was hit the *Anna O.* capsized, rolled over and sank. Captain W McMullen of the *Bonilla* acted swiftly to rescue the crew of the sunk ship.

Anna V. Fagan[a,44] 159140 Rosalind Hildred says that "Bruce Hildred, his brother Rolf, father Phil and some friends drove an old bus to Carbonear, Newfoundland to retrieve the 62' x 9' Grand Banks four dory schooner *Diane Gail* (then registered as the *Anna V Fagan*) which Bruce had bought from Max Powell of Carbonear. She was 52 tons, then with two 6-cylinder Acadia engines. She was built in the 1930s, reportedly one of the last of the fishing schooners built for sail. In 1977 they brought her to British Columbia via the Panama Canal (stopping in Bermuda to repair storm damage) and arrived in Ganges in September with a load of soapstone and agates. Bruce fished prawns, long lined for dogfish research for the Nanaimo Biological Station, and various other pursuits until she sank at the Vesuvius (Saltspring Island) dock in 1980, due to hitting a big bolt sticking out of a piling, in a storm with super high tide."

---

a   Built as *Diane Gail*; then *Anna V. Fagan*

Annapolis (HMCS)[45] On January 17, 2015 this RCN destroyer was sunk as an artificial reef in Halkett Bay, Gambier Island BC. The Annapolis lies on the bottom perfectly upright. Bottom depths at low tide range from 105 ft at the bow to 98 ft at the stern.

Annie Sophia[a] 126630 On January 03, 1932 this tug while owned by Oscar Orpana, Vancouver BC suffered an explosion near the northern island in the Ragged Islands group in Malaspina Strait BC and was destroyed by fire off the Copeland Islands BC.

Annie St. Leon 137951 On April 14, 1924 this tug owned by John L Hunt & GH Harwood, Vancouver BC was destroyed by fire in the North Arm of Burrard Inlet BC. At the time of the incident she had been towing twelve sections of booms.

Annie Tuck[46] 141545 Drew Clarke reports that "This old fishpacker now (in 2018) a wreck on the beach up in the jungles east of Alert Bay was built in 1919 with no butt joints in her hull. She had one-piece planking from stem to stern." Her interior was rosewood on yellow cedar frames. Exterior was painted fir plywood. Originally constructed as a two-masted schooner with an elliptical stern, carvel planking, five bulkheads. She was oak-ribbed and sheathed in gumwood and the bow was iron plated.

The *Annie Tuck* transiting the mouth of the Nitinat River into the Strait of Juan de Fuca. (Image from the MacFarlane Family collection)

Anscomb 177385 In January of 2004 this passenger and car ferry owned by The Ministry of Transportation, Victoria BC sank to the bottom of Kootenay Lake after a cold snap in the weather caused pipes on board to burst allowing lake water to rapidly fill the vessel.

---

a   Built as R.J. Skinner; then Annie Sophia

Anthony J.[a] 155260 On March 26, 1982 this fishboat owned by John A Secord Sr, Surrey BC capsized and sank while passing through Seymour Narrows.

Anyox[b] 150273 In 1917 as Anyox she was in service carrying copper concentrates on Pacific Coast owned by the Coastwise Steam Ship & Barge Co. Ltd., Vancouver BC. On August 26, 1925 she rammed the tug *Radius* while she was towing a gravel scow during a severe rainstorm and sunk off Prospect Point. In 1933 she was chartered as an Alaskan trading schooner by the Hudson's Bay Company to supply Point Barrow AK, damaged by ice. She was later destroyed by fire off the Wangpoo River in China and declared a total loss.

Arbory 141543 On May 3, 1959 this halibut fishboat owned by Mrs Clara Nilsen, Vancouver BC was stranded in Principe Channel BC.

Arbutus[c,47] 153214 On September 13, 1959 she developed engine trouble and was carried by the winds and currents onto rocks at Trial Island in Juan de Fuca Strait. The lightkeeper, Douglas Franklin and his assistant rowed a dory out from the island and rescued John Biddle. The boat was pulled off by the tug *Trooper*, but she had suffered damage to the hull and quickly sank in deep water.

Archer[48] On March 16, 1894 this bark sailed from Victoria BC in ballast for Oregon. She encountered a gale off Cape Flattery. Her ballast shifted and she went on her beam end drowning three crew members. The remaining crew departed in a ship's boat and were picked up by the ship *John C. Porter*. Weeks later the wreckage was found by the *Maude* and towed into Clayoquot Sound. There she was righted, by the tug *Pioneer* towed her to Victoria where she was repaired and sold.

---

a   Built as Jessie Island No. 10; then Anthony J.
b   Built as Anyox; then Salvage Queen; then Sheng Li
c   Built as Anna E.; then Arbutus

Arctic Fox II 371702/OR22FBS This charismatic vessel was often seen at the Gibsons Government Wharf where she was rigged as a long-liner or prawn/shrimp boat. This vessel was featured in the film Free Willy 3 in 1997. On August 11, 2020, this fishing vessel registered in Oregon, foundered and sank west of Ucluelet BC in heavy weather. There was a crew of three, two of whom were deceased, and the bodies were recovered. The survivor was rescued by a US Coast Guard helicopter.

Arctic Taglu[49] 368381 The Transportation Safety Board of Canada states that "On the morning of October 31, 1995, the tug *Arctic Taglu*, pushing the loaded barge Link 100, was inbound from Swartz Bay, BC, to her berth in the Fraser River. The wooden fishing vessel *Roxana Glen*, participating in the salmon fishery opening, was engaged in repositioning the nets off Steveston Island, BC in daylight and in calm and clear weather, the Link 100 and the *Roxana Glen* were involved in a collision. The lone operator of the fishing vessel, who was thrown overboard, subsequently was rescued by another fishing vessel. He suffered minor injuries. The *Roxana Glen* was a constructive total loss; the Link 100 sustained superficial damage."

Argo No. 2 (US) On June 21, 1898 this passenger freight vessel owned by the Cleveland-Alaska Gold Mining & Milling Co. was traveling in company with the *Argo No. 1* when she broke away and foundered in Dixon Entrance.

Argosy[50] 225267 (US) On July 19, 1930 this US power cruiser owned by Dr Rich, Tacoma WA was stranded near Cape Mudge BC. She was returning south after having been a contestant in the Seattle-Prince Rupert Race.

Ariadne[51] 116454 On January 16, 1929 this vessel owned by Frank & Harry Gagne, Courtenay BC burned at Quathiaski Cove off Quadra Island BC.

Ariston 156479 On July 19, 1941 while owned by Robert HF Pollock, Salt Spring Island BC she was stranded in Belize Inlet BC.

Armentieres (HMCS) In the winter months of each year the Royal Canadian Navy stationed a small warship at Bamfield. This vessel was intended to work with the lifeboat to assist vessels in distress. Lieutenant CD Donald, a very prominent name in west coast history, was in command and carried out extensive patrols of the coast. On one such patrol, September 2nd, 1925, he was passing between Refuge Island and Bazett Island in Pipestone Inlet relying on a chart drawn by Captain GH Richards RN in 1861. An uncharted rock was hit by the hull despite it being high tide. The ship passed part way over the rock before contact was made immobilizing the vessel with the bow afloat. As the tide started to fall Lieutenant Donald ordered ropes and cables to be made fast to trees on the shore tin an attempt to prevent the ship from sinking by the bow. The strain was too great, and the cables all broke or tore out the trees from the ground. The vessel sank despite the efforts and on the rising tide she was submerged. Her sister ship, HMCS *Thiepval* and the salvage tug *Salvage King* carried out a successful recovery operation. In 1978 she was engaged in carrying tourists from St Maarten to St Barts. In 1980 she was engaged in the drug trade. She was lost somewhere in South America.

The tug *Salvage King* attending the wreck of *HMCS Armentieres*
(Image from the collection of the Maritime Museum of British Columbia)

Arthur B.[52] 126735 On March 23, 1910 this freighter, owned by Hamilton Weeks, Vancouver BC, foundered off the *Sandheads Lightship* at the mouth of the Fraser River BC. She appeared to have been having engine problems at the time of the incident. Five members of the crew were lost in her sinking. The crew of the lightship heard the cries of the drowning men, but the tidal rip was so fierce that they could not launch their boat to go in assistance.

Asbjurg 159038 On May 27, 1976 this fishboat owned by Hjalmar PK Pedersen (MO), Vancouver BC foundered and sank seven miles east of Clarke Pt (Brooks Peninsula VI) BC. She was beached and declared a constructive total loss with one life lost.

Athero[a] 133707 On September 05, 1927 this power cruiser yacht exploded off the Barnett Oil Tank, near Port Moody BC. One person was killed. As a wreck she was salvaged and rebuilt by John Willard, Vancouver BC.

Atlantic Harvester I[b,53] 807736 Early on October 18, 2014, this landing craft capsized and sank just north of Campbell River, BC. One crew member, Kyle Benoit, was rescued by a zodiac launched from a passing Alaska State Ferry vessel; despite extensive search, two others were missing/presumed dead: Captain Barry Sewid and Mike Kelly

Audrey B.[c,54] 154793 This vessel was built as a rum runner in Nova Scotia and operated on the Pacific Coast after being seized and released after posting bond after landing illegal alcohol off New York at Christmas 1930. Although apparently not successful as a trader she did heroic work in the arctic as a charter freighter for the Hudson's Bay Company in 1936, 1937 and 1938 when their vessels were damaged, sank or could not operate because of extreme ice conditions.

---

a   Built as Sutil; then Athero
b   Built as Marine Link II; then Atlantic Harvester I
c   Built as Audrey B.; then Tarfran; then Audrey B.

After return to Vancouver in 1939 she was converted to a fish packer and operated as such for Nelson Brothers from 194–1962. She was then sold and became a floating home to the Tarris family and others in North Vancouver. After been sold again she was taken to the Fraser River in the early 1980s where she blew-up, burned and sank in the Fraser River just east of Tilbury Island. She was rumored to have been used as a meth lab.

The freighter *Audrey B*. (Photo with permission from the Fisherman Publishing Society Collection-UBC. B1532/458/1)

Avro[a] 141433 On January 22, 1921 this fishing vessel collided with the tug *Fearless* in the North Arm of the Fraser River. On September 19, 1924 she burned at Village Island BC. In 1931 as the *Avro* she was registered as a recovered wreck.

Azena[55] 170766 On December 4, 1940 this troller fishboat owned by Stanley Burke, Vancouver BC foundered at sea between Bamfield and Tofino BC. Her crew were presumed dead: William and Bert Hendricksen and Charles F Bugge (a clam buyer from Seattle WA). Clam boxes washed up on Lennard Island and her small flat-bottomed dinghy was found on the beach at Hequiat Village.

Azores 141712 On December 5, 1930 while owned by John Demitris, Vancouver BC she was destroyed by fire one mile south of Gabriola Pass BC.

Azores II 140910 On October 28, 1924 while owned by Cassimir Edwards, Prince Rupert BC she was destroyed by fire at Low Isle, off the Queen Charlotte Islands BC.

---

a   Built as Mamook; then Vivro; then Avro

Azuma[56] 134098 On December 7, 1927, this fishpacker, burned at Paisly Island in Howe Sound BC. On October 7, 1928, while under charter to the Canadian Fishing Co. Ltd., she foundered in a gale off in early morning off Pender Harbour BC while en route to Vancouver from Toba Inlet. The two crew members escaped safely.

B. & M.[57] 134077 On December 11, 1928 while loaded with a cargo logging chains and stumping powder, this tug, owned by the M.R. Cliff Tugboat Co. Ltd., Vancouver BC, burned to the waterline near the Traill Islands. The vessel's master perished in the fire.

B.C. Adventure[58] 320337 On March 6, 1979 this fishboat owned by North Shore Shipping Services (B.C.) Ltd., Burnaby BC foundered at the entrance to Nootka Sound BC.

B.C. Bird 150876 On March 12, 1977 this fishboat owned by William A Block, Vancouver BC sank 7 miles west of Bowen Island BC.

B.C. Boy 131032 On March 7, 1938 this tug, owned by Pacific (Coyle) Navigation Co. Ltd., Vancouver BC, was in a collision with the *Canuck* in the steamer channel in Discovery Pass opposite the mouth of the Campbell River BC.

B.C. Clipper[59] 170421 This fishing vessel is thought by some sources to have served as an auxiliary vessel in the Royal Canadian Navy during the Second World War. On August 11, 1969 the Canadian halibut vessel *B. C. Clipper*, owned by Stansor Fishing Co. Ltd., Vancouver BC, suffered an explosion of liquefied gas off Kodiak. Toxic fumes made it impossible to fight the resulting fire and the five survivors abandoned ship. They were forced to remain in the frigid water for four hours when their life raft inflated upside down, but all were rescued by the fishboat *Peggy Jo*. The B. C. Clipper had delivered 100,000 pounds of halibut to Kodiak and was outward bound for the fishing banks when the accident occurred. Winston Tucker of Vancouver BC, his son Clarence Tucker and Charles Stanley of New Westminster BC were lost. Five others survived on an overturned life raft until rescued by the fishing vessel *Peggy Jo*. The vessel sank two miles southeast of Two Headed Island southwest of Kodiak AK.

B.C. Lady[a] 171799 On April 18, 1976 this seiner owned by Babcock Fisheries Ltd., Vancouver BC had an engine room fire and burned on the south side of the Malaspina Peninsula at Ragged Island BC.

B.C. Lass[60] 194639 On September 26, 1956 this fishboat exploded and burned at the mouth of Return Channel near Bella Bella BC.

B.C. Producer[61] 178194 On March 25, 1975 this dragger/halibut boat capsized in the vicinity of Cox Island off Cape Scott with the loss of four crew members. Crew member James Tomkins survived.

B.C. Queen 179435 On September 29, 1977 this fishboat was destroyed by fire at the Entrance to False Creek (Vancouver Harbour) BC.

B.C. Rose[b] 156895 On February 25, 1949 this fishboat was destroyed by fire one mile west of Enterprise Reef in Georgia Strait BC.

B.C. Rover 178201 On November 21, 1979 this ex-fishboat owned by Paine Hardware Ltd., North Vancouver BC, sank in McIntyre Bay in the Queen Charlotte Islands BC.

B.C. Safari 344771 On October 18, 1972 she was in a collision with the B.C. *Standard* at Cape Mudge BC. She capsized and sank off Qualicum Beach BC on April 08, 2006. The skipper, Glenn Arkko was lost. The Transportation Safety Board of Canada[62] reported that "At about 1713 on the evening of 08 March 2006, the fishing vessel B.C. *Safari* was making way in the Georgia Strait between Deep Bay and French Creek, British Columbia, when it capsized and sank. The master, who was the lone operator, is missing and presumed drowned.

---

a   Built as B.C. Lady; then HMCS B.C. Lady; then B.C. Lady
b   Built as Mary Rita; then Helen-Side; then B.C. Rose

B.C. Standard[a] 312098 On October 18, 1972 she was in a collision with the fishing vessel B.C. *Safari* off Cape Mudge BC. In 1973 she was laid up when Standard Oil of British Columbia contracted with Seaspan International to transport cargoes by tug and barge. In 1979 her register was transferred to the British Virgin Islands. She was scrapped in 1991.

B.C. Troller[b,63] 172500 On July 3, 1956 the fishboat B.C. Troller (Captain Alf Styan), collided with the New Zealand freighter *Waitemata*, seven miles south southeast of Lennard island. Captain Alf Styan and his son Ken were riding at anchor when the freight hit them with a powerful glancing blow damaging their entire superstructure. She was rolled over on her side but was righted in a damaged condition. She reached Port Alberni where she was rebuilt and returned to service. The *Waitemata* did not stop and carried on course.

B.C.P. III 154533 On December 11, 1931 this workboat owned by Olier Besner, Prince Rupert BC suffered an explosion south of Dundas Islands BC.

B.C.P. IV 154534 On March 27, 1934 this workboat owned by the Packers Steamship Co. Ltd., Vancouver BC suffered a fire at 5 miles north of Sechelt BC.

B.C.P. 43 154551 On December 15, 1973 this fishboat owned by David Carpenter, Bella Bella BC capsized and sank in a 60-mph gale while in Catala Channel, 30 miles northwest of Bella Bella BC. Five lives were lost. On August 31, 1978 she sank in Seymour Narrows BC.

B.C.P. 44 154552 On October 11, 1948 this fishboat owned by Alfred N Scow (MO), Alert Bay BC was stranded at Sea Otter Cove on the west coast of Vancouver Island BC.

---

a   Built as B.C. Standard; then MacVie
b   Built as Frances R.; then B.C. Troller

B.C.P. 46[a] 138358 On October 31, 1934 she was stranded on the west coast of Vancouver Island at Sea Otter Rocks, Clayoquot Sound BC. In 1935 she was raised by the Pacific Salvage Co. (*Salvage King*) repaired and sold to Nelson Brothers and renamed as Western Pilot. She ran aground on Blunden Island Reef, was towed to Ahousat BC, and sank. The Captain and cook perished. Later, on October 4, 1959 she was aground at Race Rocks BC.

B.C.P. No. 1 152754 On October 22, 1928 she burned while berthed alongside the ferry wharf at Sidney BC.

Bacalhao[64] 153318 On December 6, 1938 this fishboat owned by Vince Zanchi, Vancouver BC burned at Keats Island in Howe Sound BC. The crew Jack Fiomingo and Vince Zanchi were severely burned in the incident. The fire was caused by an engine backfire while they were travelling to a cod-fishing site. Their fire extinguishers were inadequate for the purpose and they were forced to abandon ship in a small dinghy. The *Bacalhao* was beached on Keats Island by the strong wind.

Bagpipes[b] 176221 In April 1972 this fishboat owned by Ronald H Daly (MO), Alberni BC sank in Georgia Strait BC.

Ballena[c,65] 100635 On November 13, 1920 she burned out at CPR Pier H in Vancouver BC when early in the morning a fire was discovered by Marine Fireman, Lawrence Smith in the engine room caused by a 'blow-back'. Captain Larson, the night watchman, awakened a dozen of the sleeping crew who managed to escape safely over the bow to the dock. But four of the men were forced toward the stern eventually hanging off in a perilous state to escape the heat. Unexpectedly, a line handler, W.C. Hastings, accompanied by HB Hammersley, on his boat appeared at the stern and rescued the men. Hastings was awaiting the arrival of a liner at Brockton Point when he saw the

---

a   Built as Chuckwalla; then Western Pilot; then B.C.P. 46
b   Built as Ruthken; then Bagpipes
c   Built as Joan; then Ballena

conflagration and proceeded over to see if there was something he could do. This was a brave act as the fire had become intense and there was burning oil on the water. The Chief Engineer, Alex Perrie, had been asleep but made his way to the engine room through the smoke to start the pumps to try to save the vessel and had them working before he was driven out by the fire. Smith, the Fireman, tried to get his clothes before evacuating and was killed (perhaps suffocated by the smoke). The fire spread to the *Bowena*, laying alongside, which was damaged by her proximity to the fire. The *Ballena* sank at the wharf and was salvaged and was later broken up by the Vancouver Dredging & Salvage Co.

The ***Ballena*** sunk at the Union Steamship Dock, Vancouver BC (Photograph from the James Crookall Fonds in the City of Vancouver Archives CVA_260-1807)

Bantry Bay[66] 150315 On July 2, 1935, at 2:30 pm while proceeding north to a cannery she caught fire west of Center Point. The sea was calm when the vessel burned off the Wood Bay relief camp near Half Moon Bay BC. Four members of the crew were killed, believed drowned: Carl Peterson; Harry Pallant; Harry Johnson; and Jonas Webb. Seven others rescued: William Oram (Master); James Thom (Engineer); James McKinley.

Baracuda III 198922 On August 18, 1961 the stove in this fishboat owned by Alexander Znotin, Gambier Island BC exploded five miles off Pender Harbour five miles off Cape Coburn in Malaspina Strait BC.

Baranof[a,67] (US) On July 26, 1952 this passenger vessel owned by the Alaska Steamship Co. collided with the freighter *Triton* off Gabriola

---

a   Built as Santa Elisa; then USS Santa Elisa; then Santa Elisa; then Baranof

Island BC two miles off Entrance Island. Two crew members of the *Triton* were killed. The *Triton* owned by the Gratsos Brothers of Ithaca Greece was bound for Japan with a cargo of iron and the *Baranof* for Alaska. Both vessels were severely damaged in the incident.

Barbara Boscowitz[68] 083454 On April 1, 1883 she was launched, under Captain Warren as master. In 1899 she operated on the Victoria, Stewart, Skagway run carrying passengers. On September 16, 1898, under command of Captain John Steele, she was wrecked after stranding on a rock at Browning Island, in Kitkatlah Inlet BC. She had been carrying a cargo of salmon and was caught in the swift current. The crew and passengers were rescued by the *Princess Louise* and brought to Victoria BC. After the removal of her cargo she rolled over and was laying on her side and was almost covered at high tide. Captain Warren supervised the salvage of the vessel and she was put back into service. On October 02, 1904 at 10:30 pm she struck a reef off Harbledown Island, Alert Bay BC and sank. The passengers panicked in an uproar as the vessel heeled over to starboard. Someone cut the falls to a lifeboat and it plunged into the water killing four young First Nation girls who were passengers. Other passengers who had fallen into the water were rescued by First Nations people in canoes. Order being restored on board all the remaining passengers disembarked in lifeboats and safely reached the shore. In 1904 she was salvaged by the B.C. Salvage Co. and towed to Esquimalt Harbour.

Barbarossa 320210 In the Fall of 1989 this seiner, owned by Howard Morris, foundered in a storm, and sank near Lasqueti Island BC.

Barkerville (HMCS) She was employed by the RCN as a harbour tug at Prince Rupert, BC. On December 17, 1945 she capsized and sank at the entrance to Bedwell Bay, BC while towing HMCS *Hespeller* to her mooring in the boneyard.

Barkley Sound On February 20, 1946 this fishing troller owned by Gil Wenige foundered on the east corner of Maitland Island in Ucluelet Harbour BC.

Barkley Sound[a] In 1942 she was commissioned into the RCN Fisherman's Reserve as HMCS Barclay Sound. Al Hoskins[69] stated that "The Barkley Sound is now a sunken wreck, alongside some logs in South Bamfield Inlet."

Barmar[b] 170399 On August 18, 1979 she sank in Tekerne Arm (Redonda Island BC) and was refloated September 15, 1979 by Julian Matson (in *Argonaut II*) and John Naylor (in *Tree Isle*). The hull was repaired and refloated October 10. 1980. The hull was repaired and refloated October 10. 1980. John de Boeck[70] states that "the *Clavella* was a beautiful, strong and sleek vessel. From 1980 to 2002, we logged over 43,000 hours from Georgia Strait to Cape Scott and Central Coast to Langara Island, and everywhere between. She sank in winter 2003 in 90+ knot winds, at a dock near Port Hardy, Refloated and taken to Campbell River, she was to have been repaired on insurance, until the insurance company screwed us. She was there 6 years before being holed by a broken-free aluminum herring skiff in a gale. The skiff jammed between her and the dock, tearing through four planks that ran below the water line. Next time she came up, it was off to the wreckers."

Barnard Castle (UK) In 1881 she was under charter to Dunsmuir, Diggle & Co. and made two voyages per month to California. In 1883 her charter expired. On November 21, 1886 while en route from Nanaimo to San Francisco she struck Rosedale Reef three miles off Discovery Island BC. She was beached and remained there several months before breaking up. In 1886 her engines were salvaged by Whitelaw Salvage Co., San Francisco CA. Her cargo of coal became a source of fuel salvaged by enterprising local settlers.

Barnston[c,71] 126791 In 1937 this dredge owned by The Corporation of the Township of Richmond, Eburne BC was destroyed by fire.

---

a   Built as Barkley Sound; then HMCS Barkley Sound; then Barkley Sound
b   Built as Barmar; then HMCS Barmar; then H.C. 115; then Clavella
c   Built as Dredge Barnston; then Barnston

The *Barnard Castle* wrecked on Bentinck Island (Image from the collection of the Maritime Museum of British Columbia 1886_000095)

Baroda 098301 On August 29, 1901 this British-built bark was wrecked at Coquille OR USA. She sat on the beach for two months before she was salvaged and put back into service After the 1,417 ton-ship sank, it was raised and rebuilt into a barge. On September 3, 1910 as a coal hulk carrying 2,800 tons in Esquimalt Harbour, she caught fire. When the blaze could not be contained, she was towed to Magazine Island and sunk in shallow water. In 1910 she was re-raised at Esquimalt BC.

Barrson[a] 121770 On March 12, 1924 this tug, owned by T.W. Barr & Son, burned at Myrtle Point, Bowen Island BC. The crew was saved by the St. Clair. She had been towing booms or aircraft spruce en route for Vancouver at the time of the incident.

Bayview 141183 On July 14, 1955 this fishboat owned by Daniel Wedge, Prince Rupert BC struck a submerged object and sank off Stephens Island BC.

Bear Island[72] 157138 On May 13, 1962 this fishboat owned and operated by Captain Olva Tahtinen, Madeira Park BC, sank at Dixon

---

a   Built as Takara Maru; then Barrson

Entrance BC near Masset. She was overwhelmed by heavy seas and sank quickly. The owner climbed the mast as the vessel sank but was picked up by another fishboat that was nearby.

Bearcat No. 1[73] 179068 On December 8, 1951 this tug, owned and operated by Ray Molyard, Lulu Island BC, exploded and burned to the waterline in the North Arm of the Fraser River, opposite Angus Drive Vancouver. The Master had just finished cleaning a clogged fuel line when gas fumes ignited. He was in the wheelhouse but still suffered injuries from being knocked off his feet.

Beatrice H.[74] 152667 On September 29, 1953, while under command of Captain James Ryan, this fishing vessel capsized in a heavy storm and foundered off Oneanda River in the Queen Charlotte Islands BC. Captain Ryan was missing after the incident. Two crew members (Sid Crosby and Sonny Benyon) were rescued by the *Greyfish*.

The *Beaver* not long after her wreck while she was still largely intact. (Image from the Major Matthews collection of the City of Vancouver Archives AM54-S4-1---: S-3-18)

Beaver This iconic steamer was launched May 1835 and sailed in brigantine rig for the Pacific under command of Captain David Home, via Cape Horn. She arrived at Fort Vancouver April 10, 1836. She generated steam in two boilers for her steam engines May 1836. Additional accommodation was fitted in 1860 and she became a passenger, mail and freight vessel operating between Victoria and New Westminster and Fort Langley. She was chartered to the Royal Navy as a hydrographic survey vessel in the 1860s. She was returned to her owners in 1870. In 1874 she was converted to a tug and sold to a company under the command of one of the owners, Captain Rudlin. She was licenced to carry passengers in 1888 and served the logging camps of Burrard Inlet. She ran aground at the entrance to Vancouver Harbour on July

25, 1888 in what is now Stanley Park. The wreck remained as a prominent local landmark until July 1892 when the wake of the passing steamer Yosemite caused it to slip off the rocks and sink.

Becherdass Ambiadass This bark-rigged sailing ship was originally in trade to India. She sailed from Shanghai China to Moodyville in ballast under command of Captain Williams for a load of lumber. She was stranded on July 27th, 1879, during a dense fog in a small cove five miles south of Cape Beale Light on a reef in Pachena Bay one-half mile west of Pachena Point. at 1:45 am, as the second mate was preparing to tack, she struck bow on and immediately commenced to leak badly. She dragged over the reef, settling hard aground in a little cove inshore, and at daylight First Nations people rescued the crew. Captain Spring, who was at Cape Beale with the *Favorite*, went to the scene and took the crew, and some of the sails, etc., to Victoria. The wreck was sold to Henry Saunders for $180. Local people took much of the gear before the ship could be salvaged.

The *Belcarra* (Photograph from the Major Matthews collection in the City of Vancouver Archives AM54-S4-_B0_P455)

Belcarra[a] 111986 On September 17, 1910 this tug owned by Terminal Steam Navigation Co. Ltd., Vancouver BC was stranded on the rocks

---

a   Built as Unican; then Belcarra

in heavy fog in Agamemnon Channel BC. She was a steamship which carried the travelling post office Burrard Inlet on Burrard Inlet and Indian Arm.

Belfast[75] 116782 On July 09, 1911 this freighter owned by Thomas G. McBride, Vancouver BC was loaded with Lime from Texada Island south bound for Seattle WA USA. When she arrived at Dodd Narrows, Captain Norman McLeod was forced to wait for the change of tide. Shortly after she stopped in False Narrows a fire was discovered in the forward hold with no way to control it. Water had contacted the lime and heat of the reaction caused the fire. The crew put the wheel over and she was sailing in ever decreasing circles chased by the tug *Bermuda* with the crew huddled at the bow trying to escape the flames. The engineers had been driven out of the engine room before the engines could be stopped and she was travelling at a high speed. She was run ashore while the crew retreated astern. Quickly the fire enveloped the vessel and crew had to be rescued by the tug Bermuda. She was a total loss.

Belize[76] 189261 On January 19, 1961 she ran aground at the Lions Gate Bridge at Calamity Point in Vancouver Harbour. She sank during the change of tide while still aground during the salvage attempt. The crew, Captain and Mrs Edward Gark had lived aboard.

Belle Isle Sd 325661 On September 2, 1976 this fishboat owned by Kenneth Williamson (MO), Minstrel Island BC broke up and sank off Estevan Point BC.

Belltree[77] 141119 On March 28, 1928 she exploded and burned 15 miles west of Race Rocks in Juan de Fuca Strait BC. Her two crew members who were drifting for three hours in Juan de Fuca Strait were rescued 15 miles west of Race Rocks by the steamer *Admiral Farragut*. The crew of fishermen: Harold Neave (Kyuquot) and David Clay (Vancouver) were travelling from Vancouver to Barkley Sound at the time of the incident. During the night they were having engine problems when an explosion occurred. The vessel was considered a total loss.

Belvidere[78] (US) On November 29, 1886 this American ship was stranded on a reef at Bonilla Island under command of Captain JS Gibson in dense fog and a heavy sea while running from Wilmington for Departure Bay in ballast for a cargo of coal. She was pulled off and then sank in 21 fathoms off the Lyle River.

Benmohr[79] (UK) On March 11, 1900 this steamer, while under Captain A Wallace, struck Benmohr Rock (then an uncharted un-named rock) while proceeding to sea from Oyster Bay BC to San Francisco CA. Her pilot at the time of the incident was Captain James Christensen. The ship suffered no damage, and she was able, after inspection, to proceed on her voyage. The Benmohr was lost on October 16, 1914 in the early days of the First World War, captured and sunk by the German raider SMS Emden in the Indian Ocean.

Bentinck[a] 133740 On June 1, 1941[80] she was stranded approximately 3 miles off the mouth of the Tlell River in Hecate Straits BC. They departed Prince Rupert for Queen Charlotte City. They ran onto the rocks in the dark after being unable to find the entrance to Skidegate Inlet. In the falling tide they were unable to operate the ship's pump which had a broken spark plug. At first, they did not believe the situation to be serious and awaited the rising tide, but the seas got rougher and they launched the ship's boat, but it drifted away. The crew fashioned a rough raft and set out on it paddling with hands and feet. Four men died of exposure in the incident: Frank McRae (construction engineer); Peter Lorentzen (Prince Rupert contractor) and John Barker (Deckhand). Captain CJ Couture, Robert Morgan, William Notation and AE Richards were washed ashore and survived on Graham Island.

Bering Straits 323263 On December 17, 1989 this river tug owned by Rivtow Industries Ltd., Vancouver BC capsized and sank while towing a loaded gravel barge. RCMP divers recovered the body of Captain Robert Lee after she capsized and later salvaged.

---

a   Built as Pacific; then Bentinck

Bervin[a,81] 100205 She was prefabricated by J. McArthur & Co. and Bow McLachlan Co., Glasgow Scotland. She was brought to Vancouver on the *Grandholm*. In 1892 she was assembled at Union Shipyard, Coal Harbour, Vancouver BC by Henry Darling. On June 22, 1892 she was seized by US Customs in a sealing dispute. She was towed from Sitka to Port Townsend WA. On May 26, 1909 she caught fire off Cape Roger Curtis on Bowen Island. In 1918 she lost her propeller in Queen Charlotte Sound and drifted until she encountered the Venture which took her in tow to Alert Bay. In 1959 she was sunk as a breakwater at Trinity Bay, Malcolm Island BC.

Beryl 140929 The Beryl foundered and sank on November 17, 1920 while attempting to cross Nitinat Bar BC towing a boom of logs from Nitinat Lake. She started taking water while working for Nitinat Lumber Co., Victoria BC and the skipper cut the tow then signalled to the tug *Prosperative* which had been waiting offshore to take charge of the logs and rescued the crew of the tug.

Bethune[b] 150314 In 1941 she was seized from her Japanese owners by the Canadian Government. In 1942 her ownership transferred to His Majesty the King. She collided on September 07, 1969 at Swiftsure Bank with a Russian trawler but resulted in little damage. Her Atlas Imperial 4-cylinder 60bhp engine is held at the Cowichan Bay Marine Museum.

Betsy Nell On August 09, 1974 this fishboat troller owned by Dixon Sam of Opitsaht BC foundered one mile south southwest of Lennard Island BC.

Betsy Ross[82] 157139 This ex-ship-rigged vessel was converted to a log barge in service carrying hog fuel and wood chips between Port Alberni, Chemainus, to Port Townsend and Port Angeles WA USA.

---

a   Built as Coquitlam; then Bervin
b   Built as Navigator; then Bethune

She was added to a breakwater at Oyster Bay on Vancouver Island at the end of her life.

Bighorn 177771 On June 28, 1948 this tug owned by Ted Poole, Dick Poole, Joe Poole & Don Poole; and George Walsh, Hopkins Landing BC foundered and sank off Valdes Island BC five miles south-east of Gabriola Passage.

Billy B. 173378 This tug owned by the Active Tug & Barge Ltd., Campbell River BC pushed a barge to carry cars and passengers between Buckley and Denman. On October 28, 1967 she had an engine room fire and burned at the Hole-in-the-Wall (in Okisollo Channel) and became a complete loss.

Billy B. II 194942 On October 9, 1965 this fishboat owned by Kenneth P Maxwell, Bamfield BC ran aground in Barclay Sound BC and became a total constructive loss.

Billy S. 153380 On April 18, 1931 this tug owned by William J Scratchley, Vancouver BC suffered an explosion in Dog Bay on Hernando Island in Baker Pass BC.

Bingamon[83] 152550 This log barge, converted from an unfinished wartime freighter, was equipped with cranes and winches for unloading cargo and was designed to transport logs from the Queen Charlotte Islands to mainland mills during the winter months. Insurance on ordinary log rafts and Davis Rafts was difficult or impossible to obtain during the winter months. On July 06, 1928 she suffered a fire at Muchalat Inlet, Nootka Sound BC. On December 29, 1929, in tow of the tug *Czar*, she went ashore near Sand Heads in dense fog while carrying a cargo of logs. River currents took her up on the sand. Some of the logs were removed and she was temporarily freed only to ground again. In 1929 while owned by Coyle Towing Ltd., Vancouver BC she was scuttled as a breakwater.

Birds Eye Cove[a] 170761 This rail car barge owned by Ame Bentzen, Duncan BC had and external steel framework to strengthen the wooden hull while carrying heavy railcars. On June 18, 1963 she began to leak, took on water and capsized in Juan de Fuca Strait. She was beached and converted to a breakwater in Saanich BC.

Black Bass[b,84] 158929 In 1960 this tug owned by Gulf of Georgia Towing Co., Vancouver BC capsized and sank off Coal Harbour BC. She was going to the aid of the tug *Le Beau* which had run aground on Dead Man's Island at the time of the incident. Captain Douglas Appleton and Ted Rattenbury managed to climb onto the bottom of the hull and were rescued.

Black Fir[85] 312116 On March 9, 1963 this tug, owned by Texada Towing Co. Ltd., Vancouver BC, sank about 5 miles off Gower Point BC (near Sechelt) while running light to Blind Bay BC. Her 4-man crew escaped in a life raft.

Black Prince[c,86] 178832 On June 21, 1972 this tug foundered and sank in 65 feet of water at Latona Beach, Gambier Island BC. She foundered close to the dock. Earlier in the day the tug reported that she was taking on water and had to be pumped out at a logging camp. As he approached the dock at the Latona Beach church camp observers noted the tug awash and slowly sinking. When she was within 30 feet of the dock the engine stalled and she went down within 10 seconds. Linwood L Brandon drowned in the incident.

Black Wolf[87] 152904 On April 13, 1929 this log barge, owned by the Pacific (Coyle) Navigation Co. Ltd., Vancouver BC, was stranded on Robertson Island, Skidegate Inlet BC when she dragged her anchors during a strong gale.

---

a   Built as P.G.E. No. 2; then Island Tug 102; then Birds Eye Cove
b   Built as Knockabout; then Knockabout II; then Black Bass
c   Built as Marjorie L.; then Black Prince

Blatchford[a,88] 151195 John Campbell reports (British Columbia Nautical History Facebook Group 01/12/2014) that "the *Blatchford* was the first of eleven surplus United States Shipping Board wooden steamship hulls to be brought to BC to become the first fleet of log barges. There had been questions about whether *Blatchford* or *Addison* was the one brought to Powell River for breakwater use, but I found that all the Powell River Co. documents referring to the hulk called it the *Blatchford*. She sank in the late thirties and caused no end of trouble in the log pond and was finally blasted to pieces. Problems encountered with the Blatchford had a direct impact on the decision to not use the Malahat in the breakwater. Interesting about the hull is that it was first converted into a lighter with conveyors and a grain elevator before becoming a log barge. They thought it might be useful for loading grain ships without having to bring them into the dock."

Blue Boy[89] 170534 On May 1, 1950 this fishboat exploded and burned near the Gorge Park in Victoria BC. She burned to the waterline and was beached at the Gorge Bridge. No one was reported on board at the time of the accident.

Blue Fjord[b,90] 171629 On December 3, 2006 she sank close to the head of Toba Inlet, during wintertime when the weather was very cold. She hit a hemlock pole end-on, and the butt-end came right into the engine room. She went down in 2 minutes, the owner/skipper (Blue Fjord Charters Ltd., Ladysmith (and Nanaimo) BC) was alone, and jumped in the tin skiff off the roof. He grabbed a portable generator for heat. He was picked up the next morning suffering from exposure.

Blue Otter 155252 On March 18, 1941 this workboat owned by Samuel Prest, Chilliwack BC burned at Chilliwack Rock in the Fraser River BC.

---

a   Built as Blandford; then Blatchford
b   Built as C.G.S. Milwin; then P.M.L. 15; then RCMP M.L. 15; then Blue Fjord

Blue Seal[91] 155253 On February 25, 1939 this tug, owned by B. & K. Logging Co., burned in Powell Lake BC. She sank two miles up the lake when she caught fire while berthed next to a tank containing 3,000 gallons of gasoline. The tug, under the command of Captain George Lawson, had just arrived at the log pond when the fire broke out after an explosion. Captain Lawson and his helper were working on a nearby boat at the time of the incident.

Blue Star[a] 138364 On August 12, 1979 this fishboat owned by Raymond Kierce, Prince Rupert BC grounded in East Skidegate Channel BC and was run up onto the beach there.

Blue Waters[92] 319936 On June 6, 1977 the fishboat *Blue Waters* was in a collision with the fishing vessel *Centennial 77* and sank in Queen Charlotte Sound BC. The crew of two from the *Centennial 77* were rescued.

Bluenose III 194684 On October 21, 1963 while owned by Henry M Mann, Minstrel Island BC her bottom was ripped open and she sank.

Bluenose V 188306 On April 24, 1971 this fishboat owned by Kazauki Yoshihara, Lulu Island BC capsized and sank in Georgia Strait BC.

Bobbie B. 152545 On February 15, 1934 this tug owned by Alva M Snider Jr, Vancouver BC was destroyed by fire between Third Beach and Siwash Rock in English Bay BC.

Bon Accord 094908 On September 30, 1898 a huge fire destroyed New Westminster. She was tied up at the wharf and fire was consuming the sheds on the wharf when the firemen arrived. The *Bon Accord* quickly caught fire along with two other steamers (the *Gladys* and the *Edgar*). The three steamers drifting down the river set each dock and vessel alight as they touched the shore.

---

a   Built as Wales Island No. 7; then M.R.B.; then Blue Star

Bonabelle[93] 158583 Drew Clark states that "In 1982 she sank in False Creek where Science World is located today. I refloated her with the help of Jim and Cliff Munich. A year and half later she sank again at the same spot—this time for good. She was a bare hull at that point—stripped to the deck. Her old Buda engine straight eight still ran but she could not have been around as a yacht after that date."

Bonanza 348608 On July 3, 1980 this fishboat owned by Anthony A Knott, Terrace BC foundered and sank in Queen Charlotte Sound.

Bonnie Prince 193424 On October 10, 1972 this fishboat owned by Clarence Wells (MO), Vancouver BC sank at the mouth of the Fraser River BC and was a total loss.

Boobyall[a,94] 219685 (US) On December 29, 1929, while inbound from California, she grounded on the rocks in the First Narrows of Vancouver Harbour in dense fog. This wooden freighter carrying a cargo of shingles and paper operated by the Pacific Steamship Co. was registered at Seattle WA USA. On May 11, 1929 she caught fire two miles east of Discovery Island near Victoria BC (in Haro Strait) and her crew of 26 battled the flames which came dangerously near her fuel tank. Four hours after the fire broke out the Salvage King arrived to tow her to Esquimalt, after removing her officers and crew of 26. Her fire was so fierce that explosion was a serious possibility and to protect the powder magazine and sawmill in Esquimalt Harbour she was towed out to Albert Head where the *Salvage King* fought the fire for 36 hours. She was already considered a total loss and the decision was being made to scuttle her. Before she was beached at Rosebank many of her cargo of shingles were discharged into scows. Except for this the whole ship was considered a total loss. The wreck was taken over by the Pacific Salvage Co. and her engines removed.

Border Queen[a,95] 156604 this barge (an ex-freighter) owned by Mayo Singh, Paldi BC, ended her life as part of the breakwater at Oyster Bay BC.

---

a   Built as Rosalie Mahony; then Border Queen

Borgund 155173 On July 10, 1971 this fishboat owned by Anthony D Fay (MO), Queen Charlotte BC sank off Cape Edenshaw.

Borniti[96] 154558 On August 7, 1927 this 'speed launch' owned by Orleans Shippers Ltd., Vancouver BC exploded and burned in English Bay BC and sank off Jericho Beach. She was carrying a large amount of gasoline fuel, but the cause of the explosion was undetermined. Her master, Captain Laurent Vereecken (1927), said that they were returning from a voyage to Vancouver Island. Some mystery surrounded the event when witnesses reported two unidentified men rowing away from the wreck soon after the outbreak of the fire.

Boston She was an American vessel captured by Chief Maquinna on March 22, 1803 in Nootka Sound. All but two of the crew was murdered. John Jewitt, the ship's blacksmith and her sailmaker, Mr Thompson, survived and taken prisoner. She was accidentally burned and exploded. The exact location of her wreck has never been discovered and is the object of ongoing investigations by underwater archaeologists.

Bowena[a,97] On November 13, 1920 she was damaged when an early morning fire spread from the *Ballena* to the *Bowena* in Vancouver Harbour. On April 29, 1923 she caught fire while berthed at North Vancouver, doing damage to the steering gear and controls to the engine telegraph.

Bowie[b] 384135 After shaking down in the Caribbean Sea she operated on patrol and escort duty between southern Florida and Guantanamo Bay, Cuba. In June 1945, as the PCS-1405 went to the Pacific, where she was based at Pearl Harbor, Hawaii, for some six months. Returning to the West Coast in February 1946, she was modified for survey work Decommissioned in August 1946, transferred to the US Coast and Geodetic Survey (USC & GS). In 2010 she apparently sank in the mouth of the River.

---

a   Built as City of Nanaimo; then Bowena; then Cheam
b   Built as USS PCS-1405; then USCGC Bowie; then Bowie

Bravado[98] 347955 On March 25, 1975 this herring seiner, while under the command of Captain Rick Johansen, capsized 25 miles ESE of Sandspit while herring fishing with the loss of 6 crew members.

Brigadier-General M.G. Zalinski[a] 218268 (US) In 1946 this freighter ran aground and sank in a storm in Grenville Channel BC. The wreck was discovered about 2000 when leaking oil was discovered on the surface. The wreck was found by a submersible ROV and the leak was repaired. In 2013 the hull began to leak oil again. In July 2013, the Canadian Government announced that a "significant environmental protection operation" would be undertaken to clean up the wreck site. By December 4, 2013 35 tons of fuel oil was recovered from the wreck and the environmental protection operation came to an end and the *Brigadier-General M. G. Zalinski* was declared free of oil and safe for the environment.

Bruce Brown[99] 14K17621 The Transportation Safety Board of Canada reports that "During the night of 10/11 June 2002, the 8 m log salvage vessel *Bruce Brown* was towing a 37 m float from Barnes Bay, on Sonora Island, to Blind Bay, off Malaspina Strait. During the passage, when the *Bruce Brown* was northwest of Powell River, BC, the vessel took on water and sank. The two persons on board were found some distance from the tug, one had succumbed to hypothermia and the other to drowning."

Bruce I[100] 154368 On February 28, 1976 this seiner owned by William A Campbell (MO), Burnaby BC sank about 300 yards west of Cape Beale BC. Two of the crew evacuated in a rubber life raft while the other two scrambled onto rocks below the lighthouse. The lighthouse keeper heard shouts and called out the *Banfield Lifeboat* who picked up Captain Stanley Beale and crewman Randy West from the life raft. A rescue helicopter from the US Coast Guard in Port Angeles WA carrying a powerful 'night sun' searchlight located picked crewman Reid Dobell and pulled him off the rocks. The rescue was carried out at night in driving snow. They began the search for the fourth

---

a   Built as Lake Frohna; then Ace; then Brigadier-General M.G. Zalinski

man Rusty Waters. The accumulating snow caused an engine failure forcing a dangerous landing inside the reefs off Cape Beale. The helicopter remained afloat despite the rough seas while the lifeboat navigated through the obstacles and two of the crew (a father and son, Martin, and Cliff Charles) launched the Zodiac and rescued the crew of four and Dobell. Crewman Rusty Waters was lost in the incident. Martin Charles was subsequently awarded the Canadian Medal of Bravery and decorated by the US Coast Guard.

Brunette 094902 She was a tug originally owned by Brunette Saw Mills Co. Ltd., New Westminster BC. Terry Gustafson[101] reports that "she was stripped and went to an oyster farm in Okeover Inlet where she eventually sank."

Burns (USS) DD.171 (USN) This warship was scuttled to become part of the breakwater at Oyster Bay BC.

The *Burrard Chief* (Photograph by Dusty Rhodes in the John MacFarlane collection)

Burrard Chief 141702 On June 6, 1930 this tug owned by Island Tug & Barge Ltd., Vancouver BC was stranded in Sansum Narrows when the tug Hopkins with the aid of a derrick scow successfully refloated her. On June 19, 1930 she towed the salvage equipment to refloat the SS *San Diego* ashore on Danger Reef. On September 4, 1948 she was stranded in Porlier Pass BC and was later salvaged.

Brynje[102] On December 16, 1935 about 5:00 pm this Norwegian freighter collided with the *North Vancouver Ferry No. 2* carrying a full load of cars and passengers. The freighter was undamaged and proceeded to sea. The ferry reached her dock under her own power. She had to be drydocked to repair the damage.

Byzantium[103] 025794 She arrived in Victoria on December 24, 1867. Under the command of Captain Rufus Calhoun, she fished in the

Queen Charlotte Islands from a base in McCoy Cove. The base closed about 1878. On October 19, 1871 she struck a reef while transiting in a gale in Weynton Passage BC. She took on water and was abandoned by her crew. Apparently when she drifted off the reef, she was discovered by First Nations people who took her behind Malcolm Island and salvaged fittings and equipment. She was reported to have drifted off toward Queen Charlotte Sound.

C.C. Perkins[104] In March 1881 this schooner was caught at night on an underwater ledge and as the tide receded, she careened over on her side. On the rising tide she filled with water. Her cargo damaged by the water was removed and landed on the beach. The lightened vessel was eventually righted and repaired. She was destined for the Taku mines.

C.D. Rand[105] 100193 On November 13, 1903 this sealing schooner owned by the Victoria Sealing Co. Ltd., Victoria BC was driven ashore in a storm at Kyuquot Sound BC where she struck Dead Man's Island at 9:00 am. She then proceeded towards the settlement at Kyuquot, damaged and leaking badly but reportedly sank in Kyuquot waters before reaching shore.

C.E. Dant[a] On September 4, 1972[106] The freighter *C.E. Dant* (operated by the States Lines) on a voyage from Seattle to Longview collided with the freighter *Aegean Sea* in Juan de Fuca Strait. The two freighters remained stuck together with the bow of the *C.E. Dant* in the port side inflicting serious damage to the forward holds of the *Aegean Sea*. Salvage operators waited for favourable tides so the vessels would be in shallower water in case they had to be beached. They were separated after 67 hours locked together. The *C.E. Dant* proceeded to Seattle under her own power.

C.P. Yorke[107] On December 11, 1953 this tug, under the command of Captain Roy Johnson, struck Tattenham Ledge at Thormanby Island during a blizzard. The barge she was towing collided with her

---

a   Built as C.E. Dant; then Santa Ana; then Cape John (T-AK-5022)

and knocked a hole in her hull causing her to sink in 40 fathoms of water. Tragically, her crew of six were lost with only Captain Roy Johnson surviving. The tug was later salvaged by the Recovery Arrow Giant. She was towed in submerged condition into Buccaneer Bay and pumped out.

C.S. Holmes She carried supplies to US government posts in Arctic Alaska in 1914 under her master Captain John Backlund. In 1922 she was used by Roald Amundsen on his Arctic expedition. In September 24, 1926 she ran aground on Church Island west of Race Rocks BC while rum running. She was salvaged by the MacFarlane Brothers Towing Ltd. tug J.W.P. of Victoria BC and beached at Becher Bay for repairs. After her wartime use by the US Army, she was dismasted and reduced to a barge and severely hogged. In 1952, as a barge, she was lost off the BC coast. Her hull was eventually found three miles north of Estevan Point in 1975 by Rod Palm.

Cadboro (UK) In 1826 she was registered at London UK. In early 1827 she made her first northern trading voyage arriving at Fort Vancouver under command of John Pearson Swan. Later in 1827 she was the first ship to enter the Fraser River. In 1837 she entered Cadboro Bay and Victoria Harbour in 1842. In 1850 she was seized by US Forces at Nisqually. She was sold in 1860 to Captain Edward Howard for $2450 and used to transport lumber. She sank in a storm near Port Angeles October 6, 1863.

Cadzow Forest (UK) Built at Port Glasgow, Scotland, in 1878, this ill-fated barque had once been the command of Captain McInnis. On January 4, 1896 while attempting an inbound crossing of the Columbia River bar, this British barque was pounded by heavy seas. The conditions were so ugly that the pilot could not be removed by the pilot schooner. The vessel suffered heavy damage and drifted northward at the mercy of the elements and was lost with her entire crew. The derelict later drifted as far as the British Columbia coast where it foundered.

Camosun I[108] 121204 In 1907 she was the first coastal vessel to have a Marconi wireless installed. In 1908 she was re-registered to Canada from the UK. On March 7, 1916 she ran ashore on Lima Point, Digby Island, at the entrance to Prince Rupert Harbour. The passengers were taken off to Prince Rupert. She was refloated again on March 22, 1916 by the British Columbia Salvage Co. In 1918 she lost her propeller after hitting a deadhead in Queen Charlotte Sound. On January 23, 1923 while southbound she collided with the *Princess Beatrice* in Grenville Channel. She was damaged from her boat deck to the waterline but sailed on to Vancouver. In 1923 she ran aground near Brockton Point. The passengers were removed by the Vancouver Fire Department who used a big ladder truck and the passengers crawled ashore using the ladder. In 1925 she was with the *Prince John* on the Queen Charlotte Islands (now Haida Gwai—Prince Rupert trade. On March 22, 1930 she ran aground on Calvert Island but floated free again six hours later.

Camosun II[a] 124202 In 1907 she was in trade in northern Scottish waters. On October 15, 1940 she collided with the Italian ship *Lido* in the First Narrows. Later, as the *Cairo*, she smuggled Jewish immigrants to Palestine. In 1952 she was broken up.

Campaspe[b] 130859 On May 6, 1927 this tug owned by Thomas Marshall, Vancouver BC burned at Nanaimo Harbour BC. She was salvaged and put back into service.

Canada[109] 099675 In 1925 she was chartered by the Argentine Government and travelled (Captain Walter A Meyer) in a trans-Pacific convoy, with the *Canada* (Captain Walter Tinn) for Colonel Pedro Zanni to Japan. On November 9, 1941 she was in collision with the Alaska cruise liner *North Coast* 1.5 miles off Narrowstone Island in Puget Sound WA USA. The *North Coast* fouled the tow line of a Davis Raft that pulled the *Canada* under water. The crew was taken off by the *North Coast* and transferred to the *Snohomish*.

a   Built as St. Margaret; then Prince Charles; then Camosun II; then Cairo
b   Built as Fannicol; then Campaspe

Canadian 122533 On February 08, 1932 this tug owned by William Reynolds, Nanaimo BC foundered in tow of the tug *Ironbark* approximately 1.5 miles off lower end of Bowen Island in the Georgia Strait BC.

Canadian Clipper 372621 On September 16, 1979 this fishboat owned by Ron Burridge, Delta BC was destroyed by fire in Georgia Strait BC.

Canadian II[a,110] 327149 She operated as a passenger vessel on Harrison Lake. Later she operated at Bella Bella. Jody Louise reported: "She sank at her berth at MK Bay Marina [in Kitimat BC]. She was salvaged by Wainwright Marine and Adams Diving and then she was cut up at Kristoff's scrap metal yard in Port Edward. "

Canadian Inventor[b,111] 141705 On August 27, 1923, this workboat owned by Harry T Devine, Vancouver BC, was in a collision with the workboat V.M.D. in Burrard Inlet, Vancouver Harbour BC. The V.M.D. was crushed and sunk at the Government Dock when the tide pushed the freighter up against her. The owner of the workboat and his crewmember had to leap for their lives to escape.

Canadian National No. 1[c] 145356 On August 24, 1928 she collided with the *North Vancouver Ferry No. 3* in Burrard Inlet BC. In 1962 she was broken up.

Canadian National No. 3[d] 150998 On August 26, 1925 this tug was rammed by the *Anyox* while towing a gravel scow during a severe rainstorm and sank off Prospect Point near Vancouver BC. She was raised and taken to Beach Avenue Shipyards for repair. In 1927 she was re-assembled at Kelowna BC by Vancouver Drydock and Salvage Co. In 1953 her register was cancelled on the advice of the owner

---

a Built as Caltex Lumba Lumba; then Lumba Lumba; Bella Bella; then Canadian II
b Built as Canadian Inventor; then Sekiho Maru
c Built as HMS Finwhale; then Hopkins Bros.; then Canadian National No. 1
d Built as Radius; then Canadian National No. 3

who reported that she was beached and broken up at Vancouver BC in July 1941.

Canadian National No. 5 156887 She was cut in two and made 'trailerable'. In 1966 she was carried out to the Pacific coast on flat cars. On February 11, 1990 she was lost in a snowstorm in the Georgia Strait. Four crew were reported missing. It was surmised that she crossed a towline that then caused her to founder.

Canfisco 188582 On March 12, 1975 this fishpacker owned by The Canadian Fishing Co. Ltd., Vancouver BC grounded, was beached off the entrance to the Koeye River (Namu) BC. One life was lost and afterwards she was broken up.

Cannery Bay On November 8, 1978 this fishboat was reported missing, presumed lost, at Tofino BC with the loss of one life.

Canora[112] 138800 She was a double ender hull design with two propellers at each end. Adam Harding stated: "The *Canora* was sunk in Home Bay, at the southern entrance to Rivers Inlet." Charlotte Cooper stated: "it was turned into a fishing resort called Big Springs. It tried to sink one night in during a summer when there were guests and staff on board. I arrived for work in the morning to find it half sunk. They managed to pump it out and get through the summer. A couple winters later it went down completely."

Canuck[113] 155234 On March 7, 1938 this fishpacker carrying a cargo of clams, owned by William C. Splan of Vancouver BC, was in a collision with the tug *B.C. Boy* in Discovery Pass opposite the mouth of the Campbell River BC. She was declared a total loss.

Canyon No. 6 322491 In March 2001 this tug sank in Queen Charlotte Sound.

Cap Rouge II[114] 348903 On the morning of August 13, 2002, the commercial salmon fishing vessel *Cap Rouge II* was bound for the entrance of the main arm of the Fraser River, BC. When the vessel was approximately two miles south of Sand Heads Light, it capsized while carrying seven persons on board. Two persons abandoned the vessel and climbed into a skiff being towed by the fishing vessel. Five persons, including two children, remained within the overturned hull, and drowned.

Cape Breton (HMCS) K.350 The ship was paid off in January 1946 and in 1947 she was sold. In 1948 she was hulked at Kelsey Bay BC and placed in the breakwater there.

Cape Breton (HMCS)[a] On October 20, 2001 this Royal Canadian Navy ship was sunk as an artificial diving reef. A short section of the stern and her engines were removed before the ship was sunk by the Artificial Reef Society of British Columbia near Snake Island in Nanaimo harbour.

Cape Cleare[115] 255112 (US) She was registered in Juneau AK. On February 12, 1927 she foundered on the northeast side of Langara Island, at Dixon Entrance BC. On July 23, 1973 she grounded off Pitt Point in Grenville Channel BC.

Cape Fairweather 369482 On March 17, 1997 this fishboat owned by Kenneth Stearn, Logan Lake BC foundered and sank in Queen Charlotte Sound BC.

Cape James[116] On October 16, 1940 this fishboat went ashore near Vivian Island when she hit a submerged object, probably a rock. They hit so violently that the crew were thrown to the deck from their bunks. Captain Sandy Taylor and his crew of three were rescued.

Cape Knox 172343 On September 10, 1971 this seiner owned by The Canadian Fishing Co. Ltd., Vancouver BC burned and sank in the waters surrounding Haida Gwaii (formerly Queen Charlotte Islands).

---

a   Built as HMS Flamborough Head; renamed as HMCS Cape Breton

Cape Mudge[a] 153163 On February 03, 1991 this seiner owned by the Canadian Fishing Co. Ltd., Vancouver BC foundered and sank off Port San Juan BC.

Cape Norman[b] 176887 On December 16, 1961[117] she foundered near Maude Island, Nanoose Bay BC on voyage carrying a load of herring from Deep Bay to Steveston. She sent out SOS signals reporting that she was going down about 15 miles northeast of Nanaimo. The last message heard, picked up by the *Adriatic Star*, reported that "The dinghy has capsized. Three of the crew are in the water." Silence followed. They were thought to have been making for shelter at Maude Island, near Nanoose Bay at the time of the tragedy. An overturned dinghy and a floating lifejacket were later found by searchers. Lost were Captain Tom Wilson; Engineer Dave Falconer; Boyd Fuerst; and Bob Sherbourn. In total, the crew left behind 12 children.

Cape Scott[c] 106769 In 1908 she was brought to BC for halibut fishing. She was dismantled in 1946 at British Columbia Marine Ways. Her engine was transferred to Pacific (Coyle) tug *Newington*. In 1946 her hull was beached at Oyster Bay for use as a breakwater.

Cape Spruce[d] 194651 She is reputed to have served in the USN as a submarine chaser during the Second World War and later converted to a barge. In April 1980 she sank at Porteau Beach BC in Howe Sound.

Cape Swain[118] 150854 On October 7, 1931 this halibut schooner owned by Sinclair Pierce, Prince Rupert BC, burned in Tuck Inlet (an extension of the Prince Rupert Harbour BC). The crew was cutting firewood and the fire could not be extinguished.

---

a   Built as Cape Mudge; then Mi-Lyndo; then Cape Mudge
b   Built as RCASC Colonel Greer; then Cape Norman
c   Built as Celestial Empire; then Cape Scott
d   Built as a US Navy submarine chaser (name not known); then Cape Spruce

Cape Wolf[119] 177362 On October 31, 1947 she was wrecked one mile west of Port San Juan BC.

Caper[120] 312831 On June 16, 1964 this tug owned by Richmond Tug Boat Co. Ltd., Richmond BC exploded at the east end of Mitchell Island in the Fraser River. Captain Al Brown jumped to a log boom when his boat exploded and burned. The tug was, at the time, in service as a dike patrol vessel for the North Fraser Harbour Commission.

Capilano[121] 100203 On October 1, 1915 she sank off Harwood Island BC in the Georgia Strait. She had hit a rock, but the damage was thought to be minor. Some cargo was discharged at Vananda and then she put to sea again. When she was near Mittlenach Island it was noticed that she was taking on water. The crew took to the boats and rowed to Powell River.

Capilano 141709 On Saturday evening, May 24, 1952, the fishboat *Kanawaka* was rammed by the passenger vessel *Capilano* four miles east southeast of Gower Point BC. The fishing vessel was three hours out of Vancouver bound for Prince Rupert. The *Capilano* put a lifeboat in the water and rescued the crew of six. The hull of the *Capilano* was eventually condemned and she was purchased by Mahood Logging Ltd. and sunk at Lang Bay to become part of a breakwater protecting the booming ground there.

Capilano[a] 198366 On September 29, 1973 this tug owned by Warren L Kerr, Quesnel BC foundered in Williston Lake BC with the loss of one life.

Capt. J. Fiddler[122] 391283 On October 07, 1991 she capsized and foundered 20 miles south southwest of Cape Beale BC. The four-man crew was forced into a life raft that was picked up by the *Cape James* in US waters west of Cape Flattery WA.

---

a   Built as Gypo II; then Capilano

The *Carelmapu* drifting in distress (Image from the collection of the Maritime Museum of British Columbia 000097)

Carelmapu 076548 The *Carelmapu* was sailing inbound from Honolulu to Puget Sound for a cargo of lumber under Captain Fernando Desolmes. She was wrecked On November 23, 1915 in Shelter Bay east of Portland Point. The vessel made landfall 16 miles south of Cape Beale early on the morning of November 23rd. At 6:30 am they signaled Pachena Light in hope of picking up a tug to tow her through Juan de Fuca Strait. The day was spent tacking back and forth in light wind awaiting a tug. By 6:00 pm the wind was a hard-southeast gale, and her sails were carried away. About 1:00 am the wind shifted to the southwest when land was four miles away. She dropped her anchors. The steamer *Princess Maquinna*, under Captain Gillam, appeared and the crew began abandoning ship. Then the biggest squall broke and the ship was carried across the corner of one of the numerous reefs, bringing up on the rocks about 70 yards from cliff. The ship went over on her beam ends and the hull broke in two at the after hatch. Twenty of the crew and twenty-four passengers that were listed aboard were lost; only five crew and the ship's dog were saved. As of 2020, a piece of the bow and steel debris remain in the rocks and can be seen at low tide. Much of the ship was salvaged in 1919. Tofino nautical historian Ken Gibson[123] spoke with Mike Hamilton whose brother Harry survived the wreck. Hamilton told him that Harry was aboard the *Princess Maquinna* as she anchored ahead of the *Carelmapu* which was dragging her anchor toward Cox Bay. In the screaming sou'wester Captain Gillam was easing his ship back, playing out the anchor chain, to get a rescue line across on the more sheltered side. One lifeboat had capsized already. Suddenly a severe gust struck, ripping the anchor winch a few inches from the deck rendering the steam power and gears useless. Gillam's attention swung to his ship and passengers. One of the crew was selected and given a 'hang saw'. He was lashed to the starboard and port bar link chain between swells. Harry was one of these men and said that he was buried in water most of the time. Mean while Gilliam ordered a full head of steam and had already started to move the ship forward when the chain parted. He gave the order "Full Ahead". Another witness to the storm that night was Jack MacLeod who had sailed around Cape Horn and was with the lifeboat service. He was on Cox Point on the shore and related that the wind and waves were so violent that even fish had been washed into the woods.

The *Carelmapu* in distress (Image from the collection of the Maritime Museum of British Columbia 000098)

Cardena[124] 150977 She was a popular Union Steamship Co. passenger vessel. On March 14, 1946 she ran aground at Port Clements BC. On November 4, 1950 she was stranded at Estevan Point BC and later salvaged. In March 1952, the *Cardena* grounded on mud flats under the Lions Gate Bridge and, in early 1953, struck a rock in Patrick Channel, near Sullivan Bay in the Broughton Archipelago. Then, in the fall of 1953, again under Lions Gate Bridge, the ship collided head-on in heavy fog with the CPR liner *Princess Elizabeth*, leaving a 20-foot gash in the *Cardena*'s bow. Following the collision, the two conjoined vessels managed to manoeuvre into the sheltered waters of English Bay, away from the busy shipping lanes beneath the bridge.

All the passengers had donned life jackets, but they remained aboard for the four hours it took to separate the ships by cutting torch. On December 20, 1946 she went aground near Balmoral Cannery at the mouth of the Skeena River. She was hauled off after three days by the *Salvage Princess* and *Cape Scott*. In 1961 she was broken up by Capital Iron & Metals Co. Ltd., Victoria BC. Her hull was towed to Powell River and ballasted with gravel where she served as a floating breakwater. She was then towed to Kelsey Bay for the breakwater there.

The *Carina No. 1* breaking up in the surf at Nitinat Narrows BC with her stern section upper right corner of image. (Photograph from Richmond Archives # 2001 34 9 139)

Carina No. 1 314873 On October 17, 1985 this seiner grounded and stranded and was declared a constructive total loss at the entrance to Nitinat Narrows BC.

Carluke[125] 173622 On August 21, 1955, at 2:35 am, this fishing troller owned by Joseph & John Norman (JO), New Westminster BC was sunk in a collision with the Japanese freighter *Kashii Maru* five miles south of Nitinat off the entrance to Juan de Fuca Strait. The boat was anchored near the Swiftsure Lightship and the two brothers were asleep at the time of the collision. After spending two hours adrift in the ship's boat the crew were picked up by the freighter.

Carlyle B. 155117 On May 30, 1934 this fishboat owned by JCB Shannon, Vancouver BC was in collision with the *Imperial* 2.5 miles northeast of Nelly Point, McKay Reach BC.

Carlysle IV[a] 153338 On August 12, 1933 this fishboat owned by Boyd Shannon & Captain John B Shannon, Vancouver BC was stranded in Queen Charlotte Sound BC. She was rebuilt as a beam trawler, for Gulf of Georgia Cannery operations.

Carlyle IV 158561 On October 16, 1939 this fishboat owned by Carlyle B Shannon, Vancouver BC foundered and sank off Cape Mudge BC.

Carmal[126] On November 24, 1965 this fishboat was destroyed by fire off Bowen Island BC. Her owner, Oscar Vallstrom, was sleeping when the fire broke out, possibly in the oil stove. He fought the fire with an extinguisher but was forced to evacuate in a dinghy. The Bowen Queen stood by while Vallstrom was rescued by the CCGC *Mallard* and took the *Carmal* in tow, but she sank in deep water.

Carol C.[127] 178876 On October 14, 1952 this fishboat was stranded off Steamer Point, Nootka Sound BC.

Carol M 152903 On March 12, 1933 this fishboat owned by Yahei Takenaka, Vancouver BC was stranded half-way between Clo-oose BC and Nitinat BC, about one-half mile offshore.

Carrier Dove[128] In May 1910 this vessel nearly burned to the waterline 30 miles offshore while awaiting return of her fishing dories. A fire started in the engine room caused by a blow-out of an elbow joint in the exhaust. Water playing on the fire caused her to heel over. The engineer opened the seacocks which carried burning gas to other parts of the ship. The crew all sustained burns from fighting the fire. Once the fire was extinguished, they shaped a course to Bull Harbour where repairs were made. On February 13, 1912, this schooner ran aground and was left high and dry between Seymour Narrows and Chatham Point.

Cash-In 176223 On March 31, 1958 this troller burned and sank in Trevor Channel in Barkley Sound.

---

a   Built as Yip; then Carlysle IV

Cassiar[a,129] 103472 On January 12, 1910 she ran aground in Surge Narrows. Lifeboats were slung out but two hours later she refloated and continued underway. On August 16, 1917, at 2:30 am she was aground on Trivett Island in Simoom Sound BC. She was badly damaged, and passengers were put into the ship's boats and rowed to Simoom Sound. Many of the passengers were picked up three days later by the *Cowichan*. At daylight only her bow was visible. She was pulled off into deep water, turned around and pulled up onto the beach where she was patched and pumped out. In 1931 she was converted to a floating dance hall on Lake Washington. In 1940 she was destroyed by fire.

Cassiar 29 189624 On August 15, 1960 this fishboat owned by The Cassiar Packing Co. Ltd., Vancouver BC burned approximately 2.5 miles west of Weak Point BC.

Cassiar 33 320912 On September 17, 1971 this fishboat owned by the Cassiar Packing Co. (1962) Ltd., Vancouver BC grounded and sank off Bonilla Island BC in Hecate Strait.

Cassiar 64 348383 On March 20, 1976 this fishboat owned by Cassiar Packing Co. (1962) Ltd., Vancouver BC foundered on Hannah Rocks in Queen Charlotte Sound.

Cassiar No. 1 190090 In 1972 this fishboat owned by the Cassiar Packing Co. (1962) Ltd., Vancouver BC was reported as sunk off the Cassiar Cannery.

Cassiar No. 12 193719 On September 6, 1964 this fishboat owned by the Cassiar Packing Co. (1962) Ltd., Vancouver BC was swamped and sank near Kitson Island in Edye Pass BC.

Cassiar No. 41 327125 In June 1976 this fishboat owned by the Cassiar Packing Co. Ltd., Vancouver BC was destroyed by fire in Prince Rupert Harbour.

---

a   Built as J.R. MacDonald; then Cassiar; then J.R. MacDonald

Castlegar[130] 130556 On November 13, 1913 this tug owned by Canadian Pacific Railway Co., Montreal QC was in a collision with the yacht *Skookum* on Okanagan Lake BC. In 1925 she was broken up (engine and boiler sent to Roseberry BC).

The *Catala* on Sparrowhawk Reef (Photograph from the Stuart Thompson Fonds in the Vancouver City Archives AM1535-CVA_99-1968)

Catala[131] 152822 On November 9, 1927 this passenger vessel, while under the command of Captain AE Dickson, ran aground on Sparrowhawk Reef in Cunningham Passage. She sat high and dry at low tide with the tug *Cape Scott* standing by and all her passengers disembarked. The grounding was so gentle that it was not apparent until she was observed not to be answering the helm. She became so impaled on the rock that salvors had to blast away 300 tons of rock inside the ship's hull before she was removed to dry dock. She was floated off a month later a high tide. In 1962 she served briefly as a hotel ship in Seattle WA for the Century 21 Exposition moored at Gray's Harbour WA USA. In 1965 she was wrecked in a storm on the Pacific coast of Washington State.

Catala Isle 314804 On May 25, 1975 this fishboat owned by Moses Cox (MO), Kyuquot BC was holed and sank.

Caterpillar Chief[a] 153074 On December 22, 1951 this tug owned by Nanaimo Towing Co. Ltd., Nanaimo BC foundered 3/4 of a mile southwest of Popham Island and sank rapidly in Howe Sound BC after a hatch cover was torn off by waves during a storm. The crew of four escaped in a small boat and were rescued by the tug *Magellan Straits*.

---

a   Built as Hyak; then Caterpillar Chief

Catre No. 1 325621 In 1966 this work boat owned by The Cattermole-Trethewey Contractors Ltd., Vancouver BC sank in the Skeena River and was a total loss.

Caygeon[132] On June 04, 1928 she burned at the oil float at Butedale BC.

Cecilye 138525 On December 10, 1929 she burned at Moodyville in Vancouver Harbour BC. In 1930 she was rebuilt from a recovered wreck by George W Roberts, Vancouver BC.

Cellulose 194188 This tug owned by Western Sales Ltd., Vancouver BC and sank two miles northwest of Pine Island BC. The vessel was a total loss.

Centennial 71[133] 331140 On June 6, 1977 the fishboat *Blue Waters* was in a collision with the fishing vessel *Centennial 71* and sank in Queen Charlotte Sound BC. The crew of two from the *Centennial 71* were rescued.

Chakawana[a] 130441[134] On December 02, 1931 this former rum runner owned by E Hisaoka, Vancouver BC suffered an explosion in Health Harbour at the entrance to Knight Inlet BC. She burned and was a total loss.

Challambra[135] 219331 (US) On June 16, 1927 this motorship owned by Pacific Motorship Co. Inc., Tacoma WA USA was stranded on Whitecliff Island, BC, 15 miles south of Prince Rupert, at 3:00 am. She was en route from Seattle to Alaska when the incident occurred. She was left wedged between two rocks, and the strain on the hull caused her to leak and a temporary patch was put over the hole. Much of her cargo was lightered off. The *Salvage King* was sent to recover her. She was towed to Esquimalt for repairs that proved too costly. In August she was advertised for sale. On November 18, 1927 she burned at her berth in Seattle WA. Firemen built rafts to float inside the water-logged hull to reach a smouldering fire inside her boiler-room that

---

a   Built as Chakawana; then RNWMP Chakawana; then CASC Chakawana; then Chakawana

went on for several days. She was declared a total constructive loss and was broken up.

Chamiss Bay[a] 154926 This seiner owned by British Columbia Packers Ltd., Richmond BC and Christie Packing Co. Ltd., Vancouver BC sank March 09, 1981 and was declared a constructive total loss.

Champion This schooner spent time in Alaska trading and hunting seals and sea otter. She was the first vessel to engage First Nations as a hunting crew, a practise that later became an industry-wide standard. In 1887 she was owned by Chief Peter of Neah Bay WT USA. In the same year, she was wrecked near Nitinat on Vancouver Island while attempting to cross the Nitinat Bar. One crewman, the Mate Cultus George, was lost.

Champion 107728 On October 18, 1903 this wooden workboat owned by Samuel K Champion, Vancouver BC burned in Oyster Bay, Ladysmith Harbour BC.

Charis 329204 On July 21, 1981 this fishboat owned by J & W Fishing Ltd., Victoria BC burned and sank off Triple Island BC.

Charles B. Kinney 125691 This American barque sailed from Port Townsend WA for Australia with lumber on November 20, 1886. She was seen drifting in December 1886 off Cape Beale BC by the lighthouse keeper who reported that an abandoned hulk had drifted ashore one mile east. The seas were heavy, and the ship broke up that night, with the wreckage drifting away. Among the wreckage on the beach was a broken quarter board with the letters "Charles B." Thirty crew members were lost.

Charles H. Cates VI[b] 154945 On March 4, 1949 this tug was struck by the anchor of the *Olga* in Vancouver Harbour BC knocking one of her crew into the water.

---

a   Built as Chamiss Bay; then HMCS Chamiss Bay; then Chamiss Bay
b   Built as Charles H. Cates VI; then Skookum Chief

Charleston (USS)[136] C.22 (USN)/ CA.19 (USN) The *Charleston* was stripped down to the waterline and then sold to the Powell River Company, Ltd. On October 25th, 1930, the ship was towed to Powell River, British Columbia, to serve as a floating breakwater for a large logging mill. The hulk was ballasted, anchored, and periodically pumped out to keep her afloat. The following year, she was joined by the hull of the cruiser USS *Huron* (formerly *South Dakota*). In 1961, heavy weather caused the *Charleston* to partially flood, and her hull was towed to Kelsey Bay, on the north coast of Vancouver Island where the hulk was run ashore to serve as a breakwater.

Charlotte 103909 She was launched August 3, 1896. In winter 1896 she was at Steamboat Landing, but the lay-up was occupied by the *Victoria*. The *Victoria* was purchased and demolished to make room for the *Charlotte*. She hit a rock in Fort George Canyon on July 15, 1910 and sank in Fort George Canyon. She was brought back to Quesnel and abandoned there. The boiler was salvaged and used in a sawmill at Quesnel and later abandoned. The boiler was put back into operation in the 1930s in the Cariboo Gold Quartz Mine at Wells, operating until the 1940s.

Charlotte Straits[a] 193766 On July 19, 1980 this workboat owned by Olympic White Logging Ltd., Victoria BC was destroyed by fire at Cypress Bay near Tofino on the west coast of Vancouver Island BC and was a total loss.

Charlottetown (HMCS)[137] K.350 (RCN) At the end of her life she was made part of the breakwater at Oyster Bay BC.

Charmaine 313992 On July 12, 1963 this fishboat owned by Thomas M Widrig, Seattle WA USA exploded and burned 35 miles due south of Tofino BC and was destroyed by fire through misadventure.

---

a   Built as USATS TP-225; then *Artic Queen*; then *Charlotte Straits*

Charmer[a,138] 100793 In 1892 she collided with Willamette and was beached at Bush Point, towed to Victoria. In 1902 she made her 3000th voyage. In 1907 she was involved in a collision with CPR trans-Pacific steamer *Tartar* (both vessels heavily damaged). On December 03, 1908, the *Charmer* ran afoul of a fully loaded barge in tow of *Bermuda* in the First Narrows and ran ashore to save her. On hitting the beach, the crew swung out the boats in preparation for evacuating the passengers and crew. The Chief Officer in one of the ship's boats sailed to a large coal barge alongside the Empress of Japan who brought the longshoremen and the barge back to the *Charmer* to unload her cargo. Two large kedge anchors were dropped astern and at low water the hole in her side was patched and the water pumped out. The *Bermuda* also suffered damage. The barge she was towing was owned by Macdonald, Marpole & Co. It was thought that the *Charmer* hit the barge first which swung her around toward Bermuda. In 1916 she rammed and sank the CGS *Quadra* in fog off Nanaimo.

The Charmer showing collision bow damage (Image from the collection of the Maritime Museum of British Columbia 000099)

Chaudiere (HMCS) On December 5, 1992 she was deliberately scuttled by the BC Artificial Reef Society in Sechelt Inlet BC where she is now an artificial diving reef.

Chehalis[139] 103065 On June 21, 1906 while she was chartered to Robert E. Bryce this tug owned by GT Legg (MO), Vancouver BC

---

a   Built as Premier; then Charmer

collided with the Princess Victoria off Brockton Point (First Narrows) BC and sank. This generated a significant court case as the Chehalis was cut in two. The Princess Victoria was overtaking the Chehalis and collided with this tug in the stern, sinking it immediately. Of the crew of 14 on board, seven were drowned: Dr WB Hutton (Registrar of the Manitoba Medical College); Mrs Bryce (wife of the Purser of the Cassiar); PJ Chick (retired Purser); Charles Benwell (a young boy); Crawford A White (deckhand); and two unnamed Japanese firemen.

Chehalis[140] 150553 On July 25, 1932 this tug owned by Launcelot B Noel, Victoria BC, and Captain William Schade (JO), Victoria BC suffered a fire one mile west of Arbutus Point, Gulf of Georgia BC and burned to the waterline. Her crew of six escaped harm. The tug with a boom of 1,000,000 board feet of logs was waiting for a tide change to enter Sansum Narrows when a fire started in the engine room. Three members of the crew were sleeping and had to dress before they could get into action. Within 5 minutes the fire had enveloped the vessel. Captain William Schade and his two sons were aboard the tug at the time of the incident. The logs were from Mud Bay on their way to the Sidney Lumber Co. mill.

Chelhosin[141] 130805 On August 20, 1915 two prospectors returning from a trip up the coast in a small canoe were caught in a tidal rip and capsized. They clung to the overturned canoe for several minutes with no hope of rescue when Samuel E West started swimming ashore which took him more than an hour. He secured a rope and was swimming back out to his stranded friend when the Chelhosin passed close by. Her backwash created such a swell that Francis Pike of Courtenay was washed off the canoe and drowned. On February 5, 1935, the Chelhosin collided with the Princess Charlotte off Point Atkinson. They sighted each other through dense fog in time to avert a major disaster by altering course and diminishing the shock of the collision. Neither vessel took on water and both were able to enter the harbour under their own power. On November 7, 1949 in a thick fog while inbound she ran aground on Siwash Rock Vancouver BC refloated. Nineteen people were injured and all 53 were rowed ashore. The radar operator on the Lions Gate Bridge tried to warn the vessel several times by radio of the danger of her course but to no avail. The Chelhosin carried both radio and radar at the time. The hull was temporarily patched, and she was towed into the harbour. In 1951 she was scrapped at San Francisco CA USA.

The *Chelhosin* ashore (Photograph from the Williams Brothers Photographers Collection in the Vancouver City Archives AM1545-S3-CVA_586-8506)

Chemainus 126509 On October 14, 1911 this tug owned by Victoria Lumber & Manufacturing Co., Victoria BC caught fire in Jervis Inlet. On November 24, 1945, this tug owned by Straits Towing & Salvage Co., Vancouver BC was wrecked near Lund BC at the Ragged Islands. The hulk was dynamited.

Cheslakee[a,142] In 1910 she was completed at Belfast NI UK. The *Cheslakee* capsized on January 17, 1913 at the wharf at Vananda BC with the loss of 7 passengers and crew. The incident did not surprise many on the waterfront as she was considered to have been top heavy. She lay on the bottom with only her mast and funnel showing above the water. She was salvaged, rebuilt, and renamed as a much more stable craft serving another 33 years on the British Columbia coast.

---

a   Built as Cheslakee; then Cheakamus

Cheyney[143] 152739 On October 8, 1929 this motorboat burned about 800' from the Charles Creek Cannery wharf at Kingcome Inlet BC. The engine backfired and burned to the water's edge. The Engineer jumped in the water to escape the flames.

Chief Malibu[a] 176483 She served as a patrol vessel in the Royal Canadian Navy during the Second World War. In 1952 as a work boat owned by Hamiltair Ltd., Pender Harbour BC she sank in Princess Louisa Inlet, BC.

Chief Seegay[144] 155171 She formed part of the pre-war Fishermen's Reserve Fleet. She was mobilized as a Fishermen's Reserve vessel from 08 Nov 1939 to 27 May 1940 as a tender to HMCS *Givenchy*. On March 19, 1975, this fishpacker owned by Priority Seafoods Ltd., Vancouver BC foundered and sank two miles off Bordelais Island at the entrance to Barkley Sound resulting in a total loss. Her crew evacuated in a life raft and were rescued by the *Banfield Lifeboat*.

Chieftain[145] 094820 On October 9, 1947 this tug, owned by Pacific Coyle (Navigation) Co. Ltd. (The Red Band Fleet), Vancouver BC, grounded on Calamity Point shoal. (The newspapers noted that to that date more than a dozen vessel had grounded there in the previous year.) She was beached as a hulk at Gambier Island BC.

Chieftain III[146] 320258 In February 1975 a gale caught the tug and her loaded barge in Malaspina Strait BC en route from Squamish for the MacMillan-Bloedel pulp mill at Powell River. The barge was carrying 250 tons of liquid caustic soda in below deck tanks and four railway cars of chlorine. The barge capsized at the north end of Texada Island. The submarine *Pisces* enabled a subsequent salvage operation attempt, but the rail cars are still on the bottom with their cargo.

---

a Built as HMCS Q.127; then Chief Malibu

Chilcotin Princess[a,147] 371935 On September 1, 1977 she collided with the fishboat M.M. (which sank) between Egg Island and Pine Island in Queen Charlotte Sound BC. It was reported by JD Jordan that "She spent her final years tied to the dock in Namu. She was moved to Shearwater after the Coast Guard was concerned for her sinking. They dismantled her at Wainwright Shipyard, Prince Rupert in 2015."

China Hat[148] 138163 On September 24, 1949 this fishpacker, while under command of Captain Charlie Strom and owned by British Columbia Packers Ltd., Vancouver BC, was stranded in heavy fog near Mexicana Point on Hope Island BC. The captain and his crew of two were rescued by a small boat dispatched from Bull Harbour.

Chinook II[b,149] 197867 On April 5, 1962 this passenger car ferry suffered minor damage when she was stranded, in fog, on Snake Island. The passengers were evacuated safely—and the vessel was refloated safely on the next high tide.

Chiquita Mia 150752 On April 13, 1925 this fishboat owned by George Monfret, Vancouver BC burned off Granite Island, in George Strait BC.

Christella 131026 On July 13, 1913 this excursion boat, owned by the Inland Transportation Co. Ltd., Vancouver BC, was destroyed by fire at Vancouver BC.

Christiania (Norwegian Registry) On February 26, 1924 this freighter was stranded in Barkley Sound BC.

Chuckwalla[c,150] 138358 On October 31, 1934 she was stranded on the west coast of Vancouver Island ran aground on Blunden Island Reef, Clayoquot Sound BC. Captain Morris Lawler and James Thomas

---

a   Built as HMCS Laymore; then Chilcotin Princess
b   Built as Chinook; then Chinook II; then Sechelt Queen
c   Built as Chuckwalla; then Western Pilot; then B.C.P. 46

died. She was towed to Ahousat BC and sank. The engineer, Carl Smith, was washed overboard with a dinghy but managed to reach shore safely. The vessel was en route from Hecate to Kildonan towing another vessel. In 1935 she was raised by the Pacific Salvage Co. (*Salvage King*) repaired and sold to Nelson Brothers and renamed as *Western Pilot*. On October 4, 1959 she was aground at Race Rocks BC.

Chuckwalla On October 16, 1961 this fishboat burned and sank in the Juan de Fuca Strait. Two crew members were rescued by the US Coast Guard and taken to Port Angeles WA.

Chummie II[151] 138357 On April 14, 1926 this workboat owned by Wallace Shipyards Ltd., North Vancouver BC hit the Second Narrows Bridge in Burrard Inlet and sank. She was raised two days later.

Chuqualla[152] 134062 On October 26, 1938 this tug, owned by Charles F Deeks, Stewart BC, broke her anchor chain and she drifted on the rocks at Water Island BC.

Cilla[a] 133877 On August 17, 1945 this workboat, owned by Peter Ambrose, Vancouver BC, was stranded 1.5 miles west of McKenny Island off Aristazabal Island BC.

City of Ainsworth 096998 In April 1897 she foundered in Kootenay Lake off Kaslo BC. She was raised and sold. On November 29, 1898 she capsized off Pilot Bay, BC in a storm with a loss of nine lives. She was chartered by International Navigation & Trading Co. on the Nelson to Bonners Ferry service.

City of Clinton 138772 On May 12, 1931 this workboat owned by CH McKinnell, Vancouver BC burned one-and one-half miles west of Galiano Island BC.

City of Lund[153] 126545 She was the third tug built by the Thulin Brothers. In 1910 she was damaged by fire. In March 20, 1920 this

---

a Built as Sonrisa; then Cilla

tug was broadsided by the passenger vessel *Admiral Evans* heading through Discovery Passage in heavy fog. Her stern was cut off and the tug sank in Duncan Bay. On April 27, 1931, while owned by St. Clair Towing Co. Ltd., Vancouver BC, she burned near Snug Cove, Bowen Island BC off Whitecliffe BC.

City of Panama[a] (US) On October 09, 1874 she was grounded in Victoria Harbour BC. She was lightened and released without damage. On Thursday, June 22, 1876 returning to San Francisco from Victoria BC she collided with the *Zealandia*. "The steamer City of Panama arrived from Victoria about ten o'clock last evening. When coming into the Pacific Mail Steamship Company's wharf, she ran into the steamship *Zealandia*, inflicting considerable damage, though not as great as at first reported. It appears that the City of Panama came in at first at the head of the dock ; but her master, receiving some instructions, backed out into the stream, and making a turn, carne back up to the dock to take position aft of the *Zealandia*, whose bow was pointing toward the head of the dock. Whether from some misunderstanding of the bells, or for some reason that has not yet been explained, she went head on against the port side of the *Zealandia*, striking her about abreast of the after hatch, twisting and forcing in a number of her plates, for a space of about fourteen feet in length and one foot in breadth, just above and below the water line. To use the expressive language of one who was present, there was a hole big enough for a man to crawl through, if he felt like doing so. Canvas was immediately got out, and hung over the opening to prevent the influx of water; but one of the compartments, the steamer being divided into several, filled rapidly, and they soon settled, until the stern of the steamer was on about a level with the wharf, while the bow was high above it. After inflicting the damage, the City of Panama, which seemed to suffer trifling, if any, injury, went out into the stream at a considerable distance from the wharf.—The mails were placed upon a boat and taken ashore. When the full extent of the damages of the *Zealandia* were ascertained, a force of forty men was gathered, and worked all through the night, "listing" the steamer, so that the

---

a   Built as City of Panama; then Crowley; then Olga M.

injured plates should be brought above the waterline. When this is completed temporary repairs will be made, and the compartment pumped out. It is then likely she will go into the dry dock for complete repairs. It will take from one to two weeks to repair damages."

City of Seattle[154] 126635 (US) This passenger freighter of the Pacific Coast Steamship Company, went hard on the rocks at Trial Island, off Oak Bay at around 4:15 am on September 20, 1906 while enroute from Seattle to Victoria. She was traveling at full speed when she rammed the rocks. The 39 passengers, remained on board until an initial attempt to remove her by the salvage vessel *Salvor* and tugs *Pioneer* and *Pilot*, proved unsuccessful. The passengers were then removed and billeted in Victoria hotels. The steamer *Maude* was brought alongside just before noon to remove cargo from the forward holds, in attempt to lighten the ship for the next attempt to remove her from the rocks. She was eventually refloated and towed to Esquimalt.

The *City of Seattle* at Esquimalt BC. (Photograph from the Major Matthews collection in the Vancouver City Archives SGN 310)

City of Vancouver[a] 073624 On January 02, 1902, this collier loaded with 2,400 tons of coal from Ladysmith BC for the Treadwell Mine at Juneau AK, she stranded on a reef at the entrance to Milbanke Sound, (on a rock laying between Gray and Green Islands) where she broke up and sank. At the time she was owned by J Dunsmuir, Victoria BC. (The TSBC reports the location as between Gray and Green Islands in Chatham Strait BC). Her forward section was jammed in the rocks with the afterpart still afloat. After a few hours, the bow was submerged, and the stern sank too. Six crewmen were lost including the Captain. The rest of the crew of 20 were rescued by the *Cottage City*. The Pilot, TW Roberts, was lost.

---

a   Built as Bristol; then City of Vancouver

Clarksdale Victory[155] (US) On November 24, 1947, while on a voyage from Whittier AK to Seattle WA she broke in two and her stern sank. The rest of the hull ran aground on a reef near Hippa Island, near Graham Island in the Queen Charlotte Islands BC. Rescue attempts were made but found no survivors on the beach and no evidence of life on the bow which was breaking up. There was a loss of 49 men, but four survivors were found in the remains of the bow section. With a death toll of 49 lives, this was the worst Pacific Northwest marine disaster of 1947. She was driven off course by strong winds and ran aground in 50-foot seas, her stern section sank quickly after grounding taking most of her crew to a watery grave. The steamship *Denali* launched a boat in a rescue effort, but it swamped and its eight-man crew barely escaped with their lives. The Coast Guard cutters USCGC *Wachusett* and USCGC *Citrus* rescued four survivors and the bodies of three of the victims. The only survivors remained on the forward part of the ship, some of which remains over 70 years later.

Cleeve[156] 103170 In 1917 this tug, owned by William N Coughlin, Vancouver BC, collided with the passenger steamer *Prince Rupert* in Burrard Inlet near the Grand Trunk wharf. On December 6, 1923, this tug owned by Benjamin Gilbert & William McConnell (JO), North Vancouver BC was in a collision with the *Temparsan Maru* in Burrard Inlet BC. On April 24, 1925 she was destroyed by fire in Billrose Bay, off Lasqueti Island BC.

Cleveland (US) On December 6, 1897 the brigantine-rigged auxiliary steamer *Cleveland* under Captain Hall was steaming from San Francisco to Puget Sound. She lost her propeller near the mouth of the Columbia River and was forced to rely on her sails. She was forced north until the Cape Flattery Lighthouse was sighted. They fired distress rockets and displayed distress signals. Approaching Cape Beale Lighthouse, they repeated the distress signals. She was driven on by the wind and currents toward Starlight Reef. On December 9, 1897, the ship's boats were provisioned and trailed astern and the crew abandoned ship. The ship drifted toward the reef while boats took refuge in the George Fraser Islands. Only the captain's boat made it to safety, they others vanishing in the storm. They rowed on to

Ucluelet awaiting the end of the storm. In the calm that followed they rowed out to the wreck on the reef. They discovered that First Nations people had already salvaged more than 100 tons of cargo. Travelling to Alberni, overland by horse to Nanaimo and by train to Victoria he intercepted the CGS *Quadra* about to leave on a 10-day trip. A diver on the ship was able to repair a hole in the hull and the vessel was refloated. One of the missing lifeboats with its crew turned up safe at Hesquiat after being at sea for three days. While there they assisted Father Brabant in the construction of a new church there. Another boat was picked up by the Quadra in Clayoquot Sound, but the last boat was never found.

Cliff Point[a] 172323 On June 19, 1945 this fishboat owned by The Canadian Fishing Co. Ltd., Vancouver BC burned at the Cow Bay Float, Prince Rupert BC.

Cliff Point 329498 On March 7, 1977 this fishboat took on water and foundered 6 miles south of Passage Island in Howe Sound BC. She was on charter to the Canadian Fishing Co. Ltd., Vancouver BC at the time of the incident.

Clinton[b,157] 140937 On January 15, 1922 this passenger ship was in a collision in dense fog with the tug *Clinton* near the entrance of First Narrows, Vancouver Harbour which caused the *Clinton* to founder in Burrard Inlet BC. The crew of the *Clinton* climbed up onto the bow of the steamer to save themselves from the sinking tugboat. Captain LH Fraser was the last to leave the tug.

Cloyah[158] 151127 On December 11, 1927 this Canadian Government fishery patrol vessel owned by the Minister of Marine & Fisheries, Ottawa ON burned at Tuck Inlet BC. She had been en route to Prince Rupert BC at the time of the incident. Her Engineer, Christopher Eyolfsen suffered burns on his face and arm. The three men on

---

a   Built as Cliff Point; then Pursuit II
b   Built as Daring; then Clinton

board took to the lifeboat: Captain W Strachan (Master); C Eyolfsen (Engineer) and Captain R Eburne. They stayed nearby until all the gas tanks had exploded and then put a line on her and towed the burning boat to the beach.

Clutha[159] 111957 On May 12, 1925 this tug owned by Captain WS Wooster & Murdock Young, New Westminster BC struck the Fraser River Bridge at New Westminster BC and sank with a small donkey engine in 30 feet of water. A big piledriver hit the bridge and was knocked over striking the *Clutha* which was lashed to the scow of the piledriver. Captain M Young and the Mate Walter Robinson saved themselves by stepping onto the scow when they saw the collapse occurring. The deckhouse of the tug was completely smashed.

Clyde 094898 On April 23, 1890 she was caught in a sudden gale while anchored in English Bay. She was blown ashore and broke her twin screws. On December 25, 1890, her load of lime caught fire in Vancouver. In February 1896 she again caught fire off Point Grey and burned to the waterline.

Coast Harvester 393579 On September 01, 1987 this fishboat owned by Sylvester S Drozozik, Vancouver BC foundered 3 miles off Hot Springs Cove BC.

Coast Quarries Jr. 155072 On June 2, 1945 this tug owned by The Coast Quarries Ltd., Vancouver BC was sunk in a collision with the tug *Sea Lion* off Sechelt BC.

Coaticook (HMCS) K.410 (RCN) In 1949 she was in service as a breakwater at Powell River BC. In 1961 she was towed back to Victoria BC for scrapping by Morris L Greene. During the tow she was damaged and started taking water. Greene convinced the underwriters to let him sink the vessel. He put four cases of Forcite into the vessel off Race Rocks and she blew up, sinking her.

Cobb 175457 This troller fishboat owned by Adriaan P Barnum, Parksville BC used to berth at Bamfield BC while it was active. On October 14, 1975 she foundered and sank at La Perouse Bank BC (off Ucluelet BC).

Cohoe 130852 On August 23, 1943 this fishboat owned by The Packers Steamship Co. Ltd., Vancouver BC was in a collision with the *Ada II*, two miles due west of the Kinahan Islands QCI BC.

Colby 116404 On December 24, 1932 this fishboat owned by WA Wadhams, Vancouver BC burned in Koprino Harbour, Quatsino Sound on a beach close to the Cannery.

Colleen K.[a,160] 192022 On March 10, 1976 this tug grounded and capsized at False Creek Vancouver BC. On December 12, 2012, the Canadian Coast Guard (CCG) received a report that an old 13-metre steel-hulled tugboat, the *Colleen K*, had sunk at Port Simpson Marina in Northern British Columbia. The *Colleen K* was raised by the contractor on December 16, placed on a barge and taken to Wainwright Marine Services shipyard for survey and assessment. Subsequently, the CCG contracted with Wainwright Marine to remove all hydrocarbons from the tug, deconstruct and dispose of the debris in accordance with the applicable federal and provincial regulations.

Collinson[161] 153158 On November 10, 1975 this fishboat owned by Lewis Clifton (MO) and Arnold J Clifton (JO), Hartley Bay BC struck a log and sank and declared a total constructive loss two miles west of Cummins Point BC. Dirk Septer stated "Almost two years after the Broken Arrow/Lost Nuke incident south of Prince Rupert, on May 21, 1952, Lewis Clifton, a First Nations halibut fisherman from Hartley Bay, made a gruesome discovery off Ashdown Island. His fishing vessel *Collinson* hooked onto a parachute, bearing US markings, entangled with some human bones and tree branches. Though at that time no positive identification could be made, it was believed the remains might be of an airman from the giant intercontinental B-36 bomber.

---

a   Built as Forres; then Colleen K.

The Prince Rupert detachment of the BC Provincial Police held the parachute and remains until the US authorities picked them up. "

Coloma 05796 (US) An American bark, 852 tons registered at San Francisco CA USA, this 168-foot vessel was owned by the Pacific Shipping Co. She was en route from Everett WA for San Diego CA with a cargo of lumber. She was wrecked off Cape Beale on December 7th, 1906 on rocks off Cape Beale, BC. The crew was saved by Minnie Patterson from Cape Beale Lighthouse and her crew of ten was picked up by the Canadian Government vessel *Quadra*.

Columbia[162] 0126880 (US) This sternwheeler burned on August 2, 1895 opposite Sayward BC on the Columbia River (just north of the US Border). Her engines were salvaged and installed in the Kokanee.

Columbia (HMCS) She was a *Restigouche*-class destroyer that served in the Canadian Navy 1959–1974. On December 22, 1996 she was sunk as an artificial reef off Campbell River BC by the Artificial Reef Society of British Columbia.

Colusa[163] 125169 (US) She was reported to have gone aground on Bonilla Point November 1899 but apparently, she was confused with the *Vidette* or some other of the vessels that were wrecked in that period. On December 12, 1899 under command of Captain Ewart she was reported to have sunk off Sitka Sound AK. An American bark, she was travelling en route to Puget Sound. Heavy southeast gales drove her up to Alaska. The crew abandoned her in a small boat in which they spent four terrible days: the Captain, his wife, and 13 crew members with their black cat mascot Jonah. The *Colusa* had left Hawaii in October, sailing to Esquimalt for repairs. She was off Cape Flattery on November 14th when a heavy southeast gale raged until the 22nd. At that point they were within 3 miles of Vancouver Island labouring heavily so much that the water in the bilge turned the ballast to mud. The pumps were working constantly, bringing up ballast and the ship was growing ever more tenderly. The ship developed a strong list to port. By December 10th they had been driven to the entrance to Sitka Harbour. They crew requested that the Captain abandon ship. The Captain perceiving no hope put everyone in the ship's boat and within 30 minutes they had lost sight of her. They travelled in the *Cottage* City to Seattle from Sitka.

Combat[a,164] 172518 In 1940 this seiner was chartered from Combat Ltd., Vancouver BC by the RCAF and used as a supply & salvage vessel (Type II) at Ucluelet, BC. The charter however was paid by the RCN and the crew was supplied from the RCNR Fishermen's Reserve. In 1941 she was officially transferred to the RCAF Western Air Command Marine Squadron based in Vancouver BC, crewed by RCAF Marine personnel. She had been on a voyage from the Queen Charlotte Islands to the mainland in very windy weather and a tide that had turned against the wind. She was wrecked on March 10, 1965 in Hecate Strait BC with seven crew lost: Gunnar Mourn; James E Kelly; John Leland; Harold Dahm; Walley Leighton and Hans Lehmann.

Comet[165] 096982 On May 25, 1905 this tug was wrecked (aground) at Theodosia Arm, Malaspina Inlet BC. The crew shored her up with timbers as the tide fell but the timbers gave way on her starboard beam and she fell over on to the rocks suffering extensive damage. She was uninsured. Her machinery was salvaged for use in another vessel.

Comet[b,166] 112812 In 1962 this ex-four-masted bark, converted to a log barge, was beached as part of the breakwater in Royston BC.

Comet[c] (US) This ex-US Army tug while owned by the Alaska, British Columbia Transportation Co. in civilian service she towed car barges between Wards Cove AK and Prince Rupert BC. In 1968 she burned and sank off Prince Rupert BC. She was raised and towed to Seattle

---

a Built as Combat, later HMCS Combat, then RCAF M.350 Combat, then Combat again
b Built as Comet; then Orotava; then James Dollar; then Pacific Forester; then Island Forest; then Crown Zellerbach No. 2
c Built as USATS L.T. 393; then Mikiala; then Comet

WA. She was abandoned on the mud flats of Puget Sound near Port Haddock WA USA.

Commodore Straits[a] 122363 In 1942–1945 she was chartered to the United States Army Transportation Service towing barges to the Aleutian Islands. In 1942 she was converted from coal to oil. On December 10, 1955, this tug owned by Straits Towing & Salvage Co. Ltd., Vancouver BC struck rocks at the Rosette Islets and sank when a train barge in tow rammed her.

Como F. 153079 Matt Embree[167] stated that in October 1993 she sprang a plank and sank at Rose Spit BC with the loss of a deckhand during a violent storm. He reported, "I have post traumatic stress syndrome and struggle every day because of this event. After it sank, we drifted for 12 hours until the *Tequila Sunrise* picked us up—it was too rough for the Coast Guard to come."

Comrade 25325 (US) She was registered at Port Angeles WA USA. On February 02, 1911 she burned off Cliff Island in Queen Charlotte Sound BC.

The ship's boat recovered from *HMS Condor* found in 1902. (Image from the collection of the Maritime Museum of British Columbia 000100)

Condor (HMS) On December 2, 1901 the British sloop of war HMS Condor departed Esquimalt for Honolulu. She carried a complement of 130 officers and ratings, although Victoria sources claimed she had embarked an additional 10 men as supernumeraries just prior to sailing. She sank off Cape Flattery in 1901 at Latitude 48°15N and Longitude 125°40W with 140 casualties.

---

a Built as Commodore; then Commodore Straits

Confidence 368701 On October 27, 1980 this fishboat owned by Kari Holding Co. Ltd., Vancouver BC foundered and was abandoned at sea and presumed sunk in Hecate Strait BC.

Connaught[168] On the night of April 14, 1883 this British Bark was driven ashore at Royal Roads (Victoria) during a high gale en route to the Cape of Good Hope with a cargo of lumber from Burrard Inlet. The Connaught, 698 tons, under command of Captain Simpson, was wrecked at Albert Head with 500,000 feet of lumber aboard. Afterwards Welch, Rithet & Co. purchased her wreck for $900.

Connie Jean 176799 On February 17, 1969 this fishboat owned by Murray C. Steen, Vancouver BC burned and was abandoned at Rosang Harbour off Dundas Island BC.

Connie-Kay[169] On June 28, 1966 this American seiner sank during a storm at Nanoose BC in 120 fathoms of water. She hit a submerged deadhead. She began to fill with water. The US fishboat Momentum attempted to tow the boat to Maude Island but the towline broke in the heavy seas. Her crew of six were all rescued by another American boat.

Constance[170] 094899 October 2, 1915 this tug owned by John Hind, Vancouver BC and under commander of Captain Harry Smith foundered at Traill Island in the Gulf of Georgia. She was carrying passengers while towing the disabled un-registered launch Monroe (also carrying 18 passengers) to Pender Harbour. Her crew of 7 and 12 logger passengers escaped to the launch and were saved. The weather was rough, and the tow line parted several times, but the launch was picked up each time. When the Constance started taking on water the crew abandoned ship to the launch as the tug sank.

Constance 117016 On May 08, 1914, at 8:00 am, she struck a submerged floating object while underway in Prevost Passage BC (one mile west of Turn Point) travelling from Victoria to Vancouver BC. She rapidly filled with water and sank within 50 minutes.

Coogee II 134073 On July 19, 1936 this workboat owned by Pacific Mills Ltd., Vancouver BC burned at the head of Cumshewa Inlet, Moresby Island QCI, BC.

The *Coolcha* aground at Albert Head (Photograph from Alberni Valley Museum pn05466)

Coolcha[171] (US) This freighter was registered in San Francisco CA USA. On February 13, 1923 she was stranded at Albert Head BC. She was leaking badly in the forward hold. The crew were rescued safely. She had been en route from San Francisco to Nanoose to load lumber when she lost her course in a driving snowstorm. She was later salvaged by the Algerine but with a broken back and taken to Esquimalt where she was patched up. In May two American tugs, (the *Humaconna* and the *Dolly C.*) arrived to tow her to Seattle for breaking up.

Coquitlam[a,172] On June 22, 1892 this steamship was seized by US Customs in a sealing dispute. She was towed from Sitka to Port Townsend WA. On December 18, 1897 she was stranded at Lama Passage and was salvaged. On May 26, 1909 she caught fire off Cape

---

a   Built as Coquitlam; then Bervin

Roger Curtis on Bowen Island. In 1959 she was sunk as a breakwater at Trinity Bay, Malcolm Island BC.

Cordelia (US) On January 19, 1878 while en route from San Francisco to the Coquille River this tug disappeared. On March 09, 1878, her hull was found bottom-up on the west coast of Vancouver Island.

Cordova[a] 330420 This ex-USN & RCN minesweeper was sunk as a diving hulk in Porteau Cove in 1992 as a dive attraction. This vessel is frequently referred to by her last held name the *Nakaya*.

Corene I 154647 On March 17, 1931 this tug owned by Harold I. Duncan, Vancouver BC exploded in Otter Bay on North Pender Island BC.

Cormorant II[b] 179594 The Canadian Fishing Co. Ltd., operated this vessel owned by The Canadian Fishing Co. Ltd., Vancouver BC out of Butedale as a 'scout' boat—the "eyes and ears" of the company. On July 22, 1963 she burned after hitting the rock bluff on Lewis Island adjacent to the mouth of the Skeena River.

Corner Brook (HMCS) In June 2011 the RCN submarine HMCS *Corner Brook* ran aground during exercises off Vancouver Island and suffered damage to her bow—the pressure hull was reportedly intact. This incident brought forward pre-maintenance work on the submarine, in expectation of a previously planned extended 2.5-year planned maintenance program which has been developed for all the submarines in its class.

Coronado[173] 077461 On November 20, 1913 she foundered in the Gulf of Georgia BC while in tow of the tug *Clayburn* sailing from Ladysmith to Vancouver. The *Coronado* which had been converted to a barge carried a crew who hoisted distress signals seen by the tug.

---

a   Built as USS YMS 420; then HMCS Cordova; then Cordova; then Harbour Queen No. 1; then Nakaya
b   Built as RCAF M.197 Cormorant; then Cormorant II

She began sinking and when finally gone the crew were in a lifeboat that was picked up by the tug and taken to Vancouver.

Corsair She ran Long Beach to Mexico cruises, however in the summer of 1948 Pacific Cruise Lines switched the Corsair to Alaska service, sailing out of Vancouver, British Columbia where she was the very first ship ever to provide a deluxe two-week cruise to the Inside Passage. On November 12, 1949 she struck a rock was beached at Acapulco Mexico to prevent her from sinking, but she was not salvaged before she sank.

Cottage City[174] (US) In 1899; after seven years carrying passengers between New York and Portland; Maine; the Cottage City was purchased by the Pacific Coast Steamship Company and put into service carrying gold miners between Seattle and Skagway; Alaska. On April 26, 1908 while transiting Seymour Narrows and bucking a strong tide she hit bottom and went aground and listed heavily to starboard. Her false keel, wedged in the rocks, broke off as she continued to list. This allowed her to slide off the rock into deeper water. Panicking passengers rushed to don life preservers but the vessel was able to proceed to Vancouver and then on to drydock in Seattle. On January 26, 1911, the steamer Cottage City foundered on the reef at Cape Mudge under Captain AC Jansen. She was caught in a blinding snowstorm and heavy fog and went on a reef off Quadra Island. She had been en route from Seattle WA to Skagway. The 38 passengers and the crew were taken in small boats to Campbell River BC by the tug Salvor. The ship was equipped with radio telegraph equipment, so an SOS call brought help from Victoria, British Columbia, and Port Townsend, Washington.

Cougar King[a] 330585 On May 9, 1979 this fishboat owned by Clive E Amos, Victoria BC foundered and sank at La Perouse Bank off the west coast of Vancouver Island BC.

---

a   Built as Beacon Hill; then Nootka Lady; then Beatrice Mary; then Beacon Hill; then Cougar King

Courser 096997 In 1892 this sternwheeler worked on the Fraser River service. Later she moved to the Stikine River in 1898 going as far as Telegraph Creek. Afterwards she towed logs from Harrison Lake to Harrison Mills. She was powered by a steam engine salvaged from the steamer *Colonel Moody*. In 1905 she sank near Cheam BC after striking a stump. In 1905 she was broken up with her engines going to the steamer *Cheam*.

Cowichan[a,175] 126210 In 1923 she ran aground in Welcome Pass and destroyed her stem and crumpled her shell plating. On December 20th, 1925, this passenger/freight vessel owned by Union Steamships Ltd., Vancouver BC sank in 50 fathoms of water after a collision in dense fog with the *Lady Cynthia* at Roberts Creek. No lives were lost, 14 passengers and the crew of 21 on the Cowichan were quickly transferred to the *Lady Cynthia*.

Cowichan Gap 141795 On August 13, 1928 this fishboat owned by Minosuke Yamamoto, Steveston BC burned in the Queen Charlotte Islands.

Craig Foss[176] 838359 The Transportation Safety Board of Canada states that "At 0110, 28 May 1995, the fishing vessel *Eagle*, southbound on passage from Ketchikan, Alaska, to Seattle, Washington, collided with the loaded rail car barge *Aqua Train*, which was under tow astern of the tug *Craig Foss*, northbound from Prince Rupert, BC, to Whittier, Alaska. The collision occurred two miles east of the northern tip of Melville Island, Chatham Sound in moderate visibility. There was no injury or pollution because of the occurrence. The *Eagle* sustained minor damage to her anchor, which was housed on the forecastle head, and the Aqua Train sustained superficial scraping and denting to the hull. "

Crest[177] On July 25, 1929 the American tugs *Crest* and *Kingfisher* were en route from Chemainus to Seattle tandem towing (in bridle) a boom of logs. They ran up onto Atkin's Reef (east of Walker's Hook

---

a   Built as Cariboo; then Cowichan

between Galiano Island and Saltspring Island. They were high and dry until the rising tide lifted them both off safely.

Criterion I[178] 155111 On April 5, 1930 she struck a submerged log one-half mile of Blenkinsop Bay, in Johnstone Strait BC. She had been en route to Vancouver from a northern logging camp having been delayed by bad weather. After hitting the log, the boat began to sink immediately, and the two-man crew launched the dinghy and made their way to Port Neville.

Croatia[a] 176504 On September 23, 1977 this fishboat owned by Peter Spika, Vancouver BC was declared a total loss after suffering a fire at Northeast point Texada Island BC.

Crofton[b] 126895[179] In October 1953 she dragged her anchor off Point Grey BC with a rock barge in tow she was saved by Captain RH MacDonald in the Emerald Straits. On March 28, 1959, while chartered to the Burton Mining Co., she burned to the waterline at Herbert Inlet, on the west coast of Vancouver Island.

Crown Forest 72–68[c,180] 392962 While crossing Skidegate Narrows, the Crown Forest 72-68 listed to starboard until the vessel capsized. The crew of two was in the wheelhouse. The operator escaped from the wheelhouse and climbed on the capsized hull. He was unable to find his companion after a search above and below water. The operator was rescued a short time later. The body of the missing crew member was later recovered from the wheelhouse by a diver, but resuscitation attempts were unsuccessful.

Crown Zellerbach No. 1[d,181] 099434 In 1914 this sailing vessel was interned at Santa Rosalia, Mexico. After the war she was awarded to Italy for war reparations. She was converted to a hog fuel barge. On

---

a   Built as Lady Marr; then Croatia
b   Built as Burin; then Crofton
c   Built as CZ-72-68; then Crown Forest 72-68
d   Built as Somali; then Alsterdamn; then Adolph Vinnen; then Mae Dollar; then Pacific Carrier; then Island Carrier; then Crown Zellerbach No. 1

June 16, 1945, her cargo caught fire at Alberni and the barge was sunk to extinguish the fire but not before considerable damage was done. Sold for $9000 to the Powell River Co. in 1945 as a breakwater hulk, she was removed from the breakwater in 1954 for repairs to be used as a barge again. In May 1969 she was sold to Capital Iron & Metals Ltd. of Victoria for demolition but was towed to Alaska to become a pier for the Alaska pipeline project. This plan fell through and she was taken instead to Seattle in October 1971.

Crystal No. 2 320895 On June 09, 1975 this gillnet fishboat owned by Howard EE Willson (MO), Port Clements BC foundered in Hecate Strait BC.

Cummins[a] 130875 On February 6, 1954 this passenger ferry owned by Mike Sakich, Vancouver BC struck a submerged object at the junction of Sydney and Shelter Inlets and sank in Sidney Inlet BC.

Cuprite[182] 138307 On January 06, 1958 this tug, ender command of Captain Jack Nicholles, foundered in fog in a riptide off Brockton Point in 175' of water, having turned over while towing a log boom. The skipper and deckhand were in the water for two hours before the skipper and his Mate, John Peeley, were picked up by a lifeboat lowered by the *Princess of Vancouver*.

Cyrus This American brig was travelling from Steilacoom (Puget Sound) to San Francisco with a cargo of lumber under command of Captain Mitchell. Weather conditions were extremely poor and adverse winds caused her to be stuck in the Juan de Fuca Strait for six days sailing against the wind. When her cargo shifted, she entered Port San Juan for shelter. Her anchor chain parted, and she was driven onto the shore. She was lost with all hands at the head of Port San Juan near the Gordon River on Vancouver Island December 23, 1858. Both anchors were lost in the bay when the chains parted before she was wrecked.

---

a Built as Fraser Ferry No. 1; then Maid of Ecoole; then Cummins

Czar 103907 In 1940 she was converted to a barge. In 1942 owned by Nelson Brothers Fisheries Ltd., Vancouver BC she foundered. Her hull was sunk off Prince Rupert BC where she was a derelict on the mud flats. The propeller and shaft were on display outside the Prince Rupert Museum.

D.C.F. No. 1 138180 On October 4, 1923 this fishboat owned by Deep C. Fisheries Ltd., Prince Rupert BC foundered five miles south of Gibson Island, Grenville Channel BC.

D.H.T. No. 3[a,183] 179054 On October 22, 1997 the skipper of the tug *Fraser King*, which was towing the barge D.H.T. No. 3, became disoriented at night after the tug's radar broke down. The skipper called a shore station, reported his position, and requested guidance. Several vessels and aircraft proceeded to assist; however, the search was prolonged because the tug and barge were some 23 miles from the reported position. Although a helicopter attempted to direct the tug, in an area for which the tug had no nautical charts, the barge went aground. Next morning the barge refloated, and the tow was resumed. The barge's shell plating was damaged by the grounding and it took on water and sank.

D.L. Clinch This American schooner sailing from Port Townsend bound for San Francisco under command of Captain WR Perriman with a cargo of lumber. On November 10, 1860 she was being driven on to a lee shore and struck a rocky reef about 200 metres from shore near Sombrio Point, on Vancouver Island. She was swamped by heavy seas when the vessel began to break up. The crew were trapped on board. Later the captain and six others reached shore on a makeshift raft. Attempts to walk out to Sooke were unsuccessful and the crew returned to the wreck. A First Nations canoe arrived on the scene which delivered them safely to Sooke.

---

a   Built as B. No. 1; then Pacific Barge 36; then V.P.D. No. 31; then Dillingham No. 252; then D.H.T. No. 3

Dagan[a,184] 329311 Ken Lund reports that this power-cruiser yacht (ex-fishboat) was "burned and sunk."

Daisy[185] 088375 On March 18, 1909 this tug, owned by Albert Berquist and Captain Fred Anderson, Sidney BC, was stranded on Tumbo Island BC and later salvaged.

Daleson[b,186] 172099 On October 25, 1979 this troller fishboat foundered off Pachena Bay BC in extraordinarily strong winds. The patrol vessel *Laurier* took on David Hegstrom, the OIC of the Banfield Lifeboat Station to offer local knowledge in the incident. This ship saved two crew members of the *Daleson*.

Dance This schooner was believed to have been wrecked during the storm of November 10, 1860 in which the *D.L. Clinch* and *John Marshall* were also lost near Bonilla Point on Vancouver Island. The *Dance* was thought to have gone ashore 8 miles west of Port San Juan. Remains of the vessel, including her name board were recovered by the schooner *Ino*. No bodies were recovered.

Danny & David[187] 323670 John McLean reports that "this fishboat sank and then broke up in Prince Rupert and her the aluminium wheelhouse is on the Active Pass now (2015)."

Dar Kat[188] 331925 On September 16, 1972 this combination troller fishboat, owned by Herbert J Forsyth, Surrey BC, caught fire and sank at Lasqueti Island BC in Georgia Strait.

Dardanella[c] 313882 On December 11, 1966 this fishboat owned by John A Wood, Hammond BC exploded and burned at the Pitt River Bridge BC and was a total loss.

---

a   Built as Dolphin Queen; then Boy David; then Dagan
b   Built as I.L.C.; then Daleson
c   Built as Miss Cogmor; then Dardanella

Dare 157063 (US) On December 23, 1890 this three-masted schooner owned by Simpson Bros & Co., while under the command of Captain FA Berry in transit from San Francisco in ballast for Tacoma to load lumber, was wrecked near Bonilla Point (2.5 miles west of Carmanah Point) during a thick fog. All hands were saved.

The steam tug *Daring* (Photograph from the John MacFarlane Collection)

Daring (VI) 122375 The steam tug *Daring* (ON #122375) was purchased from the Gulf of Georgia Towing Co. in 1926 by MacFarlane Towing Ltd., of Victoria BC. She had been built in 1907 with a 16nhp coal burning steam engine. At first this vessel was employed towing booms for the Stella Lake Logging Company from Elk Bay to Victoria, but the Great Depression caused their mill to close. They then contracted to the Canadian Packing Corporation towing scows of pilchards to the reduction plant at Ceepeecee on Esperanza Inlet. The tug had just bunkered coal, so she was fully laden. One of the duties of the engineer was to break up the clinker in the fire box so that they could be removed. Apparently after this was done, he stowed the red-hot slice bars under the firebox resting them on the wooden ribs of the vessel. It was said that Eastwood had the habit of vacating the engine room between the stoking of the engine to the upper deck. On this occasion he was sitting in the head reading for some time when he noticed that the space was getting very warm. He tried to return to the engine room, but it was already too late. The hot slice bars had ignited the wooden hull. It was then too hot and smoky to either fight the fire or to enter the engine room to shut off the steam to the engine. Another operating error was that he had failed to shut off the steam to the towing winch which turned out to be helpful. This allowed the crew to haul in the tow line and bring one of the scows along side. When it was close enough the crew jumped into scow which was full of fish. Captain MacFarlane put the helm hard over before leaving the bridge so that it steamed in a circle for a long time, nearly ramming the scow on several of the passes. The tug cruised in a wide circle until it burned to the waterline and sank. The work boat was launched but it was crushed between the tug and the tow. Captain MacFarlane swam back to the tug and climbed aboard and single handed launched the lifeboat which was secured to the scow. The crew of the *Daring* was quickly rescued by the *Imlac*, (a pilchard fish boat), but Captain MacFarlane remained aboard the scow (standing up to his neck in rotting pilchards) to prevent a potential salvage claim from their rescuers and others. He was picked up the next day when the scow was towed into port. For his efforts, the company gave MacFarlane a cheque for $75.00 as a reward for standing by the scow. The manager of the fish plant gave Captain MacFarlane his personal set of binoculars as a token of thanks.

Dart[189] (US) This small sealing schooner was owned and crewed by First Nations people from Neah Bay WA USA. In April 1895 she was stranded near Seven Mile Creek close to Carmanah Point dragging her anchor. The theory was that she had broken her anchorage in in the lee of Ozette Rocks WA and then went out sealing in small boats. The wind came up and carried the vessel away to Carmanah about 25 miles away where she was brought up short on the Canadian side by the anchor on the chain.

Dashing Wave[190] 006533 On March 16, 1920 this old schooner converted to a barge, owned by McNeill & Libby, went ashore in Duncan Bay BC. She had been waiting for a tide change so she could transit

Seymour Narrows when with her tug, the San Juan, went ashore at Shelter Point. The San Juan managed to get back into deeper water on her own. She had been en route from Seattle to the Libby salmon packing plant at Taku AK loaded with cannery supplies.

The *Dauntless* ashore between Ladysmith and Chemainus May 1908 (Image from the collection of the Maritime Museum of British Columbia P3266_349)

Dauntless[191] 111599 In 1901 she was built for log towing for the Fraser Mills. On November 25, 1903, this tug ran on the rocks in Euclataw Rapids. She was salvaged by the Maude with a diver using jacks to raise her. A temporary ways was built under her and she was pulled off into deeper water. On June 19, 1908 while towing logs bound for Anacortes while under command of Captain George Marchant, she grounded on Ballingall Rock after hitting the reef below Walker Light on Trincomalee Channel. Fortunately, the current carried the boom around the vessel, and they did not collide. She failed to float off the rock on the high tide. The B.C. Salvage Co. tug *Salvor* was engaged to salvage the tug. A diver was sent down to patch up any openings and powerful pumps de-watered her. The *Salvor* was then able to pull her off. The engines had become inoperable, so she was towed back to port by the tug Fearless.

David Bruce[192] 318646 On September 21, 1972 this troller fishboat, owned by Emil Ronlund, Port Alberni BC, was destroyed by fire and sank at Winter Harbour VI BC. Her two-man crew (Captain David

Ronlund and Ray Haslam) escaped uninjured in a life raft 73 miles southwest of Winter Harbour BC.

David III [193] 176270 This troller fishboat used to berth at Bamfield BC while it was active. On July 29, 1973, this fishboat collided with a deadhead and sank within 3 minutes while heading for Bamfield at Lone Tree Point in the Alberni Inlet BC. Lamb was picked up by a sports fisherman who had to be paid to turn around and take Gordon Lamb to Port Alberni.

Deardot [a] 189220 On May 13, 1964 the exhaust manifold split open and this power cruiser caught fire. The owner fought the fire but hailed the nearby BC ferry *Queen of Tsawwassen* who rescued him. After a few minutes he transferred to a nearby fishboat which put a line on the *Deardot* and began to tow her to the beach. The towline snapped and the boat immediately sank.

Debbie Kathleen K. [b] 150649 In 1944 she sank off Ten Mile Point and was salvaged by the RCN crane and derrick barge B.D. 6. On January 07, 1967 she was destroyed by fire caused by a short-circuited battery and sank while at anchor at Gambier Island BC and was a total loss.

Deborah 130497 On November 2, 1921 this fishboat, owned by Olaf Onse, Mill Bay BC, foundered in Hecate Strait BC. Her two-man crew just had time to get matches and throw a gun into the skiff when she sank. They rowed to a rocky reef where they were marooned for a week. They had no shelter and were kept drench by driving rains. They shot ducks and dug clams for food. Making their way to Lucy Island Light they finally were rescued.

Deer Park 195239 This tug was designed with a tunnel stern, for moving the barge *Arrow Park*. She was shipped by rail to the Arrow Lakes. On November 17, 1956, this tug owned by Interior Tug & Transport Co. Ltd., Revelstoke BC foundered and sank off Spanish

---

a   Built as Beljay; then Deardot
b   Built as USS S.C. 293; then Etta Mac; then Grant Lindsay; then Debbie Kathleen K.

Banks while towing logs. On September 4, 1980, this tug owned by Rivtow Marine Ltd., Vancouver BC sank in Douglas Channel near Hawkesworth Island BC.

Deerleap[a] 155107 Andrew W. McLimont (President of Winnipeg Light and Power) used this large power cruiser extensively to cruise the Inside Passage with private hunting and fishing parties. Gertrude Spencer was the wife of Victor Spencer (owner of Spencer's Department Stores. In 1943 she was chartered by the RCAF and in 1944 she was returned to her owner. In 1956, she reportedly ran aground in front of the Empress Hotel in Victoria and, in the winter of 1957, the boat sank to the bottom of the harbor in Port Angeles, Washington but was later salvaged.

Del Norte This sidewheeler freighter's twin oscillating steam engines were salvaged from the American sidewheeler *Republic*. On October 21, 1866 she was aground in Porlier Pass (Canoe Reef). Her wreck remains lay in water of 15m-25m in depth.

Della C.[194] 134279 On September 08, 1930 this tug, owned by Island Tug & Barge Ltd., Victoria BC, burned one mile west of Macaulay Point BC (near Victoria Harbour)—the two crew members were saved. She had been towing a scow of gravel from the pit as Albert Head when gasoline being refuelled in the engine room ignited. The crew fought the fire with buckets of water before they were forced off the boat by the flames. They jumped aboard the scow and cut the tug adrift. Despite this the burning tug remained alongside and threatened to ignite the scow. The tug *Island Comet* arrived and took the scow in tow. The burning tug sank about one hour later in deep water.

Delma II[b] 193623 On November 6, 1979 she foundered and sank in 30 fathoms off Amphitrite Point BC from an intake of water below the waterline and was declared a constructive total loss.

---

a   Built as Deerleap; then RCAF M.592 Deerleap; then Deerleap
b   Built as Arnold No. 1; then Delma II

Delmar[a,195] 154332 On November 2, 1950 this seiner owned by Harry Martinich, Ladner BC was stranded three miles south of Carmanah Point BC in Juan de Fuca Strait. The vessel developed a leak, hatches had been opened to dump the catch when the vessel was swamped by a huge swell. The vessel sank killing Captain Henry Martinick, North Burnaby BC and John Canick, the cook. The rest of the crew were saved.

Delphinium 134063 On October 5, 1934 this fishboat while owned by The Royal Fish Co. Ltd., Prince Rupert BC was stranded at Whitesand Island BC and later salvaged by Captain Charles Currie. In 1944 she was lost off Vargas Island BC.

Delta Star[196] 328423 On November 20, 1977 this seiner owned by Michael H Wilson, Ladner BC foundered in Porlier Pass BC. The crew of five were picked up by nearby fishermen. They were transferred to the Coast Guard vessel and taken to Fernwood Point on Saltspring Island. The *Atlin Post* tried unsuccessfully to get a line on the overturned boat. She sank in 25 fathoms of water.

Denali[b,197] 220759 (US) In 1935 this passenger freighter owned by the Alaska Steamship Co. was registered in New York NY USA. On May 19, 1935 she was stranded on a reef at Zayas Island BC. This Alaska Steamship Co. passenger freighter was carrying a cargo of 100 tons of dynamite, Road machinery and other items. Fire was starting to consume the vessel when she sank. She broke up and slid into deep water leaving only her forepeak on the reef. Seven passengers, 23 crew members and 4 stowaways were safely taken off the vessel by the *Cyane*. Captain Thomas E Healy and Frank Howseth, the radio operator and others stayed behind. The *Cyane* evacuated most of these leaving Captain Healy, Chief Mate WE Cleasby, and Third Mate J Lawton behind. They followed the others the next day when it was apparent that there was no hope for the vessel.

---

a   Built as Ryuo; then Delmar
b   Built as Jeptha, then Denali

Departure Bay[a] **(HMCS)** 153296 In 1941 she was seized from her Japanese owners by the Canadian Government. In 1942 she was appraised at $7,500. In 1942 her ownership transferred to His Majesty the King. In 1941, shortly after being requisitioning, she was seriously damaged by fire and submersion in the Fraser River. She was repaired at New Westminster, BC. In 1942 she was appraised at $7,500. In 1942 her she was commissioned into the Royal Canadian Navy Fisherman's Reserve. She was employed for general patrol from Esquimalt BC. She underwent extensive repairs after being burned and sunk while in naval service.

Des Brisay[198] 126554 On March 15, 1922 she was swamped by heavy seas at Gonzales Point off Trial Island BC while towing a lumber scow to Esquimalt. The sinking occurred so quickly that the boat could not be launched, and the crew ended up in the water. They gripped the hawser to the scow and managed to climb aboard for temporary safety. The tug Superior got a line aboard the scow under difficult conditions. Three of her crew were picked up by the government launch M. & F. They were A Worth (Chief Engineer); Mr Brownlie (Mate); and Mr Mills (Second Engineer). Captain Warren was picked up by the CPR steamer Otter. The Chinese cook, Mr R Lee, was reported missing and presumed drowned. She was salvaged by the Pacific Salvage Co. from 75 feet of water by Pacific Salvage Company. A diver was sent down and slings for lifting were placed under the hull. On August 24, 1939 she sank off Fiddle Reef (Oak Bay) due to water intake through an open hatch after she was stranded.

Destiny III[b] 314883 She was the first whale chaser imported by Taiyo Gyogyo K.K. to work in British Columbia. Some time while owned by Reginald Carnaby, Port Mellon BC, she was sunk in Howe Sound BC near Port Mellon.

---

a   Built as Departure Bay; then HMCS Departure Bay; then Melvin E. II; then Luanna S.; then Belmac II

b   Built as Fumi Maru No. 5; then Katsu Maru No. 5; then Katsu Maru No. 5; then Westwhale 5; then Destiny III

Detour 320930 On April 08, 1980 this tug owned by Hakki & Kelly Enterprises Ltd., Queen Charlotte City BC foundered while on a voyage from Queen Charlotte City to Peel Inlet and was beached in Skidegate Channel with two lives lost.

Dewy Mist 194918 On September 7, 1977 this fishboat owned by Grant S Goodfellow (MO), Prince Rupert BC foundered near Petrel Rock, Chatham Sound BC.

Diane H. No. 2 331018 On March 6, 1977 this tug owned by George Harlow, Ladysmith BC burned in Switzer Cove, on the east side of Hecate Strait BC and was declared a total constructive loss.

Digby Island Ferry[a] 157211 In 1958 this passenger-car ferry took her last scheduled ferry trip while owned by The Corporation of the City of North Vancouver, North Vancouver BC. On April 16, 1972 while owned by the City of Prince Rupert, Prince Rupert BC she sank in Georgia Strait BC.

Discovery (HMS)[199] On 1 April 1791, HMS Discovery left England with HMS Chatham. Both ships stopped at Cape Town before exploring the south coast of Australia the Discovery's naturalist and surgeon Archibald Menzies collected various plant species. The two ships sailed to Hawaii where Vancouver met Kamehameha I. Chatham and Discovery then sailed on to the Northwest Pacific. She aground in early August 1792 on hidden rocks in Queen Charlotte Strait near Fife Sound. Within a day Chatham also ran aground on rocks about two miles away.

Discovery[200] 061305 In 1890 this schooner was wrecked at Jordan River (VI) BC and became a total loss.

Discovery Isle (Hong Kong) On December 5, 1950 this power cruiser owned by Captain Ernest Godfrey Beaumont, Victoria BC foundered off Gonzales Point in Haro Strait BC.

---

a   Built as North Vancouver Ferry No. 4; then Prince Rupert Airport Ferry; then Digby Island Ferry

Dola[201] 122517 This tug owned by Dola Tugboats Ltd., Vancouver BC towed a railway barge from Vancouver Harbour to Ladysmith or Jayem (Nanoose Harbour). On October 29th, 1953 she was sunk in the fog in Howe Sound in a collision when she was hit by the *Lady Cynthia*, owned by the Union Steamship Co. Ltd. The *Lady Cynthia* took the crew of nine from the tugboat as she sank. The *Dola* was outbound for Squamish with a barge carrying Pacific Great Eastern Railway cars. The *Blackbird* II picked up the *Dola*'s barge.

Dollina[202] 172532 On August 28, 1952 this seiner, owned by Dollina Fisheries Ltd., Vancouver BC, was stranded, while under command of Captain Norman Fiddler, on rocks at Rose Point, Graham Island BC. Big waves soon broke her up. Her crew of eight were saved by the seiner *Kodiak*. A compass deviation of only half a point caused her to run ashore.

Dolly In 1832 this small sailing vessel was stranded on the north coast of the Queen Charlotte Islands and broke up.

Dolphin II[203] 141276 On February 06, 1932 this halibut fishboat, owned by Peter Byrne, Prince Rupert BC, suffered a fire one mile offshore of Stephens Island BC. Captain Peter Byrne and his brother William Byrne were both saved by rowing in a dory through a fierce snowstorm to Prince Rupert BC.

Dominion[204] This bark left Honolulu for Victoria but was never heard of again. A missionary walking near Clo-oose found the name-board that had washed up on the beach.

Don Q. 130844 On October 2, 1975 this fishboat owned by Hugh MacLean (MO), Vancouver BC was in a collision and sank at La Perouse Bank BC (11 miles SW of Ucluelet BC) and was a total loss.

Donald D.[a] 126941 On November 2, 1916[205] this coal barge was stranded in very heavy weather 8 miles west northwest of Pine

---

a Built as Ivy; then Donald D.

Island, Queen Charlotte Sound BC. Her crew of 5 men and one woman were saved by the Prince John. She sailed southbound in ballast from Anyox in tow of the tug *Dola* under command of Captain Verge. The towline parted and efforts get a line aboard failed. The *Dola*, running short of coal, had to abandon the barge, and run for fuel at Alert Bay. By this time, the Donald D. had drifted 30 miles when the Prince John, alerted by naval radio stations, came alongside to rescue the crew 20 miles west of Cape Calvert. The Prince John stood by the barge for some time but efforts to get a line aboard failed so the barge was abandoned, and the Prince John proceeded to Prince Rupert.

Dora[206] 157000 (US) This freighter under the command of Captain Fred A Hovick was bound for western Alaska with supplies for her owners, the Bering Sea Fisheries Co. for their cod fishing outstations. She was carrying a cargo of coal, oil, and general freight. She struck a rocky ledge that extends out into the channel. On backing off she began to take water, and the Captain's hopes of reaching Port Hardy were rapidly revised. She came to rest on a sandy bottom with only her masts showing above the water having slipped after the evacuation of her passengers and crew to the shore. Efforts to remove the wireless set from the ship to set it up on shore were about to be successful when relief arrived. The American steamer *Admiral Rodman* and HMCS *Thiepval* arrived in quick succession to give aid to the survivors who were waiting on shore. The *Admiral Rodman* brought the survivors back to Seattle. On December 28th, Marsh & McLennan, the insurance agents asked for bids from salvagers.

Dora II 154514 On October 12, 1932 while owned by owned by Henry White, Masset BC her engine backfired off Cape Cook VI about twelve miles offshore.

Dora-bel II 173899 On September 9, 1950 this fishboat owned by Levitt Comeau, Sooke BC struck a deadhead and sank at Sheringham Point BC.

Dorbarth[a] 178819 On December 30, 1954 this fishboat owned by Julius Barth, Vancouver BC capsized 1.5 miles south of Green light near the Arm Jetty, Georgia Strait BC. On December 25, 1965 she was stranded on Stephens Island BC and she was later salvaged from her stranding. In 1980 she was reported to have been lost at sea and her owner deceased.

Doreen M.[207] 153326 In 1927 this tug, owned by the MacFarlane Towing Company, Victoria BC, was operated by Captain George A MacFarlane in the Cowichan Bay booming grounds. On July 05, 1928, while owned by Cathels & Sorenson, Victoria BC, she foundered at Secretary Island off Sooke BC while in tow of the seiner *Faith of Sechart*, in 35 fathoms of water. She had hit a submerged snag at 3:00 am. She sank in 30 fathoms of water and powerful currents swept her wreck out to sea.

Doreen M. II 318976 On July 03, 1981 this troller fishboat owned by Silver Harvest Fisheries Ltd., Victoria BC grounded and sank on Starlight Reef.

Doric G. 173503 On August 27, 1954 this troller fishboat owned by Randel Christney, Bamfield BC foundered one mile south west of Helby Island in the Deer Group, Barkley Sound.

Dorothkalon[208] 138677 On March 31, 1925 this tug, owned by T.A. Kelly Logging and Lumber Co. Ltd., Vancouver BC, was stranded on Cumshewa Rock, Moresby Island (QCI) BC with the loss of the Engineer Jimmy Clark.

Dorothy Engvick[209] 153289 On November 23, 1932 this fishboat, owned by Engvick Ltd., Vancouver BC, foundered and sank off Texada Island. She was salvaged and repaired. In 1937 her register was closed, and she was licenced. On May 14, 1970, this fishboat sank in Johnstone Straits off Ragged Island and was a total loss.

---

a   Built as David Scott; then Dorbarth

Dorothy K[a] 314033 On February 11. 1970 this fishboat owned by Mitchell H Gillis (MO), Vancouver BC burned at Cape Roger Curtis, Georgia Strait BC.

Douglas Fir 141422 On May 12, 1948 this work boat owned by William Raby, New Westminster BC burned in the North Arm of the Fraser River BC.

Dreamerie[210] 154334 On March 31, 1932 this halibut fishboat owned by Norman C. Nelson and Richard Nelson (JO), New Westminster BC was stranded on Whyac Beach three miles from Clo-oose BC. She developed engine trouble while fishing and Bill Babcock at the Nitinat Cannery called out the *Banfield Lifeboat*. The crew of the *Dreamerie* dropped anchors but there was a heavy sea running and they started to drag. When it was obvious that the boat was going to end up on the beach the crew evacuated in a small boat. The crew were: Captain Bert Hansen; Art Hansen; Albert Olsen and Charlie Smith.

Drumrock[b,211] 099316 This log carrier barge (ex-sailing ship) owned by BL Johnson, Vancouver BC, was carrying a cargo of several million board feet of logs in tow of the tug Cape Scott. While under tow by the *Pacific Monarch* she went ashore and broke her back. On February 3, 1927 she was stranded at Takush Harbour, Smith Inlet QCI BC. In March 1927, the workboat *Skookum* sank while engaged in wrecking the remains of the *Drumrock* when she ran on a deadhead.

Drumwall[c,212] 152746 The Puako a four-masted barkentine of 1084 tons and 1400 M capacity, was built at Oakland by W. A. Boole & Son in 1902, another of the skysail yarders operated by Hind, Rolph & Co. She was laid up at Victoria in May 1921, and in 1926 she was sold to the Pacific Navigation Co., Vancouver, and converted to a log-barge under the name of *Drumwall*. She was in service carrying

---

a   Built as Daf; then Dorothy K.
b   Built as Helwig Vinnen; then Persimmon; then Drumrock
c   Built as Puako; then Drumwall

hog fuel and wood chips between Port Alberni, Chemainus, to Port Townsend and Port Angeles WA USA. She was added to a breakwater at Oyster Bay on Vancouver Island at the end of her life.

Duchess This freighter owned by Captain Frank P Armstrong was powered by a steam engine which was brought from Montreal and had been used in a ferry on the St. Lawrence River for 45 years previously. She sank in 1887 after a severe wreck near the Canyon Creek rapids. She sank again three weeks later, which caused her to be dismantled in 1888 with her engines going to the second Duchess.

Duchess of Argyle[213] On October 11, 1887 this British four-masted bark, 1,700 tons, inbound from Liverpool via San Francisco to Burrard Inlet, was wrecked in fog five miles southeast of Port San Juan, near Sombrio Point. She was commanded by Captain HE Heard and was sailing with a part-cargo to load lumber. She was stranded in poor visibility near Bonilla Point at Cullite Cove on Vancouver Island and was pounded to pieces in the heavy surf.

Dunsyre[214] 098965 On November 18, 1936 this old sailing ship that had been converted to a barge owned by Island Tug & Barge Co., Victoria BC broke her towline from the tug *Anyox* and went ashore at Kains Island (in Quatsino Sound). She drifted for nineteen hours travelling more than 75 miles from the spot where her towline broke. The crew: Captain W Billington; Roy Larkin; and Alan Heater awaited what they presumed would be their doom when no assistance appeared. These old barges carried a crew because they had to be steered when they were being towed and often required pumping out the bilge when leaking. Her three-man crew was saved but she was a total loss.

Dunver (HMCS)[215] K.03 (RCN) In 1948 when she was sold to Wagner Stein & Greene to be stripped. The remaining hulk was then sent to Royston, British Columbia to be used as part of the breakwater.

E.K. Wood[216] In November 1912 this four-masted lumber schooner, owned by the E.K. Wood Lumber Co., Bellingham WA USA, under

Captain Hellquist was wrecked at Barrier Island BC. Her deck load of lumber was so huge that the strain opened her seams, and she broke her back. Her sails were blown away and even jettisoning her cargo could not save her. The spanker boom fell crushing the lifeboat leaving the crew only one small dinghy.

E.P. Burchett 326601 On January 11, 1979 this tug owned by Weldwood of Canada Ltd., Vancouver BC sank in Jervis Inlet BC and was a total loss.

Eagle (US) In 1865 this trading schooner was arrested by HMS *Clio* and a court was held on board at Port Simpson (conducted by William Duncan JP). She was a sloop whose Master, the Mate and the Cook were each fined for trafficking in illegal alcohol to First Nations people at Port Simpson British Columbia. The Master was fined 500 pounds or 5 years in prison, the Mate and Cook were each fined 100 pounds or one year in prison. She was attacked and burned at Owaykeeno in 1868 and Captain Knight and two crew members were murdered.

Eagle (US) On September 11, 1918 while under the command of Captain Fred Inborg this halibut schooner was lost on the southwest end of George Fraser Island (previously Shelter Island) near Amphitrite Point when she ran ashore in a dense fog while en route for Ucluelet Harbour. The crew were all saved.

Eagle Mar 192407 On August 07, 2019 this power cruiser owned by Natural High Venture Corp., Salt Spring Island BC was burned at Long Harbour, Saltspring Island BC. She burned to the waterline and sank—no one was aboard at the time, and the cause was unknown.

Eagle VI 153005 On November 21, 1944 this tug owned by Harry Bruno, Vancouver BC sprang a leak and sank near the Ballenas Islands BC after hitting Rudder Rock.

Earl 094906 This tug owned by Pacific (Coyle) Navigation Co. Ltd., Vancouver BC ended up as a hulk on the shore of Texada Island BC.

Early Field[a] 153080 On October 8, 1976 this seiner owned by Early Field Fishing Co. Ltd., Ganges BC grounded and sank near Neck Point in Georgia Strait.

East Bay No. 1 154374 On January 7, 1954 this seiner owned by Paul J Perttula, Vancouver BC was in a collision in Seymour Narrows with the Ross Prince which was wrecked near North Vancouver BC.

East Bay No. 2 154375 On July 12, 1936 this seiner owned by William C. Splan, Vancouver BC burned at Fiddlers Point in Chancellor Channel BC.

Eastholm[217] 134071 On December 1, 1937 at 4:00 pm in heavy fog this old coastal freighter owned by Frank Waterhouse & Company of Canada Ltd., Vancouver BC was in collision with a scow being towed by the tug *Tarzan* under command of Captain James Aitken at English Bay BC. She was so severely damaged, with a hole in her starboard bow, that after partially submerging, she sank on December 2nd off Siwash Rock during efforts to tow her to shore in 100 feet of water. Captain GG Brown and his crew of nine were saved by the *Venture* from the ship's lifeboat. The *Eastholm* had been bound for Seattle with a cargo of hides and canned salmon for trans-shipment to Asia. She was salvaged by the West Coast Salvage Co. crew in the *Cherrypicker*. On August 24, 1970 she was destroyed by fire and sank in Pendrell Sound BC.

Eastview (HMCS)[218] K.665 (RCN) At the end of her life this warship was scuttled and made part of the breakwater at Oyster Bay BC.

Echo II 134090 On January 24, 1924 this tug owned by William J Hawkins, Vancouver BC burned at Bear Island BC.

---

a   Built as Early Field; then HMCS Early Field; then Early Field

Ed. Glen[a] 194940 On June 18, 1978 this fishboat owned by Ralph L Brown (MO), Shawnigan Lake BC sank off the west coast of Vancouver Island.

Edenshaw[219] 150851 On December 1, 1939 this fishboat owned by Douglas Edenshaw, Masset BC foundered and sank between Egg Island and Pine Island BC, one half mile from Storm Island QCI. This fishboat under command of Captain Douglas Edenshaw sprang a leak in her engine room during a fierce southeast gale near the Queen Charlotte Islands. Pumping and bailing efforts by the crew proved ineffective and the crew evacuated in the lifeboat. The crew of three made for the Egg Island Lighthouse, about 14 miles away, and the rough sea was constantly threatening to swamp the little boat which at one point was half full of water. The light keeper looked after them for 4 hours until a passing cannery tender picked them up.

Edgar 100682 On September 30, 1898 this sternwheeler was destroyed in the New Westminster waterfront fire disaster. She was destroyed along with the *Bonaccord* and the *Gladys*.

Edward Lipsett 150671 On September 22, 1951 she caught fire in Ogden Channel, Schooner Passage BC.

Edwin[220] (US) This bark loaded with lumber sailed from Utsalady WA for Adelaide Australia. In 1874 under Captain Hughes, she became water-logged in the Strait of Juan de Fuca and sank. The Captain's wife was killed by the shifting lumber, and his two children and the Chinese cook were washed overboard. The Captain and 8 men climbed to the foretop and hung on for three days—finally going ashore in Hesquiat BC. The First Nations people there at Hesquiat under Chief Matlahaw saved most of the crew and received a silver medal from the Canadian Government and a reward from the United States Government. The hull ended up on the beach at Itloune Point

---

a   Built as Ronrico; then Ed. Glen

and its cargo provided the material for the new mission there. The Captain's wife was buried at Hesquiat BC.

Eemdyk[221] On October 15, 1925 this freighter owned by the Holland America Line went aground in dense fog on the eastern side of Bentinck Island. She went ashore at midnight outbound from Tacoma for Antwerp in a blinding fog. She was not carrying cargo in the damaged hold which had taken on some water. Her bow was firmly held by the rocks in almost the exact spot the *Siberian Prince* went ashore three years previously. This is the so-called zone of silence where fog signals care often not heard by ships. The big tug *Salvage Queen* proceeded to the scene of the incident. Part of her cargo was lightered away, and she was refloated several days later.

Egret Plume[222] 134124 On December 3, 1935 she exploded and was destroyed by fire while alongside the Shell Oil fuel dock at Alert Bay BC. The owners (Mr & Mrs JP Burridge) had the vessel under charter to several Vancouver wholesale warehouses travelling between Vancouver and Prince Rupert.

Eider (US) On October 25, 1941 this US Fish & Wildlife Service cutter ran aground on Green Top Island outside Prince Rupert while en route Ketchikan to Seattle.

Eight Bells[223] 150728 On October 8, 1947 this seiner, fishing for the Anglo-British Columbia Fishing Co., was stranded and destroyed by fire at Vere Cove, Thurlow Island BC. The seven crew members, including the captain's wife (who also served as the ship's cook), took to the skiff when the fire broke out while the vessel wallowed in heavy seas. They were picked up by a nearby seiner and transported to Vancouver.

Eiko[224] 154389 On October 5, 1962 this seiner, this seiner owned by The Canadian Fishing Co. Ltd., Vancouver BC, capsized in Dodd Narrows BC. She capsized and slowly sank in 400 feet of water. The crew of 4 made calm but harrowing escapes. Two were trapped below decks and discussed the best way to escape, swimming out through a skylight into the darkness. The other two were thrown into the water and freed a skiff that was trapped under the vessel. One put on a life preserver and swam the half a mile to a log boom—it took 90 minutes. Boom workers pulled them out of the water.

El Paso 192498 On November 16, 1983 this fishboat owned by Robert A Pottie, Campbell River BC experienced a fire two miles south of Cape Beale and sank.

El Phileen 227911 (US) On July 22, 1960 this vessel was destroyed by fire at Bull Harbour BC.

Elcoa[a] 173605 On August 1, 1970 this vessel was destroyed by fire at Von Donop Inlet, Cortes Island BC and was a total loss.

Elf[b,225] On January 14, 2014, an old wooden tug, Elf, sank near Passage Island, British Columbia. The tug Elf was itself under tow from Squamish to the Fraser River to be demolished. The Coast Guard raised the boat and towed it before it sank a second time near Point Atkinson, BC. It was not raised again, as authorities pegged the cost between $650,000 to $2 million.

Eliza Anderson (US) In 1882 she sank at a wharf in Seattle WA. In 1882 she was raised and overhauled by Captain Tom Wright. She was placed on the New Westminster to Seattle run. In 1884 she was in competition with the *Olympia* on the Victoria run. In 1885 she was seized by Collector Beecher in Port Townsend for carrying illegal Chinese immigrants. She was acquitted of the charges. In 1897 she sailed to Alaska for the Klondike Gold Rush. She sailed without a compass. At Comox BC she went out of control and rammed the ship *Glory of the Seas*.

---

a   Built as Paramount II; then Beegee II; then Elcoa
b   Built as Elf; then Foss No. 15; then Karlyn; then Skookum Cache; then Elf

Elizabeth J. Irving 080901 She was powered by a steam engines from the Royal City. On her second run she caught fire at Hope while landing and had to be cut free from the dock to save the town. She floated to Italian Bar where she was stranded and burned to the waterline. In 1881 she was owned by the Pioneer Line (John Irving), New Westminster BC. Her life was short—she was launched June 18, 1881 and burned at Hope BC September 29. 1881.

The *Aleutian Native* next to the sunken hull of the *Ella McKenzie* (Photograph from the Major Matthews Collection in the Vancouver City Archives AM54-S4-Bo_P206.1)

Ella McKenzie[a,226] 130498 On April 28, 1939 this tug, owned by McKenzie Barge & Derrick Co., Vancouver BC, sank after a collision with the American tanker *Aleutian Native*, under the command of Captain Samuel B Wellington, west of the Burrard Street Bridge in Vancouver Harbour. The tug heeled over after the collision and the tanker threw lines to her to arrest the capsize. Despite this she sank with only the top of her mast showing above the water to mark her resting place. Captain A Jorgenson and the mate, Les McIntosh, escaped in the dump scow they had been pushing. The Engineer, Howard W Randall, was knocked overboard by the impact. He was caught under the hull of the tanker and narrowly missed being cut up in her propeller. The *Ella McKenzie* was later raised and put back into service.

Elmatra[227] 154841 On March 30, 1934 this power cruiser, owned by Thomas G. Denny and Roy C. Denny (JO), Esquimalt BC, exploded and burned in Saanich Inlet at Brentwood BC while fishing for salmon. When the engine stopped, the gas tank was found to be empty and they spilled gasoline during refuelling. Two of the passengers

---

a   Built as C.F.P.; then Ella McKenzie

jumped overboard and the owner stayed aboard until rescued. The report noted that they also lost a twenty-pound salmon that they were hoping would earn them a bronze button award from the Victoria and Saanich Inlet Anglers Association.

Elnat 188603 On January 9, 1975 this power-cruiser yacht owned by Victor F MacLenny, Vancouver BC burned in Vancouver Harbour and was a total constructive loss.

Elola 126329 On October 16, 1915 this workboat owned by Herman G Estay, Vancouver BC burned one mile north of Island Point BC.

Elsa May[228] 122505 On May 24, 1931 this sailing sloop, owned by Noel Jones, Vancouver BC, was stranded on the Flat Top Islands in Georgia Strait and was a total loss. She was participating in a race across the Georgia Strait sponsored by the Royal Vancouver Yacht Club but when the wind died the fleet anchored at the Flat top Islands. Anchored in an exposed position she drifted ashore.

Elsie[229] 117012 On August 23, 1964 she foundered and sank so suddenly in Queen Charlotte Channel, Howe Sound BC, that the skipper and two crew members were forced to don lifejackets and jump into the water. They were rescued by passing speedboats.

Elsie Bradford[a] 100802 On November 4, 1911 she foundered near Entrance Island BC in transit from Gabriola to Nanaimo while towing a scow of gravel. The scow sprang a leak and while sinking damaged the schooner which filled with water and sank pulling down the scow. Captain Alf Bradford, the master, and his crew of three escaped in the ship's boat.

Elva M. No. II[b,230] 154595 This vessel sank in November 2016 and was finally scrapped and destroyed in October 2018.

---

a Built as Selma; then Elsie Bradford
b Built as Handy Billy; then Elva M No. II

Embla[a,231] 155179 On January 29, 1960 this fishboat, owned by Ole C. Anderson, Masset BC, exploded and burned at Prince Rupert Harbour BC. Three bodies, charred beyond recognition, were discovered in the wreck. The explosions occurred at the oil dock and the blazing hulk was towed across the harbour and beached, where she burned out.

Emblem No. 1[232] 154510 On June 12, 1931 this fishboat acting as a cannery tender, and owned by Pietro A Bruno, Prince Rupert BC, foundered and burned in Naden Harbour, Moresby Island BC. The crew were landed safely.

Emerald Straits[b] 190804 On April 18, 1969 this tug owned by Straits Tug Ltd., Vancouver BC sank and was later raised by salvagers at Howe Sound, BC. Three men were lost; one was washed overboard and swam to shore.

Emily Harris (Vancouver Island Registry) Owned by Harris Carroll & Co., Victoria she was the fourth steamer built in the Colony of Vancouver Island. Her boiler exploded on August 14, 1871 killing Captain Frain under mysterious circumstances on a voyage from Nanaimo to Victoria BC. Foul play was suspected but after investigations was never proven.

Emily Jade[c,233] 347965 Mike Pearson stated that "She piled up hard on warrior rocks. The crew was asleep at the wheel I believe. Fred Chandler owned it at the time, and she was on the hard for some time. Freddy Letts helped Mike rebuild the woodwork that was destroyed in the impact with Canada. Both Fred's are not with us anymore. They were real nice guys." Scott Kristmanson stated that "A couple years before Warrior Rocks the same thing happened in Eddie Pass area but wasn't written off by the insurance company.

---

a   Built as Cedric; then Embla
b   Built as Bering Straits; then Emerald Straits
c   Built as Rose Helene III; then Dyre Straits III; then Emily Jade

She was sunk and put back together at McLean's Shipyard in Prince Rupert BC."

Emily Parker (Vancouver Island Registry) In 1856 this trading schooner burned at Clover Point, Victoria BC.

Emma[234] 040390 This combination tug passenger freighter did a whaling expedition for Joseph Spratt and in 1881 she did a passenger run to Nanaimo BC. In 1885 she towed logs at Chemainus BC. In 1890 she struck a sunken scow in Victoria Harbour, sank, and was raised and repaired. On October 11, 1891 she was wrecked on Trial Island BC. Bound for Nanaimo with two scows in tow, she struck a rock off Trial Island in fog. She sank again. The wreck was sold to TJ Burns for $4,500 "for the benefit of all concerned."

Emma 040390 She mainly towed barges between Comox and Nanaimo BC. On October 11, 1891 while en route from Victoria to Nanaimo she struck a rock and was wrecked at Trial Island BC. Her wreck was sold for $270 to Captain McCloskey of the steamer *Mascotte*.

Emma R. 150581 On October 2, 1923 while owned by owned by Frank F Burdett, Vancouver BC she burned one half mile north of White Cliff in Howe Sound BC.

Emma Utter[235] (US) This three-masted schooner was towed out of Aberdeen WA on February 9, 1904 by the tug *Traveler* from Grays Harbour WA bound for San Francisco with a large load of lumber. She began to leak almost immediately. A survivor claimed that she touched the bar on the way out. A storm cause waves to wash over her. She was in a desperate condition and the crew evacuated the ship leaving one man accidentally behind. The crew were not seen again. The wind and currents carried the vessel to Clayoquot where he was rescued by First Nations people. On February 16, 1904 she was stranded at Lennard Island BC.

Empire Cannery[236] 134631 On August 18, 1946 this fishpacker burned two miles east of Sheringham Point BC. A fire broke out in the galley forcing the crew to evacuate the ship which burned for hours to the waterline. She sank in 36 fathoms of water.

The *Empress of Canada* hard aground with salvage tugs alongside (Photograph from the collection of the Maritime Museum of British Columbia MMBC_993.017.2892)

Empress of Canada[237] 146215 The *Empress of Canada* departed Southampton England on September 18th, 1929 for a voyage with ports of call that included Cherbourg to New York then on to the west coast of North America via the Panama Canal for stops in San Francisco, Vancouver and Victoria, BC. Most of her passengers had been picked up two days before when she called at San Francisco CA. On the morning of October 13th, 1929 as she was approaching William Head to undergo inspection at the Quarantine Station, she ran aground at Albert Head. The *Empress of Canada* remained fast for a considerable part of her length and developed a starboard list. The tugs *Salvage King*, *Burrard Chief* and *Hopkins* worked together for two days to move her off the rocks. There was, for two days, much concern that a southeasterly gale might come up, in which case she would doubtless have been lost. Fortunately, the weather remained favourable. She was moved to the graving dock in Esquimalt as Yarrow Ltd. secured the contract to undertake repair work. Following repairs at the Esquimalt graving dock the *Empress of Canada* returned to her trans-Pacific run. As a result of this accident the Canadian Government erected a lighthouse and fog signal at Albert Head.

Emy S. II 314892 On September 5, 1973 this fishboat owned by Kazuo Sakauye, Toronto ON exploded and fire in her engine room at Tofino Harbour BC.

Enilada[238] 126432 On November 23, 1923 this work boat was being used to convey non-union longshoremen to their workplaces during a strike. She collided with the Holland-America Line freighter *Dinteldyk* in Vancouver Harbour. On July 18, 1926, this vessel collided with the Robert H Merrick in Vancouver Harbour. On December 2, 1928 this vessel, owned by Captain William McMullen, was destroyed by fire in the engine room off Point Atkinson. The Captain and three crew members fought the fire until they needed to evacuate in the ship's dinghy when the steamer *Coaster* appeared and took them off. The tug *Hustler* tried to put a line on the vessel to beach her, but the heat of the flames was too intense, and she had to withdraw. The vessel eventually sank. She was salvaged by the Pacific Salvage Co. tug *Skookum*.

Enterprise 083441 In 1861 she was built at San Francisco for trade with Stockton but brought north to operate on Puget Sound. In 1861 she was owned by William Curry and Peter F Doling. In 1862 she was moved to Victoria for competition with the Hudson's Bay Co. vessel *Eliza Anderson* on the Puget Sound run. In 1862 she was purchased by the Hudson's Bay Co. for the Victoria to New Westminster run. In 1864 she was on the Victoria to Sooke run for the Leechtown Gold Rush. In 1883 she was incorporated into the Canadian Pacific Navigation Co. Ltd. In 1884, for a brief time, she operated in opposition to the *Amelia* on the Victoria – Nanaimo run. On July 28, 1885 she was in a collision with the *R.P. Rithet* and sank at Cadboro Bay BC with a loss of two passengers.

Enterprise (US) In the Autumn of 1874 this freighter was wrecked off Sooke Harbour BC while under command of Captain John Peterson.

Eric Roy[239] 153008 On September 18, 1934 this halibut fishboat, owned by Captain Sinclair Pierce, Prince Rupert BC, burned 5 miles southwest from Buck Point QCI BC. The crew of five were all rescued safely. She had been running at full speed when the fire broke out in the engine room. They rowed for five hours to reach Skidegate Inlet where the fishpacker *Bonilla* picked them up and took them to Butedale. The fisheries patrol cruiser *Senapa* carried them to Prince Rupert.

Erie 100686 In 1910 this work boat owned by John Leckie & FE Kinnell, Vancouver BC sank while in in Arrow Lakes service.

Erika[a] 7377854 (Japan) On October 17, 1979 she collided with the Second Narrows Bridge in heavy fog knocking a section of the bridge just north of the lift span into the water. The bridge was closed until March 4, 1980.

Erin II 111827 In 1913 this tug owned by CA Elliott & William Payne, Harrison Hot Springs BC sank, was raised, and then sank again.

Erne 156886 On July 14, 1960 this fishpacker owned by Harbour Services Ltd., Vancouver BC sank in Discovery Passage BC. Her hull is buried in the beach of Capilano Shoal BC.

Ernest Todd[b] 178240 She was a former US Navy Accentor Class minesweeper converted for use in the fishing industry. On March 19, 1975 while owned by J.H. Todd & Sons Ltd., Vancouver BC she foundered while en route to Vancouver with a cargo of herring, three miles SSW of Pachena Point and was a total loss.

Ericsson (US) Early in her life this vessel sank in storm off New York. On being raised the *Ericsson* was fitted with new engines. In 1851 the Ericsson-cycle engine was used to power a 2,000-ton ship, the caloric ship *Ericsson*, and ran flawlessly for 73 hours. The combination engine produced about 300 horsepower (220 kW). It had a combination of four dual-piston engines; the larger expansion piston/cylinder, at 14 feet (4.3 m) in diameter. On November 19, 1892 she while bound for Nanaimo from San Francisco for a cargo of coal she was stranded at Folger Island in Barkley Sound BC. In the Juan de Fuca Strait, a gale drove her onto the Vancouver Island coast into Barkley Sound. The captain went ashore to use the newly installed telegraph line to Victoria at Cape Beale Lighthouse to request assistance. The vessel's bow was on a rock while her stern was awash. The steamer *Alert* offered assistance which the crew declined assuming the captain had

---

a Built as Japan Erika; then Erika
b Built as USS AMc-99; then Norcrest; then Ernest Todd

made alternate arrangements. But the captain could not get his message through and the departure of the Alert left them helpless. Three days later the lightkeeper managed to get a message through and the tug Lorne picked up the survivors. The ship was destroyed by waves.

Esdud[a] 111782[240] She fished on the Grand Banks to 1897. In 1898 she was brought out around Cape Horn to the Pacific Coast for the gold rush. In 1929 she was abandoned as a derelict at False Creek. In 1939 she was stripped of any valuable metal and was taken to Long Beach on Texada Island and installed as a floating breakwater. In 1943 she was scuttled at Texada Island BC.

Estelle[241] 097167 On February 03, 1894 this vessel owned by Mayor Andrew Haslam, Nanaimo BC, exploded and sank at Cape Mudge, Quadra Island BC with the loss of 8 crew members (all hands). She was carrying boom chains and dynamite in the cargo—and local First Nations people reported that they had heard an explosion. It was thought that she was caught in a tide rip, and that seawater bursting into the engine room hist the boiler and caused an explosion.

Etta White[242] 064154 On October 29, 1920 she burned and sank in Princess Royal Channel 10 miles north of Swanson Bay BC. She had been towing a boom of logs to Ocean Falls. The Captain and crew were picked up by the tug *Commodore*.

Eunice D. 192466 On August 19, 1971 this fishboat owned by Marvin L Ladret, Cumberland BC sank in Okisollo Channel.

Eurana[243] (US) On March 10, 1927 this freighter owned by the Isthmian Line hit the Second Narrows Railway Bridge and caused $80,000 damage. She hung on the fixed span for nearly two hours, but salvage engineers had her removed to a safe anchorage. The bridge was not put out of commission. She was outbound for New York at the time of the incident with a cargo of lumber.

---

a   Built as Nellie G. Thurston; then Esdud

Eva D. 320300 On April 11, 1964 this fishboat experienced an explosion in her bilge in Sakinaw Bay BC.

Eva Marie[a,244] 088370 On June 13, 1910 this schooner, owned by Victor Jacobsen, Victoria BC, was stranded on Green Island BC but later salvaged. She grounded in shallow water between Speaker Rock and Helmcken Island.

Explorer[245] 0054 (Vancouver Island) This schooner, owned by Robert Burnaby of Victoria BC, for service carrying passengers and freight. On February 15, 1863, this schooner grounded near Valdes Island, but the vessel was able to free herself. A short time later she hit more rocks the force of which caused her to take on water. Overnight she shipped some heavy seas that carried away the ship's boat. The boat was later recovered, and the passengers and crew landed all the freight and valuables awaiting rescue. Many days later the passengers were rescued by the sloop Box. The wreck broke up.

Explorathor 818502 The Transportation Safety Board of Canada[246] states that "On the morning of 23 July 2009, the passenger vessel *Explorathor* departed Steveston, British Columbia, with 34 persons on board for a whale-watching excursion. At 1252, on the return journey, the vessel struck a submerged object off Croker Point, Saturna Island, British Columbia, and began to take on water. Passengers and crew were transferred to another whale-watching vessel. The *Explorathor* subsequently flooded and sank in Campbell Bay, Mayne Island, British Columbia, at 1334."

F.G. 170621 On December 18, 1964 this fishboat owned by Inga S Cousins (MO), North Burnaby BC sank at Port Moody BC.

F.G. Alder 150445 On February 9, 1923 this work boat owned by The Minister of Lands, Victoria BC burned at Powell River BC.

---

a Built as Teaser; then Rainbow; then Eva Marie

F.G. Balsam 150657 On January 28, 1928 this workboat owned by The Minister of Lands, Victoria BC was stranded at Fairfax Point on Moresby Island BC in Boundary Passage Georgia Strait.

F.G. Birch 150447 On April 3, 1927 this work boat owned by The Minister of Lands, Victoria BC was stranded at Mystery Reef BC south of Lund BC.

F.G. Maple 150444 On July 3, 1926 this work boat owned by The Minister of Lands, Victoria BC burned off Hood Point at Bowen Island BC.

F.M. Yorke 178238 On April 5, 1948 this tug owned by F.M. Yorke & Son Ltd., Vancouver BC was stranded and sank in Howe Sound BC.

F.R.P.D. Co. 10 194406 On March 21, 1977 this piledriver owned by Fraser River Equipment Co. Ltd., New Westminster BC exploded and burned at Reed Point, Port Moody in Burrard Inlet BC resulting in one dead and one injury.

Fairview[247] 103473 On July 01, 1896 this sternwheeler owned by WB Cousens had been out with an excursion party at Okanagan Landing BC. By the time the fire was discovered it was impossible to stop it, and soon the whole vessel was involved. She burned to the water's edge at the Okanagan Landing dock and was declared a total loss, and only insured for about half her value.

Faith of Sechart[248] 154420 On December 8, 1949 this seiner, owned by Dinko Anzulovich, Vancouver BC, foundered at Entrance Island BC in Georgia Strait. The crew of three abandoned ship in the skiff and were rescued off Nanaimo. She had been operating as a fish-packer for Nelson Brothers and had 50 tons of herring on board.

Falcon 090808 On January 08, 1896 this tug, owned by Susan E Cooper, Victoria BC was sunk near Gonzales Point BC.

Falcon III 175710 On March 7, 1973 this fishboat owned by McCallum Sales Ltd., Vancouver BC sank off Tofino BC.

The *Famous* (Photo from Fisherman Publishing Society Collection-UBC 1-0013664)

Famous[a,249] 098073 In 1890 she was in the North Sea and Baltic trade. On November 10, 1901 she ran aground in Chilkat Inlet AK because of careless navigation. In 1924 she was stranded. In 1926 she was aground at Skeena River and salvaged by Vancouver Dredging and Salvage Company. In 1927 she re-entered service under charter to Frank Waterhouse & Company of Canada Ltd. In 1929 she was stripped of steel and brass and beached at Bedwell Bay. In 1932 she was sunk by Pacific Salvage Company in Burrard Inlet on orders of Vancouver Port Authority.

Fancy Free[250] On February 7, 1957 this tug burned and sank off Halkett Point, Gambier Island BC while beachcombing for logs. The owner of this converted fishboat, Ron Crook and his assistant, Stan Wilkinson, evacuated in the boat's dinghy. They had only been in the small boat a few minutes when they were rescued by the tug G.M. Flyer.

Fantasy This gillnet fishboat left Nanaimo BC on May 05, 1955. She foundered on May 06, 1955. The crew of two (J Scouler and E Digerraud), had been clinging to the side of the vessel for about nine hours when they were rescued by the RCAF Nimpkish (M.975), and

---

a   Built as Amur; then Sunderland; then Famous

transferred to a Canso flying boat for removal to hospital. The vessel was then towed to Sechelt.

Farquhar 126205 On January 15, 1930 she was lost with all hands in the Georgia Strait while towing a barge from Bellingham WA to Vancouver BC. Part of the wheelhouse was washed ashore on Stewart Island WA and the barge itself landed on Saturna Island.

Favourite In 1888 this schooner was chartered by the government to carry lumber and building materials to First Nation settlements on the west coast of Vancouver Island and lumber and bricks for the church at Friendly Cove. She was one of the first vessels to employ First Nation hunters and boat steerers. In May 1893 she was a sealing schooner that carried the survivors of the wrecked whaling schooner *Jane Gray* from Cape Cook to Victoria. In 1919–1920 she was damaged in a storm and sank in Sydney Inlet BC.

Fawn[251] 100495 She was a sealing schooner owned by Victoria Sealing Co. Ltd., Victoria BC and built near the head of Horseshoe Bay (just past the mill) at Chemainus BC. She was wrecked on Catala Island when she broke from her anchorage and was salvaged in 1902 by Sprott Balcom for the Victoria Sealing Company. She continued sealing through 1905. At the end of that season, October 1905, she was lost with all hands on Carmanah Point BC—a combination crew of First Nations people from Friendly Cove, Ahousat and Esperanza Inlet.

Fearless 107247 In 1921 this steam tug owned by Joseph Mayer (MO), New Westminster BC was in collision with the gasoline tug *Mamook* in the North Arm of the Fraser River. In 1942 she was re-engined as a diesel for deep sea towing, In 1990, while owned by Michael G Greenwood, White Rock BC, she was reported to have filled with water and rolled over at Mike's Marina in Ladner BC.

Feelin' Free 369192 On January 30, 2017 this fishboat owned by T.C. Rockfish Ltd., Campbell River BC burned at Port Neville BC. Chet McArthur[252] reported that "This boat caught fire and quickly engulfed the vessel last Mon in the Johnstone Strait. The skipper and crew escaped, and the vessel drifted into Port Neville aflame. It ended up hitting a neighbour's wharf and got tangled in the anchor line."

Ferida[a] 126543 On December 17, 1928 this tug owned by R Hartlew, Bamfield BC sank two miles southeast of San Juan Light BC.

Ferngulf[253] On May 2, 1959 this 8,800-ton Norwegian freighter experienced an explosion and fire while in Vancouver Harbour, her crew of 30 was taken off by the A.P. Knight. Six men were injured and burned. Sailors from HMCS *Saguenay* and the submarine USS *Capitane* volunteered to go aboard to fight the fire led by Commander Ken Lewis RCN. The witnesses said that the explosion blew the hatches open and destroyed staterooms.

Fibreboard[b,254] 098300 On January 26, 1942 while she was under tow with a cargo of hog fuel for Port Alice when her towline snagged bottom, parted and she was driven ashore at Lawn Point BC in a fierce gale. She broke in two on the beach. Captain James W. Cates had to leap for his life into the stormy seas.

Fidalgo (US) In May of 1912 she collided with a scow which was being towed alongside of the tug *Sadie*. She was holed and quickly beached to save her. The *Fidalgo* was described as an oddly constructed vessel, a shallow flat-bottomed craft with sternwheel. Forward she had an elevator which is used to assist discharging. It seems she transported bales of hay for the most part, from the sound to Victoria.

Fidelater In 1863 she was put on the Portland to British Columbia ports run. In 1864 she arrived on the British Columbia coast, at Victoria from England under sail. In June 1865 she collided with the *Alexandria* off Clover Point Vancouver Island. In 1869 she was seized by the US Government. In 1876 she was lost on the California coast.

---

a   Built as Harrison Queen; then Ferida
b   Built as Robert Duncan; then William T. Lewis; then Fibreboard

Finback II[a] 195790 On September 5, 1956 this fishboat owned by Fergus Walker, Victoria BC exploded and sank 8 miles southwest of Esperanza Inlet BC.

Fir Leaf 141308 On November 10th, 1955 this fishpacker owned by H. Bell-Irving & Co. Ltd., Vancouver BC burned in Johnstone Straits, BC and was declared a total loss.

Five Princes[255] 176242 On December 22, 1971 this fishboat owned by Five Princes Fishing Ltd., Prince Rupert BC foundered at Chatham Sound BC.

Five Star[256] C02439BC On June12, 2014, the small crab fishing vessel *Five Star* was underway in adverse sea conditions near Kelsey Bay, British Columbia, when the crab catch stowed on deck shifted. The vessel listed to port, capsized, and eventually sank. The master and the one crew member on board abandoned the vessel. The crew member swam to shore. The master was lost at sea and is presumed drowned.

HMS Flora hard aground (Image from the collection of the Maritime Museum of British Columbia)

Flora (HMS) On December 5th, 1903 HMS *Flora* hit a submerged rock, settled in a basin of rocks, and developed a list of 8° to starboard. The event hit the newspapers worldwide and articles recounted day by day events in her salvage. The officers were apparently mistaken in their calculations of the position of the ship. A seagull perched on a black spar buoy was confused with another marker and ship ran up on the rock becoming stranded. HMS *Grafton*, Flagship of Rear-Admiral Andrew Kennedy Bickford RN, (Commander-in-Chief of HM Ships and Vessels on the Pacific Station (carrying his flag in HMS *Warspite* and

---

a   Built as Wimoweh; then Finback II

HMS *Grafton*) appointed in 1900.)) arrived with salvage gear. Pontoons built by the crews of HMS *Grafton* and HMS *Egeria*. Four big centrifugal pumps were placed in the after end of the vessel to remove water. Big anchors were placed from the stern in preparation for dragging the hull into deeper water. They were placed next to her stern with the intention of preventing it from settling deeper into the water too soon in the process. This effort failed when one of the hawsers parted and could not be replaced before the tide changed. Scows arrived to lighten ship by removing stores and coal onto lighters and scows delivered by tugs from Victoria. Her guns were removed as well. On the sixth attempt the vessel was moved for the first time, moving some six feet, but again a hawser parted, and some bitts on HMS *Grafton* gave way under the strain. on the morning of December 10th, with HMS *Grafton* and *Egeria* and some unnamed tugs pulling together and with the engines of HMS *Flora* powered up and screws pulling astern she was moved into deeper water. HMS *Flora* sailed to Union Bay where she re–shipped the coal that had been removed, remounted her guns, and reloaded her removed stores. She left under her own power for Esquimalt, escorted by HMS *Grafton*. At Esquimalt she entered the drydock in HM Dockyard for inspection and repairs.

Flora H.[257] 154353 On June 11, 1965 this seiner owned by The Canadian Fishing Co. Ltd., Vancouver BC was wrecked at Fraser Reach BC. Fred Rogers stated that she hit rocks and sank at Kingcome Point BC.

Florence II[258] On October 8, 1947 this seiner owned by J.H. Todd & Sons Ltd., Victoria BC capsized outside Growler Cove with the loss of two crew members. She apparently drifted and became a derelict, with her engines still running. She was laying on her port side with only a small portion of her stern showing. She was in danger of drifting onto Hanson Island where she would have broken up in the surf. Later in the day the *Emma K.* encountered her and with great difficulty put a line on her and towed her into Parson Bay. During the tow she righted herself although she was full of water. Cedar logs were lashed to her sides and by the morning of October 10th she had been pumped out. She was then towed 150 miles into Vancouver BC. The *Emma K.* claimed the value of the vessel plus damages to their own.

Florence Filberg[a] 176286 In 2007 this tug burned and sank in Sooke Harbour BC. She had been anchored there in the harbour and many observers considered her to be a derelict at the time.

Florencia (Peru) This brig, while under command of Captain JP de Echiandeia, was sailing from Utslady WA for Callao carrying a cargo of lumber. She encountered a gale off Cape Flattery on December 12th, 1860. She was swamped and kept afloat only by her cargo of lumber. The master, cook, supercargo and a passenger were drowned in the ordeal. The vessel drifted into Nootka Sound and the rest of the crew escaped after anchoring. She was taken in tow by HMS *Forward* but had to be cast off when the Forward developed boiler trouble. On December 31, 1860 she drifted into what became known as Wreck Bay. The wreck was sold by the Mate (the Master having drowned) to Captain Charles Edward Stuart (who owned a trading post at Ucluelet) for $100. This deal was later repudiated by authorities in Victoria.

Flyer 107712 In November 1934 this tug owned by Monarch Towing & Trading Co. Ltd., New Westminster BC sank alongside a dock in New Westminster

Flying Fish No. 2 194217 On January 7, 1956 this fishboat owned by James Hovell, Quathiaski Cove BC burned in Discovery Passage BC.

Forest Friend 156447 / 219452 (US) About 1950 she was condemned, and the Crown Zellerbach Lumber Co. used her as a breakwater at the Comox booming grounds. She was scuttled as a breakwater at Royston BC in the late 1950s. She is now covered with rock and fill.

Forest Pioneer[b,259] 323880 Michael Coney (1983) claimed in his book that she was originally named as *Clayhurst*, but there does not seem to be evidence for this as the *Clayhurst* was a reaction ferry being built in the same yard around the same time as the *Forest Pioneer*. This

---

a   Built as USATS LT-144; then Florence Filberg
b   Built as Forest Pioneer; then R.C.S.C.C. Grizzly No. 158

conflation of names has been endlessly repeated causing confusion. In 1977 she was sold to the Royal Canadian Sea Cadet Corps—an organization that was not eligible to own a registered Canadian vessel. She was then licenced. Christopher Lars states that "in 2000 she sank in front of the Gillnetter Pub, (on the Fraser River) and she was later salvaged."

Forest Pride[a] 170779[260] On January 27, 1944 this barge had been adrift for two days in a storm carrying 600,000 feet of logs for the Kelly Logging Co. operation being towed by the tug *Newington*. She broke adrift in a heavy storm carrying her crew, Joseph Pash and Frank Wilson, with her. They were later rescued by naval vessels. A big American tug tried to put a line on her, but it parted. The *Newington* picked up her two and resumed her voyage.

Forest Surveyor[b] 177372 During the Second World War this supply vessel was operated by the Canadian Army Pacific Command Water Transport Company of the Royal Canadian Army Service Corps; On May 30, 1947, this vessel collided with the *Merry Sea II* at a wharf in Campbell River BC. This vessel is no longer registered in Canada, and her Canadian Register was closed November 23, 1999.

Fort Camosun On June 7th, 1942 a Japanese submarine, the IJNS I–25, was spotted off Langara Island by several individuals including the light keeper. The Fishermen's Reserve vessel HMCS *Moolock* undertook a brief search but made no contact. On June 7th, 1942, the IJNS I–26 (under command of Minoru Yakota) torpedoed the freighter *Coast Trader* outbound from Port Angeles WA to San Francisco. Survivors were rescued by the US fishing vessel *Virginia I* and HMCS *Edmunston*. The IJNS I–25 (under command of Meiji Tagami) was running on the surface to recharge her batteries and just about 0230 on June 26th she fired one torpedo into the *Fort Camosun*. The crew abandoned ship in boats and as they left the ship two shells from the submarine's deck gun hit the ship. The Japanese submarine broke

---

a   Built as Fort Cedar Lake; then Forest Pride
b   Built as RCASC Colonel Ward; then Forest Surveyor

off the attack fearing that aircraft would arrive. The Fort Camosun sent a distress message but the closest naval vessels, HMCS Edmunston and HMCS Quesnel, were six hours steaming time away. At dawn, the Fort Camosun was still afloat and on an even keel when the naval vessels arrived. HMCS Quesnel detected sonar signals and laid down a pattern of depth charges. HMCS Edmunston picked up two boatloads of survivors. She was joined by HMCS Vancouver and the USS Y-994 who unsuccessfully continued the search for the submarine. The Canadian tugboat Dauntless arrived with the USN tug Tatnuck to salvage the Fort Camosun which was still afloat. The tow was exceedingly difficult, and she was taken to Neah Bay for temporary repairs. The Canadian tug Canadian National No. 2 arrived and towed the Fort Camosun to the Graving Dock in Esquimalt Harbour.

The **Fort Camosun** after being torpedoed with salvage tug and **HMCS Edmunston** alongside (Image from the collection of the Maritime Museum of British Columbia)

Fort Douglas[261] 168338 At her launching at Victoria Machinery Depot Co. Ltd. she ran aground stern-first when her propeller hit a harbour protection wall. She was caught by a stiff breeze before the tugs could get her under control. She was the first vessel to be launched without a traditional launching ceremony—and her accident was attributed to this by superstitious mariners.

Fort Ross 157174 On June 16, 1953 this freighter owned by John R Cooney, Burnaby BC ran ashore at Bear Point, Johnstone Strait BC. She was salvaged and beached at Elk Bay for repairs. On December 19, 1976 she sank at Corinto, Nicaragua.

Fort Yale[a] On April 14, 1861 this sternwheeler owned by the Yale Steam Navigation Co., Victoria BC had her boiler explode near Union Bar on the Fraser River killing the Master and four others. She was renamed as *Fort Yale*, rebuilt, and re-launched at Victoria October 15 1861.

Four Strong Winds[b] 133737 In 1981 this fishboat owned by Helin Enterprises Ltd., Nanaimo BC was reported as having been destroyed by fire in Holiday Passage and was a total loss.

Francis Cutting 126897 On January 11, 1924 this tug, under command of Captain C Hansom, foundered in a dense fog on Watson Rock in Grenville Channel BC. The tug owned by Empire Pulp & Paper Mills Ltd. owner of the Swanson Bay pulp mill had been proceeding from Swanson Bay to Prince Rupert BC. She slipped back into deep water and the Canadian National barge carrying a cargo of pulp she was towing was stranded on the beach.

Fraser 103159 On September 08, 1910 this tug owned by Fraser Sand & Gravel Co. Ltd., Vancouver BC burned in Woodward's Slough. She was used by the Canadian Hydrographic Survey in British Columbia occasionally as a houseboat from 1920–1923.

Fraser King[c] 190595 The Transportation Safety Board of Canada[262] reports that "on 22 October 1997 the skipper of the tug "*Fraser King*", which was towing the barge "D.H.T. No. 3", became disoriented at night after the tug's radar broke down. The skipper called a shore station,

---

a   Built as Idahoe; then Fort Yale
b   Built as Fredelia III; then Four Strong Winds
c   Built as Virginia G.; then Sorter VI; then Fraser King

reported his position, and requested guidance. Several vessels and aircraft proceeded to assist; however, the search was prolonged because the tug and barge were some 23 miles from the reported position. Although a helicopter attempted to direct the tug, in an area for which the tug had no nautical charts, the barge went aground. Next morning the barge refloated, and the tow was resumed. The barge's shell plating was damaged by the grounding and it took on water and sank."

Fredna 131143 In 1949 this work boat owned by Bloedel, Stewart & Welch Ltd., Vancouver BC sank in Great Central Lake BC.

Freiya[263] 141542 On August 19, 1965 this seiner owned by Nelson Bros. Fisheries Ltd., Vancouver BC was stranded and sank near Cracroft Point in Johnstone Strait BC after hitting a rock. Captain Douglas Drake and his four crewmen were rescued from the beach by the tug Geronimo.

Freno[264] 133720 On August 8, 1918 this tug burned one-half mile north of Whitecliff Point in Howe Sound BC. She was beached on Boyer Island, where she rolled over when the tide came up and sank. In 1918 she was salvaged by Vancouver Dredging & Salvage co., Vancouver BC. In November 1918 her wreck, which lay at MacDonald, Marpole & Co. in Coal Harbour was put up for sale to salvagers.

Funkis 172473 On July 2, 1954 the skipper of this fishboat, Trygve "Red" Peterson, apparently fell asleep at the wheel, while he was heading for Estevan from Ucluelet. She was wrecked at Portland Point in the same spot as the troller Restless 19 years later, sinking in 20 feet of water.

Furious II 154824 On January 2, 1933 this fishboat owned by Frank Hyde, O'Brien Bay BC burned at Grappler Sound BC.

G.B. Church[a] 168870 This freight boat served in World War II as a supply ship provisioning the allied effort in Europe. Continental Explosives was a subsidiary of Canadian Industries Ltd. (CIL). For the last ten years of her life above water, the G.B. Church was owned by #267866 British Columbia Ltd., Vancouver BC and was moored in the Pitt and Fraser rivers near Vancouver, slowly deteriorating through neglect. She was struck from the Registry on June 26, 1992. On August 10, 1991 she was sunk as an artificial reef by the Artificial Reef Society of British Columbia at what is now known as Church Reef.

G.R. Hughes[b] 133716[265] On April 24, 1912 her gasoline tank exploded and two of the crew were severely burned. Afterwards she was repaired and was renamed as the G.R. Hughes. On December 24, 1913 she was wrecked on Secretary Point, Hope Island BC. She was two weeks out on a halibut fishing trip southbound with 2,000 pounds in the hold when the incident occurred. She broke her shaft and started drifting in a southeast gale. Anchors were dropped but they failed to check the vessel's drift toward shore. Once she hit shore, she broke up very quickly. They crew rowed to shore in dories and then bushwhacked two miles to reach Bull Harbour. They dragged a dory with them intending to row to Port Hardy once they reached Bull Harbour. However, the schooner *Emma H.* was at anchor there and they received a hot meal. The Henrietta arrived and the men transferred over and were taken to Vancouver.

Gabby One[c] 323878[266] On July 31, 1977 she collided with the freighter *Californian* and sank in Juan de Fuca Strait (in US waters). Captain Bruce Petrie and Paul Legallais, and Richard Gauthier were rescued. They had just sold a catch and were heading out when they saw two freighters six miles distant. Visibility was limited in heavy fog. They

---

a   Built as Cerium; then G.R. Velie; then G.B. Church
b   Built as Rosene; then G.R. Hughes
c   Built as Lady Doris; then Gabby One

turned and headed for shore and the Californian also turned and ran over them.

Gabriola Flyer[267] 176786 On October 4, 1953 this fishing troller owned by Antti Jouppila (MO), Ladysmith BC collided with the tug *Western Challenger* and sank at Tofino BC. She rammed the tug about 10 feet from her stern, filled with water and sank within a few minutes. The tug was undamaged but lost part of her pumping gear and lines in the salvage attempt.

Gabriola Pass 158924 In 1941 she was seized from her Japanese owners by the Canadian Government. In 1942 her ownership transferred to His Majesty the King. Ian Estabrooks reports that on August 25, 1966 she sank at Malcolm Island BC.

Gail C. 176760 On September 9, 1976 this fishing troller owned by Howard A Orcutt (MO), Vancouver BC was destroyed in a fire in the engine room 9 miles offshore at Long Beach (VI) BC.

Galaxy No. 1 320899 On November 15, 1965 this fishboat owned by Alfred S Ward (MO), Masset BC sank off Masset BC.

Gale Winds 323284 On January 1, 1966 this vessel owned by Robert S Lamont (MO), Garden Bay BC was destroyed by fire in Garden Bay BC.

Galiano (HMCS)[a] 136047 We all know about the loss of HMCS *Galiano* at the end the First World War—lost to the wild weather of the Pacific coast. But here are two pictures which show her fast aground—at Cobourg Spit (Royal Roads). She was attempting to aid the Norwegian bark *Wulff* (Captain Salveson) when she dragged her anchor during a heavy gale. While trying to get a hawser aboard the sailing vessel she accidentally fouled her own propeller leaving her to the wind to drive up on the beach. There were repeated efforts to extract her from the beach over several days by the tugs *Swell* and

---

a   Built as CGS Galiano; then HMCS Galiano

Protective (her hull was partially embedded in the sand). The bark Wulff did not go ashore and remained swinging on two anchors in the Royal Roads. The Master refused assistance from the tugs and as the wind changed direction, he sent his crew aloft to set sail and he was able to move into deeper water. The Wulff underwent repairs in the drydock and then loaded a cargo of lumber for South Africa from the Cameron Lumber Co. HMCS Rainbow put a heavy hawser aboard the FPC Galiano. After large pumps removed water from the hull of the stranded vessel and the arrival of a high tide the cruiser managed to pull her free. The salvaged vessel resulted in a major repair contract for Yarrows Ltd. in Esquimalt BC. Extensive repairs were required including 16 new plates. The damaged floors and frames adjacent to these plates were removed and repaired. The stern frame was removed, welded, and straightened with a new rudder stock fitted. Other fittings and machinery had to be overhauled and repaired. As HMCS Galiano she sank in a storm at the end of the First World War and it raises the question as to whether her hull was somehow compromised in strength by the damage incurred in 1915 causing her disappearance with all hands. The Navy took great efforts to state officially at the time of the official inquiry into the sinking that "It can be safely assumed that the loss was in no way attributable to any failure on the part of the machinery or weakness of the hull and structure of the vessel; immediately before encountering this heavy gale, she was to all intents and purposes a sound and efficient vessel."

HMCS Galiano driven ashore in a storm at Royal Roads (Image from the collection of the Maritime Museum of British Columbia P4961)

Galleon 320058 In late April 1985 this fishboat owned by Griffin Fish Ltd., Port Alberni BC was destroyed in a storm near Milbanke Sound BC.

Gambier Isle 176238 On September 13, 1965 this fishboat owned by British Columbia Packers Ltd., Vancouver BC burned off Chatham Point in Johnstone Strait BC.

Gander[a] 141539 In November 1953 she foundered in the Fraser River near Annacis Island BC. She was raised and refurbished. In July 1966 she sank near Nanaimo while towing a self-dumping log barge. In 1971 her register was closed, and she was licenced.

Ganges 121763 On Junes 12, 1911 this power cruiser owned by JJ Malcolm and Peacy, Ganges BC burned at Ganges Harbour BC.

Garden Bay 194949 On August 22, 1967 this fishboat owned by Archibald McDonald, North Vancouver BC caught fire from leaking gasoline, burned and sank off Sand Heads in the Georgia Strait BC and was a total loss.

Garza (Chile Registry) On November 13, 1874 this ship-rigged vessel hit a rock at the head of Esquimalt Harbour BC while on a voyage from Burrard Inlet to Melbourne Australia and was a total loss valued at $32,000. She was salvaged.

Gatineau (HMCS)[b,268] H.61 (RCN) At the end of the Second World War she was laid up in the ship boneyard at Bedwell Bay in Indian Arm BC. Her hulk was scuttled to form a breakwater at Royston, BC.

Gem of the Ocean 018710 (US) This American bark sailed out of Newburyport MA USA was wrecked near Sombrio Point in July 1870 while traveling from Seattle to San Francisco in foggy weather with a cargo of coal under command of Captain Hawse. She struck off Vancouver Island, eight miles southeast of Port San Juan, in August 1879 and became a total loss. She had been laying broadside to the waves on a reef 25 meters from shore. Captain Hawse and his crew

---

a Built as Cedar King; then Trojan II; then Gander
b Built as HMS Express; then HMCS Gatineau

escaped and reached Port Townsend in a small boat. Her salvage rights were sold at Port Townsend.

Gene 131144 On July 10, 1930 this workboat owned by Walter C. Hanson, Butedale BC burned in Deep Cove, on the North Arm in Burrard Inlet BC.

General (US) On June 2nd, 1898 this barge was being towed by the steamer *Rival* when she foundered. Afterwards her crew of twelve was rescued by the *Rival*.

General George S. Simmonds[a] In 1922 this freighter, a US Army transport, was the flag ship of the Admiral Line. In 1943 she was used as a US transport vessel for Second World War service. She went ashore on Malcolm Island. Almost no details were publicly reported for wartime security reasons.

General T. Co. 156611 On March 27, 1942 she burned to the waterline in the Flat Top Islands (Georgia Strait) and was beached, where her engine was salvaged.

George McGregor[b,269] 177387 On November 26, 1949, while towing scows from Bamberton, this tug, owned by Victoria Tug Co. Ltd., Victoria BC, sank off Trial Island with the loss of 6 of 7 of the crew, including Captain John Mason.

George S. Wright[270] (US) In 1863 she ran on the Portland-Victoria route. On January 25, 1873 she sank in Queen Charlotte Sound BC while enroute from Alaska to Portland. Her wreckage was found at Cape Caution. It was believed at the time that the survivors were murdered by the inhabitants of Kimsquit Village. In 1877 Captain Alfred Dudower arrived in Nanaimo which information he received from Chief Charley Hamsett who visited him on the sloop *Ringleader*

---

a   Built as Columbia; then Great Northern; then H.F. Alexander; then General George S. Simmonds
b   Built as USATS ST-170; then E-170; then George McGregor

and recounted the events. Hamsett claimed his information came from a Wakena First Nations man who worked on the *George S. Wright* as a coal passer. The ship was enduing a terrific gale while transiting Queen Charlotte Sound. A huge wave broke over the ship putting out the boiler fires. The boats were lowered and all, but one was swamped. The occupants reached shore. They lit a signal fire which was seen by Wakena people who attacked and murdered the ship's survivors. In the summer of 1877, the Kimsquit village was shelled by HMS *Rocket* in a punitive action and destroyed.

Georgia She was a cannery tug. In 1896 she foundered in a storm in Queen Charlotte Sound BC. Four men used the lifeboat to reach Cape Calvert BC the following day.

Georgia Belle[a] 327206 On August 6, 1972 this passenger vessel owned by West Coast Salvage & Contracting Co. Ltd., Vancouver BC sank off Stuart Island BC.

Georgiana In 1851 this schooner sailing from Puget Sound with gold prospectors anchored in Skidegate Channel. A gale came up during the night and she was driven ashore. Her crew of 5 and 22 passengers were rescued some weeks later by the schooner *Demaris Cove*.

Gerard C. Tobey[271] On July 4, 1914 while under command of Captain Charles Brown, she struck Ripple Rock at 9 o'clock in the morning and was held fast for two hours. She had been in tow of the tug *Amur* at the time, but the current was too strong for the tug to come to their aid. The crew of six and Mrs Tobey took to a lifeboat that was made fast to the wreck with a painter. The current was too dangerous to attempt to row to shore. At 11:30 the ship righted herself and slid off the rock, and the crew scrambled aboard. They drifted safely through the narrows. As they approached Cape Mudge, they realized they were sinking, and the vessel went down by the head in 45 fathoms of water. The crew were picked up by the *Amur*.

---

a   Built as Kayen; then Georgia Belle

Geraldine R. 133767 On December 20, 1923 this workboat owned by The Minister of Lands for British Columbia, Victoria BC was destroyed by fire on the BC coast.

Gettysburg[272] On the night of April 14, 1883 this American was driven ashore at Royal Roads (Victoria) during a high gale. She was in ballast and was blown ashore on the east side of the lagoon. In the morning she had a large hole in her bow and her main and mizzen masts were gone.

Gi-Kumi II[a] 134092 On August 03, 1950 this workboat owned by Knud S Knudsen, Victoria BC exploded in Prince Rupert Harbour at the Standard Oil dock.

Gigilo[b,273] 154554 On October 17, 1961 this fishpacker, under command of Captain Peter Phillips, was sunk off the southern tip of Bowen Island after collision with the barge Island Express being towed by the Lloyd B. Gore. The Gigilo's engineer, Fred Wilkins, was lost in the incident. The Gigilo was beached, subsequently salvaged, and put back into service.

Gilboa[274] 176884 On February 12, 1957 she lost her rudder 4 miles northwest of Lennard Island Light BC. Captain George Chamberlain and his father were collecting scrap brass and iron when the incident happened and began drifting. The boat caught fire, burned, and sank. They two men were rescued after their boast sank near Vargas Island.

The tug *Gillking* (photograph from the Walter E. Frost Fonds in the City of Vancouver Archives CVA 447-4771)

Gillking[c,275] 178776 In 2003 this tug was towed to Bamfield. She lay at Ostroms Machine Shop when her pumps failed,

---

a   Built as Wekeninnish; then Gi-Kumi II
b   Built as Gigilo; then Mandolin Wind
c   Built original name unknow; then Columbia King; then Gillking

and she sank. (She may have been towed later to Ladysmith Harbour where she was scrapped.) Al Hosking reported that "she was so rotten there were small alder trees growing out of the deck and needed a generator or shore power to keep pumps running. . . . someone had unplugged her from shore power, and she sank at the old McMillan's dock."

Givenchy[a] 141343 In 1918 This Battle-class trawler was commissioned as HMCS *Givenchy*. In 1919–1938 she was owned by the Minister of Marine & Fisheries, Ottawa On and served as CGS *Givenchy* as a Fisheries Protection Service vessel. She was re-commissioned as a tender to the Royal Canadian Navy Fishermen's Reserve 1940–1943. On June 22, 1938 she struck a rock near Prince Rupert BC was freed shortly afterwards. She is said to have been broken up in the USA in 1953.

The *Givenchy* on the rocks near Prince Rupert BC (Image from the collection of the Maritime Museum of British Columbia 000101)

Glacier Queen[b] 176902 Built as a Castle-class warship she was laid up in the ship boneyard at Bedwell Bay in Indian Arm BC at the end of the Second World War. Converted to civilian use she became a passenger cruise ship. In 1967 she collided with the *Nicherei Maru* near Prince Rupert BC. In 1973 she was proposed for conversion to a hotel and restaurant ship at Bethel AK. On November 08, 1978 she sank in Cook Inlet AK USA. in January 1979 she was raised, towed to sea, and scuttled.

---

a   Built as HMCS Givenchy; then CGS Givenchy; then HMCS Givenchy; then Givenchy
b   Built as HMS Walmer Castle; then HMCS Leaside; then Coquitlam; then Glacier Queen

Glad Tidings 088371 She was a schooner-rigged steam vessel used by William Oliver and Thomas Crosby as a mission vessel out of Port Simpson 1884–1903. Her steam engines were installed in Victoria BC. On January 20, 1903 she was wrecked in a gale at Shushartie Bay, Queen Charlotte Sound while being towed by the Barbara Boscowitz.

Gladys[a] 76323 (US) In 1885 she was transferred to Canadian Registry. She was transferred to the Fraser River in 1894. On September 30, 1898 burned at New Westminster BC when a huge fire destroyed much of New Westminster. She was tied up at the wharf and fire was consuming the sheds on the wharf when the firemen arrived. The *Gladys* quickly caught fire along with two other steamers. The three steamers went drifting down the river and set each dock and vessel alight in turn when they touched the shore.

Glen Fruin On December 8th, 1880 the British bark *Glen Fruin* was sailing with a cargo of coal from Newcastle Australia bound for Portland Oregon. She had encountered heavy storms near the equator which opened some of her seams. She was driven from the mouth of the Columbia to Barkley Sound and was abandoned in leaking and sinking condition. It is said that the vessel came to rest on Danger Rock (later renamed as Hornby Rock) in the entrance to the Sound. When nearing the Columbia southerly winds drove her northward out of her course. The crew reached King Island where they waited for a week until rescued by the schooner *Favorite*.

Glendale V[b] 172338 In 1941 she was seized from her Japanese owners by the Canadian Government. In 1942–1944 she was commissioned into the Royal Canadian Navy Fisherman's Reserve as a harbour service auxiliary craft as HMCS *Glendale V*. On September 4, 1976 she foundered in Finlayson Channel off one mile NE of Jorkin Point BC.

---

a Built as James McNaught; then Gladys
b Built as Glendale V; then HMCS Glendale V; then HMCS Dalehurst; then Glendale V

Glenholme[a] 176898 In 1953, as the *C.P. Yorke*[276], she was operating in car barge towing. On December 11, 1953 she struck Tattenham Ledge off Buccaneer Bay. The barge she was towing collided with her and knocked a hole in her hull causing her to sink in deep water. She was salvaged by the *Recovery Arrow Giant*. She was towed in submerged condition into Buccaneer Bay and pumped out. Her crew of six were lost and only Captain Roy Johnson survived.

Glenorchy[277] (UK) In December 1896 this 4-masted bark was sailing for Australia from Port Blakeley with a cargo of lumber. She was thought to have foundered. In July 1897, the CGS *Quadra* found floating wreckage. A kisbee ring marked with the ship's name inscribed washed ashore in the vicinity of Cape Cook BC.

Glenshiel[b] 176554 She was employed as an RCN Harbour tug at St. John's Newfoundland and later in August 1945 as a Harbour tug at Quebec. On June 06/07th, 2007 she sank at Nakwato Rapids in Seymour Inlet BC. In July 2016 she was still listed as active in the Canada Register of Shipping.

Glimpse (US Registry) The bark *Glimpse* was built at Newbury, NY, in 1856. In 1859 she was wrecked on Clover Point at Victoria, Vancouver Island. In the fall the bark *Glimpse* ran aground near the entrance to Victoria Harbour and was sold to Henry Roeder, who repaired her at Port Ludlow and operated her for a short time afterward. The old bark *Glimpse*, which had remained a wreck for many months on Clover Point, Victoria, was afterward re-fitted and ran for thirteen years in the San Francisco and Puget Sound trade.

Gloom No. 2[c,278] 156478 On March 24, 1941 this fishboat suffered an explosion and fire while refueling in Ucluelet Harbour BC. She was cut adrift, and attempts were made to try and sink her to extinguish

---

a   Built as CNAV Glenholme; then Scanlon; then C.P. Yorke; then Trojan; then Glenholme
b   Built as HMCS Glenora; then Lotbiniere; then Glenshiel
c   Built as Gloom No. 2; then Margaret C.

the fire to protect the fuel storage tanks. She burned to the waterline. The brother of the owner was severely burned in the incident.

G.M. Flyer 193782 On October 15, 1958 this tug burned in Horseshoe Bay BC and was later salvaged and repaired.

Gofer 369493 On April 21, 1976 this salvage vessel, owned by JGD Gotoski, Nanaimo BC, foundered off Porlier Passage in Georgia Strait BC.

Golden Bear[279] (US) In 1937 she was damaged in a storm off the coast of Oregon while en route to Seattle. She was so severely damaged that she could not be put back into operation, so she was stripped down and had her engines removed as a cement barge. While unloading a shipment of cement for the Puget Sound Naval Shipyard, the former *Golden Bear* capsized and sank. After salvage she was towed to Oyster Bay BC and placed in the breakwater.

Golden Stream[280] 141029 On February 24, 1929 this fishboat was adrift in a rough sea off Marble Bay on Texada Island. The boat was set on fire from the galley stove which broke loose from its fittings and overturned. Hot coals from the stove ignited gas and oil in the bilge. Captain James Cartwright and the Engineer Neville Kirk jumped overboard and struggled ashore through the surf.

Good Hope No. 1[a] 153003 On June 4, 1957 this fishboat owned by Robert A Breaks, Prince Rupert BC burned in Ogden Channel BC.

Gore Rock[281] 314753 On March 30, 1975 this gillnetter owned by Stephen B Parent (MO), Lasqueti Island BC grounded and was drifting offshore in conditions that were described as 'incredibly rough seas.' when she sank at Fisherman Bay near Cape Scott on northern Vancouver Island BC. The two crew members were saved by another fishing vessel.

---

a   Built as Joan W.; then Good Hope No. 1

Gospel Light[282] 192062 On January 02, 1971 this mission boat owned by The Pentecostal Assemblies of Canada Inc., Toronto ON was destroyed by fire off Crab Island at Holberg BC in Quatsino Sound. The Reverend Charles Benterud was returning two members of his congregation home in Holberg when the oil cooking stove exploded. CFB Holberg sent vessels to the rescue and found people in the water and still on board. Mrs Ruth Miller and 3-year old Rita Benterud were killed and the rest of the people on board were injured. The mission boat was beached but she was a total loss to the fire.

Grace Darling She foundered and broke up on the rocks at Inkster's Bay in 1960 in a storm. She was owned by the Canadian Pacific Railway employed moving granite from the Vernon Granite & Marble Co. quarry near Vernon BC.

Grand 152767 On February 20, 1960 this fishboat owned by Seymour Packing Co. Ltd., Vancouver BC was destroyed when she drifted ashore in a windstorm.

Grand Prix 327870 On April 23, 1978 this troller fishboat owned by Seppo J Pekkonen (MO), Coquitlam BC grounded and sank in Clayoquot Sound BC (west of Tofino) and was declared as a constructive total loss after being salvaged.

Grant[283] 203825 (US) On December 27, 1911 this halibut fishing vessel under command of Captain EE Crockett and owned by the San Juan Fishing & Packing Co., Seattle WA USA sank at White Rock, north of Banks Island BC. She had 30,000 pounds of halibut on board at the time of the incident, travelling south bound from the halibut fishery to Seattle. Travelling through some of the worst sea conditions that the crew had ever experienced they sought shelter. They anchored inshore but strong gusting winds caused the anchor to drag. They struck the rocks with violent impact and sank within 15 minutes in 4–5 fathoms of water. The crew of 40 men took to their dories after a distress message had been sent by radio. They drifted for several hours before being picked up by the fishing vessel Falcon.

She had a rough journey through storms while taking the men back to Prince Rupert.

Grappler[a,284] 061301 On Pacific Station 1860–1868 she arrived at Esquimalt July 12, 1860. She remained in commission until June 1868. On April 29, 1883 while under command of Captain John F Jagers she was destroyed by fire four miles from Seymour Narrows. The fire started in the engine room behind the boiler. The crew started the donkey engine to run fire hoses and pumps. About 70 lives were lost, and many of those were Chinese labourers on their way to canneries up the coast. The efforts to control the fire caused panic among the passengers. When the captain realized that the efforts to fight the fire was hopeless, he ordered the ship beached.

Gray[b] 124395 On October 19, 1948 this whale catcher was sunk as part of the breakwater at Oyster Bay BC.

Gray Lady[285] 126422 On July 9, 1925 this tug, owned by Pacific Tug & Barge Co. Ltd., Vancouver BC, exploded and fire at the entrance to Simoom Sound BC. Her crew of two were saved.

Great Admiral[286] On January 27, 1907 while outbound with a cargo of lumber from Puget Sound this freighter was lost off Cape Flattery but her remains were found two years later on the west coast of the Queen Charlotte Islands BC. Her crew were rescued by the British ship *Barcore*.

Great Northern V[287] In December 1939 Captain George W Skinner while serving with his son Hugh Skinner in the fishpacker *Great Northern V* he was wrecked on a reef about ten miles west of Cape Cook BC. One crew member, Ted Bernard, was drowned and the two Skinners drifted up on the beach. Wet and without food he walked south until the younger man was spotted by a search plane and

---

a   Built as HMS Grappler; then Grappler
b   Built as Petriana; then Gray

rescued by a boat from Winter Cove. The senior Skinner was rescued by a party from Port Alice BC after three weeks. He survived and returned to sea in a fishpacker.

The *Great Northern* (Photograph from Fishermen Publishing Society online UBC archive BC_1532_683_1)

Great Northern 3[a,288] 153110 On November 25, 1942 this fishpacker foundered between Cape Roger Curtis and North Arm about 8 miles from Point Atkinson and 5 miles off Bowen Island (Georgia Strait). She was taking a load of herring to Nanaimo at the time of the incident. She hit a submerged object and took on water, gradually settling until the crew made distress signals. The crew of three was rescued by William MacDonald in the gillnetter *Francis S*.

Green 131339 In the 1960s this whale catcher owned by Deepsea Fish Co. (Max Lohbrunner), Victoria BC sank at her berth below the Johnson Street Bridge in Victoria Harbour from rusting-out, not being pumped-out and overloading with scrap being stored aboard. She has now disappeared from her site north of the old Johnson Street Bridge in the Inner Harbour of Victoria BC. For several years navy clearance divers trained on the wreck and would, from time to time, detonate ordnance on it during training exercises. This

---

a   Built as Oceanic I; then Great Northern 3

hastened its demise. With construction of the new Johnson Street bridge all traces of it are now gone.

Green Sea[289] 141523 On July 24, 1931 this seiner, owned by Northern Packing Co. Ltd., Vancouver BC, foundered about 200 yards off Cape Beale BC. She was loaded with pilchards when she was swamped.

Green Hill Park[a] On March 06, 1945 this newly built wartime freighter caught fire and exploded. She was beached off Stanley Park in Vancouver Harbour. She was refloated and declared a constructive total loss. In 1967 she was broken up in Kaohsiung Taiwan ROC.

Greenwood 103913 This sternwheeler owned by the Bank of Montreal; Montreal QC operated in Okanagan Lake service. In 1897 she was in Skaha Lake service between Penticton and Okanagan. On February 1, 1899 she was laid up and burned at Okanagan Falls BC.

Greyfish[290] On September 29, 1953 this vessel capsized off the Queen Charlotte Islands after rescuing Sonny Beynon and Sid Crosby from the sinking *Beatrice H*. They and the crew of the *Greyfish* were picked up by the American crab boat *Amalac* and taken to Masset.

Growler (US) In 1866 this schooner, under command of Captain Horace Coffin, left Victoria BC en route for Sitka and was wrecked off Cape Murray in the Queen Charlotte Islands under Captain Horace Coffin.

Gryme[291] 130855 This small freighter was seized in 1911 by Canadian fisheries patrol cruisers. Tried in Admiralty Court she was sold to Victoria interests. For many years she transported guano for the Vancouver and San Diego Navigation Co. Ltd., running between Ensenada Mexico and San Diego CA. For many years she disappeared from public view and was presumed to have been lost. In the late 1930s she was involved in the transport of tuna. She was said to have operated as a rum runner supply ship operating out of Ensenada

---

a   Built as Fort Simcoe; then Green Hill Park; then Phaeax II; then Lagos Michigan

Mexico. (Some reports say she only supplied the vessels with legitimate cargoes.) In 1940 the owners tried to register the vessel as the *Mureda* but this application was declined by Canadian federal authorities. During the Second World War she was a naval vessel based at Vancouver BC. On September 11, 1986 she went ashore on North Thormondby Island BC and was declared a total loss. She broke up while grounded on a big rock.

Gudvangen 156829 On August 26, 1963 this fishboat owned by John J Mclean, Prince Rupert BC exploded at the south end of Arthur Pass BC.

Gulf Coaster[a] 331112 The Transportation Safety Board of Canada reports that "The helicopter accommodation barge *"Trailer Princess"* was being moved by the tug *"Gulf Coaster"* to a new logging camp location in Mackenzie Sound, BC. After nightfall, as the tug endeavoured to tow the barge through the narrow winding channel of Kenneth Passage, the tug struck and grounded on rocks and was holed below the waterline. Another tug in the vicinity towed the undamaged barge to its destination. The *"Gulf Coaster"* sank during attempts to refloat her but was later refloated and brought to Campbell River for repairs. No one was injured but diesel fuel escaped from the sunken tug."

Gulf Log Patrol[292] 189299 On May 23, 1965 this log salvage vessel owned by the Gulf Log Salvage Co-operative Association, Vancouver BC burned and sank in Indian Arm BC. The crew saw smoke coming from the engine room in mid-afternoon and when they opened the door there was a mass of flame. Captain Art Younger and Roy Campbell battled the flames with a fire extinguisher but were unsuccessful. They were taken off by a passing pleasure boat.

Gulf Master[293] 320270 On January 11, 1967 this vessel sank suddenly in a storm in the Gulf of Georgia at Traill Island BC near Sechelt BC with the loss of 5 lives. Lonnie Berrow stated "Among those lost were

---

a   Built as Gulf Coaster; then Robina B.; then Gulf Coaster

Captain Forrest Anderson, the Mate Rodney Seymour, the Engineer Richard Mcphail, and the deckhand Robert Ayotte and an unnamed second deckhand. The only body recovered was that of Mate Rodney Seymour."

The *Gulfstream* on Dinner Rock (Photograph from the Major Matthews Collection in the Vancouver City Archives Bo P301.2)

Gulf Stream[a] 172512[294] On October 11, 1947 while under command of Captain Jack Craddock she was wrecked off Powell River BC on Dinner Rock. They left Westview at 7:30 pm bound for Refuge Cove. At 8:30 pm they hit the rock while the Second Mate was on watch. The vessel hit Dinner Rock at speed and climbed high in the air as they came to rest with the stern submerged. In two and half hours 32 survivors were pulled off Dinner rock by the cool action of the crew of the fishboat *Betty L.* under Captain Robin West. Mrs Katherine Elliott, Lyle Elliott; Mrs Sylvia Fleck, Jeanie Pavid, and Douglas Lipsett were lost.

Gulfstream II[b] 176474 She sank in Porpoise Bay on September 7th, 2018.

Gulf Trader[c] 179077 As USS Apc-15 she earned one battle star for World War II Service in the Asiatic-Pacific Campaign. As *Black Trader* she was seen in use as a live aboard in the Fraser River delta area up until the mid 1990s. She is reported to have sunk in a Fraser River Slough in 1998 after capsizing while owned by Ronald Y McMillan (MO) Richmond BC.

---

a   Built as USS Wenonah; then Blue Water; then Gulf Stream; then Stranger; then HMCS Wolf; then Gulf Stream
b   Built as HMC ML Q.125; then HMC M.L. 125; then Malibu Tillikum; then Yorkeen; then Campana; then Jormholm; then Gulfstream II
c   Built as USS APc-15; then Gulf Trader; then La Belle; then Black Trader

Gull Wing[295] 152944 On December 22, 1932 this patrol vessel under the command of Captain AFL Lloyd owned by The Minister of Marine & Fisheries, Ottawa ON was stranded between Campbell River and sank off Quathiaski Cove BC.

The steam yacht *Gunhild* (Photo by Walmis Newman (in the Robert Lawson Collection))

Gunhild[a] 130757 On August 25, 1925 this patrol vessel owned by The Minister of Public Works, Ottawa ON was destroyed by fire two miles south of the Dean River, Kimsquit BC.

Gurd Island 313088 On August 24, 1973 this fishboat built and owned by Rasmus T Tysse, Oona River BC grounded in Graham Island BC.

Gustav[296] 176505 On November 10, 1977 this fishboat owned by John A Trail (MO), Victoria BC was declared missing presumed lost while en route from Prince Rupert BC to Victoria BC. Four persons were lost.

Gwilym 126470 On July 15, 1909 she suffered an explosion and fire in Oxford Bay, Bute Inlet BC.

Gypo 190670 On June 6, 1958 this tug owned by Ray Grumbach, Alberni BC exploded and burned alongside the dock at Bligh Island BC.

Gypsy Lass[297] 391727 The Transportation Safety Board of Canada states that "In the evening of February 14, 1994, in heavy weather conditions, the skipper of the *Gypsy Lass* was unable to restart the main engine after stopping for a precautionary change of fuel filters

---

a   Built as Margaret; then Gunhild

before entering Edith Harbour, British Columbia. Another fishing vessel, the *Royal Pride*, was called for assistance, but the *Gypsy Lass*, which had been carried into shoal water, grounded a short time after the *Royal Pride* arrived on the scene. While standing by, the *Royal Pride* was subsequently disabled by kelp fouling her Kort nozzle and she also grounded. The fast rescue craft *Point Henry No. 2* which came to their assistance was swamped while attempting to rescue the crew of the *Royal Pride* and was beached. The crews of the three vessels were rescued by a US Coast Guard helicopter."

H. & L.[a] 179073 On September 07, 1972 this tug owned by West Bay Towing & Salvage Ltd., Lund BC dragged her anchor, settled on a rock, burned, and subsequently sank in Mickmicking Inlet BC while in hand logging operations.

H. & R. 152662 On October 27, 1932 while owned by Mary and Isabella Shrubsall, Prince Rupert BC she foundered at Hammond Rocks, Dundee Island BC.

H. & R. II 195232 On October 22, 1965 this tug owned by H. & R. Towing Co. Ltd., Port Coquitlam BC was in a collision with the *Princess of Vancouver* and sank in Fairway Channel BC off Nanaimo BC.

H.G.A. On July 17, 1921 this vessel was burned in Mozier Cove, Chancellor Channel BC.

H.O. No. 10[b,298] 178227 On January 05, 1974 this floating fuel barge, moored in Vancouver Harbour, exploded, and burned in Coal Harbour BC. Three men were killed in the incident: barge attendant John Campbell; and Clifford Dawley and Edgar Attard who were on board a power cruiser refueling at the float. Tugs at the scene of the incident towed the barge away so that other fuel barges in the vicinity would not be affected.

---

a   Built as USS Progress?; then H. & L.
b   Aka Home Oil Fuel Barge

H.O.G. 122200 In 1937 this sloop-rigged sailing yacht owned by Cyril H Green and Frank Hatt (JO), Elgin BC was reported to have sunk and was a total loss.

Halcyon III 312885 On July 10, 1963 this tug was in a collision with the tug Jordan one-half mile south of Junction of the Columbia and Illecillewaet Rivers BC.

Hanac[299] 126614 On March 04, 1927 this tug, owned by Rupert Marine Products Ltd., Prince Rupert BC, grounded on Hodgson Reef while towing a scow of lumber. The scow went adrift after the tug grounded. Captain Jim Morrisson and Engineer Ralph Moore rowed in a small boat to Port Simpson to telephone to Prince Rupert. In the morning the Viner, under command of Captain James Thomas, went in search of the *Hanaco*. But she had disappeared, probably broken up and sunk.

Hanna S. 178203 On October 22, 1980 this fishboat owned by Conrad H Wolthuis, North Vancouver BC burned at Winter Harbour BC.

Hansema[a] 172475 On May 18, 1958 this fishboat owned by Ross J Hansen, Port Alberni BC burned. (In 1959 her register was closed, and she was licenced as 13K67460.) On June 25, 1976 she sank in Queen Charlotte Sound BC.

Harbour B.B. 154566 On August 11, 1929 this seiner owned by Bubji Hisioka, Vancouver BC was destroyed by fire between Village Reef and Satellite Passage BC in Barkley Sound.

Hardy Maid[b] 192046 On March 10, 1969 this fishboat owned by Wayne Watson, Powell River BC burned at Merry Island BC in Georgia Strait.

---

a   Built as Sampo; then Hansema
b   Built as Lana; then Hardy Maid

Harken No. 10[300] 816476 On September 28, 2015 this tug, owned by Tidal Towing Ltd., Port Coquitlam BC, sank in the entrance to the North Arm of the Fraser River around 5 am near Sand Heads, north of the Tsawwassen Ferry Terminal. She was en route to Shelter Island Marina and Boatyard in Richmond. Her crew of two were rescued after boarding a small aluminum boat they were towing.

Harlequin 323502 On August 24, 1972 she was destroyed by fire off Lennard Island BC. The fire was put out by the Shark Salvage Co. She was then swamped by the wake of the Tofino Lifeboat while being towed into Tofino. She was raised and stripped. Her hull was sunk between Stone Island and Neilson Island in Tofino Harbour BC.

Harlequin II 179639 On August 24, 1965 this tug owned by William B Crabbe (MO), Minstrel Island BC burned and sank in Fitzhugh Sound at the mouth of Safety Cove and was a total loss.

Haro Straits[a] 320295[301] She was converted from a Second World War tug owned by the US Army Transportation Service. On February 27, 1972, this tug owned by Rivtow Marine Ltd., Vancouver BC foundered off Point Roberts in Georgia Strait BC when two barges pulled her down off Point Roberts in a gale. Nine months later she was raised, her engine was rebuilt and sold, and her hull was put up for sale. After the accident was purchased by Bill Church who then decided to sell it out of the towboat fleet. It sat in Steveston harbour for a few years as an unfinished conversion project, renamed Outlaw V.

Harris No. 1[b] 133847 On May 29, 1927 this fishboat owned by Alfred Harris, North Vancouver BC exploded and burned at Second Narrows Bridge in Burrard Inlet BC.

---

a   Built as a US Army Transport Service tug; then Santrina; then Haro Straits; then Outlaw V
b   Built as Tamokichi; then Harris No. 1

Harry S. 130918 On July 7, 1927 this tug burned at Second Narrows, Burrard Inlet BC. It was reported that her hull was used as in-fill for the supports for the Second Narrows bridge.

Harstine II 383248 On December 9, 1979 this workshop barge owned by D.J. Welding & Marine Ltd., Sidney BC was abandoned at sea and sank in Juan de Fuca Strait.

Hartfield[302] (UK) On February 5, 1908 all hope was given up for this overdue bark at Victoria. She was 104 days out from Valparaiso Chile and had a crew of 26, all presumed lost. She is thought to have capsized after her cargo shifted off Vancouver Island, where wreckage was found.

Hatsue Maru No. 55[303] 102614 On December 18, 1978 this fishboat burned in Queen Charlotte Sound with the loss of one life.

Hatta II[304] 158551 On September 30, 1972 this fishboat, owned by Henry J Hall, Campbell Island BC, foundered off Chatham Point in Johnstone Strait BC. Her crew of two were rescued.

Hattie Young[a] 077098 In 1898 she worked on the Fraser River purchased to replace the steamer *Bon Accord* (#094908) that was destroyed in the fire at New Westminster of 1898 first as the *Josie Burrows* and then as the *Hattie Young*. On December 08, 1900 while proceeding upriver a fire broke out in the hold beneath the boiler. That caught a large cargo of hay being carried and the fire spread rapidly. The flames were all over the boat in a few minutes. Captain George Magar tried to run her ashore, but he had to leave his post before she reached the bank. She burned out and sank in several feet of water opposite Marsh's Landing on the Fraser River.

Hatzic[b] 083445 In March 1889 she was seized by the United States Government in the Bering Sea. She was taken to Port Townsend and

---

a Built as Josie Burrows; then Hattie Young
b Built as Dolphin; then Hatzic

sold by the US Marshal and re-registered in the USA. She was wrecked February 16th, 1902 while sailing from Kyuquot under Captain Daley and his Mate Pat Farley, with wreckage found on Triangle Island. The crew were all Kyuquot men and all hands were lost.

Haysport No. 1[305] 130857 On July 23, 1919 this fishboat owned by Deep C. Fisheries Ltd., Prince Rupert BC foundered off Graham Island in the Queen Charlotte Islands BC when she ran aground in Skidegate Narrows. She had 9,000 pounds of fish aboard at the time of the incident.

Haysport No. 2[a,306] 134127 In 1923 this schooner made one three-month rum running trip. While owned by Harry L Higgins, Prince Rupert BC she was lost near Bella Bella BC on January 26, 1925 near the entrance to Milbanke Sound BC.

Hazel B. #3[307] 215503 (US) This fishboat was registered at Wrangell AK. On May 24, 1949 she was stranded at Beavon Point, Stikine River BC.

Hazelton *Victoria Daily Colonist*, 27 Mar 1901. "Steamer *Hazelton*, the sternwheeler being built by R. Cunningham & Co. for the Skeena river trade, was launched a few days ago and is at Spratt's wharf, where work is being hurried forward on her in order to get her north to being work by April 20. Captain Bonsar, master of the river steamer *Monte Cristo*, which last season made a good name for herself on the Skeena, is to command the *Hazelton*, and is superintending the construction of the vessel, which he expects to be able to take north from here by April 15. The steamer has the lightest draught of any of the sternwheelers that have been launched here, for when she was launched she did not draw more than eleven inches of water, and when her machinery has been placed in her, it is expected that she will not draw more than sixteen inches, having a draught almost light enough to float on a dewy marsh."

---

a   Built as *Roosevelt*; then Haysport No. 2

Hecate Ranger[308] 318654 On July 30, 1979 this patrol boat was aground on Datum Rock in Chatham Sound while towing a helicopter barge. They had just gotten underway towing a barge, when they hit, at high water, 5:00 in the morning. A barge with crane arrived in the afternoon to lift her as she was heeled over. The tide came in and they got underway with the tow about 6:30 that evening, making no water.

Helen N. On October 23, 1976, this fishboat sank at Dundas Island on the east side near Whitesand Island.

Helena B.[a] 133252 On July 7, 1972 this vessel owned by Francis Millerd & Co. Ltd., Vancouver BC sank two miles west of White Island in Georgia Strait BC.

Helge H. 154714 This fishboat owned by Marelius Holkestad, Prince Rupert BC sank on February 3, 1933. Ross Holkestad[309] (his grandson) reported that "it sank off Bonilla Island and my grandfather rowed with three of his crew in the dory for 3 days until they got to Kitkatla to be rescued."

Henry Dennis[310] (US) This schooner ran ashore and was wedged in the rocks in San Josef Bay, Vancouver Island and was declared a total loss.

Henry Foss[b,311] 077408 (US) Dave Bartle states that "On Friday 13 February 1959 while under command of Captain Warren Waterman the Henry Foss came to a "grinding and abrupt stop on a rock near Beaver Point on Salt Spring Island. There was a 50-knot gale blowing and the seas extremely rough. The Henry Foss overturned and sank in 150-ft of water, throwing all seven men into the cold and rough water of Swanson Channel." Two men were pulled from the water. The Chief Engineer survived the exposure, but deckhand Richard Lothian died of exposure after reaching the hospital. The loss of the

---

a   Built as Iphis; then Helena B.
b   Built as John Cudahy; then Henry Foss

Henry Foss's six men was the most painful calamity in the Foss's long history of tug boating; the tug was not salvaged. Lost were Captain Warren Waterman; Chief Mate Lawrence Berg; Assistant Engineer, Martin Gullstein; Deckhand, Oswald H Sorenson; Cook, Erick W Danielson; Richard Lothian."

Hera[312] (US) On November 18th this three-masted schooner sailed under Captain JL Warren from Seattle with a full cargo of general merchandise for Honolulu including 1,800 barrels of lime, 750 bales of hay, other merchandise, and half of a knocked down church. She sprang a leak causing the cargo of lime to react with it such that the ship caught fire. The fire could not be fought as adding more water would have intensified the fire. Captain Warren ran for Clayoquot Sound arriving and anchoring 25 hours later. Within the next hour the vessel was ablaze forcing the crew to abandon ship. On November 26, 1899 she burned to the waterline.

Hercules[313] 122217 On October 6, 1957 this tug, under command of Captain Ted Forde, suddenly capsized at 0300 while towing a scow near Passage Island, Howe Sound BC. Captain Forde was drowned in the incident. A crew member, Henry Woof, swan to the scow and hung on for three hours before being rescued by the *Papco II*.

Hermit[314] (US) In March 1892 this whaling bark ran ashore 15 miles from Scott Channel north of Vancouver Island.

Hesquiat Warrior 197697 In February 1973 this fishboat owned by Michael E Tom (MO), Victoria BC sank off the west coast of Vancouver Island.

Hiack 107730 On January 17, 1904 this schooner owned by Charles E Crockett, Vancouver BC was stranded in Barkley Sound BC (at Vernon Bay).

Highland Light[315] 95318 (US) This bark was formerly in the gold rush trade between San Francisco and Puget Sound and Alaska. On November 16, 1901 she sprang a leak and foundered off Vancouver

Island BC while en route from Tacoma WA to San Francisco CA with a cargo of coal. The crew was rescued by the sealing schooner *Arilla* and brought to Victoria by the steamer *Queen City*.

Highway 99 189457 On September 9, 1970 this fishboat owned by Harold E Iverson, North Surrey BC foundered at Goose Bay River Inlet BC.

Hike 176796 On July 26, 1989 this fishboat owned by Phillip Trudeau, Vancouver BC grounded and sank on Jenny Reef in Carolina Channel near Ucluelet Inlet BC.

Hiker II 141330 On September 15, 1932 this fishboat owned by George Davis, Port Hammond BC collided with the *Princess Joan* about one-half mile northeast of the Pont Grey Buoy in Burrard Inlet BC.

Hiker III 141331 On April 16, 1931 this fishboat owned by Shirozaemon Simono, Steveston BC was stranded in Gillies Bay, Texada Island BC.

Hikeo III[316] On April 16, 1931 she was stranded off Texada Island BC. On September 15, 1932 she was in a collision off Point Grey BC.

Hilda 116783 On February 13, 1923 this tug owned by Mary Jane Blackwell, Vancouver BC was stranded on Gabriola Island BC.

Hili-Kum[a,317] 171778 The Transportation Safety Board of Canada states that "The Hili-Kum departed from an anchorage off Moresby Island, BC, with a cargo of red urchins for discharge at Port Edward, BC. En route, the weather deteriorated. On April 10, 1995, in following gale-to storm-force winds and rough seas, the vessel shipped large volumes of water on the afterdeck, settled by the stern, and sank stern first. The three crew members donned immersion suits, abandoned the vessel, and boarded a life raft. Two of the three immersion suits were defective, and the life raft capsized several times. Two of the crew succumbed to hypothermia and drowned; the survivor

---

a   Built as Hili-Kum; then RCAF M.582 Hili-Kum; then Hili-Kum

was rescued some five and a half hours later. The Board determined that the Hili-Kum proceeded to sea despite a storm warning broadcast and was being operated in following high winds and rough seas with the fish hold hatch cover not battened down. The cumulative effect of large volumes of seawater shipped on the afterdeck, the vessel's low freeboard aft, and the flooding/down flooding of the below-deck spaces aft caused the vessel to settle by the stern, lose reserve buoyancy, and sink stern first. The hypothermia and subsequent drowning of two of the crew is attributable to the poor state of repair of their immersion suits and to their exposure to the harsh weather conditions when the life raft capsized."

Hilma 320062 On October 17, 1976 this troller fishboat owned by David L White (MO), Nanaimo BC burned and foundered off Tofino BC after a fire and sank.

Hi-Tide 195257 In 1963 this fishboat owned by John R Parrish (MO), Stewart Island BC sank and was declared a total loss.

Hilunga[a] 192548 On February 16, 1956, as the Hilunga, this tug owned by The Minister of Public Works, Ottawa ON sank at Kunghiti Island, Cape St. James QCI BC. She then drifted to Aristazabel Island where she was later salvaged.

Hodder Ranger[b] 392922 On June 19, 2016 this tug owned by Active Marine Towing Ltd., Gibsons BC sank near Port Mellon BC.

Holland Rock[318] On February 23, 1959 this gillnet fishboat was destroyed by fire and sank off Gambier Island BC. Thomas Andrechuk, who was starting the engine, leaped to safety when a spark ignited gasoline in the bilge.

Holly Leaf[319] 130547 On November 4, 1939, while under command of Captain Robert G. Lawson this fishpacker owned by William C.

---

a   Built as Hilunga; then B.C. Rover
b   Built as Noble Ranger; then River Ranger; then Hodder Ranger

Gibson, Vancouver BC was destroyed by fire at Chup Point, Junction Passage, Barkley Sound BC. They were bound from Kildonan to Nitinat with ice and stores for Nitinat. The fire started in the engine room about half an hour after they left port. They crew evacuated in a small boat and were picked up by a troller.

Hope 088368 On February 17, 1891 she was stranded on Portland Island BC. Fred Rogers reported that "She sank on October 17, 1925 while working on the salvage of the freighter *Eemdyk* stranded off Bentick Island near Race Rocks. The tug was maneuvering near the ship when it was swept against the freighter in a strong tidal current and capsized. The tug was ferrying workers to the site at the time leading to the high death toll of 7 lost." George Nicholson reported that "There had been 28 workers and 6 crew on board. One of the survivors clung to a log and drifted with the tide halfway to Jordan River before being picked up."

Hope 117007 On May 20, 1928 this fishboat owned by J.H. Todd & Sons Ltd., Victoria BC burned at Inverness Cannery BC.

Hope Bay[a] 323661 On February 26, 2004 she sank at the north end of Vancouver Island BC. The Transportation Safety Board of Canada reports that "Shortly after midnight on 26 February 2004, while transiting Queen Charlotte Sound, British Columbia, the commercial fishing vessel *Hope Bay* listed suddenly to starboard and capsized. The four persons on board abandoned the vessel by jumping into the sea. Search and rescue personnel initially rescued one person and recovered the bodies of two others. The body of the fourth person was recovered later the same day. The vessel remained afloat for about 12 hours before sinking."

Hope Point III[b] 156623 She was a wooden yacht was crewed with Fishermen's Reserve personnel during the Second World War but was not a part of the Fishermen's Reserve. On August 11, 1967 she was

---

a   Built as Leroy and Barry; then Hope Bay
b   Built as Saltpetre; then H.C. 95; then Hope Point III

owned by Robert M Fraser, Vancouver, BC when she sank between Kyuquot and Tofino BC while being towed and was declared a total loss.

Horda[320] On May 15, 1901 she struck Horda Rock while on passage from Ladysmith with a cargo of coal for San Francisco from Nanaimo. The rock was found to be only 2 fathoms deep where it was shown on the chart as being 26 fathoms. On December 2, 1901 after leaving drydock for repair from her first wreck she again sailed for Oregon with a cargo of grain. She ran aground on the Columbia River Bar. She sailed back to Victoria to undergo further repairs.

Horizon[321] 170929 Ric Stacey reported that "I purchased the vessel in 1973 as part of the fisheries buyback program auction. I converted that boat from a fishing vessel to a liveaboard and cruising vessel. We lived aboard for 10 years before building our floating home. The Horizon sank at our dock in Ladner in 2002 and was a total loss."

Hornblower[a,322] 141430 In 1967 this tug, Maritime Towing Co. Ltd., Vancouver BC, burned to the waterline in the Fraser River. Her crew escaped safely. She was later rebuilt.

Howe Sound III[323] 141440 On March 15, 1946 this herring seiner owned by J.H. Todd & Sons Ltd., Victoria BC foundered one-half mile off Dallain Point, north of Laredo Inlet BC with a full load of herring. The six-man crew was safe.

Hubart 198167 On August 25, 1975 this fishboat owned by Douglas A Mace, Victoria BC suffered an explosion and fire in her engine room and burned to the waterline in Sydney Inlet BC.

Hudson Explorer 323350 On June 29, 1977 this research vessel owned by International Hydrodynamics Co. Ltd., Vancouver BC burned and sank in Goliath Bay, Jervis Inlet BC.

---

a   Built as Dollarton; then Firmac; then Hornblower; then Vigorous

Hulda O[a,324] On December 26, 1926, as the *Hulda O.*, this gasoline tanker exploded and was destroyed at the Shell Oil fuel dock at Barnet BC in Burrard Inlet. The brothers who owned the vessel, James, and Oscar Orpana, were injured in the incident. The *Hulda O.* had just taken on a cargo of 5,500 gallons of gasoline at the time of the incident. It was thought that the engines had backfired as the cause. On November 6, 1927, as the *A.G. Lilly*, while owned by the Victoria Petroleum Co. she burned to the waterline at the Government Wharf at Sturdies Bay on South Galiano Island, at Active Pass BC.

Humaconna[b,325] 218071 (US) On May 21, 1938 this big American tug, owned by Merrill & Ring Lumber Co., Port Angeles WA, went ashore near Chemainus BC. She was bringing a log boom of 36 sections of big logs from Port Angeles to Vancouver BC.

The passenger freighter *Humboldt* during salvage showing the temporary patches over the hole in her hull caused by the grounding (Image from the collection of the Maritime Museum of British Columbia _P3266_352)

---

a Built as Hulda O.; then A.G. Lilly; then Lepgec
b Built as Humaconna; then Gregory J. Busch

Humboldt 096354 (US) On September 29, 1908 this freighter went ashore on Mouat Point, North Pender Island on September 29, 1908 while en route from Seattle to Skagway in a dense fog. A radio call brought the steamer *Edith* (Captain Thomas A Miller) and she removed all the passengers. The bow was crumpled back 4 feet she was re-floated by the tug *Salvor* and JE Pharo's Puget Sound salvage steamer *Santa Cruz* and following repairs she resumed her Alaska service. She sank on August 8th, 1935. In 1909 the *Humboldt* was one of the steamers responding to the wreck of the passenger steamer *Ohio* on the BC coast. The *Humboldt* herself sank August 8, 1935.

Humming Bird No. 2 140978 On October 8, 1950 she was in collision with a boom moored in the channel at Ragged Island, Georgia Strait BC.

Huron (USS) In 1930 she was added to the floating breakwater at Powell River BC. In 1960 she sank near the current site of the YOGN '82.

Hurricane I[326] 174089 On October 12, 1984 this fishboat sank in a violent storm in Royal Roads between Albert Head and the old gravel pit. His engine failed and while trying to anchor Charles Alfred Casey was drowned when his boat capsized and sank.

Huskie[a] 137932 On October 21, 1927 while owned by Margaret A McKenzie, Vancouver BC she burned at St. Vincent Bay in Jervis Inlet BC.

Hustler[b,327] 122516 On August 11, 1925 the tug *Hustler* was towing two barges (one on either side) when the Japanese freighter *Kaikiya Maru* collided with the barge sinking the *Hustler*. The freighter hit the barge amidships so violently that tug owners, Horatio and James Robert Hodder were injured. The tug sank. The freighter was arrested

---

a   Built as Flossie S.; then Huskie
b   Built as Hustler; then Gillrock

but made a run for the sea, ignoring government and court officials demanding that she heave to. On June 16, 1938 this tug, while under command of Captain W.G. McKay, was travelling upstream in the Fraser River towing two empty scows. A half mile east of the Fraser Avenue bridge the fishboat An collided with one of the scows. The An had been drifting downriver with a gillnet set. The tug took evasive and warning measures but the bow of the fishboat hit and sank almost immediately. A police investigation concluded that Alfred Nelson, on seeing the tug approaching, he went into the cabin to start the engine. He was drowned in the incident. The *Hustler* was later salvaged. At the end of her life she was reported to have been beached and broken up in 1951.

Idaho (US) In 1886 she was in Alaska-Puget Sound-California service. In 1886 she was seized by the US revenue cutter *Oliver Wolcott* and found $48,000 of opium on board. Captain Carroll owned a fish cannery at Kassan Bay AK where after a search 11 barrels of opium were found by a party from the *Oliver Wolcott*. Three months later 600 pounds of opium was found on the *Idaho* and she was seized and placed under bond. Several hundred pounds of opium was removed from the wreck by customs officials. On November 29, 1889 she was wrecked at Race Rocks BC and the wreck drifted back across the border to Port Angeles where it sank.

Imam 189274 On June 13, 1965 this fishboat owned by Andrew Hajnal, Steveston BC was stranded at Blackney Island (Sea Otter Group) BC and she was wrecked at Birgin Rock, near Bull Harbour BC.

Imar No. 1 313923 On July 14, 1967 this fishboat owned by John Bruhaug (MO), Burnaby BC burned and sank of Cape Caution BC.

Industry[328] 064134 On January 13, 1879 this schooner, under command of Captain Jones, en route to Victoria with a cargo of Nanaimo coal, was stranded at Discovery Island BC.

Inez H.[329] 141278 On March 30, 1930 this fishboat under command of Captain O Skome and owned by Edwin Skogmo, Prince Rupert BC hit a rock and foundered 4.5 miles of Eagle Hill on the east coast of Graham Island BC.

Inez W. 2 173889 On July 10, 1975 this troller fishboat owned by Adrian R Dowell (MO), Vancouver BC sank off Ucluelet BC.

Inlet Queen[330] 130308 On April 09, 1913 she broached while crossing the Nitinat Bar during a gale and struck a rock and was beached. The *Banfield Lifeboat* attended the incident and over several hours the entire crew was saved. The Inlet Queen had been running a passenger service between Nitinat Lake and surrounding points and was inbound from Victoria carrying lumber and supplies for survey camps.

Inomar III[331] 152909 On September 4, 1937 this power-cruiser exploded 50 feet from the Shell Oil Co. Fuel Barge at Coal Harbour BC and was destroyed by fire. After she exploded local boatmen towed it away from the fuel barge and she grounded on the shore of Stanley Park. There was no fireboat, so she was left to burn herself out.

Inspiration 323576 On July 1, 1967 she burned off Point Grey BC near the mouth of the Fraser River.

Irene May II 170403 On April 18, 1980 this fishboat owned by Brian W Widsten (MO), New Westminster BC was beached on Stubbs Island (VI) BC, declared a total loss and broken up.

Iris 116787 On November 25, 1904 this tug owned by Captain John E Fulton, Vancouver BC was stranded in Burrard Inlet BC and lost in First Narrows (Vancouver Harbour) BC.

Irish Mist[a] 313791 On September 20, 1972 this fishboat owned by David Campbell (MO), Nanaimo BC foundered off Brotchie Ledge, Victoria BC in Juan de Fuca Strait.

---

a   Built as Ann A. II; then Irish Mist

Irma J.[332] 156449 On October 14, 1936 this fishpacker sank off Cape Lazo BC. RO Cole and his brother, DR Cole were returning to Vancouver loaded with fish when this vessel struck an object in the water and sprang a leak. Both men pumped but the rising water overwhelmed the diesel engine. In a desperate measure they poured gasoline over the winch and set it on fire. Then Captain Ralph Grosvold of the Seattle schooner *Blue Fox* saw the blaze and arrived just in time to remove the two men before their vessel sank in 300 feet of water. They were taken to Deep Bay.

Iron Bark[333] 150978 She is reported as having been a rum runner. On February 08, 1932 she had the Canadian in tow and the tow foundered approximately 1.5 miles off lower end of Bowen Island in the Georgia Strait BC. She ran aground on Bowen Island, filled, and sank in March 1950.

Iron Lung[a] 192047 In 1962 this tug capsized off Port Mellon BC.

Iron Belle[334] 197453 On January 2, 1959 this tug owned by Sea Lane Towing Co. Ltd., Vancouver BC sank in Howe Sound BC northeast of Anvil Island. The weather was very windy at the time of the incident and she drifted ashore.

Iron Mac II[b] 323346 On December 1, 1966 this tug owned by Iron Mac Towing Ltd., Campbell River BC sank at Cape Lazo BC in 184 feet of water with the loss of two crew members. She was salvaged and put back into service.

Ironbark[335] On September 29, 1924 Customs agents went after this launch at the Royal Victoria Yacht Club. The crew of the *Ironbark* claimed that these agents looked like hijackers and that the vessel had departed immediately under a hail of bullets from the Customs agents who claimed they only wished to inspect the ship's papers. On December 29, 1930 she hit a submerged deadhead near the

---

a Built as Remlab; then Iron Lung
b Built as Iron Mac II; then Storm Winds #1

Second Narrows Bridge and sprang two planks. On February 26, 1951 this small tug, while under the command of Captain George Thayer, struck a rock near Snug Cove in Howe Sound. She sank quickly. The captain and his crew were rescued by the *North Coaster*.

The little passenger steamer *Iroquois* with the big tug *William Joliffe* in the background. (Image from the collection of the Maritime Museum of British Columbia)

Iroquois 107822 In October 1908 she ran ashore in dense fog on Jack Island. The rising tide caught and overwhelmed her stern causing her to sink. The salvage tugs *Maude* and *William Joliffe* got her afloat and she went back into service. On April 10, 1911 she left Sidney for Nanaimo via the Gulf Islands carrying 32 passengers and crew and a cargo of general freight and tools which may have been overloaded and unstable. Between Shell Island and Roberts Point she headed for Canoe Channel when she suddenly listed and capsized. Within minutes the *Iroquois* had disappeared. Three First Nations men, William Tsouhalem, Bob Klulwhalem, and Donat Charlie saved three lives, and were awarded gold medals for bravery. The captain was charged with manslaughter for his failure to aid the women and children.

Iroquois (US) This American vessel was brought around from the east coast of the USA in 1907 via the southern end of South America by the Puget Sound Navigation Co. (aka Black Ball Line). In 1927 she was rebuilt to carry automobiles on the Seattle – Victoria run. On February 8th, 1934 she ran aground[336] buffeted by heavy winds in Victoria Harbour. At the time she was giving way to the CGS *Malaspina* when her steering gear slipped and, in the process, she grounded on a high tide. The following day big Pacific Salvage Company tug *Salvage King* (Captain Leighton Evans) pulled her off the rocks with minimal damage at high water the next day and she was able to proceed to Seattle.

The American vessel *Iroquois* aground in Victoria Harbour in 1934
(Photograph by Douglas MacFarlane in the John MacFarlane collection.)

Isabel V[a] 369176 On August 24, 1978 this fishboat owned by Gran Fishing Co. Ltd., Richmond BC struck a deadhead in Metlaktla Passage, Prince Rupert BC.

Isabella[337] 064137 This schooner was wrecked while en route from Nanaimo to Victoria December 04, 1875. She was carrying a cargo of Wellington coal for the navy when she struck shore and sank in "the rapids". In December, the wreck was righted by Captain Thain and 25 tons of coal was removed by the *Black Diamond*. She was taken to Victoria for repairs.

Isabella M. 150516 On May 24, 1933 she foundered two miles offshore from Blubber Bay, and she sank off Texada Island BC.

Isla May 249713 (US) She was registered in Seattle WA USA. On December 7, 1960 she burned in Graham Reach, south of Grenville Channel BC.

Island Brave 322963 On August 30, 1967 she foundered off Portland Point BC.

---

a   Built as Wind Song VIII; then Isabel V

Island Challenger[a] 347761 The Transportation Safety Board of Canada states that "In the early morning hours of February 11, 1995, the fishboat *Pacific Bandit* owned by Banditos Fishing Ltd., Surrey, BC, laden with about 23,000 kg of fish, was off the west coast of Vancouver Island, British Columbia, not engaged in fishing operations. The wind and sea conditions were such that the vessel was shipping and retaining seas on the main deck. The vessel listed to starboard, flooded, capsized, and eventually sank. Two crew members were swept overboard; the other two abandoned the vessel and managed to board the life raft. Three of the crew members were later rescued and one person, who was in the water without a lifejacket or an immersion suit, succumbed to hypothermia and drowned.

Island Comet[b] 111789 On September 30, 1930 while owned by Island Tug & Barge Ltd., Victoria BC she sank off Otter Cove BC.

Island Cypress[c,338] 161241 On October 14, 1963 this log barge owned by Island Tug & Barge Co. Ltd., Victoria BC while in tow of the tug Sudbury II she broke in half and sank in the Pacific Ocean.

Island Express[d] 130606 On February 25, 1965 she was in a collision with the *Tyee Shell* in Quatsino Inlet BC. In 1967 she was advertised as having a top-notch warehouse mounted on the barge with a capacity of 1500 tons and 4900 cubic feet of refrigerated space. Loading and unloading was done with a forklift, crane, and ramps with an elevator between decks. It ran on Mondays from Vancouver to arrive Wednesday at Alert Bay, Sointula, port McNeill and Port Hardy. On Thursday it called at Winter Harbour, Mahatta River, Quatsino, Coal Harbour, Holberg and Jeune Landing. On Fridays it reached Port Alice with the return voyage direct to Vancouver berthing on Monday.

---

a   Built as Pacific Bandit; then Island Challenger
b   Built as Edna Grace; then Island Comet
c   Built as Surinam; then Island Cypress
d   Built as Transfer No. 3; then Island Express; then Seaspan 630; then M.F. No. 1

Island Flyer[339] 176878 On February 17, 1948 this passenger vessel owned by Sannie Transportation Co. Ltd., Vancouver BC was stranded in Douglas Bay, Gambier Island BC. After they ran aground, Douglas Cook, the one-man crew hiked through deep snow to summon help for his passengers. She had her bottom ripped open while the operator attempted to land a passenger at his cabin. The passengers were able to step ashore.

Island Gatherer[a] 156616 On September 13, 1930 while owned by Pacific (Coyle) Navigation Co. Ltd., Vancouver BC, she collided with the Second Narrows Bridge and demolished a span north of the bascule. She became wedged under the bridge's fixed centre span. The tide rose pushing the barge up under the span, knocking it off its supports. The span hung off one side before suddenly breaking free and sinking into the depths of Burrard Inlet. Lawsuits and the bankruptcy of the bridge company delayed any attempt at repairs. The bridge remained closed for four years. Six years later, Captain Fred MacFarlane, while in command of the Island Queen in Gordon Channel one mile west of Pine Island BC, with the barge *Island Gatherer* in tow on December 13, 1936 the tow line parted during a storm in Queen Charlotte Sound. The tug ran alongside the barge suffering damage. The crew lined the side with mattresses so that Captain JR Paulson on the barge with his family (his wife and two children) could leap on board the *Island Queen*. She was in tow of the tug *Island Queen* when the winch on the barge broke and went overboard with the towline. By the time the towline was recovered, and the barge crew rescued, the barge disappeared in the darkness and vanished.

Island Girls 330291 On March 13, 1979 this fishboat owned by Ross J Michelson, Sointula BC was abandoned at sea and sank in Nootka Sound BC.

Island Maple[b,340] 161234 On October 22, 1963 while in tow of the tug Sudbury she was broken in half and sank in Juan de Fuca Strait off

---

a   Built as Alsterburg; then Walkure; then William Dollar; then Pacific Gatherer; then Island Gatherer
b   Built as Tamare; then Island Maple

Cape Flattery. She was carrying a cargo of 'black liquor', a chemical used in pulp processing which was being taken to Washington State for processing. She wallowed behind her tug for most of the day in very heavy weather and then began to sink. Once freed from the tug it split in half, the stern section turned over and the bow sank.

Island Navigator[a,341] 177383 In January 1955, as the *Island Navigator*, she struck a rock in Kyuquot Sound and was sinking. Captain George Dance beached her before she sank in deep water. In January 1968, as the *Pablo*, she was in collision with the Washington State Ferry *Hyak* in Seattle Harbour.

Island Ranger[b] 177371 On August 04, 1996 she sank in Drury Inlet, Acteon Sound BC. On November 30, 2008, this 68-foot wooden tug *Island Ranger* grounded and partially sank in Tofino Harbour, BC. The vessel lay with its port side submerged across the current, approximately 70 metres off the crab dock. On January 26, 2009, the *Island Ranger* was recovered, and the remaining fuel tanks were pumped out. The vessel was slung between two barges and moved to a remote site with less current. The owner deconstructed the vessel and disposed of the debris.

Island Titan[c] 134031 Cliff Craig[342] reports that "I operated the *Island Titan* and tugboat salvaging and dredging for over six years. The Island Titan went mysteriously missing the September long weekend of 1978, never to be seen again by my eyes. She was tied alongside Valley Towing's barge *Packmore 5000* that I had been loading with 140-foot cedar poles, waiting to load out another 60 from the sorting grounds. I had just signed a contract to do more work in the coming weeks. On the Tuesday after the long weekend in September I came back to work where the *Island Titan* should have been still tied up, but her four 2-inch tie-up lines were stretched taut and shredded. She had simply disappeared with no trace. The mystery of her fate is unsolved to this day."

---

a   Built as USATS LT-188; then Island Navigator; then Isla; then Pablo
b   Built as USN Small Tug; then Island Ranger; then Seaspan Ranger; then Island Ranger
c   Built as Transfer No. 4; then Island Titan

Islander 095093 On August 15, 1901 this passenger vessel owned by Canadian Pacific Railway Steamship Services struck an iceberg at Point Hilda, Stephen's Passage, off Douglas Island AK with loss of 42 lives. In 1934 she was raised and beached on Admiralty Island. The Islander was partially salvaged, no safe was found and her remains are still on a nearby beach. Gold seekers now think safe was in the bow section that broke off in deep water.

Ivana 171800 On February 28, 1964 this seiner owned by Albert Radil (MO), Vancouver BC foundered at off Mcinnis Island at the entrance to Milbanke Sound BC. The crew were rescued safely.

Ivanhoe 121753 In 1934 she had disappeared, apparently without a trace. In 1934 she was found in Clayoquot Sound.

Ivanhoe[343] 122547 In 1930 she went ashore at the Lions Gate during a fog. In 1939 she was used for towing logs on Fraser River for several years. In 1948 she towed the largest Davis raft ever to pass under the Second Narrows Bridge (raft of cedar from Kelley Logging Co., QCI). On September 9, 1964 she collided with and sank the US seiner Ozzie R., owned by Parr Reece, Seattle WA, near the Ballenas Islands the Gulf of Georgia during the summer fishing season.

Ivy H. 178195 On September 23, 1980 she sank in Tofino Harbour BC.

Ivy II[344] On September 23, 1980 this fishboat exploded and burned and sank after an explosion and fire in Tofino Harbour. Three members of the Frank family were injured when the engine on their boat backfired when it was started at 1:00 am.

Izumi[345] 138603 On October 10, 1939 she burned and sank at French Creek near Parksville BC. She was en route to Nanaimo fishing under charter to the Canadian Fishing Co. The crew had just fished dinner and were on deck at the time of the incident. The engineer had just oiled the engine when it backfired, and a fire broke out. When fighting the fire became fruitless, they cut the net clear and the crew of five got in the boat and were just clear of the vessel when it exploded. She sank after burning about 3 hours. The *Carlisle S.* later picked up the nets.

J & D 176678 On October 13, 1954 she burned in the Alberni Canal BC.

J.B. 156814 On January 27, 1932 she suffered a fire in Prince Rupert Harbour BC. On December 26, 1947 she burned at Brake Island BC.

J.C. Bruce[346] 126175 On August 12, 1932 this yacht owned by James Small, Victoria BC burned to the waterline after the engine backfired off Ten Mile Point BC.

J.D.K. On July 9, 1976 this gillnetter had a hole in her hull when she sank at Storm Island (Gordon Channel VI) BC.

J.K. McKenzie 154913 On October 23, 1968 this tug owned by McKenzie Barge & Marine Ways Ltd., Vancouver BC foundered, capsized, and sank in a storm in Malaspina Strait four miles south of Powell River BC. Captain Frank Symes had just radioed for another tug to help with the two chip-scow tow when she sank rapidly. The rescuing tug *Gryphon* arrived soon afterwards and found the four-man crew were in the water clinging to the lifeboat and only one was wearing a life jacket.

J.R. Morgan[a] 099584 On August 19, 1914 she went ashore on Butterworth Rocks. On June 23, 1920 she grounded in Victoria Harbour BC. On April 1, 1925 she was laying off San Francisco when she fouled the Pacific Undersea Cable, breaking communications with Asia. She was sued for damages by the Commercial Cable Company, but her owners avoided payment by transferring her ownership to a dummy company. In 1935 she was renamed as J.R. *Morgan* a rumrunner mother ship converted to a tug. In 1935 she was aground on Lasqueti Island BC. In c1940 she was used for

---

a   Built as Bruno; then Prince Albert; then J.R. Morgan

towing Davis Rafts across Hecate Strait. In 1949c she was converted to a non-powered barge. On May 19, 1950 she sank off Perez Rock, Estevan Point BC (Vancouver Island BC—48° 20'N & 126° 35'W.)

J.S.M. Transporter[a] 312025 She had a 3,000-barrel capacity for transporting fuel to marine service stations on the coast of British Columbia. On July 30, 1960, soon after she went into service, owned by the Pacific Tanker Co., she burned in Calm Channel BC and was sold by the insurers.

Jabalo[347] 155175 On March 26, 1977 this herring fishboat foundered and sank five miles southeast of Northeast Point, Malaspina Strait BC. They were rescued by the naval auxiliary vessel Lynx carry sea cadets on a weekend training exercise. The crew of three was taken off the fishboat just before she went down.

Ja-Do-Mar 178210 On December 12, 1977 this fishboat owned by Larry Boroski, Nanaimo BC foundered, capsized and sank off Long Beach (VI) BC.

Jakelyn 198071 On October 18, 1960 this fishboat owned by Jacob J Trueb, Vancouver BC burned north of Passage Island in Howe Sound BC.

James B Houston (USARS)[348] 161140 (US) On January 27, 1941 she ran hard aground on Susan Rocks in Milbanke Sound, 125 miles south of Prince Rupert. Her 23 passengers and part of her 38 crew were taken off by the USS *Charleston*. Captain Williamson and a small crew stayed aboard for a time but salvage attempts by the Pacific Salvage Co. (the tug *Salvage Chieftain*), Victoria BC failed when she slipped off the rocks and sank in 90 feet of water. She was eventually beached at Prince Rupert in July after having been suspended from four large scows by cables and still submerged 35 feet.

---

a   Built as B.A. Logger; then Pacific Barge 99; then Seaspan 802; then J.S.M. Transporter

James D. McCormack[349] 150507 This sternwheeler, owned by Canadian Western Lumber Co. Ltd., Fraser Mills BC, was retired in 1939. Her hull was abandoned on the shore of the Fraser River near Fraser Mills.

James Drummond[350] 076169 (US) On October 22, 1914 she was stranded on Dall Patch BC about ten miles south of Milbanke Sound. The *James Drummond*, southbound from Gypsum, AK with a full cargo of 2,000 ton of gypsum rock for Tacoma. She was in tow of the tug *Tatoosh*, which made an unsuccessful effort to refloat her, afterward removing 4 members of the crew, and proceeding with them to Puget Sound. Captain HA Frieze and one crew member stayed aboard to take care of her in case she should be salvaged. She was declared a total loss. By late October only her forecastle head was still visible above water.

Jane Gray[351] (US) While en route from Seattle WA USA to Kotzebue Sound AK she foundered off Cape Cook with a loss of 36. She was carrying a steam launch, the *Kennorma*, as deck cargo. The lashings were cut, and she was launched to save 27 people who reached Kyuquot BC after being adrift for 5 days. The survivors were brought to Victoria by the sealing schooner *Favourite*.

Janet Cowan This four-masted bark was sailing 121 days out from Capetown South Africa (2498 tons) under the command of Captain Thompson bound for Vancouver (Hastings Mill) in ballast for a cargo of lumber. On December 31, 1895 she was wrecked 12 miles west of Carmanah Point near Pachena Point BC. Seven lives were lost. The lifesaving telephone line was out of action and the trail was blocked by several feet of snow. It was not until the second week of January that the 14 survivors of the wreck were picked up by Captain William Grove in the tug *Tyee* and landed at Port Townsend WA USA. It was later learned that the *Janet Cowan* had made her landfall off Cape Flattery on the night of December 30, 1895, and entered the Strait before a southwest gale, being preceded by two or three other vessels. When abreast of Clallam Bay she put about and endeavored to beat to sea, but the gale and northerly currents carried the ship, which was in light ballast and high out of the water, toward the Vancouver Island shore where she struck.

Japan 107831 In 1900 she was registered at Victoria BC. On July 10, 1907 she was blown up by dynamite between Reef Point and Bold Island AK.

Japan Erika[a,352] 7377854 (Japan) On October 17, 1979 this freighter collided with the bridge in heavy fog knocking a section of the bridge just north of the lift span into the water. The bridge was closed until March 4, 1980. Years later, on December 12, 1999, the Japan Erika broke in two and sank in Biscayne Bay, off the coast of Brittany (France) taking with her nearly 31000 metric tons of fuel oil. The sinking was the worst maritime disaster in the country's history.

Jay Dee[b] 198945 On February 29, 1978 this fishboat suffered damage when she grounded and sank at Tugwell Bar in the entrance to Prince Rupert Harbour BC.

Jeanie[353] 076389 This freighter owned by Alaska Pacific Steamship Co. was registered at Tacoma WA USA. On December 19, 1913 while under the command of Captain Ed Hickman she went ashore and sank off Clarke Point on Calvert Island during a heavy fog. She had been bound for southeastern Alaska ports from Seattle. She was carrying a heavy load of deck cargo and a load of equipment in her hold. Her crew was rescued by the lighthouse tender Estevan. The hull was severely damaged to the point where salvage would have been impossible.

Jennie Bay[354] 154335 On December 24, 1938 this seiner owned by Yoshimatso Teranishi, Steveston BC foundered en route from Ucluelet to Tofino BC and was driven ashore on McKenzie Beach.

a   Built as Japan Erika; then Erika
b   Built as Larilyn H.; then Jay Dee

Jerry II 198095 On January 18/19, 1969 this work boat owned by Drake Island Logging Ltd., Duncan BC sank at Nalos Landing, Smith Inlet BC.

Jessie On September 20, 1966 she sank at the mouth of the Fraser River.

Jessie Ellen 134097 On January 29, 1924 this workboat owned by Brooks Bidlake Cedar Co. Ltd., Vancouver BC was destroyed by fire at Myrtle Point Booming Ground BC.

Jessie Island[a] 138780 On July 18. 1930 this fishboat owned by Genichi Kodama & Aikimatsu Tabata (JO), Vancouver BC was stranded on rocks 1.5 miles southeast of Cox Point on the west coast of Vancouver Island BC.

Jessie Island No. 4 153297 On December 29, 1926 she was stranded while en route from Chemainus to Port Alberni. The skipper rounded Pachena Point mistakenly thinking that it was Cape Beale. More than six lives were lost.

Jessie Island No. IX 156660 On September 22, 1966 this fishboat owned by Nelson Bros Fisheries Ltd., Vancouver BC sprang a leak, foundered at mouth of Fraser River in the Georgia Strait BC.

Jessie Island No. XI 156600 On January 18, 2010, the Canadian Coast Guard (CCG) received a report of two vessels sinking together in Ladysmith Harbour, British Columbia, following a severe windstorm. One was a 30-foot sailboat and the other a 55-foot ex-fishing vessel—*Jessie Island XI*. The vessels sank in approximately 30 feet of water. The owner of both vessels advised Canadian Coast Guard Environmental Response personnel that there was oil onboard the *Jessie Island XI*, and they deployed a containment boom.

---

a   Built as Planet; then Jessie Island

Jigger Too[a] 371084 On March 24, 1979 this fishboat owned by Thomas M Isherwood, Port Alberni BC burned at Pollys Point in Port Alberni Harbour BC.

Jinks 133726 On November 24, 1915 while owned by the Vancouver Cannery Ltd., Vancouver BC she was stranded in Queen Charlotte Sound BC.

Joan G.[b,355] 153013 In 1882 she was built as a schooner she operated as a notorious 'blackbirder' slave-trading in the Solomon Islands. Later she had an historical career in the Canadian Arctic. In 1924–1928 she was owned by Christian J Klengenberg, Rymer Point NT. In 1928–1930 she was owned by the Hudson's Bay Co., London UK. In 1931–1933 she was used for rum-running (managed by Captain CH Hudson) from the Evans, Coleman & Evans dock in Vancouver BC. In 1934 she ran aground on Sarah Island. In 1954 Captain Bill Dolmage converted her to a barge. In 1966 she sank in Cockatrice Bay, Broughton Island BC during a heavy snowfall. In 1965–1971 she was owned by Robert M Savage, Vancouver BC. Her hull was used as a shake bolt barge until wrecked off Kingcome Inlet.

Joan W. II[c] 170422 On March 4, 1940 this fishing vessel was commissioned into the Royal Canadian Navy Fisherman's Reserve as HMCS Joan W II. On May 8, 1972 while owned by Dollina Enterprises Ltd., Vancouver BC she was in a collision with the fishing vessel *All Star* off Cape Roger Curtis BC.

John Bright Bark On February 4, 1869 she was outward bound from Port Ludlow in Admiralty Inlet WT to Valparaiso Chile which struck a reef one mile west of Boulder Point outside Hesquiat Harbour near Estevan Point. In a notorious event the ship was plundered by Hesquiat people and 10 members of the crew and passengers

---

a   Built as Jigger Two; then Havorn
b   Built as Maid of Orleans; then Old Maid II; then Maid of Orleans; then Joan G.
c   Built as Joan W. II; then HMCS Joan W. II; then Joan W. II

from the ship were murdered. HMS *Sparrowhawk*, under command of Commander HW Mist RN, was sent to investigate. In the aftermath seven prisoners were brought to Victoria and two First Nations men were sentenced to death and hanged at Hesquiat BC.

John Esler[a] 130691[356] On September 5, 1948 this seiner owned by Captain John Nash, Port Alberni BC foundered and sank in Skidegate Rapids BC. In October 1948 she was salvaged by Demmy Stevens and Richard Pallant of Skidegate BC.

John Henry II[b] 134107 On April 14, 1926 this tug while owned by Imperial Oil Co. Ltd., Vancouver BC hit the Second Narrows Bridge in Burrard Inlet and sank. She was raised two days later. On November 24, 1970 while owned by Herbert W. Parker, Moresby Camp QCI BC was destroyed by fire in the Queen Charlotte Islands BC.

John Marshall On November 10, 1860 while traveling in ballast from San Francisco CA to Discovery Bay WT in Puget Sound for a cargo of lumber. She drifted ashore about 8 miles beyond Port San Juan. The schooner *Ino* recovered her name board with items of rigging and gear from the ship. No survivors of the crew of 10–12 were reported. The theory at the time was that she was abandoned at sea and became a derelict before being driven ashore.

John P. Douglas 126079 On January 07, 1909 this mail and passenger ferry owned by Alfred E Yates (MO), Vancouver BC was destroyed by fire at Harrison Mills, BC. She was trying to cross the Fraser River when she was hit by pack ice. While freeing themselves the crew found the vessel engulfed in flames made worse by the wind. Only the mail bags were saved by the crew as they hastily abandoned ship. The crew salvaged planks from the burning steamer with which to make their landing from the pack ice. Her salvaged engines went to the *Vedder*.

---

a   Built as Nakano; then John Esler
b   Built as Polarine; then Chummie 2; then Charles H. Cates VII; then John Henry II

John Rosenfeld[357] (US) On February 20, 1886 at 4:00 am, this bark owned by Arthur Sewill & Co. et al., San Francisco CA USA while under Captain James G Baker she ran on Rosenfeld Rock (Boiling Reef) while in tow of the American tug Tacoma while proceeding from Nanaimo to San Francisco with a cargo of 8,900 tons of coal. She was a total loss.

Johnny Boy 175661 In November 1973 this fishboat owned by John AF Storris (MO), Nanaimo BC sank 8 miles off Carmanah Point BC.

Johnny K. No. 1 310340 On June 2, 1965 this tug owned by River Towing Co. Ltd., Vancouver BC sank in turbulent water in the Skeena River BC and was a total loss.

Joker B.[a] 150903 She was owned by James A Brackett, Pender Island BC and towed booms from Hornby and Denman as well as towing the oil barge from Vancouver to the Comox Logging booming ground. On September 18, 1929 she sank following an explosion while towing a pilchard barge in Tahsis Channel, Nootka Sound.

Jolly Jumbo 156629 The *Jolly Jumbo* was a yacht outfitted as a traveling general store cruised the area around Beaver Cove on northern Vancouver Island in the summers in the late 1920s. On May 16, 1940 she suffered a fire in Kenneth Passage at the mouth of Mackenzie Sound BC.

Jordina[b] 197652 On October 28, 1958 this tug while owned by Gordon L Kleaman, Vancouver BC exploded and burned in False Creek, Vancouver Harbour BC. This vessel is a popular dive spot at Ellison Provincial Park, just south of Vernon BC.

Jorojen[c] 197873 On September 7, 1967 this fishboat owned by Norman Turner (MO), Victoria BC was destroyed by fire and was a total loss.

---

a   Built as 2000, later Joker B.
b   Built as Kathy K.; then Squamish King; then Bobby McKenzie; then Robina B.; then Al Vi No. 1; then Jordina
c   Built as Mary-Pat; then Jorojen

Josy 252103 (US) On November 7, 1959 this vessel was destroyed by fire off Port Hardy BC.

Josroy 176240 On March 6, 1970 this fishboat owned by John G. Lloyd (MO), Vancouver BC foundered in Sechelt Inlet BC.

Jubilee[358] This tug owned by Captain Thomas D Shorts for Okanagan Lake service towed a barge when additional cargo space was required. She sank in 1889 after being damaged in an ice thaw at Okanagan Landing BC. Her machinery was taken out and placed in the City of Vernon.

Ju-Ju[359] 173778 On 19 March 1993, the Ju-Ju, a longliner fishboat owned by Ian Andrews Dawson Creek, BC was proceeding to Kildidt Sound, BC, to shelter from a south-easterly gale. The vessel took on water below decks and sank shortly thereafter. Two of the three crew members were rescued from the water, suffering from hypothermia. The third to be recovered had succumbed to hypothermia and drowned.

Juno III 312292 On Aug 19, 1966 this fishboat owned by William TN Guiney (MO), Victoria BC and Charles P Fraser, Victoria BC burned at sea seven miles south of Cape Beale BC and sank in 100 fathoms of water.

Juskatla Belle 198140 On July 16, 1965 this tug owned by Emil Anderson Construction Co. Ltd., Vancouver BC exploded and burned at Buttle Lake BC and was a total loss.

Jyp 314755 On September 8, 1965 this fishboat owned by Nelson Bros Fisheries Ltd., Vancouver BC was destroyed by fire in Luscombe Inlet (QCI) BC.

K.V. Kruse[360] (US) In January 1940 this converted log barge owned by Gibson Bros Logging Co., Vancouver BC foundered in Hecate Strait BC when in a storm she became separated from her tug the La Pointe and disappeared.

Kaare II[361] 173579 In 1941 23 members of the Novik family travelled in this fishboat across the Atlantic to Nova Scotia and on to BC through the Panama Canal from occupied Norway. On October 23, 1963 while owned by Antonsen Fishing Co. Ltd., Vancouver BC she disappeared (with the loss of the crew of 5) at sea and was last heard of 15 miles southeast of Bonita Island, in Hecate Strait BC.

Kalamalka[a,362] 190303 In 1966 this fishboat, while under the command of Captain Con M Ethier, was in collision with the *Sea Prince* at the Sandheads Lighthouse, near the mouth of the Fraser River. She sank, was raised, and repaired. Her crew of five escaped unharmed. On December 3, 1967 she had an engine room fire and burned off Goschen Island in the northern Hecate Strait BC and sank in Willis Bay. She was at anchor at the time of the fire and the crew abandoned ship and were rescued.

Kalmor II 137944 On October 21, 1979 this troller fishboat owned by Garry GL Smith, Nanaimo BC sank after taking water south of Pachena Point BC.

Kalou I[b] 344754 On March 22, 1976 this gillnetter owned by the Cassiar Packing Co. (1962) Ltd., Vancouver BC grounded and drifted ashore near the Hannah Rocks (QCI) BC. Two lives were lost.

Kanawaka[363] 156733 She was reported to have been a rum runner operating out of British Honduras. On Saturday evening, May 24, 1952 the fishpacker *Kanawaka* was rammed by the passenger vessel *Capilano* 4 miles east southeast of Gower Point BC. The fishing vessel was three hours out of Vancouver bound for Prince Rupert. The crew had difficulty freeing the lifeboat, by the time they had succeeded the wheelhouse was filling with water. A heavy swell capsized the boat just as they launched it putting them all in the water. The *Capilano* put a lifeboat in the water, the crew of six who were in the water for twenty minutes before rescue. The impact of the collision left a large hole in the stern of the vessel filling her hold with water.

---

a Built as HMCS Kalamalka; then Kalamalka
b Built as Roddy Boy; then Cassiar 64; then Kalou I

Karen A. 197442 This troller fishboat owned by Axsel Tomren, Ucluelet BC capsized and sank in the Fall of 1963 or 1964 in Barkley Sound BC.

Karen H. 189447 On November 7, 1968 this workboat owned by Frederick Germyn (MO), Prince Rupert BC sank in Work Channel BC.

Kashii Maru[364] (Japan) On August 21, 1955, at 2:35 am, this Japanese freighter under command of Captain Matsuo Noda rammed the Canadian fishing troller *Carluke* five miles south of Nitinat off the entrance to Juan de Fuca Strait. The fishboat boat was anchored near the *Swiftsure Lightship* and the two crew members were asleep at the time of the collision. About two hours later, after a search, the freighter found the crew in a small ship's boat and rescued them.

Kaslo 107827 In 1910 this sternwheeler owned by AH MacNeill, Rossland BC sank at the Ainsworth dock after hitting a rock. She was broken up at Mirror Lake BC.

Katinka II 188578 On January 6, 1966 this fishboat owned by Joseph FR Bourget (MO), Masset BC sank at Tasu Sound, QCI BC.

Kay Charles 192069 On October 28, 1973 this fishboat owned by Robert B Lansdowne, Alert Bay BC, foundered in Seymour Channel BC.

Keego I[a] 175167 [365] On January 2, 1949 this fishing troller exploded was destroyed by fire in Buccaneer Bay, Georgia Strait BC. Towed to a beach by another fishboat, this vessel burned to the waterline. The skipper had berthed at a dock and was recharging the batteries with a small auxiliary engine when they became over-heated and exploded.

Keewenau[366] This collier went to sea in a gale. Sometime later some wreckage of spars bound together with cordage was found floating

---

a   Built as Dahinda; then Keego I

off Vancouver Island. A name board from the ship was found nailed up in a First Nations hut. Nothing else was ever found.

Kella-Lee[a,367] 393992 While returning from the fishing grounds, the *Kella-Lee* owned by Newson Fisheries Ltd., Courtenay BC encountered heavy seas off Cape Scott, British Columbia. She heeled to starboard, progressively flooded and sank shortly after 2352 on October 25, 2001. Its three crew members and the owner/operator abandoned the vessel for a life raft. A search and rescue operation rescued two crew members and recovered the bodies of the third crew member and the owner/operator, both of whom had succumbed to hypothermia and drowned.

The *Kenkon Maru No. 3* aground and sinking at Mayne Island Image (Image from the collection of the Maritime Museum of British Columbia 000102)

Kenkon Maru No. 3[b,368] On January 11, 1916 she departed from Seattle WA bound for Vladivostok via Nanaimo where she intended to bunker coal, piloted by Captain James E Butler. She ran aground on the Belle Chain Islets (Mayne Island BC) during a heavy snow storm. The Pilot was later exonerated when the ship was found to have had a faulty compass. She was also carrying a cargo of iron railway equipment for the Russian Government. Cargoes of ferrous metals can affect the performance of the ship's compass which may have contributed to the incident.

Kennecott 221096 (US) In 1923 she was under charter to the Alaska Steamship Co. On February 20, 1923, while en route to Tacoma from Cordova Alaska, carrying a cargo of copper, she ran aground and

---

a   Built as Shannon Mist; then Kella-Lee
b   Built as Ailsa Craig; then Kenkon Maru

was wrecked near Hunter Point on Graham Island in the Queen Charlotte Islands. The 30-man crew escaped by in a breeches buoy. She broke in two, the pieces drifting away and sinking.

Kenora 122326 On February 21, 1908 this tug owned by Rat Portage Lumber Co., Vancouver BC struck a rock and sank at Nelson Island BC.

Key West II[a] 198648 In 1959 she deployed a specially constructed (by CP Leckie) two-mile long gillnet for an experimental fishery in the North Pacific under charter to the Fisheries Research Board of Canada. On December 20, 1961, this seiner owned by Francis GR Thompson (MO), Gabriola Island BC sank after a collision at Point Grey BC.

Kikapoo[369] 133868 On August 12, 1924, at 7:43 am, she was in a collision in dense fog with the ferry *West Vancouver No. 5* near the Calamity bell buoy in First Narrows, Burrard Inlet BC. The *Kikapoo* was cut in half and the stern stayed afloat about 5 minutes. The crew of three was taken aboard the ferry.

Kilmeny[370] 100649 On April 21, 1906 this halibut schooner, under command of Captain Fred Fredericksen, was stranded during a storm at San Josef Bay on the west coast of Vancouver Island BC. She put in and anchored, but the storm was so fierce that the anchor dragged. Carried onto the rocks the vessel overturned. The crew of six escaped ashore and were forced to walk overland five miles to the Danish settlement at Cape Scott. Afterward they went on to Quatsino.

King David[371] 102699 On December 13, 1906 owned by John A. Walker & Co., Glasgow Scotland while sailing under command of Captain William Davidson from Santa Cruz to Puget Sound she was wrecked on Bajo Point on Nootka Island with a loss of two men.

---

a   Built as Key West; then Key West II

Kingcoe 134083 On February 6, 1928 she was destroyed by fire one mile south of the north end of Wakeman Island on the east shore.

Kingfisher This trading schooner, under command of Captain Joseph Stevenson, was arrested in April 1863 by HMS *Devastation* while running illicit whiskey to First Nations villages up the coast. The master was convicted at New Westminster and fined $250 with the forfeiture of the cargo and his vessel on May 08, 1863. In August 1864, the *Kingfisher* was burned, while the vessel was anchored in Matilda Creek at Flores Island in Clayoquot Sound and the crew allegedly murdered by First Nations people.

Kingfisher[372] On July 25, 1929 the American tugs *Crest* and *Kingfisher* were en route from Chemainus to Seattle tandem towing (in bridle) a boom of logs. They ran up onto Atkin's Reef (east of Walker's Hook between Galiano Island and Saltspring Island). They remained high and dry until the rising tide lifted them both off safely.

King Oscar[373] (US) On March 29, 1992 the *King Oscar*, a US fishpacker hit the Pearl Rocks in the Queen Charlotte Islands while travelling from Seattle to Cordova Alaska for the herring fishery. She travelled over the rocks of the reef and was caught in the surf. The Captain of the *King Oscar* tried to launch the life raft, but it was lost in the surf. The *Burnaco* happened to be nearby with another US boat the *Tracy B.* but neither of them could render assistance. The *Burnaco* was towing the *Cod Fin*, a small aluminum sea urchin diving boat.

It was small enough that her skipper, Dan Jerowsky, was able to pass through the reef to rescue the crew in a dramatic middle of the night incident.

The ***Kitimat II*** on the rocks (Photograph from the Captain Alec Provan collection.)

Kitimat II In 1993 the *Kitimat II* had come to the aid of the fish boat to the left in the image (no name recalled by the photographer) and subsequently drifted onto the reef while attempting to help. This was situated just outside Berry Inlet in Seaforth Channel.

Kitmano[374] 313732 On April 22, 1993 this tug, owned by Rivtow Marine Co., Vancouver BC, foundered off Lennard Island (near Tofino) BC. She had been taken out on a charter and sank while running light to Nootka Sound. She started taking on water very quickly for unknown reasons and the crew of three ended up in the life raft.

Kitsap[a] 126800 On April 01, 1915 this tug owned by John W Abbott, Vancouver BC burned at Barnston Island (in the Fraser River) and the wreck was hauled away afterwards.

Kitwanga 133844 On July 09, 1930 this tug owned by Packers Steamship Co., Vancouver BC burned between Ten Mile Point and Star Point at Portland Inlet BC.

Kitwinmar[b] 130801 On January 17, 1918 this ketch-rigged sailboat owned by William L Selig, Prince Rupert BC foundered on Graham Island QCI BC.

Klee Wyck[375] 194697 On August 21, 1963 at 7:00 am this power cruiser exploded and burned 300 yards from Ladysmith BC. Mr & Mrs John L Phelps, Vancouver BC jumped for their lives into the harbour. Bill Michie in a Comox Logging Co. tug working on a nearby boom rushed over and saved the Phelps couple. Gas fumes were identified as the cause of the explosion and the vessel burned to the waterline.

Knot-A-Line[c] 329566 On May 20, 1978 this fishboat owned by Loman E Daury, Prince Rupert BC was swamped and sank at Rose

---

a   Built as Eclipse; then Kitsap
b   Built as Foam; then Kitwinmar
c   Built as Jan-Marie; then Knot-A-Line

Spit in the Queen Charlotte Islands BC and declared a total loss at the time.

Kobe[376] 154372 On October 15, 1933 this seiner owned by Nelson Bros Fishing Co. Ltd., Vancouver BC suffered a fire and explosion at Retreat Cove at Galiano Island BC. The engineer, Harry Kayahara was killed instantly, and Captain Masakichi Kubo was mortally wounded. The boat was beached for repairs when the incident occurred. It is believed that the switching on of a light ignited gasoline fumes causing the explosion.

Kodiak[377] 176496 She was powered by an engine from the St. Roch. On January 20, 1958, this fishpacker owned by Arnet Boat Co. Ltd., Vancouver BC foundered approximately five miles southwest of Amphitrite Point. She was abandoned while taking on water, sinking in 46 fathoms of water.

Kokanee 103303 This sternwheeler had a reputation as the fastest of the Canadian Columbia River steamers. She was laid up in 1923 when she was purchased by Commander Richard T. Deane and moored in front of Deanshaven, his property near Riondel, as a tourist lodge. In 1930 she sank at Riondel BC.

Koko Head[378] (US) When built, this barge had a large deck house with a ramp to a single open hold below decks and double bottom ballast tanks. The barge was one of the world's largest lumber barges and hauled break-bulk cargoes to Alaska and Hawaii. Prior to purchase by Lafarge, she served as a mining barge off Nome, Alaska. In August 1975, while carrying a full load of lumber, steel, cement, tires, machinery, and containers to Nome she struck a rock in Graham Reach off Klemtu, British Columbia and most of her cargo was lost. She was towed upside down into sheltered waters by a Seaspan tug where a temporary patch was welded over the hole. The noted Canadian salvage tug *Sudbury II* under salvage master Fred Collins with the help of several other tugs rolled her over, but she flipped upside down again after her tanks were pumped out. In 1978 Seaspan towed her, still upside down, into Vancouver harbour where she was anchored off. In 1981 after six years of being upside-down she was finally righted and sold to Inspiration Mines, who converted her to a gold mining dredge. In 1989, as she was hauled out in Seattle, Washington undergoing major repairs and re-conversion from a gold dredge, she was sold to Lafarge Concrete to haul limestone from Texada Island to the US for their in-house contracts.

Kootney 111820 On April 12, 1909 this freighter owned by Sechelt Steamship Co. Ltd., Vancouver BC was stranded when her tow rope broke in English Bay, Vancouver Harbour BC.

Koprino[379] 153045 She formed part of the pre-war Fishermen's Reserve Fleet. She was mobilized as a Fishermen's Reserve vessel from September 07, 1939 to September 18, 1939. On January 19, 1943 she rammed the fishpacker *Algie*, five miles from the Ballenas Islands. At first the crew thought it was a glancing blow, but she began to fill with water. The *Koprino* took on the crew and the *Algie* sank.

Kotka[380] 176889 On September 4, 1966 this troller fishboat was stranded and sank .5 miles west of Amphitrite Point BC and was a total loss.

Kraftmac[a] 197372 On November 20, 1978 this tug owned by RSL Shipyards Ltd., Vancouver BC sank in the Pearce Canal adjacent to Winter Harbour BC.

Kuskanook 121758 In 1906 she was owned by Canadian Pacific Railway Ltd., Montreal QC. In 1906 she was in service between Nelson and Kootenay Landing. In 1914 she was in service between Nelson and Kaslo. In 1930 she took her last run. In 1931 she was dismantled. In 1931 she was sold to AD Pochin to be converted to a floating hotel at Nelson BC. She was towed to Kokanee Landing where she sank in 1936.

Kvichak[b] 161140 (US) "On 27/01/1941 she ran hard aground on Susan Rocks in Milbanke Sound, 125 miles south of Prince Rupert. Her

---

a   Built as Anglo-Canadian IV; then Kraftmac
b   Built as Kvichak; then USATS Kvichak; then USARS James B Houston; then Bisayas; then Melleza; then Regina

23 passengers and part of her 38 crew were taken off by the USS *Charleston*. Captain Williamson and a small crew stayed aboard for a time but salvage attempts by the Pacific Salvage Co. (*Salvage Chieftain*), Victoria BC failed when she slipped off the rocks and sank in 90 feet of water. She was eventually beached at Prince Rupert in July after having been suspended from four large scows by cables and still submerged 35 feet."

The *Kwatna* near the end of her life afloat in Pender Harbour BC (Photograph from John MacFarlane collection.)

Kwatna 170395 This interesting old tug was a derelict for many years in Pender Harbour and sank about 2013. She eventually sank and ended up on a beach at Madeira Park BC.

Kyac[381] 126884 On April 4, 1946 this trawler fishboat, under command of Captain Jack Steele and owned by Gerald Horncastle (MO), Victoria BC, foundered, caught fire, and sank at Kelp Reef in Ucluelet Inlet BC. Captain Jack Steele was lost in the incident, and two other members of the crew were saved after they crawled onto a floating hatch cover and rescued by Axel Kauko.

L. & H.[a] 151066 The workboat L. & H. owned by the British Columbia Minister of Public Works, Victoria BC and was stranded on the beach at Clo-oose while trying to enter across the Nitinat Bar. Captain George A MacFarlane tried unsuccessfully to pull her off the beach with the *Princess Maquinna* standing by to render assistance. Captain Fred MacFarlane in the *Snohomish* pulled her free a few days later. In 1986 at the end of her life she sank in the Pitt River and her hulk was pulled ashore on Shelter Island and burned near the Canada Lafarge Cement plant.

---

a Built as *Insboy*; then *L. & H.*; then *Point Upwood*

The workboat *L. & H.* on the beach at high tide (Photograph by Captain George A. MacFarlane from the John MacFarlane collection)

L. & M.[a] 122537 On January 15, 1970 this tug owned by Tiger Tug Ltd., Gibsons BC was destroyed by fire in Howe Sound while towing logs in Collingwood Channel. She went ashore on Bowen Island BC. She was salvaged by Fred Rogers and John Peters.

L.C.M.[b] 170786 In 1941 she was seized from her Japanese owners by the Canadian Government. In 1942 her ownership transferred to His Majesty the King. In 1981 this fishboat was owned by Ocean Fisheries Ltd., Vancouver BC and sank at Cape Scott BC and was a total loss.

L.T. 62 (USATS)[c] 192879[382] In 1944 this US Army tug was present at the D-Day landings. In 1948 she ran aground and sank at Camp Point BC. In 1950 she was salvaged. In 1951 she towed the *Restorer* (cableship) and the *Pacmar* (US tug) to San Francisco CA for scrapping.

---

a   Built as Armoco; then Sea Lord III; then La Banque; then L. & M.
b   Built as Charlotte T.M. II; then L.C.M.
c   Built as USATS Major Richard M. Strong; then USATS LT-62; then Island Sovereign; then Seaspan Sovereign

La Dene[a] 323201 In 1964 her sponsor was Mrs JCF Stewart, wife of the President of Vancouver Tug Boat Company. In 1969 while owned by Vancouver Tug Boat Co. Ltd., Vancouver BC she sank alongside in Vancouver and pulled down the *La Bonne* with her. In 1969 she was refloated and repaired. In November 2000 she was transported on a barge to Shanghai China for scrapping.

La Feline[b,383] 365089 On November 19, 2019 Terry Murphy stated that "this yacht sank today near the mouth of the Fraser River off Steveston at Sandheads. She was owned for many years by Frank Griffith (CKNW radio), then by Bill McKechnie."

Lady Billie[384] 192275 On February 1, 1970 this gillnetter sank suddenly while transiting Active Pass in calm water. The lifeboat could not be launched, and Alec Harley and Eddie Liddell were lost with the boat. Crewman Peter Kelly ended up in the water but was quickly rescued by his father, Nicholas Kelly, in the *Rose-Lind* which was accompanying the *Billie K.* in the transit.

Lady C. No. 1 177998 On August 22, 1987 she burned off China Creek BC in the Alberni Inlet.

Lady Cecilia[c,385] 152718 On December 24, 1940 she ran aground on Indian Island at Pender Harbour while turning around. On December 23, 1947 she ran onto a reef in Buccaneer Bay, Thormanby Island BC while northbound to Powell River BC. Repeated efforts to dislodge her failed. She was eventually towed off and taken to Vancouver.

Lady Cynthia[d] 152899[386] She was a Royal Navy vessel converted to passenger use. On December 20th, 1925, this passenger/freight vessel owned by Union Steamships Ltd., Vancouver BC sank in 50 fathoms of water after a collision in the fog with the *Lady Cynthia* at Roberts

---

a   Built as La Dene; then Seaspan Star
b   Built as Thina; then La Feline
c   Built as HMS Swindon; then Lady Cecilia
d   Built as HMS Barnstaple; then Lady Cynthia

Creek. No lives were lost, 14 passengers and the crew of 21 on the Cowichan were quickly transferred to the Lady Cynthia. On October 3, 1950 she collided with the *A.L. Bryant* halfway between Finnisterre Island and Whytecliff Point, Queen Charlotte Channel, Howe Sound BC. In 1957 she was scrapped in Seattle WA.

Lady Dawley[a,387] 150895 On November 17, 1928 this schooner owned by Eriksen Boat Builders Ltd., North Vancouver BC was destroyed by fire two miles from Deserted Bay, in Jervis Inlet BC. She had travelled to the Florence Ann copper mine with two men on board. They went ashore when they saw the vessel burning while at anchor. She had been a recovered US wreck some years earlier and then went into service in Canada.

Lady Flo[388] On March 06, 1977 this fishboat, while under command of Captain David Procter, burned in the Alberni Inlet near Kildonan BC and was declared to be a constructive total loss. The skipper and deckhand escaped in the launch. She had been fishing for herring at the time of the incident.

Lady Helen[b] 154505 On August 2, 1977 this seiner owned by Matthew S Hill (MO), Kitkatla BC foundered near Macauley Island, at the entrance to Petrel Channel BC.

Lady Jacqueline On December 5, 1976 this gillnet fishboat experienced an explosion and fire in her accommodation area while in the Georgia Strait near Qualicum Beach BC.

Lady Lampson On January 10, 1878 this bark owned by the Hudson's Bay Company, London UK was stranded on Scragg Rocks on the Cobourg Peninsula while entering Esquimalt Harbour. On August 16, 1893, the Hawaiian barque *Lady Lampson* struck Kingman Reef, 33 mi. NW of Palmyra Island.

---

a   Built as Imperial; then Lady Dawley
b   Built as Qitonsta; then Lady Helen

Lady Linda II 323871 On May 18, 1967 this fishboat owned by Neal A Scafe (MO), Victoria BC struck a log boom and sank at 47N 123W approximately 3 miles west of Sheringham Point BC.

Lady Marjory[a] 141357 In 1974 her heat exchanger failed and flooded the battery bank which caught fire. She was destroyed in the fire and sank off the Ballenas Islands BC.

Lady Marty On October 23, 1976 this fishboat sank at Dundas Island BC on the east side near White Sand Island.

Lady Pam[b,389] 087034 In 1883 she was owned as a clipper bow steam yacht by John A Rolls. In 1914 she was owned by the All-Red Line, Vancouver BC and sailed to the Pacific coast. On November 12, 1942, this passenger freighter collided with the *Princess Elaine* outside the Lions Gate Bridge. In 1946 while owned by Union Steamships Ltd., Vancouver BC she was withdrawn from service and scuttled as a breakwater at Oyster Bay near Comox BC.

Lady Sharon[390] On April 13, 1963 this gillnetter went missing on a voyage from Alert Bay to Village Island carrying seven people including her owner, Matthew Puglas, his wife Lucy and four children.

Lady Silica 328283 She was an early example of a ferro-cement hulled fishing vessel. On November 30, 1975, this fishboat owned by John S Upton (MO), Victoria BC struck a runaway log boom and sank two miles east of Port Renfrew BC.

Lady Van 126426 In 1925 this workboat was in competition with the Sannie Transportation Co. on the Bowen Island run. On June 8, 1929 while owned by James A Eaton, Refuge Cove BC she sank in Bute Inlet at the Homathko River.

---

a   Built as CGS Berens; then Lady Marjory
b   Built as Santa Maria; then Chilco; then Lady Pam

Lahleet 154659 On November 21, 1943 this workboat owned by Nitinat Lake Logging Co. Ltd., Victoria BC burned 1.5 miles north of Gower Point BC.

Laloni[391] 172545 On December 15, 1940 this fishboat, owned by Frank C. Dougcette, Port Moody BC, was destroyed by fire at Markdale Cannery in Kyuquot BC.

Lamorna (UK) On March 7, 1904 this ship-rigged vessel was reported stranded on Starlight Reef when she foundered after being abandoned at sea with all hands (approximately 25) were lost. She was en route from Tacoma to Queenstown with a cargo of grain. Captain Walker of the Artemis encountered this vessel, apparently deserted, off Cape Flattery still afloat under sail. It was rumored that there had been a mutiny on board, that the officers had been murdered and the crew escaped in a ship's boat. She appears to have drifted as far as Crescent City. It seems unlikely that the wreckage found on Starlight Reef could have been that of the Lamorna in view of the sightings further south.

Lance 313099 From Scott Kristmanson[392] stated that "With half a load of reduction herring going back to Rupert, blowing hard on December 10th, 1966, my uncle, Ken Kristmanson was on board. He told me that she took a roll, and they could hear snapping in the hold, then laid over on her side. Then the battle began. Life raft was deployed, and everybody made it in, then it flipped over with the sea a short time later. A couple of them ended outside of the raft and had trouble getting in past the ladder as it was covering the entrance. He attributed wool underwear (from foot to neck) to their survival. A coastal fuel tanker seen the raft, thinking that it was a buoy, then came upon them. Best set of lights they had ever seen! They were lifted onboard the tanker, given dry clothes, warmed up, and a large glass of the best onboard."

Lancia 345237 On May 22, 1977 this yawl-rigged sailboat owned by Lancia Charter Co. Ltd., Vancouver BC sank at Deserted Bay BC.

Lardeau 103891 This workboat owned by Fred Robertson Lumber Co. Ltd., Revelstoke BC sank in 1916.

Laredo 150661 On December 13, 1929 this tug owned by Star Construction Co. Ltd., Sooke BC was stranded at Ocean Front BC.

Lark In July 1786 she was wrecked on Copper Island, in what are now the Queen Charlotte Islands (Haida Gwaii), along with her crew of 38.

Larry H. 171964 On July 25, 1955 this fishboat owned by Thor Sollien, Prince Rupert BC was stranded on the west side of Rose Spit, in Hecate Strait BC.

LaSalle (HMCS) K.519 (RCN) At the end of the Second World War she was laid up in the ship boneyard at Bedwell Bay in Indian Arm BC. In 1948 she was sold, her hull stripped and scuttled as breakwater in in Kelsey Bay, BC.

Lassie III 175278 On June 25, 1975 this troller owned by Robert E Cameron (MO), Prince George BC had an explosion and fire in her engine room and sank at Bajo Reef in Nootka Sound BC.

Laura[393] 097161 On the evening of January 25, 1892 this schooner owned by Charles Williams, Victoria BC was stranded at Friendly Cove, Nootka Sound BC. It was recorded that the Master and crew barely had the time to escape the sinking to save their lives.

Laura L. II 175689 On July 14, 1958 this fishboat owned by Prince Rupert Fishermen's Credit Union, Prince Rupert BC sprang a leak, was beached in the Queen Charlotte Islands BC.

Laura Pike[394] On January 26, 1902 this vessel owned by Charles Nelson, San Francisco CA left San Francisco bound for Eureka CA with a cargo of lumber. She made several unsuccessful attempts to cross the Humboldt Bar but was found to be leaking rapidly. Staying at sea the pumps were slowly being overwhelmed. They encountered the *Nome City* which took off the crew and left the hull drifting. On March 2, 1902, this lumber schooner was sighted drifting eight miles southwest of Carmanah Lighthouse by the light keeper who noted that she was "smashed to pieces". An attempt to salvage the wreck by the *Queen City* was unsuccessful. She was blown ashore at Clo-oose where her lumber cargo washed up on the beach. She had been abandoned off Cape Blanco and then drifted north as a derelict.

Laurel Leaf[395] 130916 On October 1, 1947 this fishpacker owned by H. Bell-Irving & Co. Ltd., Vancouver BC was caught in a gale off the Sandheads Jetty and driven onto the rock wall, holed and sank. Captain Charles Nelson and his crew of four stuck with the vessel for two hours then evacuated in a small boat and made for the lightship.

Laurel Point[a] 141607[396] On October 28, 1930, while under command of Captain George Richardson, she burned in a gale off Cape Roger Curtis, Bowen Island BC. She had been en route to Bute Inlet at the time of the incident when a fire broke out in the engine room.

Laurel Whalen[397] 138367 Rick James reports that, "In 1918–1919 this five-masted schooner made two lumber voyages to Australia. In 1925 her registry was dropped. She was a hulk, storm damaged in Tahiti in the winter of 1919–1920. She was purchased by RP Butchart for use as a barge for the Bamberton cement works, converted to a floating salmon cannery for Millerd Fisheries (West Vancouver) in the mid-1920s and scuttled in the breakwater at Royston BC in 1936."

Lawrence L.[b,398] 320205 The Transportation Safety Board of Canada reports that "On 19/09/1997 While in Agamemnon Channel on passage from Jervis Inlet to Vancouver, running light without barges, the tug "*Lawrence L*" suffered a fire in the engine room. A solvent had been poured onto the side of the main engine, for cleaning purposes, and the gases ignited. The fire spread into the fibre-board acoustic tiles and wood grounds of the deckhead covering. Fire extinguishers

---

a   Built as Laurel Point; then Hyak I; then Speed The Light; then Meota
b   Built as Lawrence L.; then North Arm Voyager; then Lawrence L.

were used to put out the fire on and around the engine and to control the deckhead fire until the tug reached the dock at Earls Cove. Approaching the dock, the fixed CO_2 system was released into the engine room without stopping the main engine or shutting off ventilation. At the dock, assistance was rendered by crews of other vessels and shore persons, and a hose was used to finally extinguish the fire in the deckhead."

Lee Wang Zin 781977 (Panama) On December 25, 1979 this bulk freighter capsized in Dixon Entrance with the loss of 30 lives. During the early hours of Christmas morning 1979, the Canadian Bull Harbor Coast Guard Station, located at the north tip of Vancouver Island, BC, monitored the last transmissions from the M/V *Lee Wang Zin*. Only the SOS and call sign were received, each three times. Four hours later, a Canadian Coast Guard helicopter had located the red hull of a large, overturned vessel, about 258 mi to the northwest in Dixon Entrance, between Alaska and Canada. There were no signs of survivors, the vessel was emitting large quantities of oil, winds were southeast 30 to 40 knots and seas were 15 to 20 feet. The vessel was later confirmed to be the Taiwan-owned ore freighter M/V *Lee Wang Zin* en route from Prince Rupert with 30 crewmen, 53,310 long tons of taconite pellets, 1,111 metric tons of bunker fuel, and 67 long tons of diesel oil aboard. The *Lee Wang Zin* drifted northward 28 mi into US waters and there, at daylight on December 27, was found aground off the Kendrick Islands on the southeast tip of the Prince of Wales Island, 30 miles south-southeast of Ketchikan.

Legpec[a,399] 138531 On December 26, 1926 she exploded at the Shell Oil fuel dock at Barnet BC in Burrard Inlet. On November 6, 1927 she burned at the Government Wharf at South Galiano Island, in Active Pass BC.

---

a   Built as Hulda O.; then A.G. Lilly; then Lepgec

Lennard Island 156615 On September 8, 1979 this troller fishboat owned by Dwight E Welwood (MO), Masset BC was reported as taking on water at Dixon Entrance BC.

Lenric 174077 On September 23, 1964 this workboat owned by N.G. Duncan Logging Co. Ltd., Vancouver BC burned at Bella Coola BC.

Leona[400] 122951 (UK) She was registered in Goole, England UK brought out by Captain Ludlow. On October 30, 1915, this freighter owned by Vancouver Portland Cement Company turned turtle and sank in storm 4 miles northwest of Active Pass BC in the Gulf of Georgia. She was en route from Britannia Mines to Tacoma. It is possible that she was overloaded and that either the cargo shifted, or water entered the cargo hold. Other theories advanced concerned the possibility of striking a submerged object. Seven of the 14 crew members were drowned: Captain Ludlow; Captain Cochrane; William Anderson (Second Mate); H Cecil, (Fireman), Joe Drunnel, (Fireman), JJ Hunter, (Fireman, and an unnamed Chinese cook.

Leslie Ann[a] 154683 In 1962 this workboat owned by Mrs Elizabeth Gisbourne, Vancouver BC sank while towing an oil barge through Second Narrows. She was salvaged and refitted as a packer tug. She was stripped and sunk before 2016.

Leslie T.[b,401] 150896 On September 11, 1932 this steam tug was rounding up logs at Northeast Point, Texada Island BC. She ran into severe head winds and high waves swept over the vessel flooding the engine room. She was caught by a sudden gust of wind and the crew steered the boat toward the shore and she grounded on the rocky beach and sank. Her owner Norman Somner was drowned, while two others were saved.

---

a Built as Labouchere; then Leslie Ann
b Built as 8002, then Leslie T.

Letitia 090790 On December 07, 1904 this schooner owned by Punch Quatchiqum, Neuchatlet (Nootka Sound) BC sank in Victoria Harbour.

Leviathan II[a] 800190 On October 25, 2015 this workboat owned by Jamie's Whaling Station Ltd., Tofino BC sank with the loss of six passengers west of Vargas Island BC. She had 27 people on board at the time.

Levis (HMCS)[400] (RCN) At the end of the Second World War she was laid up in the ship boneyard at Bedwell Bay in Indian Arm BC. In 1948 her hull was stripped. At the end of her life she was scuttled as part of the breakwater at Oyster Bay BC.

Lewac[402] 153098 On February 1, 1932 this seiner foundered in heavy weather 3–4 miles off the Sunday Rocks near Estevan Point BC. She sprang a leak which the crew could not counteract. The crew were rescued by the *Percy W.* and shortly afterward she sank carrying her cargo of 54 tons of herring down 24 fathoms.

Libertad[403] (Peru) On November 06, 1899 this bark, while travelling from Chile to Vancouver carrying a cargo of nitrates for the Victoria Chemical Works under charter to W.R. Grace & Co. of San Francisco CA. She sprang a leak which continued for 40 days with a foot of water in her hold. She was damaged in heavy gales with sails and rigging carried away. Her cargo started to shift making the hull leaks worse. The crew could not keep up with the pumping. On November 6th they hurriedly took to the ship's boats but in their haste, they neglected to load water. One lifeboat with 12 crewmen aboard never heard of again. Captain Vincent D. Arenas and the remainder of the crew reached shore. They survived on mussels until barefoot and starving some days later they encountered a gold prospecting camp where they received food. The prospectors included Captain Gus Hansen; the sealing Captain known as "The flying Dutchman" who organized their rescue. The exhausted crewmen were picked up by

---

a   Built as CZ-72-112; then Crown Forest 72-112; then Leviathan II

a passing schooner and transferred to the *Queen City* for passage to Victoria. The derelict hull came ashore in Brooks Bay immediately to the west.

Liberty 172523 On November 7, 1940 this seiner, owned by Walter Carr, Victoria BC, was stranded after fouling a line in her propeller at the bluffs off Useless Inlet in Barkley Sound BC.

Lief E.[404] (US) In 1912 this halibut schooner, under command of Captain Jack Johnson, was involved in a collision in the fog with the *Prince George*, under command of Captain D McKenzie. She was struck amidships, but no one was injured. In August 1920 she burned and sank off Cape Beale BC.

Lila N. 155275 On October 7, 1944 this tug owned by the Kelly Logging Co. Ltd., Vancouver BC was believed to have struck a submerged log and sank three miles east of Pine Island, QCI BC.

Lillian M. 138175 On November 20, 1930 this troller fishboat owned by Samuel Gurney, Prince Rupert BC foundered off Long Beach near Ucluelet BC while in tow of the *Lysekil*.

Lily[405] 083443 (Some reports spell her name as *Lillie*). She was a sealing schooner owned by Morris Moss of Victoria BC. She had been seized with the schooner *Black Diamond* in 1889 in the Bering Sea by the USRC *Corwin* and the United States Government paid $40,272 in damages for illegal seizure. All hands were saved. While under command of Captain Robin she struck a rock on March 31, 1891 at Dodger Cove in Barkley Sound. She had just picked up her First Nations hunters when she struck an uncharted rock and sank. The captain and crew (including First Nations hunters) made their way to shore safely. They made their way to the Cape Beale Lighthouse and use the newly finished telegraph line to notify authorities of their situation. The steamer *Alert* brought the Captain to Victoria.

Lily 107255 In 1937 she owned by Alexander Coutts, New Westminster BC and was reported to have sunk and was a total loss.

Lincoln 210835 On June 15, 1925 she was stranded at Campania Island BC. On August 17, 1927 she exploded at Prince Rupert BC.

Linda 117008 This tug was owned by Vancouver Machinery Depot (chartered to New Westminster Tugboats), Vancouver BC. On January 04, 1944 she burned at a dock on the New Westminster BC waterfront.

Lindora[406] 214281 On April 3, 1945 this troller fishboat owned by G. Roundsell, Seattle WA grounded on Gerald Island in Georgia Strait BC. A second smaller American boat, the *Springer*, hit the same reef but suffered only minor damage and refloated herself. She attempted to pull the *Lindora* off but was unable and had to call for assistance. The two-man crew of the *Lindora* was rescued while she sank in 33 fathoms of water.

Lions Gate 153197 On December 30, 1932 this fishboat owned by Bunji Hisaoka, Vancouver BC burned at Trail Bay BC near Sechelt BC.

Little D.[a] 150966 On February 29, 1952 while en route from Ganges Harbour to Vancouver, this tug owned by the Little D. Towing Co. Ltd., Vancouver BC sank at Sand Heads Light, while under command of Captain Jack Watson.

Little Mermaid[b] 313900 On June 22, 1974 this fishboat owned by Albert J Wick, Victoria BC foundered in Juan de Fuca Strait BC.

Livingston II[c] 150320 On May 20, 1933 this fishboat, owned by Anton Martinsen, Prince Rupert BC, sank in 31 fathoms of water after stranding on the west coast of Dundas Island BC. Three weeks later she was raised by the Armour Salvage Co., Prince Rupert BC.

---

a   Built as Harris No. 3; then Little D.
b   Built as Imar; then Little Mermaid
c   Built as Livingston; then Livingston II

Lizzie G. 193315 On January 2, 1960 this fishboat owned by James J Bland, Victoria BC grounded and burned one mile north of Cape Keppel, Saltspring Island BC.

Lizzie Marshall On February 22, 1884 while under the command of Captain Adolph Bergman this American bark (434 tons) was stranded on Bonilla Point while inbound from San Francisco to Port Blakely WA. She was 14 days out of San Francisco CA. The vessel was 14 days out from San Francisco when she first sighted Cape Flattery. Fog set in and the wind died, leaving the vessel little steerageway. With a heavy swell running and no foghorn blaring on Tatoosh, the vessel lost her bearings and was carried toward Vancouver Island. Both anchors were dropped in 20 fathoms on February 21, and a boat with four volunteers was sent to Neah Bay for help. When a southeast gale came up, the vessel parted her anchor chains and went broadside on the rocks. A German sailor attempting to retrieve his personal effects was drowned. The after part of the vessel wedged tight in the rocks and afforded a means of escape for crewmen.

Llangrad[407] 130878 On April 3, 1915 she burned south of the North Arm of the Fraser River BC. She was berthed at the North Arm Jetty when a fire broke out. The crew managed to save the engine, but the rest was lost.

The *Loachraidh* while still named as the Rover (Photograph from the John MacFarlane collection.)

Loachraidh[a,408] 130294 Mike Wright reports that "She sank finally in Genoa Bay. I attended the scene at the request of the Victoria Rescue Coordination Centre. She was owned by a fellow in Ladysmith who, incidentally, let her rot away and ran her aground twice in the same day off Round Island. She was

---

a   Built as Hopkins; then Island Rover; then Rover No. 1; then Loachraidh

raised in Genoa Bay towed to Nanaimo by Saltair Marine and torn up. I believe that her wheelhouse survives somewhere."

Log Transporter[a,409] 160707 In 1961 she a Great Lakes freighter that was towed from eastern Canada by the N.R. Lang for conversion to a log barge by the M.R. Cliff Tugboat Co. Ltd. The engines were removed, and a travelling crane was fitted for loading and unloading logs. On October 24, 1961 she foundered while carrying a cargo of pulp logs in tow of the Cedarwood at Cape Mudge. She was en route from Teakerne Arm at the time of the incident. Many of the logs were picked up by the Gulf Log Salvage Association.

Lois 100200 On June 20, 1904 this work boat owned by JA Cates, Vancouver BC was stranded in Queen Charlotte Channel, Howe Sound BC.

Lois H. 322985 On September 28, 1970 this fishboat owned by Ulric H Robins (MO), Victoria BC burned after an explosion at Port Alberni BC.

Lone Ranger II[410] 178009 On August 18, 1952 this fishboat owned by Michael Williams (MO), Bamfield BC exploded at the Home Oil wharf in Victoria Harbour and her sides were blown out. Her crew of 4 escaped injury. She had just taken on fuel and exploded when the ignition switch was pressed.

Lone Ranger No. 1[411] 173786 On December 6, 1949 this fishing troller sank off Barkley Sound with the loss of 4 persons. The wreckage washed up on Diana Island. Lost were Leonard Williams, Peter Williams, Elsie Harris, and her baby girl.

Longueuil (HMCS) K.672 (RCN) At the end of the Second World War she was laid up in the ship boneyard at Bedwell Bay in Indian Arm BC. Her hull was stripped, and she was scuttled as a breakwater at Kelsey Bay BC.

---

a   Built as Eaglescliffe Hall; then David Barclay; then Log Transporter

Loom 150433 On January 5, 1924 this work boat owned by Nils Notteland, North Vancouver BC was stranded in Malaspina Strait BC.

Lord Jim[a,412] 138681 In 1925 she went ashore with the fishing schooner *Pachena* near Nitinat Vancouver Island BC. On August 27, 1937 she was in collision with the *Anna O.* 14 miles east southeast from Point Upwood, Texada Island, Georgia Strait. In 1969 she sank alongside in Vancouver and pulled down the *La Dene* with her but was later refloated and repaired. In 2010c she sank in water off Mill Bay BC.

Lord Raglan (UK) This British bark foundered in the winter of 1852, in a storm off Cape Flattery, laden with piling, lumber, and spars bound for England. The vessel was en route from Sooke, BC, carrying eight passengers including the Reverend & Mrs Staines. Some wreckage washed up on Vancouver Island.

Lord Weston This bark was wrecked in Clayoquot Sound in 1854 in Adventure Bay, on the northeast side of Sydney Inlet, 20 miles north of Tofino, on Vancouver Island. The entire crew except 3 men and the captain were rescued and brought to Victoria by First Nations of the region. The HBC *Otter* was dispatched to rescue the remaining crew December 20, 1853. Instructions given to Captain Millar of the *Otter* stated that the survivors could be found 30 miles north of Nitinat Sound, now known as Barkley Sound.

Lori Anne 313044 On July 13, 1977 this gillnetter owned by Atle H Arnsen, Prince Rupert BC while at the mouth of the Skeena River suffered an explosion and fire in her engine room and was declared a total loss at the time of report.

Lorne[413] 094809 On August 30, 1914 she was stranded with the barge *America* in tow on Kanaka Bay, San Juan Island WA USA. In 1926 she broke all records for the Queen Charlotte Islands log trade taking a Davis raft with 1,000,000 feet of logs 70 miles across Hecate Strait

---

a   Built as Bonila; then La Bonne; then V.T. No. 501; then Lord Jim

in 15 hours. The tug *Lorne* and barge *Pacific Gatherer* together were involved in a spectacular accident in September of 1930. Fast and unpredictable tide caused problems with the tow. With the captain slowing the tug down, the two vessels collided side by side and went into the Second Narrows Bridge. C.H. Cates Towing was dispatched, but their strong fleet made no headway. As the tide came in, the tug and barge slowing rose and caused the bridge span to come off its foundation. The bridge was plunged into the water.

The *Lorne* with the *Pacific Gatherer* after knocking down the Second Narrows Bridge in Vancouver Harbour (Photograph from the Stuart Thompson Fonds of the City of Vancouver Archives AM1535-: CVA 99-2152)

Lornet[a] 133696[414] On January 13, 1932, at 12:20 am, this tug, under command of Captain Gregor M Campbell, was stranded on Fraser Rock in Wellcome Pass BC while en route from Vancouver to Englewood. She turned on her side almost immediately. The crew signalled SOS with their siren and this was heard by the crew of the *Glenboro*, handling logs in Halfmoon Bay. When the *Glenboro* arrived at the wreck three members of the crew were sitting on the rail, drenched by spray. Three others were adrift in a lifeboat. At 5:30 am she sank. She was abandoned by Pacific Salvage as a total loss, but later she was salvaged by diver John Pieters.

Losmar[b] (US) On April 22, 1930 she hit and sheered the southerly span of the Second Narrows Bridge in Vancouver Harbour BC. She was eventually torpedoed by the Japanese submarine IJNS I-165 during the Second World War on September 24, 1942 about 250 miles west of Cape Comorin, India, 07°40'N, 74°15'E; of the ship's 9-man

---

a   Built as Challenge; later Kezia; later Lornet
b   Built as West Matas; then Clauseus; then Losmar

Armed Guard detachment, 3 were lost when she sank. The British ship *Louise Moller* rescued 14 survivors on October 5th; seven survivors reached the west coast of Ceylon by boat on 17 October 17, 1942.

The *Losmar* after colliding with the Second Narrows Bridge in Vancouver Harbour (Photograph from the Major Matthews collection of the City of Vancouver Archives AM54-S4-Br_P9.5)

Louise[415] 140620 (US) On July 12, 1899 she burned while at her mooring in Victoria Harbour BC. The fire started in the engine room of the *Nahleen*, but the fire department having no equipment to fight such a fire could only stand and watch the vessels burn.

Louise II 176666 On September 11, 1953 this fishboat owned by British Columbia Packers Ltd., Vancouver BC burned seven miles west of Pachena Point BC.

Louise J. 176213 On April 20, 1950 this fishboat owned by British Columbia Packers Ltd., Vancouver BC burned at Mayne Island in Active Pass BC.

Love and Anarchy[416] 814390 On the early morning of September 4, 2008, the small fishing vessel *Love and Anarchy* capsized and sank while anchored on Swiftsure Bank, 20 nautical miles southwest of Cape Beale, British Columbia. The owner and the crew member were rescued by another fishing vessel.

Lox[417] 178679 On December 14, 1950 she was destroyed by fire at Ucluelet BC. An oil-burner ignited the blaze which started to overtake the whole vessel while she was berthed at the marine service dock. She was towed away by the *Co-operator II* but the towline broke and she started to drift. This caused considerable excitement and concern as strong winds fanned this flaming mass as it moved around the harbour threatening many vessels. She grounded on the beach and finally burned out; the fire department unable to extinguish the blaze.

Loyal Chinook 158586 On August 26, 1977 this fishboat owned by British Columbia Packers Ltd., Richmond BC capsized at Seymour Harbour, Maud Island BC.

Loyal No. 1[a] 154648 She was used to carry fish for the Ucluelet Fishing Co. Ltd. (Ucluelet Fishermen's Co-operative) to Victoria, Vancouver, and Seattle BC. In 1941 she was seized from her Japanese owners by the Canadian Government. In 1942 her ownership transferred to His Majesty the King. On May 17, 1948 she sank and was declared a total loss after she foundered 1.5 miles south of Victoria Harbour BC.

Lucky Star No. 1 194412 On July 27, 1979 this fishboat owned by Lucky Star Fishing Co. Ltd., Victoria BC experienced an explosion in the engine room while in Chatham Sound BC, burned to the waterline and was declared a total loss.

Lulu 092779 On November 13, 1909 this schooner owned by G McNamee and EW Bloomfield, Vancouver BC burned 3.5nm west of Lucy Island Light (Chatham Sound) BC.

---

a   Built as Loyal No. 1; then HMCS Loyal No. 1; then Loyal No. 1

Lulu Island[a] 150971 On October 7, 1951 this power cruiser owned by British Columbia Packers Ltd., Vancouver BC capsized between Wayton Passage and Blackfish Sound, Plumper Islands BC.

Lunallilo On February 1, 1878 this bark, while en route to Burrard Inlet she was driven ashore close to where the *Lady Lampson* went ashore. She was considered a total loss.

Lupene A. 156911 In 1931 this launch, owned by James LO Anderson, Deep Bay BC, was seized by customs officials in Klaskino Inlet with a large amount of cash and a cargo of alcohol that had been smuggled into Canada. The liquor had been previously landed from Tahiti and was being bottled from drums. On November 13, 1938 while owned by Edmonds & Walker and operated by the Baronet Pass Fishing and Trading Co., Alert Bay BC, burned one half mile east of Lewis Pont Light in Johnstone Strait. Captain James W Matheson and his crew abandoned her in the dinghy. They were picked by Fred Wastell and taken to Telegraph cove BC.

Luseland[418] 137959 On October 21, 1931 this fishboat owned by Walt Saggers, Ucluelet BC was destroyed by fire one-half mile east of Beg Island at the entrance to Ucluelet Harbour BC in Barkley Sound.

Lyndona 193816 On August 15, 1964 this fishboat owned by Bruce C. Arundel (MO), Vancouver BC grounded at Shearwater Island BC, caught fire, and was destroyed as a total loss.

M.427 B.C. Star (RCAF)[b] 172348[419] On July 21, 1943, the B.C. Star had left Vancouver with 41.5 tons of gravel, cement, and other supplies for a RCAF construction detachment at Cape St. James off Kunghit Island on the southern tip of the Queen Charlotte Islands. She carried a crew of ten and three passengers. Two days later, the ship put in at the RCAF Station Shearwater near Bella Bella where she took aboard 2.5 tons of cargo and three more passengers. On July 24, the vessel departed for Cape St. James but was never seen or heard from

---

a   Built as Thomas Crosby; then Lulu Island
b   Built as B.C. Star; then RCAF M.427 B.C. Star

again. Local marine observers believed that an explosion might have sealed the fate of the B.C. *Star* and its 16 occupants.

M.872 Black Duck (CFAV)[a] She was an RCAF crash boat based at RCAF Station Comox. She was acquired by the Canadian Navy as a Canadian Naval Patrol Craft, Rescue 1965–1998. She was laid up March 19, 1998. She was purchased by the Vancouver Maritime Museum for use as a tender. Lucian Ploias[420] states that "She sank at her mooring in 2005 at the Vancouver Maritime Museum, was raised and then scrapped."

M.B.D. No. 32[421] 313699 "On the morning of 06 November 2004, the tug *Manson*, with a crew of two, was on passage between New Westminster, British Columbia, on the Fraser River and Beale Cove, Texada Island, British Columbia. The Manson had two barges in tow: the crane barge *McKenzie* and the deck barge M.B.D. 32. During the transit through the Georgia Strait, the couplers connecting the M.B.D. 32 to the stern of the McKenzie parted. The *Manson*, with the *McKenzie* in tow, attempted to recover the M.B.D. 32 but experienced steering difficulties during this process. The *Manson* capsized and sank with the loss of both crew members—a deckhand and the master. Both barges were subsequently recovered; the *Manson* has not been located."

M.M. 536935 (US) This troller fishboat was registered in Portland OR USA. On September 1, 1977 she collided with the *Chilcotin Princess* and sank between Egg Island and Pine Island in Queen Charlotte Sound BC.

M.M.C.S. Beaver[b,422] 122394 This vessel is no longer registered in Canada. In 1970 she was reported as a partially sunken derelict near Dollarton, Burrard Inlet. In 1977 she was reported as broken up."

---

a   Built as M. 972 Black Duck (RCAF); then Black Duck (C.F.A.V.)
b   Built as Leebro; then Salvor; then Island Prince; then M.M.C.S. Beaver

Christopher Cole noted that "she inherited the name but was not a replica of the original *Beaver*."

M.R. Cliff 126790 In the Spring of 1995 this old tug while owned by John R Bruce, Tofino BC sank at the floats in Genoa Bay BC.

M.T. Co. #2[a] 130803 On February 26, 1914 this tug owned by Metropole Transportation Co. Ltd., Vancouver BC burned at the B.C. Oil Refinery dock at Port Moody BC.

M.T. Co. No. 1[b] 130797 On September 30, 1924 this sloop-rigged yacht owned by AM Snider, Vancouver BC foundered in Second Narrows BC.

M.T. No. 3[c] 130907 Russ Warren423 stated that "In 1973 the work in Victoria dried up after the BCFP mill in Victoria closed followed by the mills in Esquimalt. The M.T. No. 3 sank at the dock so was re-floated, stripped then taken out to the Strait and scuttled. She was more than 80 years old at the time. There was an offer to buy and restore her. My dad, Darrell Warren said that 'she was not going to become a plaything for some rich women in Seattle.'"

Maagen[424] 126557 On December 16, 1916 this tug struck and sank the Sylvia in the First Narrows, of Vancouver Harbour. On December 16, 1915, this small Skookumchuck fishboat under the command of Captain Silvey was returning to Vancouver harbour in the evening with a cargo of fish. They were overtaking the tug *Maagen*, under command of Captain Thomas Edwards, which was towing a light scow through First Narrows. The fishboat was passing the tug on the starboard side when a strong rip current slewed the fishboat around across the bow of the tug. The tug forced the boat over on its side and it filled up with water and flooded. As she rolled past the scow

---

a   Built as the Elmo; then M.T. Co. #2
b   Built as Celtic; then M.T. Co. No. 1
c   Built as Vixen; then M.T. Co. No. 3

her house works were torn off causing her to sink. The skipper and two fishermen were in the house when the accident occurred, and Captain Silvey and George Roberts disappeared drowned. A second fisherman, Leslie Wilson, came to the surface clinging to floating wreckage and was rescued.

Mabel Girton 141149 On October 7, 1937 this fishpacker owned by Saichi Tamai, Port Alberni BC was stranded, wrecked, and sank in Alberni Inlet.

Mackenzie (HMCS) On September 16, 1995, this former Royal Canadian Navy destroyer was scuttled off Rum Island near Sidney, British Columbia, as an artificial reef.

Mae E.[425] Rick Howie reports that "My father Tom Howie owned this double-ended troller at Deep Bay BC. He only fished her for a short while before she sank, and I never heard the details of why. I suspect she was not in good shape when Dad bought her."

Magee[a] 192877 On January 8, 1972 this passenger vessel owned by Prince Rupert Ferry Services Ltd., Prince Rupert BC foundered and sank during a storm at Prince Rupert BC.

Magellan Straits[b] 194210 During the Second World War she was built by the Pacific Command Water Transport Company of the Royal Canadian Army Service Corps. Colin Henthorne[426] stated that "Magellan has reportedly sunk for the second time. The Port of Vancouver has issued a temporary work order to remove and dispose of her (North Arm, Fraser River)."

Maggie Mac[427] On March 18, 1892 this sealing schooner, under the command of Captain John Dodd, sank at Cape Scott BC with the loss of 23 persons.

---

a   Built as White Arrow; then Magee
b   Built as RCAF M.639 General MacKenzie; then Mar Bermejo; then Majellan Streight; then Magellan Straits; then Magellan

Magna[a] 150921 She was said to have been the first full diesel tug built in BC. On April 5, 1978 she sank in Cordero Channel BC. In July 1978 she burned and was declared a total constructive loss.

Maid-O-Van 178200 On October 10, 1948 this fishboat owned by Thomas E Jones (MO), Vancouver BC burned between Point Grey and Porlier Pass in Georgia Strait.

Mainland Fury[b] 188218 On February 10, 1977 this tug owned by Surf Marine Supply & Services Ltd., Vancouver BC capsized and was abandoned at sea and presumed sunk near Cape Calvert, Queen Charlotte Sound BC.

Mainland No. 3[c] 130895 On February 10, 1977 this barge (and former dredge) owned by Surf Marine Supply & Service Ltd., Vancouver BC capsized and was abandoned at sea and presumed sunk near cape Calvert Queen Charlotte Sound BC.

Mainland Prince 326678 On November 5, 1966 this tug owned by Mainland Marine Towing Ltd., Mission City BC sank south of Cape Lazo BC off Texada Island BC while towing the Coast Prince.

Major Tompkins (US) She was operating on the Olympia to Victoria run. On February 10, 1855 she was wrecked on Macauley Point at the entrance to Victoria Harbour. The crew jumped ashore as the ship broke up in the surf. The wreck was sold at auction to Robert Laing and then to the Muirs at Sooke for use in constructing a steam sawmill. The bell of the ship hung at the old Craigflower Schoolhouse in Craigflower BC.

Malahat 134655 In 1935–1945 this former 5-masted schooner converted to a barge was owned by Gibson Shipping Co. Ltd., (WC

---

a   Built as Radio; then Gryphon; then Magna
b   Built as Fury; then Mainland Fury
c   Built as Rock Cutter P.W.D. No. 1; then S.M.T.B. No. 10; then Pacific Barge 18; then Mainland No. 3

Gibson) Vancouver BC. In 1937 she was grounded in Victoria Harbour off Laurel Point blocking the channel while the tide rose while carrying a cargo of logs. In 1944 she was beached in Uchucklesit Inlet after being swamped off Cape Beale BC. In 1944 she was abandoned to sink in Green Cove in Uchucklesit Inlet by the Gibson Brothers and apparently ended up in the Powell River Breakwater where she sank.

Malleville[428] (US) This bark spent several years in the Puget Sound lumber trade. She was wrecked at Ho-Me-Is, near Estevan Point BC in October 1882. She was en route from Shanghai to Royal Roads in ballast and was driven ashore in a heavy westerly gale near Sunday Rock. Her Master, Captain Edward Harlow, his wife Abbie and their two sons were drowned along with the Mate's wife and 18 hands. In recognition of his efforts to save the lives of the crew the US Government awarded Chief Matlhaw a gold medal and $200 to be distributed among his men.

Mandala No. 1 806966 On November 15, 2019 this fishboat owned by Worldwide Seafoods Inc., Vancouver BC and G. & I. Fishing and Investments Ltd., Courtenay BC was wrecked on Cape Palmerston BC after she caught fire, was abandoned, and then drifted ashore.

Manhattan No. 2 173772 On April 29, 1980 this fishboat owned by Wilfred J Landry (MO), Vancouver BC burned and sank off Esperanza Inlet BC.

Manson[429] 344666 The Transportation Safety Board of Canada reports that "On the morning of 06 November 2004, the tug *Manson*, with a crew of two, was on passage between New Westminster, British Columbia, on the Fraser River and Beale Cove, Texada Island, British Columbia. The *Manson* had two barges in tow: the crane barge *McKenzie* and the deck barge M.B.D. 32. During the transit through the Georgia Strait, the couplers connecting the M.B.D. 32 to the stern of the McKenzie parted. The *Manson*, with the *McKenzie* in tow, attempted to recover the M.B.D. 32 but experienced steering difficulties during this process. The *Manson* capsized and sank with the loss of both crew members—a deckhand (Brian Cusson) and the master (Captain Dusty Davidson). Both barges were subsequently recovered; the *Manson* has not been located."

Manunalei[430] On October 28, 1936 this passenger vessel collided with the freighter *Temple Moat* in fog near Race Rocks BC. The *Temple Moat* suffered extensive damage and tugs took her to Seattle WA although damage to the *Manunalei* was slight.

Maracaibo 320274 On July 14, 1969 this ketch-rigged sailboat owned by James D. Milne (MO), Vancouver BC was destroyed by fire at Burnaby BC.

Marauder[a,431] 156633 As the *Hurry Home* she was said to have operated as a rum runner. Her Liberty gasoline engines were fitted with smoke-making apparatus. She formed part of the pre-war Fishermen's Reserve Fleet. She participated in the 30 January—25 February 1939 Fishermen's Reserve Training Session. She was mobilized 15 Sep 1939. In 1939 she was commissioned into the Royal Canadian Navy Fisherman's Reserve as HMCS *Marauder*. On December 18, 1951 owned by Francis Millerd and Co. Ltd., Vancouver BC she foundered, halfway between Pine Island and Scarlett Point QCI BC.

Marble Isle[432] 193627 On September 13, 1976 she was abandoned at sea and sank off the Scott Islands BC while tuna fishing. The skipper, John Pedersen, floated for a week in a life raft before being rescued 60 miles out to sea by the *G.B. Reed*. The vessel had been tethered to other fishboats anchored at Port Hardy while their crews slept. The crew had only a few minutes to abandon ship before she sank.

Margaret McKenzie[b] 152451 This tug was used for towing derricks and gravel scows. On December 19, 1968 while owned by McKenzie Barge & Derrick Co. Ltd., Vancouver BC she was damaged by fire and sank off Myrtle Point in Malaspina Strait BC. In 1984 while owned

---

a   Built as USS S.C. 308; then Hurry Home; then Marauder; then HMCS Marauder; then Marauder

b   Built as C. & S.; then Margaret McKenzie

by McKenzie Barge & Marine Ways Ltd., Vancouver BC, owned by McKenzie Barge & Marine Ways Ltd., Vancouver BC she sank after capsizing while attempting to turn around with a tow during a gale off Grief Point BC.

Margaret No. 1[a] 150859 This seiner formed part of the pre-war Fishermen's Reserve Fleet. On September 16, 1939 she was commissioned into the Royal Canadian Navy Fisherman's Reserve as HMCS Margaret I. On January 30, 1964 while owned by Perry York and Viggo Mark (MO), both of Prince Rupert, BC she foundered and capsized in Hecate Strait BC.

Margareta[b,433] (Norwegian Registry) This wooden wartime freighter was built at the end of the First World War in Victoria BC by the Cholberg Shipyard. In 1939 she was afloat in Finland as the Valborg. Kyle Stubbs stated that Valborg was renamed Margareta in 1947, still under the Finnish flag. On January 29, 1950, she collided with a floating object and sank in the Baltic Sea near Sassnitz, Germany while hauling coal on a voyage from Poland to Denmark.

Maria C. 175668 On October 10, 1974 this fishboat owned by Arne Baardsen (MO), Vancouver BC burned at the British Columbia Packers dock at Steveston BC.

Maria J. Smith On November 6, 1869 this bark sailed from Port Townsend WT with a cargo of lumber. During a strong gale and high seas her deck cargo began to shift, and her hull began to leak. Being driven onto a lee shore the crew abandoned ship and she was driven onto a reef at the entrance of Barkley Sound. The captain, his wife and children were picked up by the schooner Surprise. The wreck and cargo were sold in Victoria. The salvors refloated the vessel and she was taken in tow by the tug Politkofsky bound for Port Madison for repairs. Another gale blew up and she had to be cut adrift with Captain Smith and his crew aboard. Twelve days later the crew were

---

a   Built as Margaret No. 1; then HMCS Margaret No. 1; then Margaret No. 1
b   Built as Washington; then Cyntia; then Valborg; then; Margareta

taken off and landed at Port Townsend. The vessel drifted for some weeks being sighted at sea periodically but tugs arriving on the scene could not locate her. In March 1870 she drifted ashore on an island north of Milbanke Sound where she broke up.

The stricken *Mariechen* being salvaged (Image from the collection of the Maritime Museum of British Columbia.)

Mariechen[a] This German freighter was registered in Hamburg. She struck a rock in a snowstorm January 25, 1906 in False Bay, south of Funter on Chichagof Island, Alaska. She departed Seattle December 19, 1905 bound for Vladivostok, East Siberia (she was planning to run the Japanese naval blockade). She had a crew of 50 and a cargo of 5,000 tons of general merchandise worth $100,000 under charter to Barneson, Hibbard & Co. The vessel herself was worth $250,000. She was salvaged by the *Salvor* (B.C. Salvage Co.) and towed to Esquimalt BC. She was moved on to Seattle where she sank in Elliott Bay on April 27, 1907.

Marion[b] 122396 On November 10, 1918 this tug owned by Marion Tugboat Co. Ltd., Victoria BC burned west of Second Narrows, Burrard Inlet BC.

Mariposa (US) On October 18, 1915 she was wrecked at the entrance to Lama Pass, upper end of Fitzhugh Sound, BC. She struck a rock ledge and tore a hole in her bottom forward. Vessel was in command of Captain CJ O'Brien and was bound for SE Alaska and Cook Inlet ports with 95 passengers and a full cargo of freight. The steamer *Despatch*, under Captain SB Brunn, rescued the *Mariposa*'s passengers from the beach and took them to Ketchikan. The salvage steamer

---

a   Built as Clan Matheson; then Mariechen
b   Built as Owen; then Marion

Salvor refloated the steamer and the *Salvor* and the *William Jolliffe* later towed her to Seattle for repairs. In 1907 she was represented in Victoria BC by RP Rithet for service between Tahiti and Victoria.

The ***Mariposa*** wrecked at the entrance to Lama Pass, upper end of Fitzhugh Sound, BC. [(Image from the collection of the Maritime Museum of British Columbia 2_000104]

Marmae[434] 156880 On December 5, 1951 this seiner owned by Nelson Brothers Fisheries Ltd., Vancouver BC struck a floating object, foundered, and sank off Sand Heads BC. The crew evacuated in the lifeboat and were in the rough seas for an hour before help arrived from the *Western Cruiser*. The three crewmen rescued were: Lawrence Doving (Mate); Ralph Pennock (Engineer) and M Jackson (Cook).

Marmion[435] 102622 In 1911 she ran aground at the Second Narrows in Vancouver Harbour after hitting one of the water mains crossing from Capilano to the Stanley Park Reservoir. She normally carried cement from the tod Inlet plant and was returning there at 2 am in heavy fog when she lost her course. She got too close to shore and hit the main knocking it out. While maneuvering, the ship knocked out the second main. She had to be hauled out and had a new keel installed. On January 06, 1945 she was wrecked on St. John's Reef near Thormondby Island BC. Heavy seas were breaking over the vessel but 39 hours of timely and skilful work by the salvagers from Straits towing and Salvage Co. got her off safely. But there was so much damage to the bottom of her hull that almost half of it would have had to have been replaced. During the recovery, the derrick *Recoverer* was in danger of running aground and a motor lifeboat breaking away was smashed when it hit the shore. She was broken up at Capital Iron and Metals Ltd., Victoria BC.

Marquis of Dufferin 107444 On July 1st, 1898 while this sternwheeler was being towed to her destination on the Yukon River from Vancouver by the passenger steamer *Progreso* (Captain Gilboy). She was owned by the British America Corp. The tow was difficult, and the heavy seas caused the towline to tighten and then go slack putting strain on it. In the evening distress rockets were launched by the *Marquis of Dufferin* which had started to break up. A lifeboat was sent from the *Progreso* to rescue the ten-man crew of the *Marquis of Dufferin* which was then abandoned. Several days later she was sighted twelve miles northeast of Cape Beale by the steamer *Tartar*. She had rolled over and was standing on end with her bow submerged. Her final wreck site is not known.

Martha No. 1[436] 152734 On March 24, 1931, at 9:30 pm, this seiner owned by Shinosure Kariya, Steveston BC burned in Green Cove, Uchucklesit Inlet BC. The crew was rescued by a boat from the Green Cove Saltery.

Martha No. 2[437] 153392 In 1941 she was seized from her Japanese owners by the Canadian Government. In 1942 her ownership transferred to His Majesty the King. On September 8, 1945, this fishpacker owned by Fergus Woods, Vancouver BC was in collision with the J.O. *Edwards*, one-mile northwest of Klewnuggit light in Grenville Channel BC. She sank in 125 fathoms and her crew: Captain Fergus Woods and Frank Leask were rescued.

Marwood 301571 On 14 August 1994, this trawler fishboat was berthed at a government wharf. After being replenished with fresh water, the vessel was left unattended with about seven degrees starboard list and slack tanks. The spare trawl doors were stowed aft on the starboard side of the main deck with their top edges overhanging the ship side. As the vessel rose with the incoming tide, the spare trawl doors caught under the wale of the wharf front and water found its way onto the shelter deck by way of the open valve in the conveyor well drain line. Down flooding ensued and the vessel eventually sank at wharf. The chief engineer lost his life when he became trapped below deck.

Mary[438] (US) On September 28, 1948 this fishboat owned by Val Zitz, Seattle WA grounded in bad weather on a small island in Bull Passage. The crew escaped in a small boat. The vessel was considered a total loss.

Mary Brown[439] On June 08, 1930 the wreck of this San Francisco-based schooner was found on Banks Island BC after grounding bottom up on a reef in Hecate Strait. The cause of the wreck was never determined.

Mary Hare[440] 100796 On February 09, 1896, while under command of Captain Michael Hare, she struck a reef near Reid Island BC. She was intending to pick up a cargo of cordwood. As she approached the shore, she hit a rock. The crew went ashore for a meal while they waited for the tide to turn. It was there that they realized the vessel was burning and she soon sank and was later declared a total loss. They crew travelled to Chemainus in a small boat. Her engine was salvaged and used in another vessel.

Mary Island[441] 156972 On February 17, 1934 this seiner owned by Joseph Marinkovich, Ladner BC exploded and burned eight miles west of Point Roberts WA USA. The crew of two, J Seeley and J Corsay, were rescued and made their way to Galiano Island.

Mary Kay[442] 198651 He Canadian Registry was closed in 2011. The US National Transportation Safety Board reported (July 26, 2012) that she sank in Dixon Entrance, Alaska (54°38.015' N, 132°04.334' W), Near Cape Chacon, Prince of Wales Island, Alaska. Previously in 2012 on arriving in Bellingham WA, the Mary Kay lost operational control and consequently collided with a dock in port. The damage to the hull of the Mary Kay was not investigated, perhaps because the estimated damage was less than the required reportable amount. The Mary Kay next visited Sitka, Alaska, on July 9, 2012, where the vessel grounded twice on the boat launch (made of cement) in Sitka harbor. The National Transportation Safety Board determined that the probable cause of the sinking of the Mary Kay was the captain's failure to identify and correct the sources of the through-hull leaks.

Mary Mackin[a,443] 176287 On August 31, 1967 the Vancouver-based pocket cruise ship, *Trade Winds I*, with 10 American passengers aboard, was damaged in a collision with the tug Mary Mackin about 10 miles north of Alert Bay BC. Mark Simpson[444] reports that "She was grounded (and abandoned in 1998) on the foreshore in Patricia Bay on the Institute of Ocean Sciences lands. She sat there for many years until on July 26, 2004 she caught fire (some say it was arson). While on fire she was dragged off the beach and sank in shallow water—all this while the owner was away in jail in the United States.

Mary N. 158794 On October 11, 1950 while owned by Matteo Nicolich, Ladner BC this fishboat hit rocks and foundered at Nitinat VI.

Mary Parker[445] On December 28, 1893 this schooner under the command of Captain FL Bangs sank 3 miles off Race Rocks BC. She had been en route to Alaska. All Hands were saved, having evacuated in small boats, and rowed to Port Angeles WA.

---

a   Built as USATS LT-158; then Mary Mackin

Mary Rita[a,446] On August 17, 1933 this fishboat struck a rock and sank off Port Harvey BC in Chatham Sound. All the crew were saved. On February 25, 1949 she burned one mile west of Enterprise Reef in Georgia Strait BC.

Mary Sarita 156443 On March 16, 1938 this seiner owned by Dan Williams, Bamfield BC was stranded after dragging her anchor at Dodger Cove in Barkley Sound BC.

Mary Victoria Greenhow[447] (un-registered) This freight boat, owned by Captain Thomas D Shorts and Thomas Greenhow in 1886, was originally powered with coal oil but was later converted to burn wood because of the huge oil consumption by the original engine. She could carry 5 tons of freight and several passengers. She burned in 1886. Her engine was moved to the Jubilee.

Mary W. 152823 On July 31, 1945 this seiner owned by British Columbia Packers Ltd., Vancouver, BC was stranded off Ripple Point in Johnstone Strait BC. On November 16, 1945 she sank and was declared a total loss.

Mascotte[448] 094815 (US) This vessel, owned by JC Prevost, Vancouver BC, was involved in carrying granite blocks from Nelson Island to Vancouver BC. On August 15, 1893 while under the command of Captain Edward McCoskrie this salvage vessel was laying at anchor in Pachena Bay when the watchman discovered a fire in the galley. The vessel was carrying blasting powder and dynamite. The crew launched the ship's boats and were forced by the flames to abandon ship. The ship burned to the waterline and sank forcing them to walk to Cape Beale Lighthouse. The passenger steamer *Maude* carried the crew to Alberni.

Masonic[b] 313762 She was owned by Hi-Seas Enterprises Ltd., North Burnaby BC when she was wrecked in 1968.

---

a   Built as Mary Rita; then Helen-Side; then B.C. Rose
b   Built as Vivian A.; then Masonic

Matane (HMCS) K.444 (RCN) She was sold as surplus to Capital Iron & Metals Ltd. of Victoria, British Columbia in 1947 for stripping. At the end of her life she was scuttled as part of the breakwater at Oyster Bay BC.

Maud S.[449] 090678 On April 24, 1897 this sealing schooner, owned by Elford & Smith, Victoria BC, was wrecked in the Queen Charlotte Islands BC and became a total loss. Under the command of Captain Robert E McKiel, she ran ashore on North Island near Graham Island in a violent gale. Heavy seas battered the ship, and the First Nations hunters lowered the sealing canoes carried on the upper deck, and abandoned ship. No sooner had the canoes gone when the ship hit the rocks in the dark. Those left on board crawled forward. In the morning, the First Nations men returned and picked up the crew and took them ashore, slowly working their way to Masset. They hired a small steamer and got to Port Simpson where they were able to travel south in the *Danube*.

Maudi Morgan[a,450] 805667 On February 14, 1905, the LV 76 left New York bound for San Francisco to serve as the west coast *Relief* lightship. She was decommissioned on September 16, 1960. (In 2016 she was reportedly berthed or moored at the end of McLean Street, on the north side of the Fraser off the Lougheed Highway [BC 7]). In 2017 she sank at her berth in the Fraser River and as of 2019 was still awaiting salvage and removal.

Maui Lu[b] 150654 In 1990 (some reports say 1992) she sank in Hecate Strait BC on her way to Prince Rupert.

Mauna Kea (Hawaiian Register) On November 30, 1866 while under command of Captain David Robinson this bark, while sailing from Port Gamble to Honolulu was wrecked November 30th near Quatsino Sound. Three lives were lost. The local First Nations people attempted to hold the crew for ransom but two of them escaped and

---

a   Built as Lightship LV76 Relief/ WAL504; then Ark; then Claire Anne; then Claire Anne II; then Maudi Morgan

b   Built as Norsal; then HMCS Norsal; then Norsal; then Maui Lu

reached Fort Rupert. Word was sent to Victoria and HMS *Sparrowhawk* rescued the remainder.

Maureen R. 158569 In 1935–1950 she was the Barkley Sound pilot boat. On November 6, 1950 while owned by Reece Riley, Port Alberni BC she was lost, and her owner was drowned. Wreckage was found on Rafael Point, Flores Island in Clayoquot Sound BC.

Maverick 549879 (US) On 28 September 2012, at approximately 0430, the longliner fishboat *Viking Storm* collided with the American fishing vessel *Maverick* in thick fog, 30 nautical miles off La Push, Washington. The *Maverick* capsized and sank from the impact; 3 of the 4 crew members on board survived and were rescued by the *Viking Storm*. The fourth crew member was never found and was presumed drowned.

Mavis B. 189625 On June 13, 1966 this fishboat owned by The Cassiar Packing Company Ltd., Vancouver BC burned in Prince Rupert harbour and was a total loss. The hull was beached at Cassiar Cannery on Inverness Passage.

May Belle[451] 097158 In 1891 she was a sealing schooner owned by William Turpel, Victoria BC that had been withdrawn from trade. In 1896 she was lost with all hands off the west coast of Vancouver Island.

Mayne Express 348388 On April 14, 1981 this workboat owned by Thomas A Cook (MO), Qualicum Beach BC was destroyed by fire one mile off French Creek (VI), BC.

McCulloch 117117 On August 01, 1930 this tug owned by Julian Dale & George Thompson (JO), Vancouver BC burned near the Ballast Wharf, Nanaimo BC and sank.

McKenzie[452] 329425 The *McKenzie*, a dedicated crane barge with a large-capacity pedestal-mounted crane permanently fixed to its deck employed spuds, used for keeping the barge in position, fitted near the barge's mid-length. On the morning of 06 November 6, 2004, the tug *Manson*, with a crew of two, was on passage between New Westminster, British Columbia, on the Fraser River and Beale Cove, Texada Island, British Columbia. The *Manson* had two barges in tow: the crane barge *McKenzie* and the deck barge M.B.D. 32. During the transit through the Georgia Strait, the couplers connecting the M.B.D. 32 to the stern of the McKenzie parted. The *Manson*, with the *McKenzie* in tow, attempted to recover the M.B.D. 32 but experienced steering difficulties during this process. The *Manson* capsized and sank with the loss of both crew members—a deckhand and the master. Both barges were subsequently recovered; the *Manson* has not been located.

McR[a] 156893 In 1930 she was owned by the United Church of Canada, Toronto ON. In 1943 she was sold to the Royal Canadian Navy who employed her as a victualling depot stores boat at Halifax NS. In 1947–1958 she was owned by Duncan McRae (MO), Vancouver BC. On January 13, 1958 she caught fire and sank.

Medosa I[453] 170957 On February 12, 1976 blown by the wind this power cruiser owned by Robert and Marion Brereton, Heriot Bay BC grounded and sank at Five Fingers Island in Georgia Strait BC.

Meg Merrilees This schooner operated on the west coast of Vancouver Island in c1860. In February 1867 while en route from Whidby Island to Victoria she struck a rock off Victoria Harbour and sank.

Melanope 074550 In 1906 she ship-rigged when she was dismasted and abandoned in a storm and drifted into the Columbia River. In 1907 she was owned Coastwise Steamship & Barge Co. (Captain James Griffiths) for dismantling into barge. In 1907 she was converted to a barge. In 1911–1944 she was owned by Canadian Pacific Railway

---

a   Built as Melvin Swartout; then H.C. 166; then McR

Steamship Services as a coal barge servicing Empress-class ships in Vancouver Harbour. In 1946 she was owned by Comox Logging Company. She was sunk as a breakwater at Royston BC.

Melody B. 327833 On April 2, 1969 this power cruiser owned by Russel S Boyd (MO), Vancouver BC sank in Hotham Sound (Jervis Inlet) BC.

Melvin E.[a] 134128 In her earliest days she fished in Nitinat Lake BC. On March 13, 1976 in Goletas Channel (VI) BC she suffered a fire in the engine uptakes and was totally consumed.

Mercury On September 28, 1992 this fishboat experienced an explosion and fire in the engine room and sank in the Alberni Canal across from Nahmint Bay BC.

Mercury V[b] 197362 On July 2, 1965, this workboat owned by Charles M. Grant (MO), Earls Cove BC exploded and burned in Jervis Inlet BC.

Merlamac[454] 177361 On November 4, 1948 this fishpacker owned by Captain Westley Rainforth sprang a leak at night off Point Grey in Georgia Strait. Captain Westley Rainforth and his son Clarke were rescued by the gillnetter *Dynamite III*. A few minutes later the *Merlamac* sank in 70 fathoms about 1.5 miles off Point Grey.

Mermaid 088367 In 1902 this tug struck a rock at Newcastle Island. On March 25, 1904 she struck a rock in Jervis Inlet and sank near Moorsam Bluff.

Merry Sea[455] 130452 On November 26, 1930 this fisheries patrol vessel, owned by the Minister of Marine & Fisheries, Ottawa ON, was in collision with the passenger steamer *Princess Elaine*. The *Merry Sea* was rammed about one half mile off Prospect Pont BC in First Narrows

---

a Built as Active; then as Trapp; then as Melvin E.
b Built as Horseshoe Bay Flyer; then Mercury V

and cut in half by the impact. The crew was saved by the tug *Goblin*. The wreck was raised and dismantled.

Merry Sea II[a,456] 156914 On May 30, 1947 she was wrecked in a collision with the *Forest Surveyor* at a Campbell River wharf and sank in Discovery Passage. She was removed from the registry and abandoned as a total constructive loss. In 1950 she rebuilt and was re-registered at Nanaimo BC. In 1991 she was designated as a Vintage Vessel by the Maritime Museum of British Columbia.

Merstar[457] 173637 On April 28, 1959 this fishing troller owned by Edward Davidson, Vancouver BC exploded and sank at Calamity Shoal in Vancouver harbour approaches. Captain Edward Davidson was killed in the blast.

Mewika[458] 170618 On September 5, 1940 this trawler fishboat was in collision with the freighter *Horace Luckenbach* in dense fog between Becher Bay BC and Race Rocks in Juan de Fuca Strait BC. The fishboat capsized and sank. The crew: Captain W. Wiese, and Jack Smith, were in the water before they were rescued.

Mexico (US) On July 26, 1897 while owned by the Pacific Coast Steamship Co. she was one of the first steamers to leave Seattle WA for Skagway, Dyea, Juneau and Sitka Alaska for the Klondike Gold Rush carrying Joaquin Miller "the Poet of the Sierras". On August 06, 1897 she struck a rock and sank off Cape Chacon in Dixon Entrance BC.

Miami (US) This collier owned by the Pacific Coast Company picked up a cargo of 4500 tons of coal at Oyster Harbour and sailed for San Francisco. She struck a reef off Gabriola Island carrying coal while in transit from Ladysmith to San Francisco CA on January 25, 1900 and sank. Apparently, the marine pilot had misjudged the distance from land of the vessel while she was in Trincomalee Channel.

---

a   Built as Merry Sea II; then Curtis K.; then Merry Sea K; then Merry Sea II

Michigan On the evening of January 20, 1893, while under the command of Captain Graves, she was stranded at the mouth of what is now Michigan Creek near Pachena Point on the west coast of Vancouver Island. She was en route from San Francisco to Puget Sound with a cargo of general merchandise. There was reduced visibility in Juan de Fuca Strait and the captain lost his bearings. The vessel ran up on the beach where she was broken up in the surf and extinguishing the boiler fires. The mate travelled in a small boat to the Carmanah Lighthouse, but the telegraph line was not functioning. He travelled on to Neah Bay WA to request tugs from Port Townsend. Meanwhile in the morning the passengers and crew were moved ashore. One passenger died of exposure and was buried beside the telegraph line. The boiler, propeller and other remains are still plainly visible beyond the lighthouse at the mouth of Michigan Creek.

The boiler of the *Michigan*, in 2020, is all that remains of the wreck, the rest having been pounded to pieces by the relentless surf. (Photograph courtesy of Rick James).

Mighty Mite[459] 150767 On March 20, 1925 this tug struck owned by Captain Charles F Granholm et al., Vancouver BC drifting wood and foundered north-east of Hood Point, Bowen Island BC. The crew escaped in small boats and were picked up by the tug *Chieftain*.

Mik Mar 150904 On November 12, 1954 this ex-pilot boat burned at Union Bay, Baynes Sound BC.

Mile 83[a] 175158 On May 17, 1978, this troller fishboat owned by Edith Smit, Tofino BC was in a collision with the fishing vessel Three Sons which sank six miles southeast of Lennard Island BC.

---

a   Built as Freja IV; then Mile 83

Mill Bay A. 138680 On October 16, 1924 this fishboat foundered crossing the Nitinat Bar.

Millbank 154342 On October 10, 1974 this fishboat owned by William S Leslie (MO), Richmond BC was destroyed by fire while at Atlas Camp, Steveston BC.

Mina C.[a,460] 197361 In 1978 she sank near the Albion Ferry dock. Tim Agg recalled that "She carried explosives—on one of my two trips, we loaded dynamite at the CIL plant on James Island, and unloaded it at Jedway. The return voyage included loading frozen whale meat and sacks of whale meal at Coal Harbour, which was discharged at Steveston. That was enough to convince me that whaling should be ended. We also did grocery runs to floating logging camps."

Minerva[461] 120988 On June 18, 1936, at midnight, this sailing yawl owned by Hubert A Wallace, Vancouver BC ran ashore at Ganges Harbour, Saltspring Island BC. She had sailed to Victoria to take part in a regatta. Soon afterwards *Provincial Police Boat No. 6* tried to refloat the vessel, but they had to await high tide the following day. When the crew returned to the vessel, they noticed a leak in the gas valve. Investigating the situation someone lit a match when the gas in the bilge exploded. Within a few minutes other gas stored on board had exploded. Within half an hour the yacht was destroyed by fire.

Minnehaha[462] 096981 On April 07, 1893 this tug while under command of Captain Frank Wilkes struck Trial Island BC during a gale. Only her engine machinery was salvaged.

Minnie[463] 064150 On October 1, 1875, while crossing Milbanke Sound, this schooner was driven 150 miles offshore and took over a week to reach Fort Rupert. Another gale was encountered and the vessel, on the verge of sinking, was driven ashore at Fort Rupert to save her from sinking in deep water.

---

a   Built as Admiral Blake; then Huvik; then Timann; then Mina C.

Minnie Berna[464] 141605 In late December 1929 she caught fire while anchored at the head of Bute Inlet BC. Four hunters who had travelled north in her were ashore at the time of the incident.

Mischief II 319121 On June 22, 1977 this fishboat owned by Nelson Marriott (MO), Surrey BC burned in Higgins Passage, Milbanke Sound BC and was a total loss.

Miss Dundas 320906 On October 21, 1970 this fishboat owned by Herbert N Bryant, Prince Rupert BC foundered at Alert Bay BC.

Miss Gina[a] 369053 On April 18, 1980 this fishboat owned by William Valpy, Prince Rupert BC grounded in Prince Rupert Harbour BC.

Miss Judy No. 1 178059 On October 7, 1952 this fishboat owned by Charles Madden, Bamfield BC foundered in FitzHugh Sound south of Rivers Inlet BC.

Miss Midnite II 312902 On November 2, 1966 this power cruiser owned by Eva Creek Logging Co. Ltd., Vancouver BC sank at Bute Inlet BC.

Miss Millstream 323869 On May 20, 1970 this troller fishboat owned by David E Rolston, Victoria BC collided with a deadhead and foundered resulting in the vessel sinking southeast of Brabant Island BC.

Miss Rita No. 1 198567 In August 1976 this fishboat owned by The Cassiar Packing Company (1962) Ltd., Vancouver BC exploded at Port Simpson BC and was towed to Prince Rupert where it later sank.

Miss Robyn[465] 347962 On October 12, 1984 this fishboat capsized in Brooks Bay on the west coast of Vancouver Island BC. Patricia Malashewsky and Richard Cowlin were lost in the incident.

---

a   Built as Lady Tasha; then Miss Gina

Miss Tsawwassen 329454 On May 17, 1973, this fishboat owned by Takeshi N Yamanaka (MO), Ladner BC. was destroyed by an engine room fire while near Sechelt BC in Georgia Strait BC.

Miss Victory II 197693 On September 19, 1967 this fishboat owned by Mark Bouchard, Vancouver BC had an explosion in the engine room and sank off Carmanah Light while in Juan de Fuca Strait.

Mistann[a] 391313 This converted fishboat sank at the Yacht Club in Prince Rupert on Friday October 14, 2011. When the CCG received a report that the Mistann had sunk with approximately 1200 litres of diesel fuel and a quantity of lube oil onboard, the local Environmental Response personnel attended and deployed a boom and absorbents to the upwelling of oil between individual dock fingers at the marina. It was necessary to utilize two cranes to facilitate rigging of two lifting points on the sunken vessel from a depth of 100 feet of water. Late Monday afternoon the Mistann was brought to the surface still partially submerged and it was secured to the salvage barge. Shortly after midnight the vessel was refloated and taken to the Wainwright Marine shipyard for further assessment. In 2012 the Mistann was put up for sale in Prince Rupert.

Mistral 170772 The Transportation Safety Board of Canada[466] reports that "On the evening of 20 December 2003, the pleasure craft Mistral, with the owner/operator and 12 adult guests on board, was part of an annual event with two other vessels to celebrate the holiday season on the Fraser River near Mission. Shortly after separating from the other vessels, the Mistral collided with the deck barge Packmore 4000 under tow by the tug Tiger Shaman. The Mistral was destroyed upon impact and its occupants were thrown into the water. The crew of the tug recovered 12 survivors. One person drowned."

Misty Lady 195787 On May 19, 1980 this fishboat owned by Leonard J Dixon, Masset BC grounded north of Cape Ball (QCI) BC.

---

a   Built as Bunty; then Mistann

Mitco Surf 392751 On October 12, 1980 this tug owned by George Abernethy, & T Hemming, Queen Charlotte City BC capsized at Williston Lake BC with the loss of two lives.

Mobile City 220436 (US) On September 29, 1934 this freighter registered at New York was in collision with the San Jose at the CPR wharf Shed #7 in Vancouver BC.

Mollie G. On December 23, 1922 she burned in Georgia Strait BC.

Molly B.[a] 141726 On September 28, 1952 this workboat owned by Molly Hogan Ltd., Vancouver BC exploded and burned in Victoria Harbour BC.

Mona H. 138696 On September 20, 1928 this fishboat owned by Herb Simpson, Vancouver BC burned in Gunboat Passage at Beals Narrows BC.

Monabell 153327 On April 14, 1972 this fishboat owned by Robert Robertson, Port Alberni BC grounded on Vargas Island BC, foundered, and sank.

Monongahela[b,467] 099423 This sailing ship was rigged as a bark in layup with the Moshulu at Eagle Harbour since 1931. In 1937, after conversion to a barge, she was in service as a log carrying barge operating between the Queen Charlotte Islands and Vancouver. On December 17, 1943 while owned by Queen Charlotte Towing & Salvage Co. Ltd., Vancouver BC she was stranded and wrecked on Cape George, Porcher Island (Hecate Strait). The figurehead is in the collection at the Mystic Seaport Museum, Mystic CT USA.

Monroe[468] 138306 On October 02, 1915 this launch was in tow of the Constance which foundered and sank during a gale near Traill Island

---

a Built as Nana; then Molly B.
b Built as Balasore; then Dalbek; then Red Jacket; then Monongahela

in Georgia Strait. The *Monroe* was carry 18 men bound for a northern logging camp. She picked up the crew of seven from the *Constance* which made the *Monroe* very crowded.

Montana[a] (US) On March 16, 1901 this freighter owned by the Pacific Coast Co. while en route to Oyster Bay she struck Denman Island in Baynes Sound. She was salvaged and repaired.

Montserrat[469] In December 1894 this collier was en route with a cargo of coal from Nanaimo to Alaska. She was last reported at Cape Flattery by the light keeper in a bad storm. *Montserrat* was thought to have attempted unsuccessfully to take the *Keewenau* in tow near Tatoosh Island after she shipped a huge sea. Both ships disappeared and both nameboards washed up on the shores of the Queen Charlotte Islands.

Moonfleet[b] 347061 On December 30, 1986 she grounded and sank in Satellite Passage, Barkley Sound BC.

Moonglow 30KA5161 The Transportation Safety Board of Canada states that "The "*Moonglow*", a ketch-rigged yacht, was on passage from Tofino, BC to Victoria, BC, departed the anchorage at Port San Juan, BC at 1500, September 11, 1994. The "*Thomson*" departed Nanoose, BC on the morning of 11 September and disembarked her Canadian Navy Coastal Pilot off Victoria at 1805. The vessel was steaming on the surface in the Juan de Fuca Strait outbound for San Diego, California. At 2119, in Canadian waters off Sheringham Point, the "*Thomson*" and the "*Moonglow*" collided in dense fog. The "*Moonglow*", holed on the starboard side aft, sank quickly. The operator was rescued from the water by the crew of the submarine and treated for mild hypothermia. The submarine sustained some light damage to the starboard bow. "

---

a   Built as Willamette; then Montana
b   Built as Moonfleet; then Log Dog

Moran's No. 1[a] 154600 On November 9, 1945 this fishboat owned by Mrs Helen Moran, Vancouver BC struck a submerged object 11 miles from Porlier Pass BC.

Morning Star In 1856 this trading schooner was operating around southern Vancouver Island. In 1858 she was trading between Victoria (Vancouver Island) and the USA. In 1859 she saved the crew of the brig *Swiss Boy* in Barkley Sound who were under attack. In November 1860, she was stranded at Bonilla Point, while under the command of Captain Hugh McKay.

Morning Star[470] (US) On July 13, 1924 this American freighter, under the command of Captain JD Gilmore, had a near miss with disaster while transiting Active Pass. A huge whirlpool opened under the bow of the vessel throwing the vessel around violently within her own length. This caused the cargo to shift and the vessel lay over on her side throwing three crew members into the water. They were sucked into the whirlpool and two of them were drowned. Sprung by the force of the incident the ropes holding the forward deck cargo snapped and boxes, barrels and lumber went overboard. Steel in that cargo shifted and had to be jettisoned to enable the vessel to be trimmed properly. Captain George Maude, of Mayne Island BC, saw the vessel listing and used his vessel, the *Val*, to assist the freighter in righting herself and worked her to shelter at Goose Island. The next day he had the freighter arrested so he could lay claim to salvage. A local Japanese fisherman, Mr Yashida, also laid a claim for saving the life of the surviving crewmen who went overboard.

Morning Star[471] On Friday October 3, 1947 this gillnetter, was driven into the Fraser River Jetty and sank in a windstorm.

Morning Sunrise 392965 The Transportation Safety Board of Canada[472] reports that "On 29 June 2005, at about 1640 Pacific daylight time, while en route from the Queen Charlotte Strait to Gibsons, British Columbia, on the Sunshine Coast, the small fishing vessel

---

a   Built as D.T.; then Moran's No. 1

Morning Sunrise, with 500 prawn traps on deck and approximately 4500 kg of frozen prawns in boxes in the freezer hold, listed heavily to port and gradually sank in 152 m of water. All four crew members on board, wearing immersion suits, abandoned the vessel into a life raft and were soon picked up by the Canadian Coast Guard cutter Cape Caution."

Mosgulf[473] On September 9, 1969 in dense autumn fog this Norwegian freighter collided with the Philippines freighter *President Roxas* off Sheringham Point. She received a six-foot hole at the waterline. She proceeded to Vancouver under her own power to Vancouver BC. The *Mosgulf* had been en route from Olympia to Japan with a cargo of logs.

Mother III 326545 On March 16, 1978 this seiner owned by D.L. Larden & Sons Fishing Co. Ltd., Richmond BC experienced a fire in the engine room and sank off the north west coast of Vancouver Island.

Mount Baker 216217 (US) This freighter was registered in Los Angeles CA USA. On February 26, 1944 she burned at Berth 6, at the Ocean Dock in Prince Rupert BC.

Mount Comet[a] 178829 This tug owned by James Mckenzie, Pitt Meadows BC collided with the Pitt River Railway Bridge, sank. After her salvage she was hauled ashore and burned.

Mount Royal 111778 She was registered at Victoria BC. This sternwheeler, owned by the Hudson's Bay Company, London UK, operated on the Skeena River in opposition to the *Hazelton*. On July 6, 1907 she was caught in a cross current which drove her against Ringbolt Island, in Kitsalas Canyon where she struck a rock (Skeena River) and broke in two and capsized. Six lives were lost (passengers, and some furs were saved). Her engines went to the Inlander.

---

a   Built as Leslie; then Del Draco; then Basalt No. 1; then Jorgie; then Ocean Comet; then Mount Comet

Mr. Bill 311258 On July 31, 1964 this tug owned by Weldwood of Canada Ltd., Vancouver BC sank in the Fraser River near Quesnel BC.

Mr. Chips[474] On November 15, 1962 this log barge exploded and burned off Gambier Island BC and was beached at Cotton Bay. Ed Wray, who was on board at the time, was severely burned on his hands and face and was taken to hospital.

Mudlark[475] 100631 On November 13, 1915 this dredge (a converted dredge tender), owned by The Minister of Public Works, Ottawa ON, sank at her mooring just east of the Victoria Chemical Works. She came to rest on her port side in 20 feet of water with only the top of her spuds, funnel and house showing at low tide. A week later she was beached and pumped out. It was found that the failure of one of her spuds to slide properly on the falling tide, jamming in her socket, caused her to roll over and sink. She was salvaged and put back into service.

Muns 170391 On September 15, 1966 her anchor dragged, and this fishboat owned by John E Guthrie, Ucluelet BC, was driven ashore at Estevan Point BC and was declared a total loss.

My Buddy[a] 330257 On December 7, 1980 she was reported as taking on water in Malacca Pass, Elliot Island, Chatham Sound BC.

My Own II[b,476] 176192 On September 10, 1945 she was on a trial run when she was swamped by the wake of the Prince George in Vancouver Harbour. When Captain Gus Hegglund altered course to avoid the swell his vessel heeled over and overturned. An elderly crew member, Andrew Beaumont, died while five others fought their way clear of the wreck. Rescued were Captain Gus Hegglund; John Brynelson; John Cortez and two grandsons of the dead man. She was towed back to the wharf where she was righted with the aid of a derrick. The vessel was thought to have been carrying too little ballast

---

a   Built as Lady Carrie; then My Buddy; then Tristesse
b   Built as Pacific Clipper; then My Own II

and thrown off trim by newly installed live-bait tanks. On April 11, 1954, this vessel exploded and burned six miles north northwest of the Fraser River Lightship in Georgia Strait.

My-Way 328392 On September 24, 1976 this fishboat owned by Carl A Frericksson, Crofton BC was involved in a collision at La Perouse Bank BC.

Myrtle H. II 175276 On August 11, 1950 this troller fishboat owned by British Columbia Packers Ltd., Vancouver BC foundered above Forbes Island, near Main Bay BC.

Mystery[477] 094816 In 1903 this tug struck Schagg Rocks at Esquimalt BC and was beached just in time to prevent her foundering. She came to rest in 15 feet of water. The British Columbia Salvage Company used a large centrifugal pump into her and within minutes had her afloat again. After being repaired she dropped her tail shaft and wheel at Vancouver soon after arriving. In October 1919 she was ashore on Galiano Island BC.

N.H. 152824 On December 4, 1941 this fishpacker owned by Masao Hagewara, Vancouver BC was stranded at Mission Point BC (Wilson Creek).

N.P. 324 13K16490 On July 26, 1976 this fishboat grounded and sank at Green Top Island, Chatham Sound BC.

N.P. 341 346613 On September 01, 1977 this fishboat owned by The Canadian Fishing Co. Ltd., Vancouver BC, burned at Port Edward BC and declared a constructive total loss. One person was killed in the accident.

N.S.P. No. 14[a] 134748 In 1948 a harpoon-cannon was fitted on board this trawler by B.C. Marine Engineers and Shipbuilders. In 1956 she was hulked as a herring scow. She sank while owned by North Shore

---

a   Built as James Carruthers; then N.S.P. No. 14

Packing Co. Ltd., North Vancouver BC in Hecate Strait in 1958 while under tow.

N.S.P. No. 7[a] 192491 She earned four battle stars during her service with the US Navy in the Second World in the South Pacific. She was briefly registered as a powered vessel in 1950 but then within a few months was converted to a non-powered vessel. On December 7, 1959 she sank in Quatsino Sound BC.

N.W.D. 101 194219 On June 21, 1979 this tug owned by Tortoise Towing Ltd., Mackenzie BC had an engine room fire and was destroyed at Williston Lake BC.

Nahleen[478] 107104 On July 12, 1899 she burned while at her mooring in Victoria Harbour BC. The fire started in the engine room of the *Nahleen*, and the fire spreading to the *Louise*, but the fire department having no equipment to fight such a fire could only stand and watch the vessels burn. She had been scheduled to travel to the Yukon the next morning.

Nahleen[b,479] 133715 As the *Cullelva* she was originally built in Hong Kong as a sailing vessel converted to a workboat. In 1927 she was operated by Mr & Mrs HH Hay as a sales boat base for Marshall-Wells BC Ltd. (a hardware chain of stores). On May 3, 1929 she exploded in Barnet Passage BC fifteen miles south of Alert Bay. The *Nahleen* struck a rock and fearing that she would sink Mrs Hay, an experienced navigator and Mate in the vessel, escaped in a rowboat, her husband remaining on board. While he worked to get her afloat there was an explosion that wrecked the vessel burning Captain Hay who had to be taken to hospital in Alert Bay.

Nahmint 179478 On December 28, 1995 this former whale catcher owned by Kak Fishing Ltd., Vancouver BC sank in Gunderson Slough BC.

---

a   Built as USS P.C.S. 1452; then N.S.P. No. 7
b   Built as Cullelva; then Nahleen

Naiad[480] 122539 On January 04, 1919 this tug owned by WH Whalen, Vancouver BC ran ashore on rocks off Bull Passage, Sabine Channel, Lasqueti Island BC in fog and darkness. While under command of Captain H Lauder she sat high and dry when the crew abandoned ship. She had coaled at Nanaimo and was bound for Tucker Bay to pick up a scow at the time of the incident. The crew swerved the tug as she ran ashore so that it was sitting on a shelf. They made her fast to the shore with cables, and as the tide receded the added weight caused the cables to break and she slid off into deep water.

Nakusp[481] 103302 This sternwheeler had a troubled past. The machinery installed in her originally came from the Columbia which had burned on August 2, 1895 opposite Sayward BC on the Columbia River. In the summer of 1896, the Nakusp ran aground on Kootenay Bar and remained there for a couple of months. In December 1897 she was burned to the waterline at her berth at Arrowhead BC.

Nanaimo Brave[a] 141717 In June 1969 this tug owned by Norman W. McLellan, Fort Langley BC sank at Haney BC in the Fraser River.

Nanaimo Flyer[b,482] 134303 On August 1, 1957 the Nanaimo Flyer capsized and sank in 150' deep water in Dodd Narrows BC. It all occurred in a few seconds. Two Nanaimo sport fishermen: Wilfred T Jones and Harold Green, drove their sport boat into the churning water to rescue the crew. Saved from the cold water were Captain William Crawshaw; Mate George Shuker and deckhand Ken Dunn. She was towed into shallow water where slings were put around the vessel's hull and was later salvaged.

Nanaimo Flyer 811880 On November 4. 2001 her crew vanished overboard while towing a barge in Stuart Narrows north of Port McNeill. Lonnie Edward Berrow (British Columbia Nautical History Facebook Group 05/09/2018) states that "This incident occurred close to Stuart Narrows near the entrance to Drury Inlet in around 2001.

---

a   Built as Cliffeleine; then Catala Chief; then Nanaimo Brave
b   Built as Point Garry; then Nanaimo Flyer

The tug was found circling around with the ramp barge MBM 60 with her crew of two missing by a passing crew boat. It was speculated that the crew may have been back aft shortening up the towline and the wire may have come up hard causing the men to be thrown overboard. It was foggy that morning and this could have contributed to the accident. There was a small amount of seawater in the wheelhouse that would indicate she was heeled over at some point and the bodies were never found despite an extensive search."

Nancy L.[483] (US) On April 02, 1978 this fishboat, while on her maiden voyage, capsized and was found wrecked at Calvert Island Queen Charlotte Sound BC with the loss of three crew members. The damage to the vessel was described as very extensive and a covered life raft was missing, and immersion suits were found floating at sea.

Nanette[484] 033318 On December 23, 1860 the British bark *Nanette*, a vessel of about 400 tons burden, in command of Captain Mains, with Captain William McCulloch, as mate, was wrecked. She was consigned to Stamp & Co. of Victoria, and had an exceedingly valuable cargo, the invoice showing it to have been worth nearly $200,000. The bark was one hundred and seventy-five days out from London when she sailed lazily up the Straits when on Sunday, December 23d, and struck on Race Rocks with such force that she remained stuck there. A great effort was made to float her, but without success, and she became a total loss.

Nanoose 122397 In 1946 this tug owned by Comox Logging & Railway Company was sunk as a breakwater at Royston BC.

Narbethong[485] 134216 On March 31, 1924 the workboat Narbethong was found sunk with only her mast showing. Her owner, Captain Holmes K Freeman, was found drowned in the hull when she was later raised. She was operated on the Skeena River. On April 21, 1932 she suffered a fire at Lak Anian Island in Prince Rupert Harbour BC.

Narwhal[486] 189228 On May 16, 1961 this power-cruiser owned by Robert AD Berwick, West Vancouver BC, exploded one half mile east of the bell buoy at Spanish Banks in English Bay, Vancouver BC. They had taken a brief voyage so that a widow could scatter the ashes of her late husband. When this was done the boat exploded and the four people on board were forced to jump into the sea. A sea cadet training vessel commanded by LCDR Peter Cox RCN and his crew of cadets fought the fire, but it was too fierce, and the vessel burned to the waterline.

Nass 141721 On June 26, 1927 this fishpacker owned by Wallace diesel Ships Ltd., Vancouver BC exploded and sank alongside the dock at Quatsino Harbour BC.

Nathan E Stewart 1120997 (US) On October 13, 2016 she sank after she went ashore in Seaforth Channel, at Gale Passage, about one-mile due south of Ivory Island Light. The CCG *Cape St. James* was attending the scene. Her barge tow was intact at the time of sinking. She was still pinned to her barge in push mode. With the barge so high up being empty, all her freeboard and flotation is holding the bow of the tug out of the water.

Natural Gift[a] 327210 On August 17, 1969 she grounded at Goose Island anchorage off Rivers Inlet BC and was a total constructive loss.

Naughty Gal[487] On November 3, 1962 this gillnet fishboat was destroyed by fire off Bowen Island. The owner, Peter Sande, fought the blaze for half an hour before being forced to evacuate in a life raft. He was rescued by another gillnetter, the *Owen Sound I*.

Navvy Jack[b] 122511 On October 2, 1932 this tug owned by The Deeks Sand & Gravel Co. Ltd., Vancouver BC sank suddenly in deep water off the *Sand Heads Lightship* while in tow of another tug.

---

a   Built as Natural Gift; then North Cape
b   Built as Edith; then Navvy Jack

Navvy Jack[a,488] 176875 Leigh Cossey stated "This summer I located the *Hartville* at Kinbasket Lake near Golden BC and went to see her and take pictures. She has been laying abandoned on the beach there for 11 years now." The *Navvy Jack* capsized in False Creek when the towline attached to a barge that she was assisting for the tug *Torpedo*. The combined forces of the current and the drag of the barge pulled her uder without warning. Captain Karl W. Gursli, trapped in the cabin of the Navvy Jack, drowned in the incident."

Leigh Cossey stated "This summer I located the *Hartville* at Kinbasket Lake near Golden BC and went to see her and take pictures. She has been laying abandoned on the beach there for 11 years now." The *Navvy Jack* capsized in False Creek when the towline attached to a barge that she was assisting for the tug *Torpedo*. The combined forces of the current and the drag of the barge pulled her uder without warning. Captain Karl W. Gursli, trapped in the cabin of the Navvy Jack, drowned in the incident."

Nelbro 110 347923 In October 1974 this fishboat owned by British Columbia Packers Ltd., Richmond BC sank in Active Pass BC and was declared a total loss.

Nelda 314899 On March 12, 1980 this fishboat while owned by James E Paulik, Richmond BC foundered and was beached at James Spit (In Central Saanich) BC and was a total loss.

Nell[489] 090789 In 1887–1903 she was making monthly voyages between Vancouver and Victoria. On October 10, 1904 she burned at Georgetown BC. (She was reported in the press as having been previously twice wrecked) On February 9, 1906 she was wrecked on the beach near Tugwell Island at Jap Point BC and broke into two pieces. While the tide was out the piece containing the engines was planked up, hauled off the beach and towed to Georgetown as it was determined that the engines and boilers were not damaged.

---

a   Built as HMCS Hartville; then Portovan; then Straits; then Davis Straits; then Navvy Jack

Nellie Martin[a] 061307 In 1858 she was trading between Victoria (Vancouver Island) and the USA. In 1863 she saved the trading schooner Thorndike in Johnstone Strait from First Nations attack and towed the Thorndike to Fort Rupert. She was seized and plundered by First Nations people in 1865 at Bella Bella, British Columbia. She was in Canadian registry 1858–1871. In 1871 she was wrecked on Cypress Island.

Nellie May[490] This bark sailed from Port Madison WA on January 23, 1890 with a cargo of lumber for San Francisco under command of Captain Austin. The crew presumed lost. Her name board and other wreckage was picked up by the tug *Lorne*. A lifeboat and identified wreckage and a huge amount of lumber was washed ashore in Clayoquot Sound. Her crew of 13 men was lost.

Nellie Taylor[491] 072678 On March 14, 1891 she was lost in Howe Sound BC when she dragged her anchor in a gale and sank. No one was aboard at the time.

Nellie W.[492] On December 24, 1965 this fishboat left Port Alberni Christmas Eve with a faulty engine and no radio bound for Bamfield after the crew did Christmas shopping. It was thought that she foundered when her engine failed and she drifted into pounding seas in the Alberni Canal with the loss of 6 persons: Matthew Dennis; Richard Dennis; David Dennis; Lillian Dennis, Paul Tait and a sixth man (not named). The vessel was not found, only some floating debris.

Neptune[493] On October 22, 1978 this troller fishboat was reported missing, presumed lost, on Duncan Island (VI) BC with the loss of three lives: owner Bill Carson and another unidentified couple.

Neptune II[b] 155237 Shortly after 0400 PDT on May 9th, 2011, a fire broke out in the engine room of the small fishing vessel *Neptune*

---

a   Built as T.T. Stevens; then Nanaimo Packet; then Nellie Martin
b   Built as Snow Drift; then Neptune II

II. After their attempt to fight the fire was unsuccessful, the 2 crew members abandoned the vessel into their dive tender and issued a distress call. *Neptune* II burned to the waterline and subsequently sank in Johnstone Strait, British Columbia. There were no injuries.

Nereus[494] On August 8, 1937 this Greek-registered freighter went ashore half a mile east of Cape Beale in dense fog inbound for Port Alberni from Kobe Japan under command of Captain John Katalinos to load lumber for the UK under charter to the Anglo-Canadian Shipping Co. The crew was rescued by the *Salvage King*. While the ship was breaking up, parts were salvaged by Capital Iron and Metals Ltd., Victoria BC.

Neutron 312101 In 1969 this fishboat owned by John F Hargrove, Parksville BC caught fire, burned, and sank two miles off the southwestern tip of Calvert Island BC.

Nevilene[a,495] 130873 On October 15, 1932 the engine of this fishpacker, owned by Josip Boroevich, Vancouver BC, backfired off Mayne Island BC. This caused a destructive fire, and she was destroyed. She was en route from Vancouver to Victoria at the time of the incident. The crew of two escaped in a dinghy but they sustained serious burns.

New West No. 1 176749 On August 7, 1949 this vessel owned by James Pearcy, New Westminster BC burned while moored at dolphins at Barnston Island, Fraser River BC.

New Zealand 121766 On November 06, 1913 this vessel owned by Mrs Helen Bull, Heriot Bay BC burned at Quathiaski Cove BC.

Newcastle No. 4[496] On October 26, 1953 this fishpacker ran aground on a rocky beach at Magdalena Point near Jordan River BC. Her crew of four escaped in the ship's dinghy. High winds and pounding waves destroyed the vessel and she became a total loss.

---

a   Built as Westerner; then Nevilene

Newington[a] 110697 She sank in Burrard Inlet BC on August 26, 1959 after vandals stole her seacocks.

Nicholas Biddle[497] In 1875 this ship-rigged sailing ship sank at Race Rocks BC while en route Nanaimo to San Francisco with coal, she went ashore but was later refloated.

Nideleven[b] 310330 On August 15, 1970 this fishboat owned by Alf L Aunli, North Surrey BC sank At Georgia Point in Georgia Strait BC and was declared a total constructive loss. She was salvaged, rebuilt, and renamed as *Lady Dawn*.

Nidge[498] 122169 On December 11, 1912 this tug, owned by the Vancouver Island Power Company and under command of Captain E Fraser, was wrecked off Macauley Point (Esquimalt BC) and broken up by the heavy seas. In heavy seas and strong winds, she went ashore and was pounded by heavy seas. Her crew of five and six passengers got ashore safely through the surf. Her engines had broken down and there was no tug assistance available, so she drifted in the wind, striking the shore just past midnight. She was en route from Jordan River to Victoria at the time of the incident. She was used to carry passengers and deliver barges of construction materials during the construction of the powerhouse, dam, flumes, and other infrastructure needed for the British Columbia Electric Company's Jordan River hydroelectricity project.

Nika[499] (US) On February 15, 1923 she lost her rudder and caught fire near the *Umatilla Lightship*, and burned to the waterline. A high wind made it impossible to launch boats. The crew were saved with a breeches buoy by the crew of the tug USCGS *Snohomish* taken to Port Angeles WA. The vessel drifted while still burning and sank in Ucluelet Inlet BC.

---

a   Built as Newington; then HMCS Newington; then Newington
b   Built as Nideleven; then Lady Dawn

Nikko[500] 140901 On July 7, 1929 this fishboat owned by Hikohei Fujiwara, Vancouver BC was stranded and sank at Tow Hill, Queen Charlotte Islands BC with the loss of one person.

Nineveh[501] 018784 (US) The *Nineveh*, a British bark, was sailing out of Boston MA USA and departed Moodyville, BC on January 19, 1896 for Australia, under Captain Broadfoot with a cargo of lumber. She sprang a leak six days later and was abandoned by her crew in small boats on January 27 about 90 miles off Vancouver Island. The crew set the ship on fire to prevent her becoming a menace to navigation, she burned and then was stranded in January 1896 having drifted ashore in Wreck Bay (Florencia Bay VI). Her crew arrived in February in the schooner Compeer at Oakland CA USA. In February, the bark *Matilda* reported that she passed through masses of floating lumber 40 miles west of Cape Flattery apparently jettisoned from the *Nineveh*.

Nipigon Straits 330354 On September 14, 1971 this fishboat owned by Robert G. Willan (MO), Sointula BC foundered off the mouth of the Fraser River BC.

Nippon Current 141316 On July 22, 1928 this fishboat owned by Yoshiro Yoshido and Choichiro Yoshida, Steveston BC burned south of Nasparti Inlet on the west coast of Vancouver Island BC.

Nitinat Chief[502] 173474 On Friday December 27, 1957 she ran aground on a reef off Oak Bay BC. She had been outbound and travelling north when, after rounding up a stray boat from Oak Bay, she ran aground. She had to wait a full tidal cycle before she was able to float off.

Noah's Ark On July 25, 1977 this yacht was declared a constructive total loss after her collision and sinking at Look Out Point, Howe Sound.

Noble[a,503] 126951 She sailed as a rum runner owned by Richard Barnet Wright Pirie, Vancouver BC under command of Captain WL Kerr. She was wrecked on January 7, 1928 at Escalante Reef BC in a heavy gale. The Wireless Operator, Clifford Duchamp and Assistant Engineer Frank Bell, survived and were landed at Tofino by the *Tofino Lifeboat*. She had cleared for Mexico carrying a cargo of 400 cases and 20 kegs of whiskey (she was obviously running alcohol into the USA). It was thought that she was returning from a voyage when she met with disaster. Crew members lost in the wreck were: Captain WL Kerr; MB Wall; Harry Williams; OH Sid Elvey (cook). Early in his life Captain Kerr had rescued a man overboard and had been awarded a Carnegie Medal and $1,000.

No-Name 126081 On October 22, 1911 this tug owned by B.C. Tie & Timber Co. Ltd., Vancouver BC was in collision with the *Iroquois* in the Fraser River BC.

Nootka[504] 097164 On January 2, 1896 this schooner, owned by Charles Toquit, Nootka BC, went ashore in Nootka Sound and became a total loss.

Nootka Sound 172549 In 1941 this seiner was seized from her Japanese owners by the Canadian Government. In 1942 her ownership transferred to His Majesty the King. In 1942 after being seized from her owners she was released to the North Shore Packing Co. until an order for herring was filled. On November 3, 1943 she foundered in Georgia Strait BC.

Nootum[505] 154715 In July 28, 1931 this seiner, owned by Gosse Packing Co. Ltd., Vancouver BC, was aground near Fog Rocks, in Fitzhugh Sound BC.

Nora 122327 On October 17, 1921 this fishboat owned by Gerald F Payne, Vancouver BC was stranded in Brown Passage, Hecate Strait

---

a   Built as Lady Mine; then Noble

BC. On October 2, 1925 she burned in the north arm of the Fraser River one-half mile east of Marpole BC.

Nora Jane[506] 154548 On June 19, 1950 this tug, owned by Queen Charlotte Towing & Salvage Co. Ltd., Vancouver BC, exploded, burned, and sank out in Hecate Strait BC. Her crew of six was rescued by the *Sandy S.*, a passing fishboat. They spent an hour in the water before being rescued and then men stated that the *Sandy S.* came "just in time."

Norbessee II 156828 On August 08, 1950 this tug, owned by the Northern British Columbia Power Co. Ltd., Prince Rupert BC was in a collision with the *G.M. No. 1* on the Skeena River BC.

Nordic Queen 174062 On March 06, 1973 this fishpacker owned by the Canadian Fishing Co. Ltd., Vancouver BC in the Strait of Juan de Fuca near Port Renfrew BC with a cargo of herring bound for Vancouver.

Nordic Storm[a] 190599 This tug, was owned by Benson & Quinlan Towing Ltd., Vancouver BC at the time of her accident. On September 25, 1953 she sank in the North Arm of the Fraser River and was raised by the Pacific Salvage Ltd. After her salvage she continued in service until 1998.

Nordic Storm[b] 312068 She was used to service fish buying stations near Pender Harbour BC. On August 12, 1997 she sank.

Norma G. 154594 On July 19, 1978 this fishboat owned by Harold Smith, Lasqueti Island BC foundered and sank at Cape Caution BC.

Nornen[507] 138116 On October 5, 1968 this fishpacker owned by Patrick D Davidson (MO), Vancouver BC was destroyed by a fire

---

a   Built as Daleo, then Comealong; then Nordic Storm
b   Built as Daleo; Then Comealong; then Nordic Storm

starting in her engine room. She sank in Mayne Bay (Barkley Sound) BC. The skipper got off safely and was taken to Ucluelet.

Norpack No. 1[a,508] 154423 On November 8, 1950 this fishpacker, under the command of Captain John C Bowden, ran aground on the southern end of Denman Island BC. She was being operated as a packing tender taking salmon from Comox to Vancouver with a load of fall Chum salmon on board. Overnight she rolled over on her side and the crew were safe in a dinghy when assistance arrived. She was refloated on the rising tide.

Norseman[509] 533713 (US) On June 18, 1978 this American deep-sea crab boat ran aground on a ledge in Graham Reach, Swanson Channel BC. She slipped off the ledge she had been resting on and sank in deep water before a patch could be put on the hole in her hull. Her crew of six were all rescued safely and taken to Prince Rupert.

Nortel[510] 192479 On November 18, 1960 this cabin cruiser, owned by North-West Telephone Co., Vancouver BC, was smashed on rocks in rough weather. High winds swept her out from behind the government breakwater and wrecked against the seawall behind the Tyee Plaza.

North Arm Guardian[b,511] 174071 On April 4, 1971 this tug, owned by North Arm Transportation Ltd., Vancouver BC, caught fire and burned for 9 hours before finally sinking at Heath Point on Hope Island near Bull Harbour BC and declared as a total loss. The five-man crew was saved by the *Bull Harbour Lifeboat* and fishboats.

North Bend[512] 126621 In 1909 she was in service with the tug *Escort No. 2* freighting supplies for the construction of the Grand Trunk Pacific Railway to Prince Rupert BC. Later she became a pulp barge at

---

a   Built as Seamark No. 1; then Norpack No. 1
b   Built as La Garde; then V.T. No. 505; then North Arm Guardian

the Whalen Pulp & Paper Co. mill. On July 7, 1924 she foundered at Port Alice in Quatsino Sound BC while carrying a cargo of 470 tons of sulphur. She was lightering the sulphur from the S.S. *Carolinas* anchored offshore. On one of her trips she hit a rock and sank. The Vancouver Dredging and Salvage Co. got the contract to recover the barge. In an unanticipated subsequent tragedy their diver, AA Fagg, signalled from the depths for emergency relief and died immediately on being brought to the surface.

North Coaster No. 1 179076 On August 30, 1979 this tug owned by Garfield V White, Queen Charlotte City BC sank in Bearskin Bay QCI BC.

North Sea[a,513] 216822 (US) On February 13, 1947 she struck Middle Rock in Seaforth Channel while under the command of Captain Charles Graham. She was southbound from Ketchikan to Seattle at the time of the incident in heavy winds. The Captain and six members of the crew stayed aboard while the crew of 66 and 88 passengers were taken off by fishing vessels. The seiner *Northisle* took on 38 of them. All were taken to Bella Bella BC. The tug *La Pointe* attempted to free the vessel. The *North Sea* was stripped in situ of any useful salvage by Capital Iron & Metals Ltd.

North Sea 172386 On June 25, 1977 she was involved in a collision with an unidentified vessel and sank near Amphitrite Point BC.

North Star 094812 In 1890 she was first registered at Victoria where she was arrested for transporting illegal Chinese immigrants into the United States. In 1897 she was registered at New Westminster BC. On November 12, 1903 she sank at her dock in New Westminster BC and became a total loss.

North Vancouver Ferry No. 2[b,514] 116784 On December 16, 1935 about 5:00 pm the Norwegian freighter *Brynje* collided with the North

---

a   Built as Plainfield; then Mary Weems; then Admiral Peoples; then North Sea
b   Built as St. George; later North Vancouver Ferry No. 2

Vancouver Ferry No. 2 carrying a full load of cars and passengers. The freighter was undamaged and proceeded to sea. The ferry reached her dock under her own power. She had to be drydocked to repair the damage. On February 5, 1939, this passenger car ferry burned at Tahsis Channel BC.

North Vancouver Ferry No. 3[a,515] 130447 On August 24, 1928 this ferry, while under command of Captain Spracklin and owned by The Corporation of the City of North Vancouver, collided with the Canadian National Railway tug *Canadian National No. 1* in Burrard Inlet BC. The tug was so deeply embedded in the hull of the ferry that it took 30 minutes to separate them. There were no injuries on either vessel.

Northern Eagle[b] (US) In 1859 this barkentine burned in Esquimalt Harbour, Vancouver Island. She was abandoned there, and a Royal Navy vessel shelled her and sank her. She was afterwards raised and sold to GA Meiggs of Port Madison and rebuilt and named after his San Francisco partner as the *W.H. Gawley*. On October 23, 1880 while en route from Port Madison to San Francisco she went ashore on the Golden Gate during a dense fog and was a total loss. The captain sent his passengers ashore, and with the mate and a portion of the crew remained on board until the next morning, when they were taken off by the life-saving crew. A portion of the lumber cargo was saved. This vessel is sometimes mistakenly identified as the *Golden Eagle*.

Northern King[c] 175687 In 2017 this fishboat sank, was raised and equipment was removed from the vessel. On February 1, 2017 she was apparently scuttled near Campbell River BC.

Northern Light[516] (US Register) On February 24, 1959 this seiner sank near Cape Mudge off Campbell River BC. When she attempted to turn in heavy seas earl in the morning she capsized. Three of the

---

a   Built as North Vancouver Ferry No. 3; then N.B.F. No. 3
b   Built as Northern Eagle; then W.H. Gawley
c   Built as Pender Isle; then B.C.P. 51; then Northern King

crew were rescued by the US tug *Captain* but the master, Captain Jonas Hoddevik was lost. The vessel broke up and the wreckage was scattered along the beach 15 miles from Campbell River BC.

Northland Prince[a,517] 320164 On August 4, 1967 this passenger freighter, owned by Northland Shipping (1962) Co. Ltd., Vancouver BC, collided with the fishboat *Secord No. 1* in Grenville Channel. The fishboat sank about an hour afterwards. On August 30, 1967 she collided with the Alaska Steamship Line train ferry *Alaska*. Three passengers and a crew member of the *Northland Prince* were injured when the ship hit the train ferry broadside while underway in Broughton Strait off Malcolm Island northbound from Vancouver to Prince Rupert. The *Alaska* was transporting railway cars and freight between Seattle and Alaska.

Northholm[b,518] 148183 On January 16, 1943 this freighter, under command of Captain Frank McMahon, foundered and sank in a gale approximately one-mile northwest off Cape Scott BC. She was operated by Frank Waterhouse and Co. of Canada Ltd., Vancouver BC. Fifteen of her crew died and only two survived. She had been bound from Port Alice to Vancouver with a cargo of pulp at the time of the incident. She had developed a list, and when she entered a tidal rip she rapidly took on water making the vessel unmanageable. The survivors were: Ray W. Perry (Chief Officer) and Henry Gerbrandt (Quartermaster).

Northview[519] 193781 On February 23, 1961 this seiner, owned by Captain Joseph 'Joe' Katnich, Vancouver BC and operated for British Columbia Packers, foundered off Boat Bluff at the southern tip of Sarah Island and sank off Sarah Island BC. Lost were Captain Joseph Katnich, John Ivanich, Mario Katnich, Mario Cikes, Douglas Hill, Andrew Katnich, George Domijan and Anthony Fiamengo.

---

a   Built as Northland Prince; then St. Helena; then St. Helena Island; then Avalon
b   Built as Robert H. Merrick; then Northolm

Northwestern[a] 107145 This freighter was powered by a steam engine, from the previous *Caledonia* on the Skeena River. She was used chiefly in the Skeena River. In 1903 she was laid up. On August 24, 1908 she was wrecked in the Skeena River BC at Mile Forty-four. Her engines and fittings went to the *Omenica*.

Northwestern[b] 155177 (US) In 1907 she went ashore at Latorchu AK USA and was salvaged by the Salvor. On January 01, 1910 she was damaged when the steamship *Montara* went adrift in the East Waterway of Seattle Harbor. In 1910 she went ashore on San Juan Island WA. In 1912 she had electric lights installed in the vessel. On December 11, 1927 she went ashore at Cape Mudge BC and was refloated in 1928. On July 25, 1933 she went ashore on the beach at Eagle River AK. She was refloated a few days later when a high tide lifted her off with the help of a salvage tug. She served as a barracks ship at Dutch Harbor AK and in 1942 sustained a direct attack amidships by Japanese forces but was still afloat.

Nortonian[520] 130792 On May 15, 1938 this fishpacker, owned by Joseph & John Dodd, Vancouver BC, was stranded at Seal Rocks just off Point Atkinson BC. The vessel was located but her crew of two could not be found. She broke up on the rocks and became a total loss when her hull split in two.

Norwest I[c,521] 134215 On February 25, 1951 this tug, owned by Harbour Towing Co. Ltd., Vancouver BC, caught fire and burned to the waterline in Teakerne Arm BC. She sank in the early morning about 0230. Captain Donald Miller and his crew members, who had been sleeping, escaped safely by scrambling onto the log boom they had been towing. They were safely picked up by the tug *Ednorina* and taken to Lund.

---

a   Built as Caledonia; then Northwestern
b   Built as Orizaba; then Northwestern
c   Built as P.R.T. No. 1; then Norwest I

The freighter *Norwich City* with her superstructure and masts smashed after disastrously passing under the closed center span of the bridge. (Photograph from the Stuart Thompson Fonds of the City of Vancouver Archives AM1535-: CVA 99-1826)

Norwich City[a,522] On April 23, 1928 this freighter, owned by St. Just Steamship Co. Ltd. (Smith Line), St. Bideford UK, outward bound with a cargo of lumber, ran into the Second Narrows Bridge in Vancouver, BC. She had planned to pass the bridge at low water slack but was a few minutes late arriving. Some tidal eddies caused her to sheer off and she hit the north span. She cut through the eastern span of the bascule. She lost her superstructure, funnel, and masts. There was some damage to the bridge as well. She dropped her anchor and for half an hour she waited but no tug arrived. The building tidal current caught her and threatened to force her back across the bridge. Captain H Shotten in a bold and skilful manoeuvre slowly let out the anchor chain holding her into the current and let her slip back through the span without creating further damage. In the morning she was taken to the Burrard Dry Dock Company, where repairs and repainting were completed. This was the second collision of a ship with this bridge. On November 29, 1929 she was wrecked on the Pacific atoll, Nikumaroro Island (then known as Gardner Island).

---

a   Built as Normanby; then Norwich City

Nygaard[523] 156826 On September 15, 1933 this troller fishboat, owned by John Dybhavn, Prince Rupert BC, was stranded on Lawyer Island BC and then sank.

O.B. 141724 On November 30, 1933 this workboat owned by D.J. O'Brien Logging Co. Ltd., West Vancouver BC was stranded on Burwood Island near Gilford Island at the entrance to Viner Sound BC.

Ocean Girl[524] 150591 On September 18, 1970 this fishboat owned by Kenneth G. Morrison (MO), Victoria BC struck an unknown object, probably a deadhead, in Barkley Sound BC.

Ocean Gordon[a,525] 810194 On September 11, 2015 this tug capsized and sank in shallow water in Vancouver Harbour while towing a gravel barge. The crew were rescued by the Canadian Coast Guard.

Ocean Invader[526] On March 15, 1978 this fishboat apparently foundered northeast of Cape St. James in Queen Charlotte Strait in stormy weather. Six crew members were lost in the incident.

Ocean Pioneer[b] 320320 On August 18, 2017 she was filled with water and sank in Pender Harbour BC.

Ocean Plunger[c,527] 111547 On September 15, 1936 this tug, owned by Mrs William N Simpson, Vancouver BC, struck a submerged object in Indian Arm, Burrard Inlet BC. What is presumed to have been a deadhead she sank quickly in 90 feet of water. The crew had run a line ashore, but the sinking tug broke it forcing the deckhand and engineer to jump into the cold water. Captain Norman Bennett was on the boom they were towing making it safe as she sank.

---

a Built as Gulf Regent; then Ocean Gordon
b Built as Janice Ann; then Erin Jaye; then Ocean Pioneer
c Built as Lottie N.; then Ocean Plunger

Ocean Pride 194669 On February 23, 1965 this fishboat owned by Thomas D Birmingham (MO), Nanoose Bay BC struck and was stranded on Nepean Rock at the western entrance to Otter Channel BC. On February 25, 1964 she floated free of the rock and sank in 115 fathoms of water.

Ocean Space[528] On November 5, 1974 she caught fire and foundered off Sombrio Point BC. A seaplane landed beside the *Sea Pack*, to tell the crew they had seen a vessel on fire about seven miles away. When the *Sea Pack* arrived, the *Ocean Space* was on fire and KL Kirkland, the owner, was floating in a rubber life raft. The *Ocean Space* then foundered and sank.

Ocean Star[529] 198947 On January 31, 1966 this seiner sank at Cape Mudge BC, when she foundered off the mouth of the Oyster River south of Campbell River during a severe windstorm. It was thought that a severe gust combined with strong currents caused her to go over. Another theory was that she was riding high as she was carrying no cargo and was top heavy. Seven members of the crew were drowned in the incident: Captain William Mielty; Reino Aro; Anthony Kiiskila; Herbert Johnson; William Mackie, Norman MacLeod; and Engineer Roy Eilertson. The capsized boat was towed to land where it was righted with steel cables. She was towed to a repair yard on Quadra Island where she was put back into service.

Ocean Star III 310286 On May 20, 1977 this fishboat owned by Joseph P Thomas, Ahousat BC foundered at Mackay Harbour, Kyuquot BC and was a total loss.

Ocean Tide[a] 152540 In 1960 she was partially dismantled to a bare hull by Capital Iron & Metals Ltd., Victoria BC. In 1994 she sank off Goose Island when forward planks popped off the hull. The crew battled for 24 hours to save the ship before she was abandoned.

---

a   Built as La Reine; then Ocean Tide

Ocean Traveller[a] 171790 In 1942 this former fishpacker she was commissioned into the RCN Fisherman's Reserve as a harbour service auxiliary craft. In 1942 she served as a fireboat in Prince Rupert BC. On October 31, 1975 while owned by Ocean Traveller Ventures Ltd., Vancouver BC foundered and sank off Coal Harbour (VI) BC on the west coast of Vancouver Island BC with the loss of all hands.

Odeon[b,530] 097159 She was a former sealer. She had been a self-professed rum runner but was apparently unsuccessful, so she was refitted for fishing. On July 30, 1929 she burned about one- and one-half miles from Swale Rock Light.

Odny[531] 170537 On November 1, 1975 this trawler grounded in the Estevan Group (VI) BC and was a complete loss. One person was missing, and one was rescued.

Oelwein[532] 155090 On February 15, 1934 while owned by British Pacific Barge Co. Ltd., Vancouver BC she foundered 1.5 miles southeast of Hope Point BC in Howe Sound.

Ohara 141782 On July 25, 1969 this fishboat owned by William GE Laing, Sidney BC ran on the rocks at Porcher Island BC and was declared a total constructive loss.

The passenger freighter *Ohio* beginning to settle into deep water (Image from the collection of the Maritime Museum of British Columbia P3266_359)

Ohio[533] 019376 (US) The Ohio spent most of her career on the Liverpool-Philadelphia route she had originally been designed to

---

a   Built as Kuroshio; then HMCS Billow; then Kuroshio; then Miss Teresa; then Ocean Traveller
b   Built as Borealis; then Odeon

service. After 25 years of transatlantic crossings, Ohio was sold in 1898 for service in the Alaskan gold rush. On August 27, 1909 she struck a rock at Steep Point near Sarah Island BC en route from Seattle WA to Alaska. Her radio distress message of "SOS" was one of the first occasions that this term was used after its adoption. She was sailed on in a damaged condition for 30 minutes so that she could sink in shallow water in Carter Bay BC. Most of the passengers were saved but three persons were lost. George Eccles, her radio operator, had resigned the day before the voyage but took the trip as a favour to a friend. Her bow remaining from the wreck was a prominent landmark in this bay afterwards.

Divers working on the freighter *Ohio* in futile salvage attempts (Image from the collection of the Maritime Museum of British Columbia P3266_361)

Olympia III 154564 On November 23, 1932 this seiner owned by Toyojiro Nakamoto, Vancouver BC struck a submerged rock one-half mile from Vananda, on Malaspina Strait BC. (She might have used the official number 152750)

Olympia[a] 153289 On November 23, 1932 she foundered and sank off Texada Island. She was salvaged and repaired. In 1937 her register was closed, and she was licenced. On May 14, 1970, this fishboat owned by Enok Taksdale, Burnaby BC sank in Johnstone Straits off Ragged Island and was a total loss.

Omenica II 344898 On October 7, 1972 this barge owned by Finlay Forest Industries Ltd., Vancouver BC burned in Williston Lake BC.

Onerka[534] 156635 She was based in Fisheries District Number 2 (QCI and Skeena River). On July 26, 1930 she exploded when her engine

---

a   Built as Dorothy Engvick; then Olympia No. 3; then Olympia

backfired in Masset Inlet BC two miles south of the Watun River Cannery, on Graham Island BC. Rescuers were beaten back by the intense heat of the flames. The fire developed so quickly the crew (Captain Smith and Engineer D Woods) barely had time to get in the launch and row safely to the beach.

Onward Ho 124748 This Halibut trawler, owned by the British Columbia Packers Association, Richmond BC, went missing on January 8, 1916 off the Alaska coast and was presumed lost with all hands (34). Among the lost were Captain Fred Fredericksen, Mate H Hughes, Pilot Sid Ulstein, Chief Engineer Thomas Shiminin, Fireman Matthew Walker, Cook Jens Bendicksen Aas, and the following fishermen: P Andersen, H Aune, P Beck, B Benson, R Brandal, C Bravak, D Brown, E Edmunsen, O Hessen, J Knudsen, K Knudsen, H Larvik, O Longfelt, George Mackie, J March, O Olson, J S Petersen, H Rudd, B Schjie, S Simonsen, W Snow, M Stronstad, S Swanson, H Ulstein and H Westvik.

Ophiodon 348602 On June 25, 1975 this fishboat owned by Henry J & June McCullough, Shawnigan Lake BC grounded in Porlier Pass BC.

Ophir[535] 122531 On May 9, 1913 this freighter owned by the Lincoln Steamship Co., Vancouver BC was burned and sank in Canoe Pass at Ladner BC while under command of Captain J Johannsen. She was cut away from Brunswick's cannery wharf when her fire got out of control and beached on a sandbar where she was still burning the next morning. The coal in the bunkers was feeding the blaze. Lost in the fire were: W. Braid; William Hendrickson; John Hume; Cecil Price, WE Page, and a man whose identity could not be determined. She had been carrying a cargo including 200 coolers, 15 cannery machines, and 2557 boxes of tin plate.

Ordonez 126241 On March 6, 1939 this workboat owned by Frederick Kohse Jr, Kelsey Bay BC foundered and sank two miles west of Port Neville in mid-channel of Johnstone Strait BC.

Oriole[536] 077973 On November 14, 1889 this vessel was stranded at Point Grey at the entrance to Burrard Inlet and became a total loss.

Oriole V 189166 On September 5, 1958 this fishboat owned by Dermid Walker, Victoria BC foundered off Centre Island, Esperanza Inlet BC.

Orpheus[537] 019159 (US) In 1869 this ship-rigged vessel was sailing out of Boston MA USA. She was stranded in 1875 while in ballast en route from San Francisco to Nanaimo for a cargo of coal, on the southwest point of Tzartus Island. She was hit at night, by the Pacific (which sank). The steamer took away rigging on the sailing ship and the crew hailed the steamer to lay by them for assistance. No one answered and they sailed on. Sailing on themselves they mistook the Cape Beale Light for that of Cape Flattery and ran ashore. There was no loss of life and her anchors and rigging were salvaged.

Oscar[538] 103908 On January 15, 1913 under Captain Alexander McDonald the *Oscar* was a small steam freighter which suffered a fire in its coal bunkers in Nanaimo Harbour BC. She was carrying 2,000 cases of dynamite. The Captain steered her toward the beach on Protection Island where she blew up. She had been travelling from 10 Mile Point to Britannia and stopped at Nanaimo to bunker coal. Heading past Batchelor Point they spoke with an incoming ship who advised her wait because of the weather. The captain then noticed smoke coming from the engine room and made a run for Protection Island. When she hit the beach, the crew dropped a ladder, and everyone ran for the mine. The ship exploded—knocked over the mine head frame and fractured the rock so deeply that the mine below began to flood.

Ospika[539] 329579 The Transportation Safety Board of Canada reports that "On 5 November, 1996, at approximately 2045, after departing from the beach at Long Creek on Quesnel Lake, with five vehicles stowed on deck, the barge B-525, being pushed by the tug *Ospika*, capsized when approximately 150m from the beach. The vehicles fell overboard and sank. A deckhand sustained minor bruises during the accident. No pollution occurred. The overturned barge was brought back to the beach and righted two days later. "

Otter 107832 This freighter owned by William F Gibson, Clarke Gibson, James G Gibson, John Gibson, Albert Earson Gibson (JO), Ahousat BC was powered by a engine from the Rainbow. On October 9, 1915 she grounded near Sidney Island (Haro Strait) BC. In 1915 she was salvaged and repaired. On May 12, 1937 she burned at anchor in Malksope Inlet, and was destroyed, on the west coast Vancouver Island.

Otter (UK) She was a Hudson's Bay Company steamer sent in 1853 to relieve the *Beaver* of some of the volume of work under Captain Miller with Captain Herbert G. Lewis as First Officer and Charles Thorn as Engineer. She assisted the steamer *Triumph* in the survey of Gardner Inlet by the CPR and the Geological Survey of Canada. In the winter of 1880, she ran onto a rock at Bella Bella and sank. Diver Harmon of Victoria closed an open deadlight, and she was pumped out and raised. Towed to Victoria she was refitted and continued her work in the service of the Canadian Pacific Navigation Co. who used her as a coal hulk to June 1890. In June 1890 she was burned at Bentinck Island to salvage the metal in her.

Ououkinish[a,540] 151113 As the Alaska she was owned by USA interests. In 1914 she was a Canadian Government Ship purchased for the Canadian Arctic Expedition for Vilhjalmur Stefansson. She was employed in an unsuccessful attempt to drift over the North Pole. Instead the polar drift carried them to Siberia. On August 22, 1929, this fishpacker, owned by the Atlantic-Pacific Navigation Co. Ltd., Vancouver BC, was destroyed by fire off the west coast of Vancouver Island at Sea Bird Rocks BC carrying a cargo of fish. Her crew was Captain Joe Keegan, Harry Slattery (Mate) and H Lind (Engineer) was rescued.

---

a   Built as CGS Alaska; then Ououkinish

Our Best[541] 158900 On August 8, 1964 this tug was towing a cement barge when the fishboat Trim II hit the towline. The fishboat owner, Al Craig and Bert Blair a crew member were killed in the incident. A man and a woman were saved. The fishboat rolled under the barge but emerged afloat although the cabin was smashed. The Our Best's Mate, Doug Singlehurst dived into the water to rescue the victims and the two survivors were picked up by a Vancouver Police boat. On December 19, 1963 this tug, under command of Captain David McDonald, burned and sank off Whytecliff BC with the loss of the Mate, Edward Rhodes. The skipper was forced into the water and was clinging to the bow when rescuers arrived.

Ozzy R.[542] (US) This seiner was owned by Parr Reece, Seattle WA USA. On September 9, 1964 while under command of Captain John Kristovich, Ketchikan AK she collided with the tug *Ivanhoe*. She sank in 225 fathoms of water 10 miles southeast of the Ballenas Islands. She was south bound from Ketchikan at the time of the incident. The *Ivanhoe* was towing a pulp barge to Powell River at the time of the incident. The crew of seven was saved by the crew of the *Ivanhoe*.

P. Doreen 134220 On September 5, 1964 this fishboat owned by Wilf Landry, Prince Rupert BC sprang a leak and sank in heavy seas one-mile northwest of the Rose Spit buoy in Hecate Strait BC.

P.G. Bull 345172 On October 17, 1978 this tug owned by Point Grey Towing Co. Ltd., Vancouver BC foundered and sank in Plowden Bay, Howe Sound BC.

P.M. III 153372 On January 09, 1928 this tug owned by Pacific Mills Ltd., Vancouver BC burned at Martin River, Cousins Inlet BC.

P.W.D. 271[a] 193296 In the summer of 1961 this dredge owned by The Minister of Public Works, Ottawa ON allided with a wharf in a storm

---

a   Built as P.W.D. No. 253; then P.W.D. 271

at Fort Resolution and some planking popped off the hull and sand washed in causing the vessel to sink.

P.W.D. 585 170686 In 1966 this piledriver owned by The Minister of Public Works, Ottawa ON was reported to have been beached and left to decay on the banks of the Arrow Lakes BC.

P.Z. Caverhill[a,543] 155274 She was operated in rum runner shore boat service. In 1941 she was in collision with the CPR steamship *Princess Charlotte*. In 1945 owned by John Steffich (MO), Vancouver BC she collided with a US vessel in the Strait of Juan de Fuca and sank. She was salvaged and continued in active service until 2008.

Pacheena Prince[b] 173922 In 1992 this workboat sank at Bella Coola BC. She was hauled out at Clayton Falls BC at a dry sort on the beach where she fell over and was wrecked.

Pacific[544] (US) During the Cassiar Gold Rush many miners arrived in Victoria seeking transportation to San Francisco. It was later reported that they were carrying $100,000 in gold on board. The vessel took on an overload—132 passengers added to the 35 added in Puget Sound. Another estimate was 250 lost. It is thought that an additional unrecorded twenty passengers were also carried. The *Pacific* struck the sailing ship *Orpheus* causing considerable damage and did not stop to stand by the injured vessel. A survivor, Neal O'Halley (the Quartermaster) gave a vivid account of the disaster. The evacuation of the passengers into boats was chaotic and the boats capsized.

Pacific In January 30, 1879 this schooner was abandoned, and her crew was rescued and taken to San Francisco on the *R.K. Ham*. The vessel went ashore on the west coast of Vancouver Island.

---

a Built as Yurinohama, then P.Z. Caverhill, then Janet C., then Sleek
b Built as Allan S. II; then Pacheena Prince

Pacific On June 1, 1941 this tug owned by William P Armour, Prince Rupert BC was stranded in Hecate Straits BC.

Pacific Challenge[a] 320146 In 1996–2004 she was owned by Hi-Seas Marine Ltd., Belize City, Belize. At the end of her life she may have been owned by the Blue Whale Salvage & Deep Sea Towing Adventures Ltd. and renamed as *Bluewhale #7*. In 1996 the *Pacific Challenge* was towing the liner *Prince George* and an ex-US tanker to Japan for scrapping when the Prince George sank off Kodiak Alaska. On June 27, 2013, the Canadian Coast Guard informed the Administrator that the ex-tug *Pacific Challenge* was in danger of sinking at its anchorage off Pender Harbour, British Columbia. The owner reported that hull deterioration was the cause for the slow ingress of water, but that he was unable to respond to the incident. The Coast Guard Environmental Response personnel investigated and found that the derelict vessel contained approximately 25,000 litres of a mixture of diesel oil and sea water in its fuel tanks. There were 400 litres of hydraulic oil onboard, and a quantity of oily waste in the bilges. The tug owner was unable or unwilling to respond appropriately. Therefore, at the time of the report, the Coast Guard was in the process of trying to ensure that in the event the tug sank there would be no oil pollution damage to the marine environment.

Pacific Challenger[b,545] 347140 The Transportation Safety Board of Canada states that "On the night of 03/04 August 1993, the bulk carrier *Oakby* was proceeding from Vancouver, British Columbia, to the Victoria pilot station to disembark her pilot. At the same time, a fleet of fishing vessels, including the *Pacific Challenger*, was inbound to Vancouver from fishing zone No. 20. The winds were calm, and visibility was excellent. South of Trial Islands, both vessels altered course, one to starboard, the other to port, and they collided at 0206. No damage was reported by the *Oakby*. The *Pacific Challenger* sustained substantial damage and one crew member was injured."

a Built as Suderoy XVI; then Kos 51; then Toshi Maru No. 2; then Westwhale 7; then Pacific Challenge; then Jacqueline W.; then Pacific Challenge

b Built as Pacific Challenger; then Dedication

Pacific Coaster[a] 810484 The Transportation Safety Board of Canada states that "In the early hours of 02 December 1997, while bringing on board the final haul of a herring trawling voyage, the small fishing vessel "*Pacific Charmer*" slowly heeled to starboard before down flooding and sinking in about 55 metres of water in Pylades Channel, BC. The sea and weather conditions at the time were calm. Two of the vessel's crew and a Department of Fisheries and Oceans observer were rescued. The remaining two crew members succumbed to hypothermia and drowning. The vessel initially heeled to starboard because her intact transverse stability had been reduced by the cumulative detrimental effects of the weight of additional and spare fishing gear; asymmetric loading; free surface effects of liquids in partially filled tanks and fish holds; and fish waste water retained on deck. The dynamic effects of the weight of the trawl net cod-end being briefly suspended from a winch located above the wheelhouse caused a sudden rise in the vessel's virtual centre of gravity. In conjunction with the initial small heel to starboard, the dynamic effects were such that the vessel heeled further to starboard and remained briefly at an angle of about 40 degrees. Seawater shipped at this time down flooded through open weathertight doorways until all reserve buoyancy was lost and the *Pacific Charmer* sank."

Pacific Dolphin[546] 310268 On October 5, 1961 this tug, owned by Pacific Pile Driving Co. Ltd., Victoria BC, foundered near Steveston BC. She had been proceeding upriver from Tacoma WA with a wrapped bundle of pilings en route to a timber treatment plant. The tide was ebbing, and the bundle swung into a buoy and snagged. The tow hauled up short and the tug sank suddenly by the stern. The two crewmen, Captain Stephen Franks, and John Davies scrambled over the bow. They were rescued by the *Margaret McKenzie* which had been following them up the river. The *Pacific Dolphin* was raised and put back into operation.

---

a   Built as Pacific Charmer; then Pacific Coaster

Pacific Fortune[a] 194419 On April 27, 1967 this fishboat owned by Donald S Ansten (MO), Vancouver BC sank between Sooke BC and Port Renfrew BC.

Pacific Grizzly[b,547] 158914 On September 7, 1939 she was commissioned into the Royal Canadian Navy Fishermen's Reserve as HMCS *Vanisle*. In 2015 she sank at the dock in Bella Coola, was pulled out with an excavator and then broken up.

Pacific Home 370740 On April 18, 1981 this fishboat owned by Paul Ham, North Vancouver BC sank from a fire in the engine room in Imperial Eagle Channel in Barkley Sound BC.

Pacific Kingfisher[548] 801030 On October 17, 1985 this fishboat owned by Rivtow Straits Ltd., Vancouver BC capsized and foundered off Nitinat Narrows BC and sank. She was salvaged and put back into service.

Pacific No. 1 152811 On April 09, 1929 this fishboat owned by Pacific Coast Fish & Oyster Co. Ltd., Vancouver BC burned in Pilot Bay, Gabriola Island BC.

Pacific Pilot[c] 172309 On January 09, 1971 this tug owned by Hansen Towing Ltd., Campbell River BC was destroyed by fire and sank in Doctor Bay BC.

Pacific Ranger II 347837 On August 6, 1976 this gillnet fishboat owned by Inao Tabata (MO), Richmond BC burned off Gower Point near Popham Island (Georgia Strait) BC with the loss of one life. The vessel was a total loss.

---

a   Built as Lady Anne No. 1; then Pacific Fortune
b   Built as Vanisle; then HMCS Vanisle; then Vanisle; then B.C.P. 50; then Pacific Grizzly
c   Built as Harris No. 8; then Pacific Pilot

Pacific Sunset 174096 On February 3, 1965 this seiner owned by The Canadian Fishing Co. Ltd., Vancouver BC sank about 9 miles southeast by east of Esperanza Inlet BC and was total loss.

Pacific Traveller[549] 323588 Ed Lien stated "We came upon the *Pacific Traveller* capsized in Milbanke Sound the morning after that storm in 1985. (The skipper Leonard Egolf was lost.) Our divers searched her, nothing found. The deckhand was recovered nearby by a Coast Guard Cutter. He survived and lived to tell the story. The *Pacific Traveller* was towed to Shearwater. That was a terrible night with many boats and lives lost due to a storm that was not forecast.

Pacific Trident 368928 On November 11, 1980 this fishboat owned by Pacific Sunrise Fishing Co. Ltd., Victoria BC had a fire in her accommodation while in Hecate Strait BC.

Pacific Unity[550] (UK) On January 6, 1958 this British freighter was in collision with the *Strath*, which sank, two miles from the North Arm Jetty in Georgia Strait BC. The British freighter picked up the 7-man crew of the tug a few minutes later. They were then transferred to the tug *Iron Belle* to a rendezvous with the tug *Green Point* off Jericho Beach where an injured man was taken to hospital.

Pacific Venture[a,551] 192079 She was once billed as the "largest fishing vessel in British Columbia". In 1964 she was in service seining, dragging and halibut fishing. On March 22, 1975 she foundered and sank carrying a full cargo of 250 tons of herring off Estevan Point on the west coast of Vancouver Island. Her crew of six was safely picked up by the *Wind Song 8*.

Pacific Wave 198632 On February 17, 1958 this seiner while owned by Pacific Wave Co. Ltd., Vancouver BC was stranded on Hammer Rock BC. On October 15, 1991 while owned by Robert M Duncan, Campbell

---

a   Built as a USN YMS; then Tahsis King; then Tahsis Straits; then Pacific Venture

River BC she grounded and sank on Quartertide Rocks in Port San Juan BC.

Pacinaco I 101334 On January 31, 1959 this fishpacker owned by William Smith, Victoria BC experienced a fire in Hotham Sound BC on the middle mainland coast.

Pacinaco I[a,552] 131034 In October-November 1931 she operated as a rum runner, under Captain DJ MacDonald and Mate Jack Wolf. She was converted for use as a fishpacker at the Celtic Cannery in the north arm of the Fraser River for British Columbia Packers Ltd., Vancouver BC. On August 29, 1949 she went aground between Sechelt and Halfmoon Bay BC. She was pulled off the beach by the tug *La Belle* later in the day.

Pacinaco II[b,553] 154567 In 1930 she was reported to have been a rum runner. On August 27, 1931 while owned by owned by Clyde Reed she burned one-half mile north of Lang Bay, Malaspina Strait BC.

Paige No. 2[c] 154367 On December 15, 1957 this seiner sank off Cape Mudge, Quadra Island BC while en route from Bella Bella.

Packmore 4000[d,554] 348554 The Transportation Safety Board of Canada reports that "On the evening of 20 December 2003, the pleasure craft *Mistral*, with the owner/operator and 12 adult guests on board, was part of an annual event with two other vessels to celebrate the holiday season on the Fraser River near Mission. Shortly after separating from the other vessels, the *Mistral* collided with the deck barge *Packmore 4000* under tow by the tug *Tiger Shaman*. The *Mistral* was destroyed upon impact and its occupants were thrown into the water. The crew of the tug recovered 12 survivors. One person drowned.

---

a   Built as Donacella; then Chasam III; then Pacinaco I
b   Built as Chasam III; then Pacinaco II
c   Built as Eva D.; then Paige No. 2
d   Built as Packmore 4000; then Bagheera Bahay

Pal III 313784 On February 15, 1967 this workboat owned by James WR Whyte, Vancouver BC caught fire while unattended in Deas Slough on the Fraser River BC.

Palmarsyl[a,555] 130856 On October 9, 1959 while owned by Lindsay E Moir, North Vancouver BC, she foundered and sank seven miles north of Race Point, in Georgia Strait BC. The skipper, Captain Rod Fredericks, and his crew were rescued from a lifeboat.

Pamela[b] 154856 On April 26, 1970 this fishboat owned by John Prokopchuk (MO), Port Alberni BC foundered and sank near Pachena Lighthouse, Cape Beale BC.

Panther[556] (US) On January 17, 1874 this collier, owned by Pope & Talbot Sawmill, Port Gamble WA USA, after sailing from Nanaimo BC in tow of the tug *Goliah* hit a reef off Saltspring Island BC near Panther Point on Wallace Island while carrying 1750 tons of coal for San Francisco CA. She was declared a total loss of $25,000. In August, the wreck was sold to James Waterman, Portland OR by CJ Gilbert who retained a one-quarter share. In November CJ Gilbert dissolved his partnership with James Waterman, B Chilson and J Deyer.

Papco XIII (US) She was registered at Bellingham WA USA. On May 31, 1954 she was grounded and sank approximately one-half east of Point Young BC.

Paragon No. 1[557] 176669 On March 8, 1974 this converted fishpacker foundered in heavy seas off Kitson Island BC (8 miles south of Prince Rupert). She was carrying 28 tons of herring. Her crew of two was found dead: John Wick, and Ron Peterson.

---

a   Built as Lo Oltbee; then Palmarsyl
b   Built as Bimbo; then Pamela

Parthenon[a] 154536 On September 21, 1967 this seiner owned by H. Bell-Irving & Co., Vancouver BC sank in Johnstone Strait BC.

Partow[b] 194357 She was built as a workboat. In September 1973, she was owned by Freill Lake Logging Ltd., Vancouver BC and she sank in Rasy Inlet BC.

Pass of Melfort[558] 098683 On December 28, 1905 while travelling from Panama to Port Townsend she was driven ashore near (1/4 mile east) Amphitrite Point on the Ucluth Peninsula with the loss of all hands (35). The British four-masted steel bark *Pass of Melfort*, Captain Harry Scougall, from Ancon for Puget Sound, drove ashore on the rocks of Vancouver Island a quarter of a mile east of Amphitrite Point on the night after Christmas, and all on board were lost. The vessel was making for the entrance to the Strait of Juan de Fuca when a southwest gale drove her to the lee shore of Vancouver Island, where she smashed into the rocks with terrific force, breaking up soon afterward. Several her crew were stricken with malarial fever when she was lying at Ancon, and it was believed she came in short handed, with insufficient able-bodied men to handle her in the storm which she encountered off the Cape. In all, she carried a crew of 35, many of the bodies drifting ashore with the wreckage, being taken to Victoria by the salvage steamer *Salvor*.

Passing Cloud[559] 172522 On February 9, 1949 she foundered two miles off Cape Caution (QCI) BC. The three of the crew were saved in a small boat, but Captain GG (Buster) Brown was drowned. He was wearing heavy clothing and no life preserver and is thought to have suffered a heart attack.

Pastime 121759 In 1911 she sank in Sechelt Harbour BC near Selma Park. The crew was rescued.

---

a   Built as West River; then La Paloma; then Parthenon
b   Built as Zuleka II; then Partow

Patricia 255532 (US) On August 26, 1955 she burned at Preedy Harbour, Thetis Island BC.

Paulina II[a] 197692 On September 6, 1945 she was in collision with the *Martha II*, one-mile northwest of Klewnuggit light in Grenville Channel BC.

Pearl Harbor 154701 On September 21, 1952 this fishboat struck a submerged object and sank in Finlayson Channel BC.

Peggy B.[560] 150552 On January 13, 1926 while owned by the Smith Dollar Timber Co., Vancouver BC she burned at Lyall Point in Toquart Bay BC.

Peggy McNeil[561] 150276 On September 23, 1923 this tug under command of Captain Robert T Derever was lost when she was capsized by her tow in the Gulf of Georgia BC near Porlier Pass with the loss of five lives. The two empty scows were suddenly swung around by the current and the towline got underneath the tug causing her to capsize. The only survivor, W Ingram (the Mate), secured the scows to trees on shore and got a ride to Nanaimo on a fisherman's launch. Lost were Gus Young (Chief Engineer); A Johnson (Second Engineer); Mr McDougall (Cook); and E Manders (Deckhand).

Peggy Nell On October 13, 1983 this troller fishboat struck an object and sank west of Tofino BC.

Pelican[562] This freighter, owned by the Northern Pacific Line, departed Port Townsend for the Taku Bar in 1897 and was never seen again. Some years later the Master of the San Francisco fishing schooner Hermann found a floating bottle containing a note written by the *Pelican*'s Chief Officer Patterson. It read, "Steamer *Pelican* latitude 50 north, longitude 175 west—the ship is sinking. We are leaving her in boats. Please report us." Nothing more was found.

---

a   Built as J.O. Edwards; then Skardale; then West Hawk; then Paulina II

Pelican[563] 268035 (US) This cannery tender was registered at Seattle WA USA. On April 28, 1955, while en route for Juneau, she was stranded on a reef 4 miles north of Camp Point Light near Davenport Point on Grenville Channel BC. The crew of five men and the wife of the Captain were taken off by the American fishboat *Luna*, bound for Ketchikan. A fire broke out following the grounding.

Pelican 1[564] 170068 (US) She was laid down as the *State of Oregon* but launched as the *Oregon*. The builder was a subsidiary of the Alaska Pacific Navigation Co. which was leasing the Nilson & Kelez yard. She was a freighter, primarily used to transport goods between Washington and Alaska. In 1939–1941 she was laid up at Seattle WA. In 1946 the vessel was blown up and the wreck drifted up on the beach at Nissen Bight, at Cape Scott.

Percy W.[a,565] 154915 Bryon Taylor stated that "She formed part of the pre-war Fishermen's Reserve Fleet and participated in the 30 January—25 February 1939 Fishermen's Reserve Training Session. She was however not mobilized for active duty during the Second World War." On April 28, 1970, this fishboat owned by Nelson Bros. Fisheries Ltd., Vancouver BC grounded and broke up on Rose Spit, Hecate Strait BC.

Petersfield[566] The Transportation Safety Board of Canada reports that: "On 25 September 2009, at 2246 PDT, the open hatch bulk carrier *Petersfield* experienced a malfunction of its gyro heading feed and struck the west shore of Douglas Channel, BC. The vessel sustained extensive damage to its bulbous bow, forepeak, and collision bulkhead. There were no injuries or pollution and the vessel returned to Kitimat, BC under its own power."

Petrel[567] 121974 On December 27, 1952 this tug, under Captain Don Horie, left Vancouver for the booming ground at Gowlland Harbour with threatening weather. She sailed up the Georgia Strait and

---

a   Built as Port Essington No. II; then Percy W.

approached Cape Mudge around midnight in a southeast gale with flood tide from the north. The tug met a "vicious combination of dangerous tide rip, strong southeast wind, and heavy seas". The sea overwhelmed the tug and on December 27, 1952 and she foundered and sank in 70 fathoms just south of Cape Mudge, Quadra Island BC. She sank so quickly that there was no time for a radiotelephone distress call or to lower the boats. Seven lives were lost.

Pezuta[568] 152905 On December 11, 1928 she broke adrift while under tow by the tug *Imbricaria* (Dominion Tug & Barge Ltd. She was en route to Skidegate Inlet. She broke her tow line and was stranded at Tlell River, Queen Charlotte Islands BC. Her crew of eight landed safely in a lifeboat.

Phantom[569] (US) On November 11, 1893 she left Victoria BC for Saanich BC when in a gale she hit a tidal rip and capsized off Gordon Head and sank. The crew members were saved but the vessel was a total loss.

Phantom Lady VI 189242 On September 6, 1958 this vessel owned by Phillip H Peterson, Campbell River BC burned 1.5 miles north of Campbell River BC.

Pharaon[a] 126952 On May 22, 1917 this tug owned by Ocean Foods Ltd., Vancouver BC foundered in the Queen Charlotte Islands BC.

Pheasant 111952 In 1906 she took a contract to remove rocks from the "Beaver Dam" and the Hornet's Nest" on the Skeena River. In 1906 she was wrecked at Beaver Dam Rapids near Skeena Crossing Bridge on the Skeena River BC. On June 10, 1917 it is stated that she was stranded in Prince Rupert Harbour BC. Norman V Bennett (1997) states that she was wrecked at Redrock Canyon near the site of the Skeena Crossing Bridge and was a total loss.

---

a   Built as Petrel; then Pharaon

Phoebe J. 314035 On February 3, 1972 this fishboat owned by Alf E Jensen (MO), Tofino BC exploded, burned, and sank at Lennard Island BC.

Phyllis F. 157124 On December 13, 1957 this vessel owned by John G Wenman, Victoria BC burned at the north end of Sansum Narrows BC.

Phyllis G. II 176258 On December 13, 1948 this vessel owned by Vadem G Stavrakov, Vancouver BC foundered near Port Renfrew BC.

Picnic 126622 On March 3, 1910 this workboat owned by Ernest Easthope, Vancouver BC burned 17 miles above Lund, in Lewis Channel BC.

Pilot 072674 (US) She was seized in 1891 at Port Angeles for towing a US ship in US waters. Released on payment of a small fine. She was converted to a barge. She was in collision with the tug *Velos* in March 1895.

Pine Isle 815155 On January 4, 2013, the Canadian Coast Guard (CCG) informed the Administrator that a small vessel, *Pine Isle*, had sunk at Silva Bay, Gabriola Island, BC. The vessel sank overnight on December 31 while at anchor and was discharging oil. The vessel was reported to be abandoned and the owner could not be found.

Pioneer[570] On September 27, 1898 this fishing schooner was missing in the North Pacific. She sailed from Quatsino and failed to return home. The relatives of the First Nations crew members were performing mourning rituals when they learned from the Nahwitti band of the ship sighted at sea with skeletons lashed in the rigging.

Plouton 368755 On May 14, 1978 this fishboat owned by Peter P Karvounis, Ladner BC suffered a fire in the engine room at Moorehouse Bay, Return Channel BC. She burned to the waterline and was declared as a total loss at the time.

Plunger[a] 131152 On November 19, 1972 this tug owned by Weldwood Transportation Ltd., Vancouver BC sank off Raza Island BC while yarding a tow. The crew was alerted to the flooding in the engine room after the stove went out.

Pocroluco 137956 In July 1926 this fishboat owned by The Canadian Fishing Co. Ltd., Vancouver BC burned in Portland Inlet BC.

Point Ellice 130897 In 1913 she was in collision with the *Princess Charlotte* outside Vancouver harbour. In 1920 she was put on the Vancouver to Squamish barge service. In 1957 she was rendered unnecessary by construction of the Second Narrows Bridge. In 1957 she was sold to Capital Iron & Metals Ltd., Victoria BC for scrapping.

Point Grey 130917 In 1911–1949 this tug was owned by The Minister of Public Works, Ottawa ON. On March 03, 1949 she was wrecked in Porlier Pass BC after running onto Virago Rock in heavy fog. She was strip-salvaged by divers.

Point Grey Boy[b] 193795 On December 23, 1971 this tug owned by Point Grey Towing Co. Ltd., Vancouver BC was destroyed by fire and sank in Long Bay, Gambier Island BC and was a total loss.

Point Grey Pal[c] 153166 On August 13, 1954 this tug owned by Lorne Hurschman (MO), Vancouver BC sank about two miles off Passage Island at the entrance to Howe Sound BC.

Point Hope[d] 130310 On March 7, 1979 this ex-tug owned by Robert Jordan (MO), Vancouver BC and McDuff Holdings Ltd., Vancouver BC was destroyed by fire east of Sheringham Point BC in an engine room fire.

---

a Built as Plunger; then Gillfoam; then Plunger
b Built as Jim Hughes; then Point Grey Boy
c Built as Eriks No. 1; then Sea Pal; then Point Grey Pal
d Built as Prospective; then Point Hope

Polar Fury[a] 150554 She acted as ferry to James Island BC from Saanichton to service the powder works there. Later she was used for towing logs to Sooke BC. Mike Wright[571] reported that "She sank in Cowichan Bay under mysterious circumstances and was not salvaged."

Porcher 66[572] On December 3, 1954 this fishboat was swamped by heavy seas and sank at Ryan Point, Metlakatla BC. Two members of the crew, Ralph Clayton and Percy Stanley were lost. A third crewman clung to the mast of the boat for 16 hours before he was rescued.

Porcher G. 172326 In 1941 she was seized from her Japanese owners by the Canadian Government. In 1942 her ownership transferred to His Majesty the King. In October 1963 she was stranded at Union Bay BC and later salvaged. On January 13, 2014, the Canadian Coast Guard (CCG) informed the Administrator that the 45-foot ex-fishing vessel *Porcher G* had sunk and was discharging oil at Campbell River, British Columbia.

Port Douglas 126885 She was a tug owned by Brooks-Scanlon Lumber Co. Ltd., Vancouver BC. On February 4th, 1923 she sank in the Harrison River BC while towing a Cottonwood log boom down the river. As she started to sink, she was beached in shallow water.

Premier[b] 100793 Capacity 300 day-passengers, and staterooms for 79. In 1892 she collided with the *Willamette* and was beached at Bush Point, then towed to Victoria. In 1902 she made her 3000th voyage. In 1907, as the *Charmer*, she was involved in a collision with CPR trans-Pacific steamer *Tartar* (both vessels heavily damaged). In 1916 she rammed and sank the CGS *Quadra* in fog off Nanaimo. In 1933 she served as a dressing room for bathers at Newcastle Island. In 1935 she was dismantled, the hull was burned at Albert Head, Victoria BC.

---

a   Built as Polar Forcite; then Polar Fury
b   Built as Premier; then Charmer

President Roxas[573] In autumn fog 1969 this freighter collided in dense fog with the Norwegian freighter *Mosgulf* about 15 miles off Sheringham Point. She received a smashed bow Both vessels proceeded under their own power to Vancouver BC and sustained minor bow damage.

Primrose No. 1 177972 On July 12, 1965 this fishboat owned by William Cowpar, Queen Charlotte BC caught fire on the beach at Masset BC and was a total loss.

Prince Andrew 311869 She was seized in a drug bust in the early 1990s. In 1999 she sank in Massett Harbour (QCI) where she lay derelict on the beach.

Prince George[574] 179563 In 1952 she went aground at Ripple Point in Johnstone Strait (Captain EB Caldwell) in heavy fog suffering minor damage. She was laid up in Howe Sound for several years. On February 2, 1954 at 0630 under Captain WE Eccles she struck rocks near North Bluff in Seymour Narrows forcing her to turn back to Vancouver with serious underwater damage. She was escorted back by the big salvage tug *Salvor*. She had been en route for Ocean Falls, Prince Rupert, and Ketchikan with 232 passengers and crew on board. Captain Eccles ordered the lifeboats swung out in case they were needed at short notice. In 1975 she was outfitting at Victoria for what was expected to be her final Alaska cruise season. She suffered $400,000 in damages and the cruise season was suspended. She was subsequently purchased by the provincial government with the intention of joining her with the *Princess Marguerite*. Following a change in government she was sold to Wong Brothers for operation as a restaurant in Nanaimo BC. In 1995 she was burned out by two mysterious fires. In October 1996 she was towed to Taiwan for breaking-up by the tug *Pacific Challenge* in tandem with the USS *Kishwaukee* (AOG.9) but sank at Dutch Harbour, Unalaska Island AK USA.

Prince Rupert 122323 On August 07, 1907 this freighter owned by John Davis and Robert Jeffrey (JO), both of Vancouver BC foundered at Sechelt BC.

The *Prince Rupert* high and dry (Image from the collection of the Maritime Museum of British Columbia 000106)

Prince Rupert[575] 129743 In 1917 this passenger steamer collided with the tug *Cleeve* in Burrard Inlet near the Grand Trunk wharf. On September 20, 1920 she struck a reef four miles north of Swanson Bay in fog. She was beached where the passengers disembarked. The ship sank in deep water. The Pacific Salvage Co. tug *Algerine* with two 4,100-ton barges built a coffer dam around her and divers patched the hull. She was refloated and taken to Bullen's Shipyard for repair. On September 4, 1935 she was in collision with the *Anna J.* in Seymour Narrows BC. In 1956 she was broken up.

Prince Rupert (HMCS) K.324 (RCN) At the end of the Second World War she was laid up in the ship boneyard at Bedwell Bay in Indian Arm BC. In 1948 she was scuttled as a hulk in the breakwater at Royston BC.

Princess Adelaide[a] 126948 On July 10, 1910 she was sponsored by Mrs A Piers (wife of the Manager of CPR Steam Ship lines). In 1911 she was put into Victoria-Vancouver service. On October 13, 1918 she grounded on Georgina Point, Mayne Island BC and was assisted by the tug *Nitinat*. In 1928 she was in collision with *Hampholm*, towed to Vancouver for repairs. In 1948 she was withdrawn from service. In 1967 she was withdrawn from service and wrecked on the coast of Italy.

---

a   Built as Princess Adelaide; then Angelika

Princess Beatrice[576] On September 10, 1903 she was sponsored by Mrs F Bullen (wife of the owner of the Esquimalt Marine Railway Co.) On February 9, 1921, this vessel was running north when at 3:00 am she ran on rocks at Steep Island in Sabine Channel near Bull Passage. The *Princess Patricia* was sent to pick up the passengers. In 1904 she was put on Victoria – Seattle service. In 1928 she was stripped and scuttled by Charlie Klein as a breakwater at Mouat Bay (Texada Island) BC.

Princess Charlotte[a] 126236 In 1909 she was put into Vancouver-Victoria service. In 1925 on Alaska cruise service. In 1927 she ran aground near Wrangell Alaska. In 1935 she collided with the *Chelhosin*. In 1940 she hit rocks in Tolmie Channel. In 1941 she collided with the Provincial Forestry vessel *Caverhill*. In 1949 she was laid up at Thetis Cove BC. In 1965 she was broken up at Perema Greece.

Princess Elaine[577] 154739 In 1928 she arrived in Victoria via Panama Canal. In 1928 she was placed on Vancouver – Nanaimo service. In 1936 she was stranded on Gallows Point in fog. In 1955 she collided with the barge VT 25 at the entrance to Vancouver Harbour. On November 12, 1942, the passenger freighter *Lady Pam* collided with the *Princess Elaine* outside the Lions Gate Bridge. In 1960 she collided with the *Alaska Prince*. In 1962 she was withdrawn from service. In 1964 she opened in Blaine as a floating restaurant. In 1967 she was closed, sold, and moved to a marina in West Seattle again as a floating restaurant. In 1977 she was scrapped at Seattle WA by John Jack Gargan in Lake Union.

Princess Joan[b] 156465 In 1930–1960 she was owned by Canadian Pacific Steamships, Montreal QC. On October 5, 1930 she collided with the *Bamfield* on her first rum running trip which sank while leaving Victoria harbour two miles northeast of Discovery Island. On September 15, 1932 she collided with the *Hiker II* about one-half mile northeast of the Point Grey Buoy in Burrard Inlet BC. On

---

a Built as Princess Charlotte; then Mediterranean
b Built as Princess Joan; then Hermes

October 12, 1943 she collided with the *Squid* which was carrying 400 cases of dynamite from James Island BC to the Britannia Mine and the *Squid* sank off Point Grey BC. In 1959 she made her final night crossing Vancouver – Victoria BC. In 1959 she was withdrawn from service. In 1961 she was in service on Venice-Piraeus-Haifa run. In 1973 she was used as accommodation for North Sea oil workers at Nigg Bay, Inverness Scotland. In 1974 she was used as an accommodation vessel at Jeddah Saudi Arabia.

Collision damage suffered by the *Princess Louise* (Image from the collection of the Maritime Museum of British Columbia 3_000111)

Princess Louise[a] 072682 She was built with a walking beam engine. In 1884 she was registered at Victoria BC. She was briefly involved in carrying ore to Tacoma WA. In 1919 while owned by Whalen Pulp & Paper Mills, Port Alice BC she sank at Port Alice.

Princess Louisa Inlet[b] 176485 On December 18, 1955 this passenger vessel owned by George L Murray, Vancouver BC burned and sank in Pendrell Sound, BC.

Princess Marguerite 150910 In 1925 she made her maiden sailing to Vancouver BC. On March 6, 1930 she collided with the H.O. No. 5 at 1.5 miles north of Kelp Reefs, Haro Strait BC. In 1939 she carried King George VI from Victoria BC to Vancouver BC during the Royal Visit. In 1941 she was requisitioned for war service as a troopship. In 1942 she was torpedoed by the German submarine U-83 en route to Port Said from Cyprus with the loss of 49 lives.

---

a   Built as Olympia; then Princess Louise
b   Built as HMC ML Q.128; then HMC M.L. 128; then Princess Louisa Inlet

Princess Norah[a] 154848 In 1930 she struck rocks off Colt Island (North of Ketchikan AK) sustaining serious underwater damage. In 1931 she was stranded at Port Renfrew BC. In 1931 she touched bottom in Man Pass AK. In 1943 she was grounded at Zero Rock, James Island BC. In 1944 she collided with fish packer *Co-operator I*. In 1946 she was grounded near Comox harbour. In 1955 she was put in joint service with CNR to Kitimat. In 1957 the joint service was withdrawn. The Kodiak Maritime Museum[578] reports that "In 1964 she was towed to Kodiak Alaska by Walter Le Grue for conversion to a restaurant and dancehall. In January 1976 however, with maintenance costs rising and the ship falling into disrepair, the Le Grues closed the bar and hotel, and after several failed deals to sell it, shut it up for good. Le Grue had the hull scrapped in the late 1980s. Some of the steel went to shore up the bulkheads at TT Fuller's boat yard on the channel. The keel and bow stem remained in the ground, cut off at ground level and mostly buried beneath what is now the Salvation Army parking lot on Mission Road."

Princess Royal[579] 121988 On January 15, 1922 this passenger ship was in a collision in dense fog with the tug *Clinton* near the entrance of First Narrows, Vancouver Harbour which caused the *Clinton* to founder in Burrard Inlet BC. The crew of the *Clinton* climbed up onto the bow of the steamer to save themselves from the sinking tugboat. Captain of the *L.H. Fraser* was the last to leave the tug.

The *Princess Sophia* stranded on Vanderbilt Reef in Lynn Channel just prior to her disastrous sinking. (Image from the collection of the Maritime Museum of British Columbia 000324)

Princess Sophia 130620 This vessel was the focus of one of the most notorious marine disasters on the Pacific coast. On October 23, 1918, this Canadian Pacific passenger steamer departed

---

a   Built as Princess Norah; then Queen of the North; then Canadian Prince; then Beachcomber

from Skagway AK en route to Vancouver and Victoria. During an early morning storm, she ran aground on Vanderbilt Reef. Rescue vessels arrived quickly and stood off the distressed ship calculating a way to safely evacuate the passengers and crew. The stormy weather increased in ferocity and the rescuers departed to take shelter. During the night, the ship broke up and disappeared into the water, leaving only the mast to show her location. All 353 persons on board perished.

Procter[a] 107724 In 1899 she was in service towing railcar barges Nelson to Kootenay Landing. In 1921 she was withdrawn from service. In 1929 she was scuttled in Kootenay Lake BC.

Progressive[b] 122158 In 1917 this tug towed the first Davis log raft across Hecate Straits. In 1970 she burned in a fire that started in the galley while in Pendrell Sound BC as an oyster barge. John Dolmage[580] stated that "Our old *Progressive* was owned by Pacific Towing when she last worked and then Wes Perry bought her and turned her into a barge for his oyster operations in Pendrell Sound along with the old Burnett. They all burned up and sank in December 1970. There were two days where Wes had no insurance as he was switching brokers and that's when they burned!"

Prospect Point[581] 150432 On September 21, 1925 this tug owned by Harry Bruno, Vancouver BC burned to the waterline when her engine backfired while off the Traill Islands BC. They were bound for Hotham Sound for a tow of logs at the time of the incident. The crew fought the fire for two hours. The two-man crew evacuated in a lifeboat and although the area was brightly lit from the blaze a steamer passed them without responding to their calls for assistance. They then rowed to Sechelt.

Prospect Point[582] 383442 The Transportation Safety Board of Canada reports that "During the afternoon of 29 October 2004,

---

a   Built as Ymir; then Procter
b   Built as Progressive; then D.A. Evans; then Progressive

the commercial fishing vessel Prospect Point, with a crew of five on board, was fishing for sardines, in Kyuquot Sound, off the west coast of Vancouver Island, British Columbia. After pursing in the net, while the crew was in the process of preparing to haul in the catch of sardines, the vessel heeled to starboard and capsized, forcing all the crew members into the water. The crew members were recovered and landed on board a coastal freighter anchored in the vicinity. The vessel was subsequently recovered and towed to Steveston, British Columbia. No injury was reported."

Pullaway[583] 171781 On February 7, 1968 she was destroyed by fire at Long Bay, Howe Sound BC and was a total loss. The crew were asleep in their bunks when they awoke to find their bunk on fire, apparently caused by the galley stove. Her crew of two (Captain Ray Young and Alvin Schochenmaier) leaped to safety on the 16-section log boom they were towing.

Pull-Over 173715 On July 23, 1947 she burned and exploded at Glagia Creek, Jervis Inlet BC.

Puri M. 153409 On September 24, 1957 she struck a submerged object and sank near Bowen Island BC.

Puritan (US) On the night of November 13, 1895 the *Puritan* (a four-masted auxiliary schooner) was sailing out of San Francisco CA USA. She was sailing to load lumber at Pot Gamble WA USA. The captain lost his bearings possibly because the Carmanah Lighthouse was obscured by fog. She became stranded near Bonilla Point and waves carried way the ship's boats. Without boats the only safe way to shore was via a lifeline. Frank Knighton approached in a canoe but was prevented from taking a line. Starting from the beach he waded out with a line which was held on the beach by his wife. For several hours he tried to throw a fishing line leader to the ship and eventually the line was received by the crew. The crew were saved by a lifeline rigged from shore to the ship by them displaying a great sense of resourcefulness and determination. Once ashore the were looked after by the couple in their home. Frank Knighton and his wife (First Nations people) were awarded a money prize of $100 from the US Government for their part in the rescue. Later Knighton was awarded a medal by the British Government.

Pyeluco 154355 On March 11, 1931 she exploded between Marpole Bridge and the railroad bridge in front of gravel dock on the North Arm of the Fraser River.

Q.C. Timber[584] On May 06, 1975 this workboat owned by Q.C. Timber Ltd. capsized at Marble Island QCI. Two crew members (Roy Gerhardt and Don Mercer) were missing, and Eric Turk was killed.

Quadra[585] 096899 She came to British Columbia via the Strait of Magellan under Captain Walbran. In 1892 she struck the Quadra Rocks in the Houston Stewart Channel Queen Charlotte Islands while on a cruise to the Bering Sea in support of the sealing industry under relief skipper Captain James Gaudin. In 1897 she rescued two survivors of the *Cleveland* near Clayoquot Sound. In 1906 she rescued the survivors of the bark *Colima* wrecked at Cape Beale BC. In 1907 she was fitted with wireless equipment. On February 26, 1917 she was in a collision with the *Charmer* on a foggy day at the entrance to Nanaimo Harbour. The *Quadra* was towed to shallow water where she sank with only a portion of her superstructure and rigging left visible at high tide. The wreck was sold to the Britannia Mine Co. who salvaged her for use in the Howe Sound – Tacoma ore trade. On September 24, 1924 she sailed from Vancouver with 12,000 cases of liquor and was seized by the USCGC *Shawnee*. In 1924 she was scrapped.

Quathiaski[586] 134070 On May 17, 1965 this seiner owned by Slavko Tobako, Vancouver BC burned and sank one mile east of Point Upwood BC in Georgia Strait and was a total loss. The fire started in the engine room. Her crew of four were rescued after taking the skiff to escape the flames. They were picked up by the *Ruby Allen*. She had been fishing off the southern end of Texada Island.

Quatse II 173613 On April 26, 1968 she burned and sank at Plowden Bay, in Howe Sound and was a total loss.

Quatsino[a,587] 179614 Lonnie Edward Berrow reported that "In the 1990s she cut between a tug and tow in Seymour Narrows and was hit by the barge. They ran her for the beach in Plumper Bay but didn't make it and she sank in deep water." John Demosten states that "This was prior to 1990, because the *Western Express* had an engine room fire in March of 1990. This accident occurred sometime in August, on a Sunday night, either in 1986 or 1987. Rick Johnson was the master on the *Western Express* and was in Deep Water Bay with seine boats on either side. The *Quatsino* stern was severely damaged by a barge being towed by a southbound Crowley tug. Johnson stopped pumping, disconnected all the brailers, picked up his anchor and ran out to put bridles and a tow line onto the *Quatsino*. He began to tow her towards Deep Water Bay, but she started taking on water. There was nothing he could do but let his towline go. The *Quatsino* had quite a history and Hank Auchterlonie took her back east in the early 1970s with three BC Packer seine boats in tow."

Queen[588] (US) On September 16, 1922 this American freighter, owned by the Admiral Line, was stranded in dense fog at Whytecliff Island ledge. Her passengers were rescued by the Union Steamship *Venture*. The *Venture* got so close that the passengers and crew of the *Queen* crossed over on a gangplank. Her cargo of salmon was transferred to the *Admiral Rodman* later in the day and at high tide she was pulled off the ledge.

Queen City[589] 103842 In November 1901 this freighter picked up the rescued crew of the bark *Highland Light* from the sealing schooner *Arilla* at Estevan Point and carried them to Victoria. On September 09, 1916 she burned out at Victoria BC. On November 11, 1920 while under tow a gas tank exploded, and the hull burned. In 1920 she was rebuilt as a barge.

Queen City[590] 121980 In 1899 she brought the survivors of the wrecked Peruvian bark *Libertad* to Victoria BC. Charles Bruce was the Chief Engineer—and he sold a half interest to John Isbester,

---

a   Built as USS SC-1045; then Quatsino

Victoria BC. On April 11, 1928 she sank after striking a rock, while both owners were aboard, at Cracroft Island, Lewis Channel BC.

Queen of Alberni[591] 370066 On August 9, 1979 this car and passenger ferry ran aground in Active Pass. The captain steered too close to the shore to avoid another ferry coming from the opposite direction. As the tide fell the vessel threatened to capsize. Vehicles crashed together. In 1984 an extra car deck was added. The Transportation Safety Board of Canada reports that "On 12 March 1992, the Canadian ferry *Queen of Alberni*, under the conduct of the master, departed from Tsawwassen, British Columbia, bound for Nanaimo, British Columbia, and the Japanese bulk carrier *Shinwa Maru*, under the conduct of a British Columbia coast pilot, departed from Roberts Bank Terminal (Westshore Terminals) en route to the Victoria Pilot Station. Approximately one nautical mile south-west of Tsawwassen Ferry Terminal the vessels collided in daylight, with calm weather conditions and visibility reduced by fog."

Queen of Coquitlam[592] 370060 On October 19, 1980 this car and passenger ferry fell over while inside the floating Burrard Drydock, Vancouver BC when a support gave way. Seawater flooded her engine room, and she was left leaning against one was of the drydock, threatening to roll further over.

Queen of Hawaii 150426 On September 15, 1931 this schooner owned by Captain Bode burned two miles due west of Highest Island, Schooner Entrance, Kyuquot Sound BC.

Queen of Prince Rupert[a,593] 323870 On August 11, 1967 this car and passenger ferry grounded in fog on Haddington Reef near Alert Bay BC. About 300 passengers were evacuated and taken ashore at Alert Bay. On November 16, 1980 she began operation to the Queen Charlotte Islands. On August 25, 1982 she grounded in Gunboat Passage while en route to Port Hardy. After she was refloated, she

---

a   Built as Victoria Princess; then Queen of Prince Rupert; then Lomaiviti Princess off loaded her passengers at Bella Bella. The ship was refloated and proceeded to Port Hardy.

Queen of Saanich[a,594] 318669 The Transportation Safety Board of Canada states that "At 0818, February 06, 1992, in light airs, calm sea and fog, the catamaran passenger ferry "*Royal Vancouver*" and the British Columbia Ferry Corporation vehicle/passenger ferry *Queen of Saanich* collided head-on off Georgina Point at the northern entrance to Active Pass, British Columbia. On board the *Royal Vancouver*, which was extensively damaged, 19 passengers and 4 crew members were injured. The bow doors of the *Queen of Saanich* were also damaged."

Queen of Storm[b] 138781 In 1919 she was the tender to the fish traps at Sooke BC owned by the Sooke Harbour Fishing and Packing Co. On September 1, 1933 she was stranded at Race Rocks BC. In 1992 she was burned in a fire in the Fraser River.

Queen of the North[c,595] 368854 At 2000 on 21 March 2006, the passenger and vehicle ferry *Queen of the North* departed Prince Rupert, British Columbia, for Port Hardy, British Columbia. On board were 59 passengers and 42 crew members. After entering Wright Sound from Grenville Channel, the vessel struck the northeast side of Gil Island at approximately 0021 on March 22. The vessel sustained extensive damage to its hull, lost its propulsion, and drifted for about 1 hour and 17 minutes before it sank in 430 m of water. Passengers and crew abandoned the vessel before it sank. Two passengers were unaccounted for after the abandonment and have since been declared dead.

Queen of Victoria[d] 314040 On August 02, 1970 this car and passenger ferry was involved in a collision with the Soviet bulk carrier *Sergey Yesenin* in Active Pass BC that killed three people. In 1972 an engine

---

a Built as Queen of Saanich; then Owen Belle
b Built as Montana; then Harriet E.; then Queen of Storm
c Built as Stena Danica; then Queen of Surrey; then Queen of the North
d Built as City of Victoria; then Queen of Victoria; then Queen of Ocoa

room fire broke out while she was in Active Pass caused by a broken oil line over a hot manifold. She was towed to Burrard Drydock for repairs.

Quickstep[596] 077975 On December 25, 1882 this vessel owned by the Hudson's Bay Company was wrecked on the east coast of Prince of Wales Island 5 miles from Cape Chacon.

Quinnat 126437 This tug owned by Fred S Buck (owner of the Deep Cove Logging Co. and Cedar Creek Logging Co.) had been in service towing logs (possibly to Woodfibre). On July 12, 1925 she was destroyed by a fire that started in the engine room and she sank one mile from Whytecliffe Point BC. The crew of two were picked up in a small boat by the *Sannie* and transferred to the Lady Alexandra out of Bowen Island.

Quinsam 6[a] 319438 On March 15, 2015 this tug owned by Helifor Canada Corp., Vancouver BC sank off Cape Caution BC.

R.B. Green[b] 152820 In November 1933 she went aground in Bull Channel, Lasqueti Island. Her keel was broken, and her bilge was cracked. She was towed for repairs by the *Skookum* to the Vancouver Drydock in North Vancouver. In 1959 she foundered in heavy weather near Birch Bay WA while securing a scow. The crew went into the life rafts. On January 27, 1973 she foundered in Porpoise Harbour BC. In 2011 she was reported to be still afloat in Porpoise Bay BC—still with glass in the deadlights.

R.J. Morse[597] 100806 This sealing schooner under command of Captain George Cessford was owned by James Hunter, Victoria BC. On February 18, 1902 she foundered and capsized in the Strait of Juan de Fuca with the loss of one life (Mr Donaldson who was swept overboard). The crew were rescued by the *Penelope* and then three days later transferred to the *Umatilla*.

---

a   Built as Quinsam 6; then Log Baron (The)
b   Built as Goblin; then R.B. Green

R.P. Rithet[a,598] On July 28, 1885 she collided with the *Enterprise* near Victoria BC. About 1928 she was beached at Sturt Bay, Texada Island BC. In 1931 she was still listed in the Canada List of Shipping. An 1882 newspaper report states "Perfect in lines and model, she is finished and found in every respect in first-class style. The carving in the saloons is elaborate and ornate, while the upholstering, gilding and general finish are simply gorgeous. The staterooms are spacious and convenient provided with luxurious spring beds and fittings. In short, in the perfection of her lines the completeness of her appointments and the elegance of her design and finish the R.P. *Rithet* is truly a floating palace. She is provided with the patent hydraulic steering gear and is brilliantly lighted throughout with 'electricity' having two powerful headlights placed in huge reflectors. These lights with dazzling brilliance as the noble steamer came into our harbour on Saturday night, the New Westminster Militia band also were on board, playing a lively air. The wharves were literally crowded with people who went down to welcome Captain Irving and congratulate him upon this his last great triumph in marine architecture." In 1928 she was abandoned at Sturt Bay, Texada Island BC.

R.S. 141204 On July 20, 1959 this fishboat owned by Francis Millerd and Co. Ltd., West Vancouver BC foundered and sank at Egg Island, BC.

Radar 327140 On June 2, 1976 this fishboat owned by James l Jeannotte, Queen Charlotte City BC suffered a fire at Ivory Island (Milbanke Sound) BC. She was declared a constructive total loss at that time.

Rady 322450 On November 9, 1970 this fishboat owned by Frank Radonich and Stanley Radonich, both of Vancouver BC grounded at Savory Island BC and was a total loss.

---

a   Built as R.P. Rithet; then Baramba

Raita[a,599] (US) She was registered in Papeete, Tahiti. On January 26, 1925 while under command of Captain JH Richam and a nine-man Polynesian crew en route from Winslow WA to Papeete Tahiti with a load of lumber she was stranded and wrecked at Clo-oose (west coast of Vancouver Island) after taking on water in rough seas.

Ramona[600] 107253 In 1898 this sternwheeler was sent from her service at Wrangel AK to the mouth of the Stikine River. Later she was sent to the Fraser River. Her boiler exploded on April 17, 1901 at Henry West's Landing near Langley BC killing four persons: Engineer Richard Powers, Mrs Bailey, a First Nations man only known as 'Alec' and Mrs Hector Morrison. Six others were injured. The hull was sold to the Western Steamboat Company, and she was later rebuilt.

Ramsey Isle[601] 179561 On February 28, 1982 this troller, owned by Clarence Cootes, Kildonan BC, sank for unknown reasons with the loss of her crew, Captain Clarence Cootes, Wilfred (Shorty) Dennis Sr, Phillip Johnson, and Patrick Peters who all perished. They were running up to the Nootka area from Ucluelet for herring fishing when they encountered a storm." The bodies of her crew, who had to abandon ship without survival suits, were found drifting in the ship's dinghy a month and a half later.

Rap[602] 156894 On March 10, 1954 this fishpacker owned by John Clausen, Prince Rupert BC foundered on a reef two cables from Holliday Island BC. Captain Clausen was declared as missing and crewman Hans Grove died at the scene of the incident.

Rapid Providour[b] 346313 On March 07, 2009 this tug owned by West Coast Tug & Barge Ltd., Campbell River BC sank in Sonderland Channel with two barges loaded with construction materials in tow.

---

a   Built as Lucy; then Raita
b   Built as Point Grey Providour; then Rivtow Providour; then Island Providour I; then Saltair Providour; then Rapid Providour

Ravalli[603] 202681 (US) On June 14, 1918 the coal bunkers of this Seattle cannery tender, while under command of Captain RD MacGillivray, caught fire in Lowe Inlet BC. She was en route to southwestern Alaska. When the fire was discovered she was run onto the beach where she burned to the waterline. Her crew of 40 and 49 passengers were all saved. In September 1918 she was salvaged and towed to Vancouver BC by the tug *Georgia*.

Ray Roberts[604] 152806 She was said to have once been a rumrunner while owned by General Navigation Co. of Canada Ltd. She was fitted with a derrick for transferring cargo. On January 24, 1947 while on charter to Kelly Logging Ltd., Vancouver BC she was stranded at Port Renfrew BC.

Red Arrow 154348 On November 3, 1927 this workboat owned by salesman HS Wilder for use by the National Biscuit Co., Vancouver BC burned at Pope's Landing, Pender Harbour BC.

Red Fir[a] 085674 Her register describes her as a 'steam scow'. On October 15, 1918, this tug owned by Charles Bruce, Jordan River BC was stranded at Jordan River BC.

Red Fir[b] 121980 In 1899 this tug brought the survivors of the wrecked Peruvian bark *Libertad* to Victoria BC. Charles Bruce was the Chief Engineer—and he sold a half interest to John Isbester, Victoria BC. On April 11, 1928, this tug owned by Charles Bruce, Victoria BC (and he sold a half interest to John Isbester, Victoria BC) sank after striking a rock, while both owners were aboard, at Cracroft Island, Lewis Channel BC.

Red Fir No. 6 176280 On October 19, 1967 this tug owned by Inlet Marine Services Ltd., Coquitlam BC had an engine room fire at Tahsis Inlet BC and was a total loss.

---

a   Built as Belle; then Red Fir
b   Built as Queen City; then Queen; then Red Fir

Red Fir No. 10[a] 179091 In 1999 while owned by John L Gerry, Cobble Hill BC she sank and was salvaged at Shearwater BC.

Red Wing I 156626 On February 13, 1942 this power cruiser yacht was requisitioned for the RCAF but was found unsuitable. On February 17, 1942, the requisition was cancelled and returned to her owner on March 24, 1942. She was never taken up by the RCN." On May 24, 1961 while owned by Jervis Towing Co. Ltd., Vancouver BC she burned five miles north of Pender Harbour, Agamemnon Channel BC.

Reef Bay[b,605] 121992 On March 15, 1926 this small freighter, owned by Nelson H & ED Jean, Vancouver BC, foundered on Client Reef, (near Lawyer Island and the Oceanic Cannery) in Malacca Passage BC. She was the former sailing vessel *Emma H.* and was carrying a cargo of salted herring from the Millerd Cannery to Vancouver when she hit the rocks in the fog. Three hours later she worked herself off the rocks but sank shortly afterward in 40 fathoms of water. The crew of five lowered a boat and rowed to the Oceanic Cannery and then to Prince Rupert.

Regah 154572 On September 1, 1935 this vessel owned by the Canadian Fishing Co. Ltd., Vancouver BC exploded and burned at Pitt River BC.

Regal 4 176262 In 1975 this fishboat owned by Frank Knighton (MO), Clo-oose BC sank in Nitinat Lake BC.

Regal R 138179 In 1967 this workboat owned by Morris Benson, Ocean Falls BC broke her mooring during a storm and sank. Due to her old age and condition she was not salvaged.

Reliance (Vancouver Island register) This sternwheel freighter was launched October 8, 1862. She was built for the New Westminster to Yale run and owned by Captain William Irving, New Westminster

---

a   Built as RCAF M.446 Auklet; then Auklet; then Red Fir No. 10
b   Built as Emma H.; then Reef Bay

BC. On December 09, 1881 she struck a snag downstream from Hope BC and sank in shallow water off Wildcat Point (near Chilliwack). William Irving took off the freight, the vessel was salvaged and taken to New Westminster BC for repairs.

Reliance 103166 On July 5, 1930 this tug owned by Alva N Snider, Vancouver BC burned one-half mile east of Berry Point, in Burrard Inlet BC.

Reliant 195241 In June 1957 this tug struck a rock and capsized north of Vancouver on a charter to Kingcome Inlet BC. In October 1989 she grounded off Gower Point BC. In June 2020 she sank at Gibsons BC.

Renfrew[606] 138682 She was a seiner owned by Lummi Bay Packing Co. Ltd., Vancouver BC under Captain Nels Ford, carrying 26 employees to the Lummi Bay Cannery in Nitinat Lake BC. She was swamped while crossing the Nitinat Bar on Vancouver Island November 17, 1918 with the loss of 13 lives. Another 13 survivors were saved by First Nations people at Clo-oose BC. A court of inquiry was held to investigate the incident, but no blame was attached to the master as a result.

Rennell 138673 On August 28, 1924 while owned by R Beaumont and CH Nicholson (JO), Vancouver BC she foundered in Wright Sound BC.

Renown 189291 On April 2, 1971 this fishboat owned by British Columbia Packers Ltd., Richmond BC sank off Texada Island BC. She appears to have been salvaged and put back into service.

Resolution[607] (US) In July 1794 this American schooner was captured by the Haida Chief Cumshewa and his people in the Queen Charlotte Islands killing all but one of her crew of ten. She was destroyed by fire at Cumshewa Inlet BC.

Restless[a] 117159 In 1908 she was converted to a naval tug for hydrographic studies. In 1927 her funnel was painted green with a white

---

a   Built as Restless; then CGS Restless; then HMCS Restless; then Restless

band and green shamrock as the livery of the MacFarlane Brothers Ltd. On January 7, 1933, while under command of Captain McPhee, she burned and sank at the James Island wharf in Saanichton Bay BC. The engine and propeller were later salvaged and sold.

Restless Guy 327161 In 1970 this fishboat owned by Robert G Whyte (MO), Madeira Park BC sank in Hecate Strait.

Retirement 348003 On May 1, 1977 this fishboat while owned by Carl W. Stout (MO), and Jeanette Stout (JO), Nanaimo BC exploded and burned at the Newcastle Marina, Nanaimo BC and was a total loss.

Return 313091 On January 31, 1979 this fishboat owned by Harold C Leighton Jr, Metlakatla BC burned and then exploded in Prince Rupert Harbour BC.

Revelstoke 111777 She replaced the steamer *Lytton* on the Columbia River run above Revelstoke Narrows doing excursion and relief voyages on the Upper Arrow Lake and Columbia River. On April 15, 1915 she burned when the town of Comaplix BC was destroyed by fire.

Revere This American bark, 795 tons, was wrecked on September 9, 1883, while under the command of Captain JF Hinds in Port San Juan Harbor, BC. The vessel was bound for Port Townsend from Honolulu, in ballast. The vessel left the Islands, August 22, and off the entrance to the Strait of Juan De Fuca got into a pea soup fog. When surf was heard, the anchors were dropped but the vessel crashed ashore broadside and gouged a bole in her bottom planks. The wreck soon became a total loss, but the crew and passengers were rescued and taken to Victoria.

Reverie[608] On July 10, 1911 this schooner yacht owned by Captain G McMillan burned while alongside a wharf causing devastation of the Wallace Shipyards Ltd. in North Vancouver BC causing $150,000 in damage.

Rex II 170405 On December 10, 1958 this tug owned by Sidney Salvage & Contractors Ltd., Sidney BC sank in east Howe Sound BC after a hole was punched through her hull.

Rio III[a] 177612 In 1944–1945 she was in service with the Royal Canadian Navy as a Harbour Defence Patrol Craft. On December 3, 1946, this vessel owned by Reita Hayward, Vancouver, BC burned and was a total loss in Knight Inlet BC.

Riona[609] 154753 In 1941 this fishboat was seized from her Japanese owners by the Canadian Government. In 1942 her ownership transferred to His Majesty the King. On July 29, 1944 while owned by the Canadian Fishing Co. Ltd., Vancouver BC she sprang a leak, foundered, and sank 3/4 of a mile NE of the Kinahan Islands BC in 30 feet of water. The crew escaped.

Rippon Point[610] On August 14, 1947 this fishing scout boat exploded at Duncansby Landing in Rivers Inlet BC while taking on gasoline. The two members of the crew, Harold Malm (manager of the Margaret Bay fish plant) and J Tynjala (cook/deckhand) were hurled into the water by the force of the explosion. They had been en route to the Goose Bay fish plant at the time of the incident and the vessel was only a few weeks old having been launched by the builders.

River Chief[611] 158576 This tug was built for service on the Fraser and Harrison Rivers. On March 08, 1938 she burned in Johnstone Strait 4 miles east of Boat Harbour Light BC and was a total loss. The fire started in the engine room. She sank in 70 fathoms of water. The crew was rescued by the *Salvor*.

River Prince 190824 On May 16, 1972 this tug owned by British Columbia Forest Products Ltd., Vancouver BC sank in the Fraser River near Hammond BC and was not recovered.

---

a   Built as H.D.P.C. 37; then Rio III

Riversdale 102129 In 1914–1920 this sailing ship was interned in Santa Rosalia, Mexico as she was owned by a belligerent nation in the First World War. She was rebuilt as a log barge. In November 1961 she ended her life scuttled in the breakwater at Royston BC.

Rivtow Lion[a] 182199 The Nanaimo Dive Association (NDA) acquired the ship in early 2002, and following the remainder of the clean-up operation, and scuttled her in Departure Bay, Nanaimo on February 6th, 2005 as a shallow water artificial reef, ideal for novice wreck diver training and sport diving all year round.

Rivtow Norseman 330598 In 1969 this log barge (self-loading/self-dumping) hit Hazard Rock off Klemtu while under tow of *Rivtow Viking* (dumped load and returned to Vancouver for repair of bottom damage.) On October 21, 1971 she was stranded at Cox Island BC. In 1980 she broke a towline and went ashore in the Scott Islands on northern Vancouver Island BC.

Rivtow Rogue[b] 330409 On February 14, 1975 she foundered in the Queen Charlotte Islands BC while towing the barge *Bute #3* on a voyage from Masset to Prince Rupert BC. She sank near Triple Island still tethered by towline to the barge which remained afloat. All six crew were lost including: Captain Max Sievert (master); Cliff Moraes (mate); Howard Pierce (engineer); Andre Schmidt (cook); Allan East (deckhand); and Frank Brereton (deckhand).

Roald Amundsen[612] 210102 (US) On May 5, 1929 she burned while en route south from Alaska in Principe Channel BC. Most likely this incident was caused by an engine backfire. The vessel burned for two hours and was destroyed. Captain Angel and two crewmen evacuated in a dory and were rescued by the *New England*.

---

a   Built as HMS Prudent; then HMS Cautious; then Rivtow Lion
b   Built as Fulmar; then RivTow Rogue

Roamer[a] 156588 On July 4, 1978 this fishboat owned by British Columbia Packers Ltd., Richmond BC grounded and sank in Otter Cove, on the west coast of Vancouver Island BC.

Roaming Chief II 348500 On October 10, 1977 this fishboat owned by Bingham Fisheries Ltd., Vancouver BC suffered a fire in the engine room off Favada Point in Georgia Strait and was declared a total loss.

Robert Kerr[613] (Canada East register) In 1866 she was in the Liverpool to India trade. In 1874 she was in coastal trade in the UK. She provided refuge for people in the Great Fire of 1886 at Vancouver BC. In 1887 she was operated by the Hudson's Bay Co. between the UK and the west coast. In 1903 while being towed by the tug Mystery from Vancouver to Union Bay, she struck rocks at Ballenas and was damaged. She was towed in a leaking condition to Union Bay where she was repaired. She was wrecked near Danger Reef while in tow of the tug Coulti from Ladysmith to Vancouver with a cargo of coal. Afterwards she was coal hulk in Vancouver harbour. She sank while transporting coal under tow of the tug Coulti on the night of March 4, 1911 SE of Miami Islet located in Stuart Channel, jn the Gulf Islands. She lays just north of Thetis Island and is located on a line between Ragged Islet and Miami Islet. The UASBC has installed a plaque on her. The wreck of the *Miami* is close by."

Roberta[b] 192896 On December 12, 1961 she burned and sank ten miles west of Lennard Island BC. Her 4-man crew was rescued by the fishboat Kodiak. In 1970 this fishboat owned by Harry S Nataros (JO), Langley BC and Harry B Craig, Cloverdale BC sank at the entrance to Toba Inlet BC.

Roberta Lin[c] 312884 In 1978 this fishboat owned by Leslie D Souch (MO), Richmond BC was reported to have sunk at MacKay Reach BC.

---

a   Built as Steveston III; then Roamer
b   Built as Roberta; then Scuba Queen
c   Built as Dana N.; then Roberta Lin

Roche Point 130458 This fishpacker was originally on the mail and passenger run from Port Alberni to Barkley Sound. On November 4, 1927 while owned by West Coast Transportation Co. Ltd., Port Alberni BC she was stranded in Jervis Inlet BC. While owned by Mrs George Pellis, North Vancouver BC she foundered August 05, 1930 five miles south of Cape Beale BC.

Rocket[a] 320036 On September 22, 1970 this tug owned by Island Tug & Barge Co. Ltd., Victoria BC foundered off Victoria Harbour BC.

Rocky 176263 On May 10, 1953 this troller fishboat owned by Arthur Peter, Bamfield BC burned at her mooring in Bamfield BC.

Rocky 318967 On October 23, 1985 this fishboat owned by John H Tom, Tofino BC was involved in a collision and sank off Blowhole Bay on Vancouver Island BC.

Rodney P.[b] 141714 On October 17, 1951 while owned by Atwood E Pierce (MO), Prince Rupert BC she caught fire at Skidegate, Skidegate Inlet BC.

Rondeggen[614] She was an overhanging-gantry type design freighter for carrying newsprint from BC ports (Ocean Falls & Duncan Bay) to California for Crown Zellerbach. In August 1965 she hit a cliff at Wearing Point (at the entrance to Cousins inlet) in an accident that was caused when a log jammed in her rudder disabling her steering.

Rosallie 202681 On June 14, 1918 she was destroyed by fire in Lowe Inlet BC.

Rosarah[615] 158942 On November 17, 1949 this fishboat, owned by Olaf P Jacobsen (MO), and TW Cooper, both of Victoria BC, suffered a fire in her engine room off Sheringham Point in Juan de Fuca Strait

---

a   Built as Island Rocket; then Seaspan Rocket; then Rocket
b   Built as D.S.T.; then Rodney P.

BC. The skipper, TW Cooper, was rescued from a small dinghy by the American fishboat *Addington*.

Rose-Lind[616] In 1952 this seiner capsized in Seymour Narrows near Ripple Rock. Crewman Ned Pelser was lost. Captain Peter Kelly, Carl Berg and Frank Measure were rescued by a passing boat. She was later salvaged and put back into operation.

Rose Lorraine 197659 On December 4, 1966 this fishboat owned by William G McAllan (MO), Victoria BC sank near Brotchie Ledge after she struck an unidentified object while under tow and was a total loss.

Rose N.[a,617] 153141 n 1932 this fishboat, owned by Yoshitaro Hashimoto, Steveston BC and Yasuichiro Nakai, Vancouver BC, struck an object that pierced her hull, and she sank at Comox Bay.

Rose of Langley (UK) On February 22, 1859 this schooner foundered in the Strait of Juan de Fuca with the loss of two lives.

Rosina B.[b] 150571 On October 15, 1931 this fishboat owned by Olier Besher, Prince Rupert BC suffered a fire a half mile off the west coast of Kinahan Island BC.

Roslin 174049 On August 4, 1946 while owned by owned by Lawrence G. Chisholm, Bamfield BC she sank 7 miles south of Esperanza Inlet BC.

Ross Prince[c] 130866 On January 7, 1954 this power cruiser yacht owned by Duane Brown, Vancouver BC was wrecked near North Vancouver BC after a collision in Seymour Narrows with the *East Bay No. 1*.

---

a   Built as Rose N.; then Silver Rose; then Stromross
b   Built as Iris; then Rosina B.
c   Built as Birdswell; then P.W.; then Ross Prince

Rossland 107142 On January 25, 1916 this sternwheeler, owned by the Canadian Pacific Railway, Montreal QC, sank in a snowstorm at Nakusp BC. In 1917 she sank at her mooring. The hull was sold to Captain Forslund as a landing stage downstream from the Needles.

Rothesay[618] On May 4, 1959 this power cruiser, owned by Dr CA Armstrong, was lost on her maiden voyage with three men on a trip to Port Mellon BC. They were stranded at Sea Island and spent 21 hours waving to attract attention. Potential rescuers thought the crew were simply being friendly and ignored their plight. They were eventually rescued by the tug *Storm Winds*.

Rover 122518 On September 03, 1931 while owned by Vancouver Pile Driving & Contracting Co. Ltd., Vancouver BC she burned off Anvil Island, in Howe Sound.

Royal City She was launched March 2, 1875. In 1875 she was owned by Otis Parsons, Victoria BC. In 1875 she was sold to Captain John Irving for the Pioneer Line. She serviced Sumas Landing BC. In 1882 she was wrecked on the Fraser River BC. She lay for some time, bottom up, near the *Sand Heads Lightship*.

Royal No. 2 194414 On January 24, 1961 this tug owned by Royal City Towing Co. Ltd., Vancouver BC capsized near Canal Island in Nootka Sound and sank.

Royal Pacific[a] 173760 On March 3, 1975 this fishboat owned by Ronald V Sparrow (MO), Ladner BC foundered in Barkley Sound BC.

Royal Pride[619] 811213 The Transportation Safety Board of Canada states that "In the evening of 14 February 1994, in heavy weather conditions, the skipper of the "Gypsy Lass" was unable to restart the main engine after stopping for a precautionary change of fuel filters before entering Edith Harbour, British Columbia. Another fishing vessel, the "Royal Pride", was called for assistance, but the "Gypsy Lass", which had been carried into shoal water, grounded a short time after

---

a   Built as Royal T.; then Royal Pacific

the "*Royal Pride*" arrived on the scene. While standing by, the "Royal Pride" was subsequently disabled by kelp fouling her Kort nozzle and she also grounded. The Fast Rescue Craft "*Point Henry No. 2*" which came to their assistance was swamped while attempting to rescue the crew of the "*Royal Pride*" and was beached. The crews of the three vessels were rescued by a US Coast Guard helicopter."

Royal Vancouver[620] At 0818, 06 February 1992, in light airs, calm sea and fog, the catamaran passenger ferry *Royal Vancouver* and the British Columbia Ferry Corporation vehicle/passenger ferry *Queen of Saanich* collided head-on off Georgina Point at the northern entrance to Active Pass, British Columbia. On board the *Royal Vancouver*, which was extensively damaged, 19 passengers and 4 crew members were injured. The bow doors of the *Queen of Saanich* were also damaged. The Board determined that the bridge team of the *Royal Vancouver* did not positively identify and track a radar target and, as a result, altered course into the projected path of the *Queen of Saanich* about one minute before the collision. Contributing to the situation was the bridge team's limited experience with the catamaran's equipment."

Runnymede (HMCS) K.678 (RCN) After the Second World War she was placed in the ship boneyard at Bedwell Bay BC. In 1947 she was sold to Capital Iron & Metals Ltd. of Victoria, British Columbia for scrapping. Her hull was stripped, and it was scuttled as a breakwater in Kelsey Bay, British Columbia.

Rupert[621] On September 24, 1964 she sank at Lion Point (Portland Canal) BC.

Rustler 110606 (US) Captain Warren (Victoria BC) used this schooner for fur sealing voyages. She was driven ashore in a gale on December 26, 1887 at Nitinat south of Cape Beale on Vancouver Island while attempting to cross the bar. She was on a sealing expedition but had not taken any furs prior to her demise. All hands reached shore safely and were saved.

Ruston[a] 154921 On May 19, 1931 this fishboat owned by Martin & Kildall Ltd., Vancouver BC was stranded in Johnstone Strait BC.

Ruth B. 141551 On September 8, 1966 she was destroyed by fire at Bella Bella BC.

Ruth C.[622] 230772 (US) On February 10, 1939 while under the command of Captain Lawrence Olsen, she was bound for Ketchikan with a cargo of supplies when she sank off Chatham Point in Johnstone Strait BC. The Captain and his crew of 7 were rescued from the vessel's dory and taken to the hospital at Rock Bay. While transiting the vessel was caught in a tide rip that caused the cargo to shift.

Ruth Carlyle[b] 172498 During the Second World War she was operated by the Pacific Command Water Transport Company of the Royal Canadian Army Service Corps. She was used to transport supplies and personnel to Outer Defences Prince Rupert. On November 21, 1957 she sank off Seal Rocks, in Hecate Strait.

St. Patrick[623] (Canada) On September 23, 1892 this sloop, owned by Bob Dugdale of Nanaimo BC was wrecked after a chain of events that began with losing the rudder. They lost their rigging and were washed up on Sangster Island. The crew of the sloop, David Edwards, and Dan Macgillivray, who were out on a seal hunting trip, made a raft out of beach logs and made for Lasqueti Island. Jesse Burden and William Stevens, sailing in the sloop No. 18, picked the crew up just as their raft started to break up, and carried them both to Nanaimo.

S. & B. II[c] 190286 On August 7, 1972 this workboat owned by Alice Crossley, Victoria BC sank in Johnstone Strait BC.

S.C. 167 A00247 On September 27, 1976 this gillnet fishboat foundered, was abandoned at sea, and sank on the east side of Graham Island.

---

a   Built as Pike's Peak; then Ruston
b   Built as RCASC General Anderson; then General Anderson; then Ruth Carlyle
c   Built as L.C.V. 32; then S. & B. II

S.D. Brooks[a] 143397 In 1962 this tug owned by Kingcome Navigation Co. Ltd, Vancouver BC sank at the Kingcome Navigation dock in Vancouver harbour. In 1971 she was laid up at Onehunga NZ. Her final service was carrying out ammunition shuttles under charter to a US government agency prior to the collapse of South Vietnam, and while on a towing voyage from Singapore to the Arabian Gulf in 1976, suffered machinery failure near Colombo Sri Lanka. In 1977 she was broken up in Jurong Singapore at the National Iron & Steel Works.

The wreck of the **S.F. Tolmie** (Image from the collection of the Maritime Museum of British Columbia 1_000113)

S.F. Tolmie[624] 141617 In 1921–1923 she was rigged a barkentine she operated on voyages to the Orient and Australia. In 1928 she was converted to floating herring saltery by Nelson Brothers. She was converted to a log barge by Gibson Brothers. On December 27, 1944 she broke loose from her moorings at Ogden Point and was wrecked on Macaulay Point, near Victoria BC. She broke up before she could be salvaged.

S.S. Beaver[b] 368759 In 1966 the S.S. Beaver was created from a YSF by the Royal Canadian Navy as a replica of the original steamship the Beaver. In 1972 she was purchased by the Municipality of Langley to moor as a floating exhibit. When this proved too costly, she was sold for use a harbour cruise ship with the stipulation that she must sail to Langley at least eight times a year and be placed on display during Greater Vancouver Sea Festivals. She underwent several renovations, including the addition of a dining room and discotheque. On May 7, 2014 as a derelict she sank in Cowichan Bay BC.

---

a Built as St. Faith; then S.D. Brooks; then Haida Monarch; then Le Beau; then Unit Shipper; then Killarney
b Built as CNAV Y.S.F.-216; then S.S. Beaver

S.T. No. 4 193439 On January 26, 1954 this tug owned by Swiftsure Towing Ltd., New Westminster BC foundered between the lightship and Porlier Pass BC.

Safari II[a] 179058 In 1942–1946 she served as a crash boat for the RCAF at Jericho Beach (Vancouver) BC. On December 11, 1985 she experienced a fire in the engine room and sank three miles off Wickaninnish Bay BC.

Sailor[625] 154338 On October 20, 1928 this fishboat burned at the Nootka Cannery Wharf BC.

Salar 173750 On September 05, 1967 this troller fishboat owned by Gerry W Brooks (MO), Sooke BC was in a collision hitting a deadhead at night and sank in 50 fathoms in the Alberni Inlet BC

Salinta[626] On December 2, 1979 she was found derelict in Revillagigedo Channel with ten lives lost (Three adults and seven children) "She was found washed ashore at Tree Point December 5, 1979. The small old Canadian fishing vessel had departed Prince Rupert December 2nd on a day trip to Portland Inlet. The heavily damaged vessel washed ashore 46 miles northwest of Prince Rupert. There were no survivors."

Sally J.[627] On September 17, 1965 she was destroyed by fire and sank at Sooke BC.

Salmon King[b] 154599 On September 3, 1976 this troller owned by Marineland Enterprises Ltd., Vancouver BC was destroyed by fire after an explosion in the engine room off Effingham Island BC.

Salmon Queen 173166 In 1948 this fishboat carried milk from dairy farms during the Fraser River floods. On November 9, 1954 while owned by The British Columbia Packers Ltd., Vancouver BC she foundered in Georgia Strait.

---

a   Built as RCAF M.441 Merganser; then Safari II
b   Built as Alberta G.; then Salmon King

Salvage Boy[a] 133867 On March 27, 1934 this tug owned by Dominion Tug and Barge Co. Ltd., Vancouver BC foundered at the Gypsum Plant wharf at south New Westminster BC.

Salvage Chief[b,628] 091255 In 1885 this vessel was billed as the world's most powerful tug. On February 7, 1925 she was wrecked at Merry Island, Welcome Pass BC. She had gone there to re-float two Davis rafts which were grounded on Merry Island when she herself caught a submerged rock tearing a hole in her hull. Water poured in, the ship was quickly overwhelmed, and Captain FC Stratford ordered the crew to abandon ship. The crew was taken aboard the *Cape Scott*.

Salvage King[c,629] 179065 On October 19,1953 a fire broke out in the forecastle of this tug which burned at her berth. Crews fought the fire for five hours, slowly filling with water and then sinking at her berth and sank in Victoria Harbour. She was later raised. On April 4, 1959, this tug hit the Johnson Street Bridge, while being towed by the *Island Comet* to the breakers yard, nearly severing one main girder. In October 1959, the hulk was towed to the Comox Logging Company's breakwater at Royston BC. The scuttling there was difficult when after her seacocks were opened, she refused to sink.

Salvor[d] 179458 As an auxiliary vessel she was employed in 1950 for towing whale carcasses into the whaling station at Coal Harbour on the west coast of Vancouver Island. In 1961 she was broken up by Capital Iron & Metals Ltd., Victoria BC. The hull was towed to Royston BC and scuttled in the breakwater.

Samantha J.[e,630] 348369 On October 15, 2005 this tug owned by Jones Marine Group from Chemainus was struck by a barge she had in tow off Harmac after she lost power resulting in her sinking in about 230 feet of water in Northumberland Channel by Gabriola Bluffs. One crew swam ashore and the other leaped onto a chip barge. The ferries

---

a   Built as Princess; then Digges; then Salvage Boy
b   Built as William T. Joliffe; then Nitinat; then Salvage Chief
c   Built as USS A.T.R. 13; then Salvage King
d   Built as USS A.T.R.-68; then Towmac; then Salvor
e   Built as Northumberland Navigator; then Samantha J.

Quinsam and *Queen of New Westminster* attended the scene. The crew were able to climb aboard the barge and except for a minor cut were only a little cold, wet and shaken. They were taken ashore to a waiting ambulance. The first responders to the incident aided in the safe recovery of the barge which was attached to the sunken vessel. The vessel sank at one of the six deep sea anchorage spots preventing use by ships. Using a Remote Operated Vessel used its manipulator arms to secure a chain to the vessel's bow and two slings under the hull. She was lifted to the surface, dewatered, and placed on a barge. It was anticipated that the vessel would be rebuilt for service.

The *Sampep* burning in Port Alberni harbour (Photograph from the Port Alberni Museum pn12396)

Sampep On August 26, 1947 this freighter burned in a spectacular fire at the lumber assembly wharf in Port Alberni BC. Six tugs towed the burning freighter out into the harbour. After the fire she lay at the Ogden Point wharf awaiting repair, but she was decommissioned to the boneyard at Astoria Oregon. In 1948 she was rebuilt. Under the terms of the wartime Lend-Lease agreement she had to be restored before her return to the US Maritime Commission.

Samson V[631] 170681 This sternwheel snag boat burned and sank at her berth in New Westminster. Mark MacKenzie stated " the night watchman was drinking below by the light of a kerosene lantern which broke, setting the creosote hull timbers on fire. You can still see charred parts to her hull when you are down inside. All the decking to the engine room and the top chord of the keelsons were replaced in the rebuild."

San Juan Prince[a,632] 138489 She is reported to have towed in and out of Nitinat Lake before the Second World War and that she was turned end for end in the waves crossing the Bar three times. Michael Kaehn stated that "In December 1936 my great uncle Captain Jim Olson had a heart attack and died on the deck, while it was approaching Bellingham WA." On October 2, 1971 she grounded in the Skeena River BC and sank.

San Pedro 115894 This freighter ran onto Brotchie Ledge while proceeding in the charge of a pilot (Captain James Christiansen) from Union Bay via Victoria to San Francisco laden with 4,000 tons of coal November 23, 1891. She could not be dislodged from the rock. The *Wellington* (Captain Salmond) proceeded to the wreck carrying a Royal Navy diver from HMS *Nymphe*. About 300 tons of cargo was removed to lighten ship. Overnight she sank where she lay. Several attempts to salvage her were unsuccessful including one by TPH Whitelaw of San Francisco CA and another by Moran Brothers of Seattle WA. The bow and foremast of the vessel were still in plain view in 1895 when she was dismantled on the spot and dynamited.

San Pedro[b] 312781 On February 28, 1977, owned by Sven Royle (MO), Nanaimo BC she exploded in the engine room and burned to the waterline at the entrance to Port San Juan in Juan de Fuca Strait.

---

a   Built as Fairbanks; then San Juan Prince
b   Built as Nu-Duck; then San Pedro

San Tomas[a,633] 170951 On February 7, 1958 this seiner, owned by Captain Walter Steen experienced a structural failure. About 8:00 am a bulkhead gave way and her cargo of 80 tons of herring shifted. The crew immediately headed to beach her at Porter Head on Moresby Island where she grounded in shallow water. The seiner *Shirley Rose* came along side and rescued the crew "without even getting their feet wet".

Sancarmella[b] 312109 On September 27, 1967 this power cruiser owned by Robert B Leatherdale (MO), Port Moody BC was destroyed by fire and sank in Indian Arm BC.

Sandheads Lightship No. 16[c,634] 121979 In February 1947 this lightship stationed at the mouth of the Fraser River was blown aground at Westham Island during a storm.

Sandra Carol[635] 192090 On November 18, 1952 this fishboat, under command of Captain Oliver Adams, foundered in a fierce gale four miles southwest of Hudson Bay Passage (in Dixon Entrance) BC. They were just about to make a set when they noticed water coming into the after hold. Her crew were rescued, and she was towed by two other fishboats, the *Burnaby M* and the *BC Producer*, to within 4 miles of the shore at Hudson Bay Point when her towline parted, and she sank in 50 fathoms.

Sandra Carol[d,636] 174047 On June 03, 2005 this fishboat, while on a voyage from Courtenay to Port Alberni, in the Swanson Channel she crossed the cable connecting two barges being towed by the tug *Ocean Warrior*. The hull was damaged by the *Barge 216*, and she sank after her owner, alone on board, had jumped on the barge and his boat was sunk by the second barge.

---

a   Built as San Tomas, later HMCS San Tomas, then San Tomas
b   Built as First Love II; then Sancarmella
c   Built as Thomas F. Bayard; then Sandheads No. 16; then Lightship No. 16; then Thomas F. Bayard
d   Built as Zorina; then Island Bell; then Sandra Carol

Sandy L. 198664 On September 03, 1971 this vessel sank at Plowden Bay, Howe Sound BC.

The *Santa Maria* on the rocks off Dallas Road in Victoria BC. (Image from the collection of the Maritime Museum of British Columbia)

Santa Maria She was an oil tanker owned by the Union Oil Co., USA. On March 17, 1938, this oil tanker ran on the reefs at 3:20 am, Tuesday morning, March 17, 1938 on Glimpse Reef off Victoria BC. The tanker had discharged her cargo of oil at Vancouver and was riding high in the water on her return to Los Angeles. She heaved to off Brotchie Ledge about 3 am to drop off Pilot Captain James Noel. Just as the pilot boat was clearing the vessel, an extremely heavy squall struck her, forcing her head inshore. Before she could gather enough steerage way to clear, she crashed on the reef with considerable force, puncturing her bottom in several places. The stranding punctured the single hull of the ship on the jagged rocks. Water flooded No. 3 tank and the port pump room. The *Santa Maria* grounded as the tide was falling and remained stuck fast all day. As the tide receded, the bow rose higher and the stern settled. The *Salvage King*, of the Pacific Salvage Company, put a line aboard the stern of the *Santa Maria*. With propellers turning slowly, the tug kept the tanker from "keeling around" as she rested amidships on the rocks. To lighten the vessel for the attempt to refloat at the next high tide, fuel was pumped out and oil from that operation covered the surface of the water around the ship. There was an especially large crowd on hand to witness the effort to refloat the tanker that evening. When four tugs—the *Salvage King*, Snohomish, Anyox and Salvage Princess—pulled with cables about 7:15 pm, shortly before high tide, the tanker slid easily from the reef into deep water. The ship had been stranded on Glimpse Reefs for sixteen hours. Damage to the *Santa Maria* was estimated to have been $75,000. The surveyors agreed that the *Santa Maria* could proceed to San Francisco where repairs would be made. The tanker then departed from Royal Roads at 9:00 pm on May 18th.

Santa Maria I[a] 158915 She was a seiner that formed part of the pre-war Fishermen's Reserve Fleet. She was mobilized September 15, 1939. In 1940 she was commissioned into the Royal Canadian Navy Fisherman's Reserve. After the Second World War she was returned to her owners. On July 25, 1960, owned by Edward J Zitko, Vancouver BC, she struck an object and sank at Butedale BC in Tolmie Channel BC.

Santa Rita[b] 210894[637] (US) On February 15, 1923 while under command of Captain OB Rolstad, this freighter was stranded on sloping rocks one mile east of Clo-oose having run ashore in reduced visibility. En route from San Pedro to Seattle the captain thought he was still in the vicinity of Tatoosh Lighthouse and ran aground at full speed at 5:30 am in thick fog. The ground swell was strong, and waves broke right over the vessel. Men from Clo-oose gathered on the beach and helped Seaman Victor Hautopp who swan ashore with a line tied around his body. Helped ashore with the lone the men on the beach quickly rigged a breeched buoy. All the crew of 30 were rescued. The hull had several large holes, and the engine room was flooded. She was not salvaged.

Sanyo[638] 141311 On November 13, 1925 this fishboat, under command of Captain Chester Coutts, burned one-half mile north of the Breton Islands, Georgia Strait BC. A red-hot coal rolled out of the stove and fell into the bilge. The gas and oil in the bilge burst into flame and she was destroyed by fire. The crew evacuated in a dinghy that was rescued by the *Moon Dawn*.

Sapphire[639] 088226 In 1887–1897 this sealing schooner, under command of Captain William Cox, was owned by E.B. Marvin & Co.,

---

a   Built as Santa Maria; later HMCS Santa Maria, then Santa Maria I
b   Built as William Chatham; then Santa Rita

Victoria BC. At 8:30 am on April 23, 1897 she experienced an explosion and fire about twenty miles off Ucluelet BC. Only Captain Cox and three members of the crew were still on board at the time. The vessel had to be abandoned even though she had boats out hunting at the time as the fire was nearing powder that was stored in the vessel. Five minutes later she was a mass of flames and exploded making a noise so loud it was heard by the First Nations boat crews that were hunting miles away. It was thought later that heat from the cook stove was the cause of the fire.

Sarah On November 8, 1891 this Nova Scotian bark, 1,142 tons, was wrecked near Pachena Point, BC while under the command of Captain Greenhalgh. The vessel was inbound for Port Blakely from Manila in ballast. She fell victim to a heavy fog and the currents placed her in jeopardy after dragging her anchors six miles east of Cape Beale. The crew escaped in lifeboats, but two lives were lost while effecting a landing through the surf. The captain, his wife and baby were among the survivors.

Saranac (USS) This naval sloop served in the US Navy's North Pacific Squadron in 1871–1873. She operated in that region until she was wrecked at 8.40 am on June 18, 1875 on the submerged Ripple Rock in Seymour Narrows off Campbell River, British Columbia. She under the command of Captain WW Queen USN while en route from San Francisco CA to Alaska while on a mission to collect natural curiosities for the Philadelphia Centennial Exposition. Her bow was immediately run into the Vancouver Island shore and made fast with a hawser to a tree, but within an hour she had sunk completely from sight. Lieutenant Commander Sanders USN, with a pilot and thirteen men, made their way on foot to Victoria.

Sardonyx[640] (UK) On June 12, 1890 while under command of Captain WJ Smith, this freighter was stranded between Skidegate and Rose Spit Queen Charlotte Islands BC. She had been en route from Victoria to the Skeena River and Nass River and ports in between at the time of the incident. On June 13 she grounded about 30 miles from Skidegate and five and a half miles offshore. The engine room began to flood and fill with water. The boats were launched, and the passengers crew were evacuated with the Captain the last to leave.

Sarn[641] 251770 (US) This fishboat was registered at Aberdeen WA USA. On August 31, 1954 she foundered 3.5 miles of Cape George, near Porcher Island BC.

Saskatchewan (HMCS) On June 14, 1997 this ex-Royal Canadian Navy destroyer was deliberately scuttled to form an artificial reef.

Satellite II[642] 310325 On August 7, 1969 this fishpacker owned by Nelson Bros. Fisheries Ltd., Vancouver BC foundered when she was overwhelmed by waves off the Rose Spit Buoy, QCI BC. Three of the crew were rescued but Patrick Bennett drowned.

Satellite (HMS) On November 3, 1884 she was stranded at Ripple Rock BC and later salvaged. In 1896 she was on the Bering Sea Patrol and in service on the North Pacific. While laying at Unalaska AK. Two seamen went fishing in a small boat. High winds suddenly came up and a larger cutter was put in the water manned by seven crew and Lieutenant Heyman RN to save the two sailors. They saved themselves but the cutter was driven ashore with the loss of all aboard.

Saturn On September 1, 1921 she burned 12 miles south-west of Freeman Passage, Porcher Island BC.

Saturna[643] 088380 On August 07, 1894 this vessel, owned by Alderman John McDowell, Vancouver BC, was stranded, burned, salvaged, and rebuilt. She had been attempting to pass under the Granville Street Bridge on her way to False Creek. While waiting for the tide to rise the crew went ashore and she caught fire. The fire brigade arrived in time to save the hull although the upper works were severely damaged. On January 3, 1911 she hit a rock while proceeding eastwards through Second Narrows while 'working the back eddies'. She was raised. On May 30, 1911 while owned by Imperial

Timber & Trading Co., she capsized in False Creek and was raised but was declared a total constructive loss.

Saturna 100505 In 1892 she was registered at Victoria BC. This vessel, owned by George Byrnes, Victoria BC, was reported as having sunk in Victoria Harbour as a total loss.

Saturna[a] 134080 this troller fishboat owned by Wayne Greer, Ucluelet BC burned after an explosion October 11, 1969 while at anchor and sank in Pipestem Inlet BC.

Saugeen 153017 On October 22, 1948 this fishboat owned by British Columbia Packers Ltd., Vancouver BC burned in Quatsino Sound BC.

Scacon[644] 312080 On October 17, 1965 this tug owned by Texada Towing Co. Ltd., Vancouver BC sank after she overturned in Tahsis Channel. The master James Andrews, swam to a log boom, while the Mate, Robert Notley, drowned in the incident impeded by his heavy boots and clothes. The tug was later salvaged. They were towing about one million board feet of wood when a tide rip caused them to capsize about 6:30 pm. Andrews was rescued about two hours later.

Scallop II 150772 On July 15, 1965 this workboat owned by Gordon F Deberri, Westview BC struck a deadhead and sank off Francis Point in Malaspina Strait BC.

Sceptre Squamish[645] In 1995 this dredge was lost in a storm off Little River when it was left by the charterer unattended in heavy weather.

Schiedijk[646] In 1949–1969 this freighter was owned by Nederlandsche-Amerikaansche Stoomvaart Mij. N.V. (NASM, Holland-Amerika Line, HAL), Rotterdam Netherlands. On January 03, 1968 she grounded on Bligh Island in 1969 while outbound from the Gold River pulp mill. The ship slipped off the reef 15 hours after

---

a   Built as Watla; then Saturna

she struck and went down in deep water. She was abandoned by her crew and sank the next day. The *Schiedijk* was on passage from Seattle to Antwerp with pulp, barley, and other food. Les Sharcott reports that "she was towed into Nootka Sound by the *Sudbury* II and a boom was placed around her and she was pumped out. The *Nitinat Chief* was left to tend her."

Scimitar 328945 On January 31, 1994 this tug owned by Gulf Towing Ltd., North Vancouver BC heeled over to starboard, took on water and sank in five minutes. The five crew members abandoned ship in the inflatable life raft.

Scopas[a,647] 152895 On October 21, 1926 this fish packer owned by Matthew Sutton, Vancouver BC was destroyed by fire en route from Port Alberni to Vancouver 2.5 miles off Albert Head, in Juan de Fuca Strait BC.

Scotch Fir 314945 On January 15, 1962 this tug owned by Texada Towing Co. Ltd., Vancouver BC burned at Tahsis and was salvaged later. On July 25, 1963 she sank near Nanaimo BC.

Scottish Lady[b] 058939 She was registered in London UK. In 1896–1897 she was shipping grain from Puget Sound WA. On January 20, 1961 she sank in Quatsino Sound BC.

Scotty 130692 In 1937 this workboat owned by Donald Burgess, South Vancouver BC was reported as having sunk and was a total loss.

Scrub[c] 141280 On September 21, 1950 this fishboat owned by British Columbia Packers Ltd., Vancouver BC foundered abreast of Copper Island, Hecate Strait BC.

---

a Built as Scopas; then Wild Rose
b Built as La Escocesa; then Coalinga; then Star of Chile; then Roche Harbour Lime Transport; then Scottish Lady
c Built as Vienna; then Scrub

Scuba Queen[a] 192896 On December 12, 1961 she burned and sank ten miles west of Lennard Island BC. Her 4-man crew was rescued by the fishboat Kodiak. In 1970 this fishboat owned by Harry S Nataros (JO), Langley BC and Harry B Craig, Cloverdale BC sank at the entrance to Toba Inlet BC.

Sea Bird This American sidewheeler was built in the eastern USA. In 1858 she travelled as far as Murderer's Bar on the Fraser River, the first vessel to do so. She arrived at Port Townsend WT on March 18, 1858. She carried passengers on the Fraser River. She ran onto a bar a few miles below Hope on what is now known as Sea Bird Bar and was stuck for four months. After her removal she burned to her waters edge at Discovery Island while en route to Victoria September 07, 1858. Her engines were salvaged and went into the steamer John T Wright.

Sea Breeze III[b] 155209 On May 8, 1969 this tug owned by Cackette Enterprises Ltd., Vancouver BC burned in Johnstone Strait BC.

Sea Comet[c] 177994 In 1944–1947 she was owned and operated by the Canadian Army Pacific Command Water Transport Company of the Royal Canadian Army Service Corps. In 1947–1951 she was owned by the British Columbia Attorney General, Victoria BC for the British Columbia Provincial Police. In 1950–1958 she was owned by the RCMP Marine Section. In 1960–1965 she was owned by Bendickson Towing Co. Ltd., Vancouver BC. In 1975–1979 she was owned by Broughton Towing Co. Ltd., North Vancouver BC. In 1980 she was owned by Fairway Towing & Salvage Ltd., Nanaimo BC. In 1983–1987 she was owned by Island Merchant Marine Ltd., Vancouver BC. Her registry closed on November 25, 1951 and was reopened 29 June 1959. On November 25, 1987 she was destroyed by fire and sank in Howe Sound BC.

---

a   Built as Roberta; then Scuba Queen
b   Built as Maple Prince; then Sea Breeze III
c   Built as Brigadier Sutherland Brown; then P.M.L. 16; then RCMP M.L. 16; then Sea Comet

Sea Crest II[a] 126894 On November 28, 1951 she was towing the barge Lucky N. carrying a cargo of furniture when she was swamped by high seas and run aground near Myrtle Point. The crew of three was saved: Captain Ben McDonald, John Argue (engineer) and Harold Price (deck hand). The tug was salvaged. In 1954 she burned to the waterline near Powell River.

Sea Dawn[b,648] 170753 On March 8th, 1967 this tugboat had an engine room fire and burned and sank between Halkett Bay and Hood Point near Bowen Island BC and was a total loss. Captain Neil Levine and Mate Art Lindsay were rescued by the *Haida Monarch*.

Sea Foam 121739 On November 30, 1926 this tug owned by Harold S Cove, Vancouver BC burned in Menzies Bay BC.

Sea Foam V[c] 170939 On April 06, 1987 this tug owned by Thompson Navigation Ltd., Campbell River BC sank after hitting a bluff in Tribune Channel BC.

Sea Fox II[d] 152801 In 1941 she was commissioned into the Royal Canadian Navy Fisherman's Reserve. In 1942 she was a tender to HMCS Givenchy. In 1943–1944 she was a tender to HMCS Chatham. On May 15, 1968, this fishpacker owned by Bute Towing Ltd., Vancouver BC burned with an oil barge in tow near North Harwood Island and was a constructive total loss. She was re-registered April 30, 1976 after a re-build as a power-cruiser.

Sea Fox II[e] 172318 During the Second World War she served as a Canadian Naval Patrol Vessel, Fishermen's Reserve as HMCS Cancolim II. In 1942 she was renamed as HMCS Flores. In 1942 she was listed as

---

a   Built as New Delta; then Sea Crest II
b   Built as Mabel Mac; then Sea Dawn
c   Built as Sea Foam I; then La Porte; then V.T. No. 502; then Damar; then Sea Foam V
d   Built as Canfisco; the HMCS Canfisco; then Sea Fox II; then Dunwurkin
e   Built as Cancolim II; then HMCS Cancolim II; then HMCS Flores; then Cancolim II; then Loligo; then Gillian Lindsay; then La Salle; then Sea Fox II

a harbour service auxiliary craft in the Canadian Naval List. In 1944 she was a tender to HMCS Givenchy II. On September 15, 1976 she grounded and sank at Anchor Island, Slingsby Channel BC. Andrew Clarke reports that "In 2016 she is now sunk at her moorings in Burgoyne Bay, Saltspring Island BC."

Sea Gull On May 12, 1889 this fishing schooner was stranded at Cape St. James (QCI) BC.

Sea Gypsy[a] 138527 On January 30, 1968 this power cruiser owned by Ronald M Jebb (MO), Langley BC foundered and sank at the Pitt River Marina BC and was a total loss.

Sea Harp[649] On October 31, 1953 this troller ran aground on Growler Point and was later salvaged by a derrick. On November 7, 1955 she burned off Sand Heads BC.

Sea Imp X[650] 806963 On September 22, 2015 this tug, owned by Catherwood Towing Ltd., Mission BC, was towing a barge in the North Arm of the Fraser River when she caught a submerged deadhead in her propeller that caused her to stop dead in the water. The barge she had in tow dragged her sideways in the current causing her to capsize and sink. The crew abandoned ship safely. The tug suffered damage but was salvaged and put back into operation.

Sea Lion[b,651] 117116 In 1925 this tug was wrecked on a rock at the entrance to the Euclataw Rapids southeast of Gillard Island. The tug *Skookum No. 2* undertook the salvage work and pumped her out and the *Hopkins Bros.* then towed her to Vancouver BC. On June 2, 1945 she collided with the *Coast Quarries Jr.* off Sechelt BC.

Sea Luck 153044 On December 18, 1975 this seiner owned by Albert Recalma (MO), Qualicum BC was destroyed by fire.

---

a   Built as Seal Cove; then Sea Gypsy
b   Built as Sea Lion; then Sea Lion VI

Sea Maid Y II[a] 173402 In 1942 she was seized from her Japanese owners for service with the Royal Canadian Air Force. At the time, her appraised value was $7,500. On November 16. 1971 she sank southwest of Nootka Light and was a total loss.

Sea Mite[b] 150981 In August 1942 with a hog fuel barge in tow from Dollarton BC she was bound for Powell River and struck a bridge pier in the Second Narrows Bridge. In 1956 she foundered off Spanish Banks, Vancouver BC.

Sea Pigeon II 318989 On October 15, 1966 this fishboat owned by Tenho A Vitto (MO), Vancouver BC and Lenni E Suo (JO), Coquitlam BC burned when her engine caught fire in Ucluelet Inlet BC and was a total loss.

Sea Pride II[c] 172296 During the Second World War she was crewed with Fishermen's Reserve personnel but was not a part of the Fishermen's Reserve. She was employed as a DEMS Training Vessel at Esquimalt. In 1943 she was a tender to HMCS Givenchy II. On October 25, 1960 she foundered off Cape Mudge BC.

Sea Prince[d,652] 192870 In 1966 the *T-W Sea Prince*, under command of Captain Norman Sigmund, collided with dragger *Kalamalka* (which sank) near the mouth of the Fraser River at the Sandheads Lighthouse. The *T-W Sea Prince* was holed but pumps kept her afloat until she reached dock and her crew of 5 was rescued. On January 19, 1984, this fishboat, while under command of Captain Robert Levy, exploded and burned three miles off Hornby Island BC when a fuel supply line near the galley stove ruptured. She sank five miles north of Sisters Island BC and Eugene Williams died in the incident. Four other crew members and the Master escaped.

---

a   Built as Sea Maid Y II; then RCAF M.430 Puffin; then Sea Maid Y II
b   Built as Kanaka; then Sea Mite
c   Built as Sea Pride II; then HMCS Sea Pride II; then Sea Pride II
d   Built as USS APc-96; then Sea Prince; then Le Prince; then T-W Sea Prince; then Sea Prince

Sea Snipe 130460 On November 12, 1926 this vessel owned by Mr & Mrs William C Lawson, Vancouver BC foundered off north end of Hanson Island, Johnstone Strait BC.

Sea Spray I[a] 173380 During the Second World War this tug was operated by the Royal Canadian Air Force. On February 28, 1969, this tug owned by Westfrob Mines Ltd., Vancouver BC sank in Hunger Harbour, Tasu Sound, Queen Charlotte Islands, BC.

Sea Venture[b] 178007 On April 2, 1976 this tug owned by William T Kelly (MO), Port Coquitlam BC burned in Pryce Channel, Redonda Island BC.

Seahome No. 1 178675 In August 1963 this houseboat owned by Tulloch Fisheries Ltd., Vancouver BC sank at Big Bay BC off Stuart Island BC.

Sea-Link Rigger[c,653] 320217 On August 06, 1995, the self-dumping log barge *Sea-Link Rigger* capsized during the unloading operation. When the load of logs would not dump, preparations were begun to bring the barge back to the upright and unload by crane. The load then started to dump, but the barge was not ejected from under the load and was rolled over onto its beam ends and capsized. Two crew members from the towing tug were on board the barge; the deckhand was rescued from the water, but the mate had to escape from a pump room of the overturned barge. The barge was declared a total loss after it sank in deep water during subsequent salvage attempts.

Sealnes[654] N-00753 (Norway) The Transportation Safety Board of Canada states that "Shortly after midnight on 19 December 1993, in good visibility, the *Sealnes* was approaching the First Narrows, inbound to Vancouver Harbour, when she collided with the Mr

---

a   Built as Sea Spray I; then RCAF M.598 Sea Spray I; then Sea Spray I
b   Built as Saraboyd; then Sea Venture
c   Built as Crown Zellerbach No. 4; then Crown Forest No. 4; then Sea-Link Rigger

Fission which was drifting in the main channel after an engine malfunction. The three crew members of the *Mr Fission* were promptly rescued by one of the tugs in the area before their capsized vessel sank. The Board determined that the *Sealnes* and the *Mr Fission* collided because both vessels were not maintaining a proper look-out and neither vessel had determined that a risk of collision existed."

Sea-Ment 329317 On October 20, 1975 this fishboat owned by Leo Suo (MO), Ucluelet BC struck a submerged object and sank in Hayden Passage Vancouver Island, BC.

Searcher[a] 178058 On June 24, 1962 this fishboat owned by Wilfred J Landry, Vancouver BC sank near Freeman Pass BC.

Seaspan Rigger[b] 395390 In 1983 this self-loading log barge capsized at King Edward Island. Her hull was split in two for recovery and she was towed to Vancouver for re-assembly. On October 15, 2002 she capsized, and her cranes embedded into the substrate on the bottom effectively anchoring her so that she could not easily be righted. Divers used explosives to detach the cranes, and with a system of cables and anchors she was righted and towed to a shipyard for repair.

Seatowne 328439 On September 6, 1976 this fishboat owned by David H Hofstad (MO), Surrey BC was destroyed by fire in the engine room off Bute Inlet BC.

Seawolf[655] On November 3, 1950 this fishboat ran aground off Comox Spit. Richard Fraser of Deep Bay BC died of a heart attack and the vessel owner Mathew Pihlea, of Comox was sent to hospital. The vessel first went aground on a sandbar and Wiloughby Pendlebury, caretaker at the spit helped to push the boat off. The boat was later thrown back onto the spit in heavy fog. The boat filled with water and the crew were unable to escape because of heavy seas.

---

a   Built as Joutsen; then Searcher
b   Built as Seaspan Rigger; then Seaspan Phoenix

Sechelt[a,656] 122338 On March 24, 1911 while under command of Captain HV James she was en route Victoria to Jordan River BC this shelter deck steamer capsized in Race Passage and sank at Beechey Head BC near Sooke. She was carrying men and material for the hydro power station which was under construction. Twenty-four passengers and five crew were killed in the incident. The actual death toll was difficult to ascertain as there were different reports of how many were aboard.

Second Life 371895 On June 28, 1977 this sailing yacht owned by Roy Looyenga, Surrey BC sank off Sand Heads BC and was a total loss.

Secord No. 1[b,657] 320272 On August 4, 1967 the passenger freighter Northland Prince, owned by Northland Shipping (1962) Co. Ltd., Vancouver BC, collided with the fishboat Secord No. 1 in Grenville Channel. The fishboat sank about an hour afterwards.

Semiahmoo 126086 On November 24, 1915 this patrol vessel owned by the Minister of Marine and Fisheries, Ottawa ON was stranded 3/4 of a mile above Beaver Cove, Johnstone Strait BC.

Senator 080902 In 1925 this vessel, owned by owned by Captain Henrick Grauer and Ingval Johnson, Vancouver BC, was laid up and then deliberately sunk by her owner at Bowen Island BC.

Sergey Yesenin[658] (USSR) On August 02, 1970 this Russian freighter collided with the British Columbia Ferry Queen of Victoria in Active Pass BC. The freighter sliced into the ferry and jammed, killing a mother and her baby who stayed on the car deck in an automobile. The incident caused large merchant vessels to be banned from transiting Active Pass.

Shamrock[c,659] 090807 She was said to have been the first steamer built at New Westminster BC. On January 20; 1896 she was mortgaged

---

a   Built as Hattie Hansen; then Sechelt
b   Built as Secord No. 1; then Henry L. II
c   Built as Mamie; then Shamrock

by Jonathan Miller (Postmaster of Vancouver BC). As the *Mamie* she struck Mamie Rock in September 1897 while travelling, under the command of Captain Henry Smith, from Quascilla Bay to Rivers Inlet with a cargo of fresh salmon. On July 25, 1908 while under command of Captain D Heritage she was towing logs from Nanoose when her tail shaft broke. The crew stuffed rags into the gland and the tug *Daring* towed her to Nanaimo for repairs. On December 08, 1926 she was struck Bear Rock at the end of Malaspina Strait late at night while en route to Bute Inlet to pick up a tow of logs. Captain ES Hicks, and his crew of eight evacuated to Bear Rock when the tug filled with water and sank. Three men rowed to Lund where the tug *Achates* was alerted to the plight of the crew.

Shane[a,660] 155084 On June 30, 1961 this troller fishboat owned by Jack Rupert, Thetis Island BC exploded and burned in Georgia Strait approximately five miles southeast of Hornby Island BC. The owner and his partner, Ken Campbell, were rescued safely. The RCAF crash boat *Mallard* took them in tow, but the boat sank in about 12 feet of water.

Shannon J. 156605 On September 17, 1941 this tug owned by John S Shannon, Vancouver BC burned at the dock in Port Washington BC.

Shark II 194226 On October 07, 1957 this fishboat owned by Edward M Forde, Port Kells BC foundered and sank in Howe Sound BC one mile north of Passage Island.

Sharon Y. 188313 On June 28, 1969 this troller fishboat owned by Hiroshi Yoneda, Steveston BC burned and sank off Carmanah Light in San Juan Strait.

Shawatlans[661] 122156 On October 10, 1909 this tug owned by the Grand Trunk Pacific Railway Co., Vancouver BC was under the command of Captain Gus Hanson. Returning from a hunting trip they anchored in the vicinity of Shawatlans Lake. About 7:00 pm the

---

a   Built as Fred C.S. No. II; that Shane

master entered the engine room carrying a lantern. Apparently, the fuel line had been leaking gasoline and the fumes exploded. The Captain was burned, and the vessel was destroyed by fire. After the accident, the Captain made his way in a small boat to a nearby camp.

Sheba II 188297 On June 30, 1972 this power cruiser owned by Francis CL Carlow (MO) and Goldie R Carlow (JO), Victoria BC had an explosion in the engine room and was destroyed by fire in the Inner Victoria Harbour BC and was a total loss.

Sheena M.[a] 800064 On June 2, 1999 at about 00:45 am, the loaded chip barge Rivtow 901, under tow of the tug *Sheena M*, struck the Canadian Pacific Railway Mission Railway Bridge which spans the Fraser River at Mission, British Columbia. The striking caused considerable damage to the protection pier and swing span of the bridge. Rail traffic over the bridge was interrupted until June 30, 1999. Marine traffic through the swing span was suspended until the same date when it was made available on a limited basis. Unrestricted maritime use of the swing span was not available until July 25, 1999.

Sheila Faye 190621 In 1972 the RCMP advised the Registrar of shipping that this fishboat owned by Stanley L Brown, Madeira Park BC burned and sank in Agamemnon Channel BC in July 1969.

Shelmerdene[662] 154635 On July 10, 1932 this power cruiser, owned by John Cowdry, Vancouver BC, suffered an explosion and burned at McNab Creek, Howe Sound BC. The boat was being moved to a safe anchorage during stormy weather when the engine exploded as it was being started. One man was hurled into the water and the other onto a log boom. The vessel burned to the waterline and sank.

Sherman[b,663] 138685 On September 8, 1942 this fishpacker, owned by John D Paul, Hartley Bay BC, foundered at the north entrance of Moose Cove in Telegraph Passage at the mouth of the Skeena River.

---

a   Built as Petro-Master; then Sheena M.
b   Built as Dreadnaught; then Sherman

The owner skipper had to break a window in the cabin of the vessel to escape from the sinking vessel. He was picked up by five other members of the crew who had launched the vessel's lifeboat. They then rowed 25 miles to the Claxton Cannery to which they had been proceeding at the time of the incident.

Shimara[a,664] 138162 On October 24, 1956 this fishpacker, owned by Captain William Burrow, North Vancouver BC, foundered in a storm and sank. The engineer was trying to restart the engine when the battery exploded, and flames spread to barrels of gasoline stored nearby. The men spent 90 minutes in a 10' rowboat on the stormy seas before being picked up by the fishboat *Nadina*. The crew of five were admitted to hospital but were otherwise safely rescued.

Shinwa Maru[665] The Transportation Safety Board of Canada reports that "On 12 March 1992, the Canadian ferry *Queen of Alberni*, under the conduct of the master, departed from Tsawwassen, British Columbia, bound for Nanaimo, British Columbia, and the Japanese bulk carrier *Shinwa Maru*, under the conduct of a British Columbia coast pilot, departed from Roberts Bank Terminal (Westshore Terminals) en route to the Victoria Pilot Station. The vessels collided approximately one nautical mile south-west of Tsawwassen Ferry Terminal in daylight, with calm weather conditions and visibility reduced by fog."

Shirlu[666] 177973 On September 2nd, 1958 this fishpacker, owned by Captain Webster A Pierce, Prince Rupert BC, was involved in a collision in Grenville Channel BC in that she got between a tug and barge in the fog and flipped under the barge, Clare Clopp and Chester Huskins were killed in the accident.

Shizu 141713 In 1941 she was seized from her Japanese owners by the Canadian Government. In 1942 her ownership transferred to His Majesty the King. On April 28, 1950, this fishboat owned by Walter Herman, Courtenay BC burned at the Nelson Brothers' wharf in Comox BC.

---

a   Built as Kildala; then Pacinaco; then Shimara

Siberian Prince[667] 135729 On July 29, 1923 this British freighter, while en route from Seattle to San Francisco, went aground in a fog on Bentinck Island. She struck on a particularly high tide and the receding tide left her stranded. They had to wait several weeks until another extremely high tide could aid the salvage process. On August 13, 1923, after 16 days she was refloated by the salvage tug *Algerine* (with the *Nitinat* and *Burrard Chief*).

Sidney No. 2[668] 126179 On December 29, 1927 this car barge, while under tow by the Chieftain with a cargo of cotton, was stranded on James Island, Juan de Fuca Strait BC. The barge was partially sunk with several cars under water. Afterwards, bales of cotton, which had been en route to the explosives plant were being washed up on the beach.

Silver Bounty 198580 On June 13, 2003 this fishboat owned by Bounty Holdings Ltd., Terrace BC sank 64km south of Sandspit QCI. Her crew of three was rescued by the Royal Caribbean cruise ship *Radiance of the Seas* after her life raft blew away in the storm.

Silver Horde 158552 On July 30, 1979 this fishboat owned by Bulkley Valley Aquaculture Ltd., Houston BC sank at Langara Point QCI BC.

Silver Triton[669] 347963 On October 11, 1984 John C Secord and his crew member Stanley T Szczuka went down with this fishing boat, the Silver Triton, in a violent storm off the west coast of Vancouver Island near Winter Harbour.

Silvey[670] On December 16, 1915 this small Skookumchuck fishboat under the command of Captain Silvey was returning to Vancouver harbour in the evening with a cargo of fish. They were overtaking the tug Maagen, under command of Captain Thomas Edwards, which was towing a light scow through First Narrows. The fishboat was passing the tug on the starboard side when a strong rip current slewed the fishboat around across the bow of the tug. The tug forced the boat over on its side and it filled up with water and flooded. As she rolled past the scow her house works were torn off causing her to sink. The skipper and two fishermen were in the house when the accident occurred, and Captain Silvey and George Roberts disappeared, drowned. A second fisherman, Leslie Wilson, came to the surface clinging to floating wreckage and was rescued.

Sir Thomas Lipton[671] This former 4-masted schooner (converted to a log barge) was in service carrying hog fuel and wood chips between Port Alberni, Chemainus, to Port Townsend and Port Angeles WA USA. On December 4, 1946 she was abandoned as a hulk on Gambier Island BC.

Skagit[672] This US barkentine, under command of Captain Lewis W Rose, was registered at Port Townsend WA USA. On October 25, 1906 while inbound from San Francisco for Port Gamble WA she went ashore and was wrecked at Clo-oose. In stormy weather they sighted Cape Beale light which they mistook for Carmanah Light. The night was very dark and visibility when they went ashore was limited in the early morning. The ship swung around until she was broadside to the waves. A man attempted to get ashore with a line but spent a harrowing 30 minutes in the surf being pounded on the rocks and the hull of the ship until he was brought back on board. Captain Rose was swept away after falling overboard. Three persons, including the Captain, were lost and Dave Logan the lineman on the Lifesaving Telegraph at Clo-oose saved 15 others.

Skeena Cat[673] 179441 On May 12, 1958 she sank southwest of Frenchman Bay in Massett Inlet QCI BC. William Tauber reports that "as a young kid living in Juskatla, I can remember the *Skeena Cat* being scuttled in Mamin Bay, about a kilometre offshore in front of Juskatla."

Skeena Maid[a] 172513 On January 26, 1959 this fishboat, owned by Norman Ryall, Vancouver, BC, sank near Janit Reef, Barclay Sound, BC and became a total loss.

---

a   Built as Skeena Maid; then RCAF M.536 Skeena Maid; then Skeena Maid

Skeena Prince[a] 176563 In 1966 she collided with a rail barge in Grenville Channel. In 1967 she collided with the train ship *Alaska* in Queen Charlotte Channel. Ken Lund[674] states that " In 1976 she was sold and taken to Panama."

Skookum[675] 134028 On November 13, 1913 this power cruiser, owned by the Okanagan Lake Boat Co., was in a collision with the *Castlegar* on Okanagan Lake BC. She was towing a scow load of cement pipe at the time of the incident. She had her whole cabin torn away and the master had his leg broken.

Skookum Cache[b] On January 14, 2014, an old wooden tug, *Elf*, sank near Passage Island, British Columbia. The tug *Elf* was itself under tow from Squamish to the Fraser River to be demolished. She was not raised again, as authorities pegged the cost between $650,000 to $2 million which was considered prohibitive. Before sinking, the *Elf* was moored alongside a barge known as the *King Arthur*, located in the Mamquam Blind Channel.

Skookum Chief[676] 171977 On May 28, 1949 this tug, owned by Nanaimo Towing Co. Ltd., Nanaimo BC, blew up near the Home Oil fuel dock at Newcastle Island BC in Nanaimo Harbour. Her crew of two were severely burned and were forced to jump in the water by the intensity of the fire. The burning hulk of the Skookum Chief was towed 1.5 miles up Newcastle Channel toward Departure Bay to burn out so it would not endanger shore properties.

Skookum I[c,677] 126323 On December 17, 1957 she struck a submerged object and sank in Victoria Harbour BC. In May 1961 this derrick barge, owned by Island Tug & Barge Ltd., Victoria BC, sank in Saanichton Bay BC and was later salvaged. She had been lifted an 11-ton propeller when a cable snapped, and the propeller smashed

---

a   Built as Ottawa Page; then Blue Peter II; then Cassiar III; then Skeena Prince
b   Built as Elf; then Foss No. 15; then Karlyn; then Skookum Cache; then Elf
c   Built as W.F. 1; then Skookum I

through the hull and she sank in 35 feet of water. She was employed removing propellers from obsolete freighters about to be towed to Japan for scrap.

Skooter[678] 188293 On September 25, 1967 this tug, owned by Captain Willie E Thuveson (MO), Burnaby BC, burned and sank in Gunderson Slough, North Surrey BC and was a total loss.

Skylge 314819 On September 13, 1967 this ketch-rigged sailing vessel owned by Klaas H Smit, Richmond BC had a fire in the engine room while in Juan de Fuca Strait off Sooke BC.

Slaven[a,679] 158257 On September 12, 1934 this cannery tender registered at Ketchikan AK hit a reef and sank 2 miles north of West Inlet on the shore of Grenville Channel BC.

Slavka C.[b,680] 117017 On May 28, 1932 this tug owned by Frank Cvitanovich, Vancouver BC burned after her engine backfired in Trincomalee Channel between Wallace and Galiano Islands BC. The crew of three escaped unharmed.

Sleipner 150598 On December 14, 1931 while owned by Charles Deving, Marpole BC she suffered a fire near Shushartie Bay in Bates Pass BC.

Slitrig 156461 On December 04, 1960 this fishing troller owned by British Columbia Packers Ltd., Vancouver BC was stranded on a rock five miles north of Muctoosh Creek in the Alberni Canal after which she slid into deep water.

Sloga I 141147 On October 5, 1930 she collided with the Princess Joan on her first rum running trip and was sunk while leaving Victoria harbour two miles northeast of Discovery Island.

---

a   Built as Slaven; then Daly; then La Salle; then Stroma; then Raccoon
b   Built as Columbia; then Chaos; then Slavka C.

Smith Isle[a] 311906 In 1980 this fishboat was owned by owned by Tobbi Gulsvik, Prince Rupert BC. She burned and sank in the early 1990s.

Smith Sound[b,681] 172530 On September 17, 1965 this seiner sank in Hecate Strait BC. She was returning to Prince Rupert when heavy seas flooded the engine. The fishboat *Twinkle* put a line aboard her but the seas were too heavy to tow the seiner. Then the Smith Sound capsized so quickly the crew did not have time to put on lifejackets. They did not carry a life raft and the skiff was full of gear. The crew jumped in the ocean together and Edward Bitman simply disappeared.

Smoky Joe 197682 On August 23, 1960 this fishboat owned by Carl Roadhouse, Vancouver BC burned in Halfmoon Bay BC.

Snohomish[c] 158954 In 1937 she towed the Alaska Packer ship *Star of Holland* from San Francisco for conversion to a log barge. She sank in Seymour Narrows in August 1941, grounding and being rammed by her tow, the tank barge S.O. No. 5. She was submerged to the top of her funnel she was refloated in October 1941 and returned to service. In March 30. 1942 she sailed to the Aleutian Islands with OTC *Barge #1* and a steel scow in tow. She returned to Victoria BC on June 26, 1942. On July 20, 1942 she departed Vancouver BC towing the *Daylight* to Valdez AK. In 1947 she was sent under command of Captain Fred R MacFarlane from Puget Sound to Buenos Aires. She was towing a 278' barge called the *Island Yarder* containing six 74' surplus US Army tugs. On arrival at Buenos Aires she was commissioned into the Argentinian Navy. In 1980 she was sold for scrap and broken up in Argentina.

---

a Built as Silver Token; then Smith Isle
b Built as Smith Sound; then HMCS Smith Sound; then Smith Sound
c Built as USRC No. 16; then USRC Snohomish; then Snohomish; then Matarasin; then Ona Sol

Snoqualmie 152525 On August 28, 1932 this fishboat was stranded on an unnamed point four miles south of Cape Scott BC. In 1932 she was broken up.

Snow Mountain[a,682] 134644 On July 18, 1929 this vessel owned by Nootka Packing Co. Ltd., Vancouver BC foundered six miles south southeast of Refuge Cove on the west coast of Vancouver Island BC. Her crew was rescued by the tug *Solander*. The *Snow Mountain* sank while in tow of the tug.

Solan 329561 On August 15, 1978 this fishboat owned by Edward J Kowaleski (MO), Richmond BC sank at Rasonia Roller Bar, near Rason Island in Queen Charlotte Sound BC.

Solander 155250 Rod Baker reported "I was aboard the Solander, as one of four crew members in December of 1968. Around midnight, we were heading up the Masset Inlet. We hit a reef and then the barge carrying 18,000 gallons of gasoline and some heavy equipment, ran over us crushing the aft cabin. Due to the damage sustained to the hull and topsides. We got a float plane to Skidegate and commercial flight back home." After 1969 she was registered as a fishboat. On June 16, 1969 she struck a rock and sank and was declared a total constructive loss. She was salvaged by Rod Palm (Tofino BC) and put back into operation in the Tofino area.

Captain George MacFarlane (r) and Chief Engineer McPhee (l) on the deck of the *Solander* in 1938 at Victoria BC (Photograph from John MacFarlane collection.)

---

a   Built as Tanana; then Snow Mountain

Sonja III 190610 On June 13, 1975 this troller fishboat owned by Michael Hanson, Kyuquot BC grounded and sank on the west coast of Nootka Island BC and was a total loss.

Soquel (US) This four-masted schooner was registered at San Francisco CA USA. On January 22, 1909 she was wrecked on the Sea Bird Rocks (Vancouver Island) BC. She had been travelling from Callao Peru to Port Townsend in ballast under Captain Henningsen (who had previously been wrecked in the Uncle John in 1899). The Captain mistook the light at Pachena Bay for the light at Cape Flattery. "Twenty minutes after she struck a mountainous wave broke over the vessel, carrying away two masts and a lifeboat and killing the captain's wife and daughter. The rest of the crew were rescued by the Leebro."[683]

Southend 154713 On October 27, 1956 this fishboat owned by Hugo Gratland, Vancouver BC burned at Lasqueti Island BC.

Southern Chief[684] On the night of April 14, 1883 this American Bark was one of four sailing ships driven ashore at Royal Roads (Victoria). She was stuck there for months, finally refloated in damaged condition after being sold at auction. In 1894 bound for Australia with lumber she sprang a leak and was abandoned off Cape Flattery—the crew was rescued and taken to Port Townsend by the tug *Sea Lion*. The vessel itself was later picked up and taken to Port Townsend but she was written off as a total loss.

Southseaman 156631 On September 13, 1935 this fishboat owned by Gerald B Hamilton, Salt Spring Island BC foundered at the entrance to Seaforth Channel, Milbanke Sound BC.

Sparky[685] In 1954 she was fishing for the Porcher Island Cannery. On October 6, 1956, this gillnet fishboat owned by Henry Krutko, Nanaimo BC was destroyed by fire when the owner was trying to restart a stalled engine. She sank, while in tow of a federal fisheries vessel, in 180 feet of water off Neck Point near Nanaimo BC.

Speedway 138449 She was reported to have operated in the rum running trade[686]. On January 24, 1925, this schooner owned by John Murray Bowman, Vancouver BC was destroyed by an explosion and fire in the Strait of Juan de Fuca (all crew saved).

Spindrift 103475 On August 19, 1976 this fishboat owned by Francis Millerd and Co. Ltd., West Vancouver BC sank at the Government Wharf in Ladysmith Harbour BC.

Spindrift III 314871 On July 25, 1964 this power cruiser owned by Robert H Davie, West Vancouver BC exploded and fire in Fisherman's Cove, West Vancouver near the entrance to Howe Sound BC.

Spindrift X 369039 On April 4, 1980 this power cruiser owned by Werner W. Schulze, Port Alberni BC sank in Mayne Bay BC.

Spirit of Vancouver Island 816503 The Transportation Safety Board of Canada reports that "On the morning of 14 September 2000 shortly after departing her berth at Swartz Bay, BC, the passenger/vehicle ferry *Spirit of Vancouver Island* increased to a customary speed and attempted to overtake the pleasure craft *Star Ruby* in the 460 m long narrow section of the buoyed channel of Colburne Passage. Neither vessel took effective collision-avoidance measures. A collision resulted. The pleasure craft sustained considerable damage and sank. The two persons aboard the *Star Ruby* were recovered and transported to a hospital, where they subsequently succumbed to their injuries."

Spokane 100684 In 1891 this sternwheeler was in service on Great Northern Railway from Bonners Ferry to Jennings MT. On July 04, 1891 she snagged at Myie Landing but was salvaged. She was used as a landing stage at Kaslo BC after the Kaslo wharf washed out in a flood in 1894. On March 25, 1895 she burned to the waterline at Kaslo BC and declared a total loss. Her engines were salvaged.

Disasters occurred on freshwater too. The sternwheeler *Spokane* on fire with the sternwheeler *Idaho* standing by (Image from the collection of the Maritime Museum of British Columbia 000116)

Spokane[687] On the night of June 29, 1911, while under command of Captain JW Guptill, she struck Ripple Rock in Seymour Narrows shortly before midnight. The fierce current caused her to swerve in the channel and she hit on the starboard side tearing a huge hole in her double hull. She was moved into Plumper Bay, but the pumps could not keep up with the inflow. She had 160 passengers on board of who 100 jumped overboard. They were rescued by the crew and brought back to the ship. Two passengers died in their stateroom: Mrs JE Strauss, and Mrs GF Williams. The pilot took a boat to intercept the *Prince George* at Grange Point. They aided the stricken ship and hailed the *Admiral Sampson*. The steamer City of Seattle also gave assistance. All the passengers were offered berths on the City of Seattle, but none wished to continue their journey and were taken on board the *Admiral Sampson* for passage back to Seattle. The *Spokane* was refloated by the Salvor and escorted her back to Seattle WA USA.

Sport II 179641 On August 8, 1965 this fishboat owned by George W. Amor, Kitimat BC was wrecked and sunk in Douglas Channel, south of Kitimat BC and was a total loss.

Spray 100676 On November 23, 1911 this workboat owned by George Rudge, Port Simpson BC foundered near Wark Island.

Spray[a] 122383 In 1967 this workboat owned by Billie K Warnock (MO), Pender Harbour BC was permanently beached at Bargain Harbour BC.

Spray No. 1 178303 On June 18, 1967 this troller fishboat owned by British Columbia Packers Ltd., Vancouver BC was reported as lost at sea.

Spraydrift 141563 On September 9, 1932 this sailing yacht owned by Gordon B Warren, Vancouver BC burned one-half mile west of Passage Island, is Georgia Strait.

Spring Mist 310332 On August 3, 1967 this troller fishboat owned by John Steiner (MO), Vancouver BC caught fire and sank in Pate Pass BC.

Sproat No. 21 319368 In 1970 this tug owned by MacMillan, Bloedel Ltd., Vancouver BC sank in Sproat Lake BC on Vancouver Island.

Squamish Pilot[b,688] 177759 On December 20, 1964 the tug Lordel under Captain James Boyd burned and exploded in Vancouver Harbour under the Second Narrows Bridge. Boyd and crewman Rene Beulieu escaped by paddling their life raft with their hands and feet to escape the burning wreck before it exploded. They were passing under the bridge at 5:00 pm when they saw smoke coming from the cabin. They had just taken on fuel previously and the fire was so intense that even the life raft was burning. The fire was extinguished by the Vancouver Fireboat. She was declared a total loss.

---

a   Built as Spray; then HMCS Spray; then Spray
b   Built as Lordel; then Squamish Pilot

Squamish Queen[a,689] 179421 On November 6, 1958 this fishpacker, owned by Anglo-British Columbia Packing Co. Ltd., Vancouver BC, foundered four miles southeast of Pachena Point BC and was lost off Carmanah Point BC. She was carrying a cargo of herring from Barkley Sound. She sank stern first after being overwhelmed by waves. Her crew of seven were rescued by the Cape James.

Squamish Rascal[b] 188305 On November 2, 1976 this tug owned by Lions Gate Tug & Barge (1973) Ltd., North Vancouver BC foundered in English Bay Vancouver BC.

Squamish Yarder[c] 194912 On June 27, 1976 this tug owned by Cross Forest Products Ltd., Hornby Island BC burned north of Hornby Island, Georgia Strait BC.

Squid[690] 116459 On October 22, 1943 this freighter was carrying a cargo of lime. Some water seepage into the hull caused a chemical reaction so that a fire broke out and she was damaged by fire at the Evans, Coleman, and Evans dock in Vancouver Harbour.

ST-239 (USATS)[d] (US) On December 04, 1944 this tug owned by Foss Towing Company, Seattle WA and under charter to the US Army was in a collision and sank at Kingcome Point BC.

St. Clair 107246[691] She was one of first tugs converted to an oil burner. On November 16, 1948 while owned by Coastal Towing Co. Ltd., Vancouver BC she was stranded at Port Renfrew BC during a storm with the loss of three lives, while towing a barge (the S.O.B.C. No. 8) in Port San Juan, during a storm. Her propeller was fouled by the towline. Her propeller was fouled by the towline. After taking on water she was swamped in heavy waves and three crew members were drowned: Carl Janson (Chief Engineer), J Leslie Hudson and Levi Arnott. (Her boiler was still visible in the 1970s)

---

a   Built as M.469 Squamish (RCAF); then Squamish Queen
b   Built as La Bette; then Seaspan Rascal; then Squamish Rascal
c   Built as Victory IX; then Squamish Yarder
d   Built as Chilkat; then Edith Foss; then USATS ST-239

St. Clair No. 2[a] 126545 She was the third towboat built by the Thulin Brothers. She burned in 1910. In March 1920 she was broadsided by the passenger vessel Admiral Evans heading through Discovery Passage in heavy fog. The tug sank in Duncan Bay. On April 27, 1931 she burned near Snug Cove, Bowen Island BC off Whitecliffe BC.

St. Dennis (US) When on March 25, 1909 the Boscowitz Steamship Co. Ltd. steamer Venture was destroyed by fire the Company chartered the St. Dennis from San Diego for the 1909 season. In December 1910 she was lost with all hands when she foundered in the Queen Charlotte Sound BC.

St. Paul In 1930 this ship-rigged vessel was towed through the Ballard Locks at Seattle WA for preservation as a museum ship by the Salt Water Aquarium and Marine Museum which officially opened to the public the weekend of June 16 and 17, 1934. In 1942 when the Puget Sound Academy of Science experienced financial difficulties she was sold for use as a breakwater at Oyster Bay BC where she was scuttled in the breakwater at the end of her life.

Stadia[692] 136166 On December 14, 1916 this launch, owned by T McLennan, foundered on Storm Island, Queen Charlotte Sound BC. Carrying two BC land surveyors and a survey crew of 4, this vessel while en route from the Koeye River to Vancouver anxious to return home for Christmas. A storm came up and the vessel sought shelter at Pine Island. She struck a rock, foundered, and broke up in the surf. The crew and passengers all made it ashore safely, and salvaged what they could from the waves, including the survey instruments. On shore they built a shelter. The surveyors, HT Garden and T Buran lit a fire to dry out. They signalled to several passing steamers without success. They tried smoke signals, flags, and other means but twelve steamers passed without noticing them. Some even scanned them with searchlights but took them to be First Nations people and carried on. They erected a 12' wide and 8' high sign constructed from blueprints that read "HELP". Also, unsuccessful this sign was

---

a   Built as City of Lund; then St. Clair No. 2

apparently taken as indicating "kelp" and steamers gave them a wide berth. On December 20th they poured a can of gasoline on the fire making a huge plume of flame that attracted the *Humboldt*, and that brought rescue.

Standard[693] On June 5, 1894 this vessel foundered off Cape Mudge BC near the entrance to Seymour Narrows while en route from Nanaimo to the Skeena River.

Standon[a,694] 158595 On September 26, 1954, at dusk, this tug owned by Coast Quarries Towing Co. Ltd., Vancouver BC, was in collision with a scow and capsized just east of the Second Narrows Bridge in Vancouver Harbour BC. Caught in a tide rip, she rolled over and sank throwing her two crew into the water. They were picked up by the nearby *Bayburn* that came to their aid and picked up the scow and secured it to a buoy.

Stanley B. 134422 On December 4, 1923 this vessel owned by Packers Steamship Co. Ltd., Vancouver BC was stranded off Gower Point BC.

Star of Chile 058939 She was registered in London UK. In 1896–1897 she was shipping grain from Puget Sound WA. On January 20, 1961 she sank in Quatsino Sound BC.

Star Shine[695] On February 28, 1976 this gillnetter foundered at night in a snowstorm in the Juan de Fuca Strait s few miles south of Cape Beale. Harold Wulff and Trent Hansen abandoned ship in a small skiff. After a long search they were located by a Labrador helicopter and rescued by the CGCC *Ready*.

Starling[696] On July 10, 1968 this US seiner, under command of Captain George R Williams, collided with the *Cape Scott* in Seymour Narrows. The collision ripped the bow off the boat, and she sank in 600 feet of water. Her crew of six had only two minutes to evacuate into a dinghy. The *Cape Scott*, under Captain Ian Simpson, suffered

---

a   Built as Curly; then Standon

damage to her port side but managed to take the crew of the Starling on board.

Stella Maria[697] On July 01, 1971 this troller fishboat foundered and sank in 50 mph wind and heavy rai off Amphitrite Point BC. Her master was rescued by the fishboat Odd Bay.

Stellar Sea 830007 On October 1, 2016 this whale watching vessel owned by Jamie's Whaling Station Ltd., Tofino BC bottom and partially sank near Warn Bay, east of Tofino BC. The Canadian Coast Guard reported that everyone aboard the Stellar Sea was removed from the boat safely and there have been no reports of pollution. The vessel was salvaged and put back into operation.

Sterling I 175452 On June 29, 1978 this fishboat owned by Raymond S Decock (MO), Port Clements BC grounded and sank east of Langara Island BC while being towed.

Storm King[698] 122165 On March 19, 1939 she was stranded at Race Rocks BC. On December 17, 1941 while under command of Captain Ed Roskelly and owned by Pacific Salvage Co. Ltd., Victoria BC, she was stranded on Trial Island BC during a gale, broke up and sank in Enterprise Channel. The captain and his crew of five made their way to shore in a boat and were later picked up by the tug *Island Rover* and taken to Victoria.

Stormer 198638 In June 1997 this tug owned by Bosquet Investments Ltd., Rivers Inlet BC sank in Menzies Bay with log barges in tow. She was caught by the tide with hatches open and sank suddenly. The crew was rescued.

Strady XII[a] 155094 On October 26, 1970 this tug owned by Stradiotti Brothers Ltd., Vancouver BC ran aground and was a total loss on Chatham Island near Prince Rupert BC.

---

a   Built as Three Queens; then Strady XII

Straits Cadet[a,699] 130493 In September 1965 this ex-tug, owned by Leslie Holmes, Los Angeles CA USA, was destroyed by fire near Roche Harbour and sank in 140 fathoms in Haro Strait. She caught fire while being towed by the tug *Point Hope* which had come to the aid of the yacht. The fire was thought to have started in a fuel storage tank. The *Point Hope* was forced to cut her adrift and the seven persons on board were rescued by the US Coast Guard.

Stranger II[b,700] 331657 On September 26, 1966 this power cruiser (a converted Fairmile owned by Marlineer Marine Inc., Pomona CA USA) burned and sank in the Strait of Juan de Fuca five miles of Port Angeles WA USA. The two men on board, Ted Tate (Pomona CA) and Lee Washburn (Long Beach CA) were rescued by the British freighter *Tetela*.

Strath 153100 On April 28, 1949 she struck a rock and sank at Point Upwood (30 miles north of Vancouver in Georgia Strait). The crew was rescued by the Macgregor which also picked up the tow of two barges. The top of the wheelhouse was visible at low tide and she was salvaged. (The Province Apr 28, 1949). On January 6, 1958 she was in collision with the *Pacific Unity* two miles from the North Arm Jetty in Georgia Strait BC.

Strathcona 107146 This sternwheeler was a sister ship of the *Caledonia* (III). She served on the Stikine River. This steamer helped start the Sidney and Nanaimo ferry route on June 24, 1902. This service was called the Sidney and Nanaimo Transportation Company (S&NT). The *Strathcona* had worked for three months of that year before she blew a cylinder on August 19, 1902. The ship was unable to be repaired, so she was retired from S&NT immediately and replaced. Afterwards she worked on Howe Sound. On November 17, 1909 she was wrecked at Page's Landing BC by striking a snag. In 1910 she was raised with pontoons and floated to New Westminster where her hull was abandoned.

---

a   Built as Cheerful; then Malaspina Straits; then Straits Cadet
b   Built as H.M.C. M.L. Q.067; then H.M.C. M.L.-067; then Fairchild; then Stranger II

Streamline[701] 141130 On December 2, 1926 this tug, owned by Mrs Angus Beaton, Vancouver BC, destroyed by a fire caused by an overheated stove near the Burrard Grain Elevator, in Burrard Inlet BC.

Sudbury II[a,702] 196261 One of the most famous and iconic tugs in the marine history of British Columbia. In 1958–1969 she was owned by Island Tug & Barge Co. Ltd., Victoria BC. In 1969–1970 she was owned by Genstar Ltd., Montreal QC. In 1970–1972 she was owned by Island Tug & Barge Ltd., North Vancouver BC. In 1972–1979 she was owned by Seaspan International Ltd., North Vancouver BC. In 1959 she towed two 10,000-ton liberty ships 5,500 miles to Japan in a tandem tow. In 1966 she towed the ROC freighter *Tainan* (an ex- Park Ship) to Esquimalt. On October 14, 1963 while towing the *Island Cypress* the barge broke in half and sank in the Pacific Ocean. In March 1966 she saved the Greek tramp steamer *Lefkipos* from being driven ashore north of Nootka. In 1974 she was towing log barges to Japan and then barges loaded with steel gas pipe to Point Barrow AK. About 500km east of Japan a towing chain broke severing an artery in the master's leg. One of the barges, the *Ketchikan*, capsized and sank. In 1982 after being employed as a fishpacker, owned by Lady Pacific Inc., Seattle WA USA, while en route to Seattle she burned in Hecate Strait.

Summerville 153076 In 1941 she was seized from her Japanese owners by the Canadian Government. In 1942 her ownership transferred to His Majesty the King. On December 27, 1969 she struck a submerged object one half mile off Coffin Point, VI BC.

Sun Dance[703] 178060 On January 26, 1951 she was wrecked in a storm near her mooring in Horseshoe Bay BC.

Sun Rise I 141277 On September 28, 1931 this fishboat owned by Tom Shimizu and Charles Nakamura (JO), Prince Rupert BC was missing in Queen Charlotte Sound BC.

---

a   Built as HMS Caledonian Salvor; then Sudbury II; then Lady Pacific

Sunbeam 122507 On December 15, 1924 this workboat owned by Veterans Products Co. Ltd., Victoria BC foundered at Sidney Island BC.

Sun Crest 176751 On May 15, 1954 this fishboat owned by Frederick W Parrott, Eburne BC was stranded and burned at Thetis Island BC.

Sundancer[a,704] (UK) On June 29, 1984 this cruise ship (a converted former Baltic car ferry) struck Maude Island in Seymour Narrows. It was beached at Duncan Bay at the Crown Forest Industries Elk Falls Mill dock. She was refloated and towed to the Burrard Dry Dock. She was declared to be a total loss but was subsequently rebuilt as the *Pegasus*.

Sun-Kist[b] 345697 On May 12, 1972 this ketch-rigged sail yacht owned by George B Gray (MO), Vancouver BC burned and sank at Popham Island BC and was declared a total constructive loss.

Sunrise II 176235 On November 22, 1976 this fishboat owned by Odd Olson, Vancouver BC experienced an explosion and fire at the False Creek fisherman's terminal in Vancouver BC and was a total loss.

Super X 154819 On April 23, 1931 this fishboat owned by the Packers Steamship Co. Ltd., Vancouver BC suffered a fire at the entrance to Ganges Harbour on Saltspring Island BC.

Superior[705] 111991 On July 08, 1902 this tug, owned by Captain GH French, Vancouver BC, was caught in a tideway while towing a boom of logs she capsized while under the command of Captain George Marchant, in Vancouver Harbour. She was towing booms of logs to Scott's Mill. She was swamped and later raised. (Captain Marchant was the skipper of the *Beaver* when she was wrecked in 1888.) The crew were rescued by a boat from HMS *Shearwater*. On August 23, 1948 she sank off Tasu Sound (QCI) BC.

---

a   Built as Sundancer; then Pegasus
b   Built as Sun-Kist; then Ho-Hum; then Trysta; then Karina I; then Swadeshi

Superior 209874 (US) On November 9, 1940 she was destroyed by fire in Dodd Narrows BC.

Superior Straits[a,706] 173188 In 1942 she was employed as a Gate Vessel (assigned to target towing and net defense duty) at Pearl Harbour Hawaii. In 1955 she was brought out from the Great Lakes to the West Coast. In the 1960s she was withdrawn from service and reduced to a barge. She sank in Vancouver Harbour about 1973 but she continued to be listed in the Register of Shipping until 2006.

Susan Sturgis She was an American registered schooner sailing out of San Francisco CA. In 1851 she came to the rescue of the *Una*, which was wrecked in Neah Bay WT. In 1852 she sailed to the Queen Charlotte Islands in search of gold near Mitchell Inlet. On Langara Island she took on Chief Edenshaw as a pilot. Off Masset they were boarded by a Haida party and taken over in a fierce skirmish and she was wrecked at Rose Spit. Edenshaw intervened on behalf of the crew, saving their lives. The vessel was stripped and burned.

Suwanee (USS)[707] She was a double-ended iron paddle steamer. She was wrecked in Shadwell Passage (QCI) BC after striking a rock on a voyage to Alaska on June 09, 1868. HMS *Sparrowhawk* came to her aid and removed the crew to Victoria. The S.S. *New World* salvaged her armament and some machinery and carried them to San Francisco CA.

Swan No. 1 311908 On August 29, 1973 this fishboat owned by Donald S Phipps (MO), Prince Rupert BC experienced an explosion in her engine room at Dixon Entrance BC.

Swifter No. 2 176743 In December 1962, this river tug owned by Rayonier Canada (BC) Ltd., Vancouver BC sank in the Fraser River with the loss of Captain Frank Mills. Crew members Ronald Pilkey was saved. She was salvaged a few days later.

---

a   Built as USS YN-77; then USS AN-58; then USS Abele; then Abele, then Superior Straits

Swiftsure III 310318 On October 1, 1968 this tug owned by Swiftsure Towing Co. Ltd., Vancouver BC sank off Point Grey BC at Sturgeon Bank.

Swiftsure V[708] 195739 On June 14, 1954 this tug owned by Swiftsure Towing Ltd., New Westminster BC sank while towing 14 sections of logs near Boundary Road in the North Arm of the Fraser River. The crew were rescued by the tug *Papco No. 2* which was operating nearby. When the booms got too close to the shore, the skipper Captain William Howes, attempted to pull them away, turned broadside to the current and capsized.

Swiss Boy This American brig was outward bound from Port Orchard in Puget Sound to San Francisco loaded with lumber under Captain Weldon. She took on water in a storm and anchored, probably at the southern end of Trevor Channel in Barkley Sound to repair a leak. On February 01, 1859 she was beached for repairs at Robbers Bay, Trevor Channel in Barkley Sound. Ohiat and Tseshaht First Nations people boarded and vandalized the ship, the ships gear and robbed the crew of their clothing and personal possessions, although the crew was not harmed and could leave. The First Nations people apparently assumed that because the vessel was sailing under American colours that it was acceptable to consider her as a prize—apparently a serious case of misunderstanding. HMS *Satellite* was sent to arrest the attackers- bringing the to Victoria where they were jailed for six months.

Sylvia On December 16, 1916 while crossing the bow of the tug *Maagen* in the First Narrows of Vancouver Harbour she was struck and capsized. Two crew drowned and a third was rescued.

Sylva King 179092 In 1975 this tug owned by Terry D Ingram (MO), Powell River BC sank in Alliford Bay BC where she was scrapped.

Syringa[709] 313658 On 18 March 2015, at approximately 1541 PDT, the tug *Syringa* took on water and sank about 40 metres north of Merry

Island, off Sechelt, British Columbia. The tug had been towing the loaded barge *Matcon 1*, which was released shortly before the sinking. The 2 crew members swam ashore and were later evacuated by the Canadian Coast Guard; no injuries were reported. A small quantity of diesel fuel was released from the tug after it sank, and the adrift barge was recovered by another tug.

T. & B. 133845 On December 5, 1923 this tug owned by Thomas R McLay, Nanaimo BC was in a collision with the wharf at Safety Cove, Calvert Island BC.

T.C. Co. Ltd. 190578 In August 1968 this piledriver owned by Todd Construction Co. Ltd., Vancouver BC capsized and sank.

T.H.L. 138777 On August 28, 1949 this fishboat owned by Granville Hollingsworth, Pender Harbour BC burned at Scotty Bay, Lasqueti Island BC.

T.W. Carter[710] 097169 On March 07, 1896 this tug, owned by Andrew Gray, Victoria BC sank off Trial Island BC. At the time of her demise she was considered to have been the smallest tug in Canadian service and she did not have enough power to buck the current at Trial Island. She stranded and sank at Ripple Point, Trial Island BC. She became a total constructive loss.

Taboo[711] 310416 The hull was built in 1958 and finished by the owners. For two years she was chartered to Bayshore Yacht Charters to raise money for the trip. On July 24, 1964, this schooner-rigged yacht exploded and burned at the eastern entrance of Ramillies Channel in Howe Sound BC. The owners had been planning a Caribbean cruise. The owner had just lit the galley stove and went into the cockpit when it exploded.

Tacol III[a] 192873 She was built for the lumber trade and for hauling general cargo. She established a record of 57 days from Puget

---

a   Built as Sophie Christensen; then Tacol III

Sound to Callao Peru. In 1953 she was wrecked at sea off Vancouver Island BC.

Tacol IV 192874 On November 4, 1950 she was stranded after she lost her chain on rocks at Estevan Point (VI) BC.

Tahsis No. 3[a] 115953 In 1906 she collided with and sank the tug *Chehalis* in Burrard Inlet. In October 1906 she ran onto a reef off Oak Bay BC. The *Salvor* arrived from Esquimalt BC and pulled her off and towed her to Bullen's Shipyard.

Tahsis Prince[b] 160634 On March 15, 1968 this tug owned by Northwest Shipping (1962) Co. Ltd., Vancouver BC ran aground at Estevan Point, was beached, and later refloated near Hequiat Village BC. In 1968 she was salvaged by Marine Surveyors of Western Canada. In 1968 she was sold as accommodation for oyster fishermen. In 1976 she was abandoned near New Westminster BC.

Takashina 134567 On November 27, 1925 this fishboat foundered near Porlier Passage, Georgia Strait BC.

Takla[c,712] 154654 On December 3, 1935 this seiner, while owned by Kristian Parkvold, burned at Deepwater Bay north of Seymour Narrows BC. she burned and sank in 10 fathoms of water. She was purchased from the insurance underwriters by Kristian Parkvold and rebuilt. She formed part of the pre-war Fishermen's Reserve Fleet. She was mobilized September 15, 1939 and commissioned into the Royal Canadian Navy Fisherman's Reserve as HMCS *Takla*. In 1942 she was appraised at $12,300. In 1944 she was serving as tender to HMCS *Chatham*. On February 7, 1951 she was stranded approximately 1/8-mile west northwest of Lucy Island, Parry Passage BC and she sank on February 13, 1951.

---

a   Built as Princess Victoria; then Tahsis No. 3
b   Built as Granit; then Columbia; then Island King; then Chilliwack; then Tahsis Prince
c   Built as Takla; then HMCS Takla; then Takla

Taku[713] 5351052 On July 29th, 1970, at about 1240 am this passenger car ferry ran aground on Kinihan Island, outside of Prince Rupert, BC while enroute to Prince Rupert from Juneau AK. The officer of the watch apparently missed a marker buoy and she hit the shore hard enough to knock over some trees. Within minutes the ESSO tanker *Nanaimo* arrived on the scene followed by two Department of Fisheries patrol boats and two fishing boats. The *Nanaimo* had been sailing just behind the ferry and witnessed the incident. The *Nanaimo* took off the passengers and transported them to Prince Rupert. All the passengers on board were evacuated safely, and the cars were transferred to the BC Ferry *Queen of Prince Rupert*. The two vessels berthed stern to stern and 58 of the vehicles were transferred to lighten ship. Commercial barges took another 13. Two commercial units, semi-trailers without drivers, were left aboard. Four tugs pulled her off the rocks. None of the 297 passengers or 45 crew were injured.

Talamaso[714] 153174 In 1928 this fishboat was in a collision with a passenger launch in the Alberni Canal. In 1930 she ran ashore at Commodore Point, Discovery Island BC. Her cargo of cannery supplies was removed the previous evening and after a three-hour pull she came free. She was pulled off by the tug *Burrard Chief* at peak high-water May 1, 1930. In 1938 she was proposed as a possible member of the Fishermen's Reserve Fleet but was not taken up by the Royal Canadian Navy. On February 24, 1968, while under command of Captain Donald Hall, she sank in Burke Channel BC northeast of Jacobsen Bay after hitting a rock and settling into water 1,200 feet deep. The five-man crew evacuated safely in a lifeboat.

Talofa II 194861 On September 20, 1976 this fishboat owned by Wayne Coward, Sidney BC grounded in San Juan Bay BC. She caught fire and sank and was declared a constructive total loss.

Tamako 154563 On September 2, 1933 this seiner owned by Tomy Nakatsuka, Vancouver BC suffered a fire at Boney Bay on Cracroft Island BC.

Tamerlane 193518 On March 15, 1959 this fishboat owned by Michael W Costello, Hardy Island BC sank at the top end of Gambier Island in Howe Sound BC.

Tamerlane 311272 In 1973 this fishboat owned by William M McMath (MO), Surrey BC and Frederick V Shade, Nanaimo BC sank at Deep Bay BC.

Tana Bay[a] 344742 On March 21, 1978 this fishboat owned by Ernest Townsend (MO), Victoria BC suffered a fire at Pearl Harbour south of Port Simpson BC. She was declared as a total constructive loss at the time.

Tania Too[b] 369081 In December 1950 this US Navy tug had her machinery removed in Pearl Harbor Hawaii. Her bare hull was towed to Tacoma WA by the *Agnes Foss*. She was re-engined and re-built. In 1985 while owned by Godwin Marine Ltd., Qualicum Beach BC she sank after hitting a deadhead off Ocean Falls BC.

Taniwha[715] 154734 On August 3, 1930 while owned by William Garrad, Tod Inlet BC she burned in Bedwell Bay, Pender Island BC.

The collision damage to the hull suffered by the *Tartar* (Image from the collection of the Maritime Museum of British Columbia P3266_341)

Tartar[716] 086336 On October 17, 1907 at 8:00 pm she collided with the *Charmer* off Sandheads in heavy fog. (The *Charmer* had her bow flattened but was able to reach port, while Tartar had to be beached in English Bay. The *Tartar* was outbound for Yokohama and the *Charmer* inbound from

---

a   Built as Novena; then Frenterprise; then Tana Bay
b   Built as USS Y.T.L. 309; then Duncan Foss; then Elaine Foss; then Cumshewa Chief; then Tania Too

Victoria. The Charmer crashed into the port bow of the *Tartar*. The *Tartar* was leaking badly, and the decision was made to beach her. The *Charmer's* damage was significant—her bow was smashed back as far as forward bulkhead. The *Tartar* apparently misunderstood the *Charmer's* signals and in the 13 minutes that elapsed from the first one there was time for both vessels to take evasive action. She was repaired at Esquimalt Drydock but did not return to commercial service. In 1908 she was sold to K. Kishimoto of Osaka Japan for breaking up.

Tartar[a,717] 124355 In May of 1910 as the *Tartar* approached the dock at Lund in the dark she went aground. The wind and tide pushed her on to the rocks. As the tide went out, she rolled on to her side. As the tide came back in, she filled with water and sank. She was later salvaged.

Tatchu[718] 153198 On August 7, 1938 this pilchard seiner owned by British Columbia Packers Ltd., Vancouver BC foundered south of Cape Flattery south of the *Swiftsure Lightship*. She sprang a leak in heavy weather. She was abandoned after all nets and gear had been taken off by the tender *Marauder*. The *Tatchu* sank in 100 fathoms. All the crew were saved.

The *Tatjana* hard aground on Effingham Island (Photograph from Alberni Valley Museum pn21573)

Tatjana[b] (Norwegian Registry) On February 26, 1924 while en route from Yokohama to Vancouver, she was stranded on the southeast side of Effingham Island (formerly called Village Island) a few hundred yards from where the *Tuscan Prince* was wrecked. She was under charter to the

---

a   Built as Tartar; then Hawser
b   Built as Tatjana; then Dramensfjord

Yamashita Kisen Kaisha travelling in ballast from Murran, Japan, to Vancouver to load lumber. Her stern sank and the prop was broken off on the rocks. The *Banfield Lifeboat* rescued the Norwegian crew of 27 off the rocks. She was later salvaged after being towed to Victoria by the *Salvage Chief* and *Burrard Chief*. The repairs in Esquimalt were extensive, requiring 200 frames and 100 plates to be replaced.

Tattnall (USS) DD.125 In 1946 this US warship was scuttled at Royston BC as part of a breakwater.

Teddy J.[719] (US) On May 04, 1962 this halibut fishboat en route to Petersburg Alaska foundered near Lucy Island BC with the loss of four US fishermen. She was owned by John R Otness, Petersburg AK, USA.

Teeshoe[720] 151193 This tug owned by Powell River Co. Ltd., Vancouver BC was used for yarding logs at Powell River BC. On December 4, 1954 she was sunk in a collision with the propeller of the Italian freighter, *Giovanni Amendola* in Georgia Strait, with the loss of three crew members: George Crooks; Captain George Ilott; and Gray LeVae. The only survivor was the Captain's 12-year-old son Fred Ilott who was found the next morning on Savary Island. The freighter had wanted the assistance of a pilot when she began to drag her anchor offshore that caused the tug to venture out—and having dropped the pilot suffered the mishap.

Telemark 190338 On September 17, 1965 this fishboat owned by Lauri Savolainen, Pender Harbour BC exploded and burned at Pender Harbour BC and was a total loss.

Templar[721] (UK) This yacht, owned by Captain CE Barrett-Lennard, was brought out from England on the deck of the ship *Athelstan* arriving in Victoria on March 01, 1860. Carrying Barrett-Lennard and his friend Napoleon Fitz Stubbs they circumnavigated Vancouver Island. The account of this voyage was published in 1862 called "Travels in British Columbia, including a yacht voyage round Vancouver Island". After being sold to Messrs Henderson and Burnaby of Victoria she departed on a trading cruise up the coast of Vancouver Island. On January 24, 1862 she was driven ashore in a gale from an anchorage in Foul Bay and was lost.

Temple Moat[722] On October 28, 1936 the *Manunalei* collided with the *Temple Moat*, a freighter owned by the Temple Steamship Co., in fog near Race Rocks BC. The *Temple Moat* was feeling her way up the Strait in heavy fog inbound from Baltimore. She made her way to Royal Roads under her own power. The *Temple Moat* suffered extensive damage, but it was all above the waterline.

Tenyo Maru In an incident, on July 22, 1991, the Japanese fishing vessel *Tenyo Maru* and Chinese freighter *Tuo Hai* collided within Canadian Territorial waters approximately 20 miles northwest of Cape Flattery. The *Tenyo Maru*, which was reportedly carrying 354,800 gallons of intermediate fuel oil, 97,800 gallons of diesel fuel, and 22,500 gallons of fish oil, sank after the collision. It initially leaked a large amount of oil and undetermined amounts were reported leaking for more than a month after the collision. Beaches were fouled with oil from Vancouver Island, British Columbia to northern Oregon. The Canadian Coast Guard brought in a remotely controlled underwater robot, the *Scorpio*, aboard the CCGS *Martha L. Black* to pump oil from the *Tenyo Maru* to tanks aboard a surface ship from the sunken ship in 100 fathoms. The *Scorpio* used the robot arms to install a suction cup and hose into a porthole leaking oil. The oil then was then pumped to a tank aboard a ship. This was one of the first occasions that GPS was used to position ships over the wreck.

Terena K.[a,723] 197700 On June 5, 1966 this seiner owned by Charles J Katnich, South Burnaby BC caught fire and sank off Rock Point in Johnstone Strait BC and was a total loss. The crew evacuated in the power skiff. The tug Island Mariner sighted her in distress, shortened her tow and approached her and picked up the crew of seven. They were later transferred to the Derek Todd and taken to Kelsey Bay.

---

a   Built as New Limited; then Terena K.

Terena Louise[a,724] 192867 On March 17, 1975 this seiner owned by RA Roberts Ltd., Vancouver BC capsized and sank in Barkley Sound while heavily loaded with herring. She was salvaged and put back into service. On March 2, 1977, while under command of Captain Mel Assu, this herring seiner took on water below the waterline and capsized about one mile off Cape Beale BC and sank. Her crew of six were rescued by the *Maple Leaf* C. and taken to Ucluelet.

Teresa Leigh 312926 On September 6, 1972 this fishboat owned by Clifford Laval (MO), Victoria BC burned and sank in Johnstone Straits BC.

Ternen 177415 On July 30, 1968 this fishboat owned by Arne F Larsen (MO), Wellington BC burned off Nanaimo in Georgia Strait BC.

Tex[b,725] 150764 On February 9, 1930 as the *Tex*, she was reported to have caught fire and sank in 600 feet of water in Howe Sound. A Captain Clarke representing the underwriters flew over the area and spotted the wreck. Pacific Salvage raised her using the barge *Skookum*. After inspection it was revealed that the vessel had been deliberately scuttled. The original owner disappeared before arrest. The wreck lay on the beach for a few years. In 1931 Pacific Salvage removed the 60hp Fairbanks Morse Co., Chicago IL USA engine and installed it in the tug *Helac No. 1*. Late in life she operated as a yarding tug at West Bay, Center Bay and Long Bay working for the Straits Towing Co.

Texada II[c,726] 156926 In 1930 she was operating as a maritime rum runner. She was fitted out with a courtroom when owned by the Provincial Police to dispense summary justice. In 1942 she was commissioned into the Royal Canadian Navy Fisherman's Reserve as HMCS *Ripple*. In 1943 she was tender to HMCS *Chatham*. In 1944 she was tender to HMCS *Givenchy*. In August 2000 she was aground in

---

a   Built as Louisa C.; then Terena Louise
b   Built as Eliza A.; then Tex; then Harris No. 6; then Pacific Yarder
c   Built as Margaret S II; then P.M.L. 14; then HMCS Ripple; then Texada II

Skidegate Channel. Brian Lande reports (British Columbia Nautical History Facebook Group 28/10/2014) that "In 1969 the Texada hit the rocks going into Winter Harbour the cook was at the wheel and never turned and he hit the rocks I don't remember the name of the rock. There was extensive damage the hull the keel had to be totally replaced and about half the planks below the water line. The *Texada* sat on the ways at Celtics Shipyards for at least nine months she was suspended with hundreds of wooden wedges to straighten her out. It must have been an amazing feat to tow her to Vancouver. I was on the *Chief Seagay* that season packing out of Bull Harbour and watched her go by. The damage was so extensive I often wonder why she was repaired." In 2000 she sank in Burnaby Narrows and was eventually salvaged by Dave Unsworth D & E Towing.

Thedford 141792 On May 20, 1930 while owned by Charles Williams, False Bay BC this troller fishboat burned between Boat Harbour and Forward Bay in Johnstone Strait BC.

Thelma I[a,727] 141275 On November 2, 1924 this fishboat, owned by Jens Dahl, Prince Rupert BC, was wrecked between Forrester Island and Cape Haddington. The crew reached Masset safely in a dory.

Themis[728] (Norwegian Registry) On May 22, 1906 she ran aground in Seymour Narrows when she became unmanageable resulting in damage to her bow. This was repaired in Vancouver before she sailed north. On December 15, 1906 while under command of Captain Kruger she was stranded on Broken Rock about 3/4 of a mile off Balaclava Island at the entrance to Browning Passage in Queen Charlotte Sound BC. She settled about two miles west of the Scarlett Point Lighthouse. Her crew of 25 (including Mrs Kruger) and her charterer, Captain FS Mackenzie, were safely rescued by the US fishing steamer *San Juan*. She had been en route from northern BC ports to Vancouver when the accident occurred. She was carrying 1,600 tons of copper ore and 200 tons of salmon.

---

a   Built as Thelma; then Thelma I

HMCS Thiepval sinking in Barkley Sound (Image from the collection of the Maritime Museum of British Columbia P3086)

Thiepval (HMCS) 141345 HMCS *Thiepval* carried out patrol duties on the west coast and assisted many vessels and mariners in distress. She assisted her sister ship *Armentieres* in 1925 when she struck a rock in Barkley Sound and in 1926, she pulled the schooner *Chapultepec* off the rocks at Carmanah Point. In 1930 she found herself a victim of the same treacherous waters of Barkley Sound and it was *Armentieres'* chance to aid her injured sister. The damage was too great, however, and by the following day the ship had foundered in 14 metres of water. The body of water in which she rests between Turtle and Turret Islands was named for her when the Canadian Hydrographic Service resurveyed the Sound in the late 1930s. The previous chart dated to 1861 when Captain Richards in HMS *Hecate* made their initial and brief survey. In 1959, the wreck was located by recreational divers and the deck gun was removed and placed on display in the village of Ucluelet. Because of her accessibility she has become an extremely popular dive site. Her contributions to the war effort and later aiding mariners remain a lively and interesting part of our BC coastal history. Years after her sinking the deck gun of HMCS *Thiepval* was recovered and put on display across the street from the Municipal Centre in Ucluelet BC.

Thistle[729] 094819 On May 24, 1907 this palatial yacht, owned by Lieutenant-Governor James Dunsmuir, Victoria BC, caught fired and was wrecked 7 miles north of Pine Island Light, Queen Charlotte Sound BC. She burned and sank while under the command of Captain Bissett. The passengers and crew all escaped safely.

Thomas Woodward[730] 024477 (US) She was originally a fishing schooner operating out of Gloucester MA USA. On November 25, 1868 she ran onto Shelter Point Reef south of Campbell River BC. The following day she broke up and sank. She was later salvaged by Captain Lewis.

Thompson (CNS)[731] SS-20 This Chilean Navy submarine was involved in a collision. The Transportation Safety Board of Canada states that "the *Moonglow*, on passage from Tofino, BC to Victoria, BC, departed the anchorage at Port San Juan, BC at 1500, 11 September 1994. The *Thomson* departed Nanoose, BC on the morning of 11 September and disembarked her Canadian Navy Coastal Pilot off Victoria at 1805. The vessel was steaming on the surface in the Juan de Fuca Strait outbound for San Diego, California, USA. At 2119, in Canadian waters off Sheringham Point, the *Thomson* and the *Moonglow* collided in dense fog. The *Moonglow*, holed on the starboard side aft, sank quickly. The operator was rescued from the water by the crew of the submarine and treated for mild hypothermia. The submarine sustained some light damage to the starboard bow. "

Thos. R. Foster[732] (Hawaii Register) On December 9, 1886 this bark left Esquimalt with a cargo of Wellington coal bound for Honolulu. On December 10, 1886 she sprang a leak off Cape Flattery in a gale. On December 18th she ran for Vancouver Island with 13 feet of water in the hold. She was deliberately beached 8 miles east of Cape Cook. The crew spent twenty-two days there before being picked up and carried to Victoria by the lighthouse tender *Sir James Douglas*. The crew had subsisted on mussels and seaweed. First Nations people carried the crew to Father Nicolaye at his mission who cared for them until their rescue.

Thrasher[a] On July 14, 1880, while under command of Captain Bosworth she was wrecked at Thrasher Rock (Gabriola Reef) near Nanaimo BC. She was en route from Nanaimo to San Francisco with 2600 tons of coal while under tow by the tugs *Beaver* and the *Etta White* and was a total loss. The HBC vessel *Triumph* was sent to assist but was unable to help. The wreck was later purchased by JF Engelhart of Victoria BC for $500 and the coal cargo for $50. The Thrasher court case was one in which the dispute between the Judiciary and the Executive of the Province over-shadowed the rights of the litigants in the case. The vessel *Thrasher* was lost while being towed from Nanaimo and the owner sued for damages resulting from negligence. In 1921 she burned in the Aleutian Islands Alaska.

Tiger[733] 024391 On the night of April 14, 1883 this British Bark was driven ashore at Royal Roads (Victoria) during a high gale. She lost her mizzen mast, and her foretopsail yard was lost. On Thursday April 26, 1883 there was an auction in Victoria BC of the beached wreck of the Bark *Tiger* at Royal Roads. The ship together with her masts, rigging, windlass, windmill pump, part cables, spare bower anchor, kedge anchor, galley, utensils, together with everything on board was offered for sale. The *Tiger* was carvel built in wood with iron knees. It was noted that also on the beach were a complete set of sails. Running and standing rigging, double, and single blocks, lamps, 4 boats and stores. The auction was by J.P. Davies & Co.

Tightline[b] 194683 In 1955 this tug, owned by George H Burt, Vancouver BC, sank in Fraser River BC. On March 22, 1977 she foundered between Kelsey Bay and Port Neville in Johnstone Strait BC.

Timisit[734] 157101 In August 1966 this power cruiser owned by George Dobson, Duncan BC was destroyed by fire at Shoal Harbour BC. The

---

a   Built as Thrasher; Then Kamchatka
b   Built as Mamquam; then Tightline

vessel had just been fueled at the marina when she exploded as the owner turned the ignition. The vessel was demolished, and the fuel dock operator was thrown into the water. A young child was severely burned in the incident. The boat was pushed away and flames on the fuel dock were extinguished before they reached solvents stored there. Fire fighters doused flames on the boat but not before she was destroyed.

Tofino 154842 On May 13, 1937 she aided when the Otter caught fire after a gas engine explosion alongside at a Malksope Inlet logging camp. On August 11, 1940 while owned by Captain Sam S Stone, Ucluelet BC she was stranded in Nootka Sound BC.

Topaz[735] 122162 On April 08, 1965 she hit a log and sank near Somerville Island (Portland Inlet) BC. Crewman Charlie Sankey, who survived the sinking because he was wearing a lifejacket swam to an island about one mile away. Once ashore he bushwhacked eleven miles to an abandoned logging camp. Here he fashioned a crude raft on which he floated 11 miles to Somerville Island where he found a rowboat. He rowed 14 miles of open water to Port Simpson. Two other crewmen (Patrick Green and Harvey Ryan) perished in the wreck.

Tonquin On September 6, 1810 this brig sailed from New York for the Pacific Fur Company under the command of Captain Jonathan Thorn (who on leave from the USN). On March 22, 1811 she landed at the Columbia River on to establish Fort Astoria on May 18, 1811. In 1811 she was attacked in Clayoquot Sound by First Nations people and was destroyed by them when the vessel exploded. It is thought that while some of the crew survived the explosion and attack, none of the crew survived to return to Astoria.

Tordo[a,736] 172556 On March 07, 1973 this fishpacker foundered about 4.5 miles west of Box Island (Long Beach) carrying herring bound for Vancouver BC. The three crew members abandoned ship and rowed to shore.

---

a   Built as Tordo; then HMCS Tordo; then Tordo

Tornado[737] 319341 On November 28, 1965 this tug owned by Mogens Johnstad-Moeller, North Vancouver BC capsized while towing a barge and sank at Second Narrows, Burrard Inlet BC. Caught in a rip current half a mile from Second Narrows she capsized while towing a barge she developed engine trouble. Radioing for help the tug *Service II* arrived to assist by pushing on the barge. Suddenly the barge started to veer off-course, so the *Service II* backed off when the Tornado capsized and sank. Captain John Stad was trapped in an air lock in the engine room. He managed to break a window and swim to the surface. Crew member John A Boyle perished in the incident. The tug was later salvaged and repaired at McKenzie Shipyards.

Torpedo[738] 153379 On February 17, 1960 this tug burned and sank at Point Atkinson BC. Captain Eric North and two crewmen fought an engine room blaze that eventually forced them into a lifeboat. They were towing three empty barges to Britannia when the fire started. The nearby tug *La Mite* quickly arrived to pour water on the blaze but picked up the crewmen from the lifeboat. She then took the burning tug in tow until the Vancouver fire tug *J.H. Carlisle* arrived to extinguish the blaze.

Towena[739] 150856 On August 07, 1929 this fishboat owned by Peter D Cameron, Prince Rupert BC exploded two miles off Port Simpson BC. She was in transit to Wales Island for seine nets. The Master and his deckhand were uninjured.

Townsend[a] 138170 In 1921 she dredged the Vedder Canal for the Marsh Construction Co. On March 14, 1957 while owned by British Columbia Bridge & Dredging Co. Ltd., Vancouver BC she was struck by a scow towed by the tug *La Dene* at the Deas Island Tunnel in the Fraser River BC.

Trade Winds I[740] On August 31, 1967 this Vancouver-based pocket cruise ship, with 10 American passengers aboard, was damaged in a collision with the tug *Mary Mackin* about 10 miles north of Alert Bay BC.

---

a   Built as P.D. Co. No. 4; then Tacoma; then Star; then Colonel Tobin; then Townsend

Trader[741] 107838 On March 16, 1923 this freighter carrying a cargo of cement from Bamberton to Vancouver was stranded off Point Grey BC in a storm. She had sought shelter in the North Arm of the Fraser River but was driven ashore on the bar near the North Arm Jetty. Her cargo was ruined. She was owned by Trader Steamship Co. Ltd., (Charlie Vincent and Fred White), Victoria BC.

Trail 103306 In 1900 this tug owned by the Canadian Pacific Railway, Montreal QC, was withdrawn from service. On June 02, 1902 she was burned out at her wharf at Robson West BC on the Columbia River.

Tramp[a] 141271 This fishboat formed part of the pre-war Fishermen's Reserve Fleet. She participated in the January 30–February 25, 1939 Fishermen's Reserve Training Session. She was however not mobilized for active duty during the Second World War. On October 24, 1980 she grounded and foundered at Comox in Georgia Strait BC.

Trebla[b,742] 150565 In 1910 she helped the William Joliffe free the stranded *Princess May* on Sentinel Island. On May 10, 1924 she was destroyed by fire that started in the engine room near Sidney BC and was declared as a total loss. She was en route to Victoria towing an old scow when she tied up for the night near James Island. The fire came on very rapidly and the crew abandoned ship in a small boat that was in turn rescued by First Nations people who had been camped near Sidney Spit.

Treis Ierarcha[743] (Greece Registry) She was stranded December 07, 1969 at Ferrer Point BC near the entrance to Nootka Sound. She was en route to load lumber at BC ports for shipment to Japan. Her hull was strengthened for the carriage of ore cargoes. She was salvaged by Lloyd Wade and Bill Lore. She was cut up and dragged to Louie Bay, loaded on barges.

---

a   Built as Fearless; then Tramp
b   Built as Santa Cruz; then Trebla

Triggerfish[a,744] 179598 This wooden coastal freighter was converted from an ex-USN sub chaser. In a 1955 incident this vessel was caught in a beam sea, heeled over and a cargo of steel plates slid off her deck into the sea off Cape Roger Curtis. On October 6th, 1956, this freighter was on a run up Howe Sound with a general cargo when she capsized and sank one mile off Whytecliff in Howe Sound with the loss of three lives: Chris Karsten; Boyne A Hay, and Chris Junker.

Trio V[b] 197855 She was a General Utility Harbour Craft at Sydney NS. In December 1946 she was transported by rail to HMCS Hunter to serve as a tender. On May 8, 1966 while owned by George R Breckon and Gaynel Luckstein (MO), New Westminster BC she sank (but was apparently salvaged and put back into service).

Triton[745] (Greece) On July 26, 1952 this freighter, owned by the Gratsos Brothers, Ithaca Greece, collided with the Alaska Steamship Co. passenger ship *Baranof* off Gabriola Island BC. Two crew members of the Triton were killed in the incident. The *Baranof* hit the Triton amidships on her starboard side. The Triton, carrying a cargo of iron ore was taken to the Esquimalt Graving Dock for repairs.

Trivar 177980 On June 14, 1961 this fishboat owned by The Cassiar Packing Co. Ltd., Vancouver BC foundered in Queen Charlotte Sound, one mile from Cape Caution BC.

Tryon[746] 193425 On August 21, 1969 this troller fishboat owned by Jeremy SP (Gerry) Dick, Victoria BC was in a collision with a Russian freighter at Big Bank. The trolling poles were snapped off by the trawl apparatus from the Russian fishboat. The Captain Dick unsuccessfully complained to the Russian Embassy in Ottawa for compensation.

---

a   Built as USS SC-730; then Kaigani II; then Seymour Narrows; then Triggerfish
b   Built as H.C. 261; then J.C.G.; then Marm II; then Trio V

Tsin Kwis[747] 154565 On November 26, 1947 this beam trawler owned by John Heale, Victoria BC exploded and burned five miles north of Discovery Island BC. The crew: J 'Buster' Heal, and Barney Dale were uninjured in the incident. The fire happened suddenly, and the two men were forced to abandon ship in a small rowboat. An RCN fireboat extinguished the fire. The skipper had just changed over fuel tanks and had pressed the starter when the fire occurred.

Tsusiat[a] 170956 On August 5, 1959 this fishboat while owned by Eugene E Farrington, Steveston BC burned at Port Hammond BC. On March 21, 1975 while owned by Thomas J Orcutt (MO), Vancouver BC she foundered while taking water off Forbes Island in Barkley Sound BC. She was beached at Forbes River BC and was declared a total loss.

Tugaway[b] 154355 On March 11, 1931 this tug owned by Amos Beckman, Vancouver BC exploded between Marpole Bridge and the railroad bridge in front of gravel dock on the North Arm of the Fraser River.

Tugaway[748] 170771 On January 23, 1943 this tug, owned by Beckman Towboat Co. Ltd., Marpole BC, struck a hemlock snag in the Fraser River that punched a large hole in the hull. Captain Buster Monk managed to get her aground before she sank. The salvage vessel *Helite No. 1* put on a temporary patch and refloated. In 1977 she was reported to have been beached and broken up at Gambier Island BC.

Tuladi[749] 126216 On November 05, 1928 this fishboat owned by Theologus N Malbhais & James E Johnson, Vancouver BC burned five miles west of the Ballenas Island BC near Parksville BC when her engine backfired. Her two crew members, T Malahais and Tom Liates, abandoned ship together and rowed two and a half miles to shore in a skiff.

---

a   Built as Welcome Pass; then Tsusiat
b   Built as Tugaway; then Pyeluco

Tuo Hai[750] On July 22, 1991, the Japanese fishing vessel *Tenyo Maru* and Chinese freighter *Tuo Hai* collided within Canadian Territorial waters approximately 20 miles northwest of Cape Flattery. The *Tenyo Maru*, which was reportedly carrying 354,800 gallons of intermediate fuel oil, 97,800 gallons of diesel fuel, and 22,500 gallons of fish oil, sank after the collision. It initially leaked a large amount of oil and undetermined amounts were reported leaking for more than a month after the collision. Beaches were fouled with oil from Vancouver Island, British Columbia to northern Oregon. The Canadian Coast Guard brought in a remotely controlled underwater robot, the *Scorpio*, aboard the CCGS *Martha L. Black* to pump oil from the *Tenyo Maru* to tanks aboard a surface ship from the sunken ship in 100 fathoms. The *Scorpio* used the robot arms to install a suction cup and hose into a porthole leaking oil. The oil then was then pumped to a tank aboard a ship. This was one of the first occasions that GPS was used to position ships over a wreck.

Tuscan Prince[751] 133543 On February 15, 1923 she was bound from San Francisco to Seattle under the command of Captain James Chilvers and a crew of 42 men. She was carrying a cargo of pig iron and coke. Radio operators heard the distress message "breaking up fast!" She became distressed off Cape Flattery in a violent winter storm. In the darkness, and uncertain of their position they hove to await daylight, anchored, and then were struck by a huge wave that knocked out the radio. In ten minutes, they were stranded on Village Island (later renamed as Austin Island) in Barkley Sound BC and quickly broke in two. Grinding on the rocks they became wedged tightly. In the thick of a blizzard her crew was rescued by the USCGC *Snohomish* using a breeches buoy. Boatswain Fox of the *Tuscan Prince* risked his life to save his shipmates he swam ashore, clambered over wet rocks through the surf with a line that he fastened to a tree. Each crew member was hauled through the surf to safety. They camped on the shore shivering in the cold until the arrival of Coxswain Brady in the *Banfield Lifeboat* who picked up the crew again by use of a breeches buoy.

The *Tuscan Prince* aground before she disappeared into deep water near Village Island (Image from the collection of the Maritime Museum of British Columbia 000117)

Tusko[a] 150670 In 1929 she sailed chiefly out of Victoria to Vancouver Island's west coast towing for Cathels and Sorenson Ltd., and independent loggers Lamont, Rutger, Baird, Frank Baker and John Quinn in the Port San Juan area. On August 5, 1930 she was grounded in the fog near Jordan River. She was refloated with the help of the tug *Daring* (Captain George A MacFarlane). In 1948 she towed a Davis Raft (25 million board feet) the largest ever towed into the Fraser River. On February 13, 1968 she was grounded on Mowat Reef. In 1973 she sank at Yuculta Rapids BC after grounding. She was salvaged and her crew rescued.

Tussler[752] 126239 On May 31, 1937 she was stranded and burned while towing a logging camp barge above Welbore Rapids at Jackson Bay in Sunderland Channel. She struck a shallow reef and was pitched on her beam ends. They were about to launch a boat and Granholm and his Mate were thrown into the boat from the deck of the tug. Almost immediately the tug burst into flames and the tug became destroyed.

Tu-Tu 329581 On December 1, 1970 this tug owned by Empire Tugboats Ltd., New Westminster BC, sank in Williston Lake BC.

---

a   Built as J.W.P.; then Swiftsure II; then Tusko

T-W Sea Prince[a] 192870 In 1966 this converted fishpacker collided with the trawler *Kalamalka* (which sank) near the mouth of the Fraser River but was not seriously damaged. On January 19, 1984 while owned by Frederick Fishing Ltd, et al, Prince Rupert BC she exploded and burned three miles off Hornby Island BC when the fuel supply to the galley stove ruptured. She sank five miles north of Sisters Island BC and Eugene Williams died in the incident.

T-W Sea Queen[b] 192059 This converted fishpacker owned by the Sea Queen Fisheries Ltd., Burnaby BC had an engine room fire, burned, and sank in Queen Charlotte Sound BC on June 6th, 1972 and was declared a total loss.

T-W Zelley[c] 193770 This converted fishpacker owned by Slavko Tabako, Joseph Longcarich and Mirko Longcarich, all of Vancouver BC sank on January 26, 1966 off Cox Point West Coast of Vancouver Island, total loss.

Twilight II[753] On March 30, 1975 this gillnet fishboat grounded in Fisherman's Bay on the north of Vancouver Island and was last seen drifting offshore south of Prince Rupert in conditions that were described as "incredibly rough".

Tyee[754] 107639 In 1899 she was a cannery tender. In 1923 she was serving Balmoral Cannery as a cannery tender. On December 24, 1923 she foundered during a sudden storm in the Strait of Juan de Fuca at Pedder Bay BC with loss of Captain Anderson; Jimmy Davis (Mate) and Jack Atill (cook). The owner Engineer, Archie Pike swam 600 yards to shore. They had left Albert Head with a scow filled with gravel at 10:00 am bound for Port Angeles. After dropping the scow there, the returned at 4:00 pm. Huge seas (20'–30') were running at Race Rocks, so they ran for shelter at Pedder Bay. But rather than shelter they faced another tide rip where they were suddenly

---

a   Built as USS APc-96; then Sea Prince; then Le Prince; then T-W Sea Prince; then Sea Prince
b   Built as USS APc-111; then Coastal Trader; then Sea Queen III; then La Fleur; then T-W Sea Queen
c   Built as USS APc-3; then P.B. Andersen; then T-W Zelley

swamped by two huge waves. The started to sink and it was all over in 5 minutes. Tee crew in the water they held onto an upturned lifeboat and Al Warner and Archie Pike were the only ones to make it to shore—the others being drowned.

Tyee Shell[755] 188392 On February 25, 1965 she was in a collision with the barge *Island Express* in Quatsino Inlet BC. The *Tyee Shell* was sailing inbound to the Mahatta River and the *Island Express* barge was rounding Salmon Island, with the *Island Commander* on its outside, outbound. They saw each other too late and the *Island Express* plowed into the port aft end of the *Tyee Shell*. One crew member on the *Tyee Shell* was crushed to death.

Umatilla 25242 (US) She was brought around Cape Horn to the Pacific coast by Captain Frank Worth in 1880. In 1896 she was in service on the San Francisco–Puget Sound route. In 1884 she went ashore at Race Rocks. In 1886 she struck a rock near Cape Flattery freed herself and was towed in sinking condition by the steam collier *Wellington* into Esquimalt Harbour where she sank. On September 29, 1896 she left Victoria BC and when near Point Wilson WA she ran onto a reef known as Libby Rock. The vessel was beached, and the passengers were put ashore. In 1907 an advertisement in The British Colonist newspaper promoted excursions in her to southeast Alaska and San Francisco. On March 07, 1918 she ran aground North of Inuboyesaki and was wrecked.

Umbrina[756] 094634 Captain Charles Campbell originally brought the schooner, built in 1881, out from Nova Scotia to British Columbia. On March 15, 1911 she was a sealing schooner in collision with the US collier *Saturn* (under Captain Smith) and then foundered in the North Pacific at 43° 50' N and 125° W sank while her hunting crews were away in their boats. The *Saturn* stood by until all the boats had returned and all 10 the crew and the 25 First Nations hunters were saved. They were all carried on the *Saturn* to San Francisco.

Uncle John[757] 0025246 (US) This American barkentine, 314 tons, was registered at Eureka CA USA. On October 7, 1899 she was wrecked near Nitinat at Tsusiat Falls. The vessel was inbound from Honolulu to the Puget Sound under command of Captain C Hemmingsen. The Captain mistook his position when he took the Cape Beale Light to be the Carmanah Light and thought he could sail safely on course. She was a total loss, but the crew managed to get to shore safely. After three days on the beach they walked out to Clo-oose they were picked up by the *Willapa* and taken to Victoria.

Unimak[758] 176507 On July 22, 1960 at around midnight this seiner was in collision with the towing cable between a barge in tow of the fishpacker Cape Flattery one mile off Roberts Creek BC. The vessel overturned and sank with its crew of four trapped inside desperately knocking on the hull in please for help. They could not be saved and drowned. Robert Pederson, the cook was thrown clear and was the only survivor. A young woman, Emily J Hornell, who was a guest onboard, was alone on the wheel at the time of the incident. Captain Wilfred Pohto had stepped into the adjacent galley moments before and returned to the bridge 'in seconds'. The three other casualties were Captain Wilfred Pohto; Bill Anderson; and Dick Joliffe. She was involved in a second sinking. On November 24, 1963 while owned by Eric V Johnson, Vancouver BC and under command of Captain Forest J Ferguson, she was in a collision with the coastal tanker *Pacific Wind*, cut in half and sank in Tolmie Channel BC. Her crew of four were rescued.

Union Maid[759] 326616 On May 15, 1976 this troller fishboat exploded, burned, and sank off Estevan Point VI with the loss of Captain Gregory Shupe.

The Soviet freighter *Uzbekistan* being pounded by heavy surf and already breaking up in 1944. (Photo from MacFarlane Family collection.)

Uzbekistan (USSR) The *Uzbekistan* was a converted Victory-type freighter turned over to the Soviet government (Northern Soviet Supply Service) under lend-lease arrangements. Originally built in

France she had been recently rebuilt in Portland Oregon and fitted for icebreaking. On April 30, 1943, this vessel was travelling from Portland OR to Seattle WA when she went ashore just west of the mouth of Darling Creek 2.5 miles east of Pachena Point. All navigational lights on the coast were blacked out after the shelling by the Imperial Japanese Navy in 1942 of the Estevan Lighthouse. She went aground at Pachena Point presumably due to a navigational error. After hitting the shore, the crew began firing their guns presumably to attract attention. Residents of the coast hearing the gunfire were fearful of another Japanese attack. The ship was so firmly grounded that the crew walked ashore at low tide. After waiting in vain on the beach for rescue after several days they walked out on the Lifesaving Trail to Bamfield. The vessel was quickly vandalized and looted. Traces of the ship's boilers and machinery can still be seen at low water at the edge of the reef and on the beach at the mouth of the Darling Creek.

The boiler of the Soviet freighter *Uzbekistan*, in 2020, is all that remains of the wrecked ship, the rest having been pounded to pieces by the relentless surf. (Photograph courtesy of Rick James).

V. & H.[760] 312913 On March 1, 1970 this tug owned by Rivtow Marine Ltd., Vancouver BC was salvaged from 215 feet of water at Clio Bay.

V.M.D.[761] 130906 On August 27, 1923, this workboat owned by Harry T Devine, Vancouver BC, was in a collision with the workboat V.M.D. in Burrard Inlet, Vancouver Harbour BC. The V.M.D. was crushed and sunk at the Government Dock when the tide pushed the freighter up against her. The owner of the workboat and his crewmember had to leap for their lives to escape.

V.T. No. 100[a,762] 198108 In 1943 this US Navy minesweeper was assigned to Guantanamo Bay Cuba. Later she grounded on a coral

---

a   Built as USS Y.M.S. 159; then Gerry Rae; then V.T. No. 100

head at Bikini Atoll in the Marshall Islands in September 1945. After repairs at Eniwetok, she was returned to the USA. She was brought to Canada after the Second World War and laid up in the 'boneyard' in Burrard Inlet. On April 22, 1956 she was burned by vandals and sank in Bedwell Bay. There were three salvage attempts and much of the valuable metal was removed including the propellers.

Vadso[a] 124077[763] This unlucky passenger freight vessel carried 50 passengers and had six accidents during her life. She also operated briefly as a cannery freighter. In 1908 she had three accidents. On February 7th she was driven ashore on Cape Lazo and afterwards towed to Comox BC for repair. On April 11th while backing out from the cannery at Beaver Cove she struck a submerged rock and damaged her propeller and twisted the sternpost. On April 22nd she went aground in Schooner Passage but floated off at high tide unassisted. On September 16th she collided with the Amur in fine weather off Trivet Point in McKay Reach damaging both ships. In 1912 she drove ashore at the No. 1 Buoy in Baynes Sound. Although considered by many as unsalvageable her salvors managed to get her afloat. The Union Steamship Co. put her in service. On January 25, 1914 while owned by The Vadso Steamship Co. Ltd., Vancouver BC, under the command of Captain Richardson, she was stranded when she hit a rock in Portland Inlet near the Nass River BC and was holed during a blinding snowstorm. She quickly filled with water and sank. She is reported to have settled in 170 feet of water. Her crew of 26 were all saved and transported back to Victoria from the Arrandale Cannery in the *Venture*.

Valencia 025998 The loss of this passenger vessel is one of the most famous on the British Columbia coast and was the worst marine disaster in the history of Vancouver Island—when 117 lives were lost. She went ashore October 23rd, 1906 ten miles east of Cape Beale near Pachena Point. She was trapped between the rock cliffs and the huge waves rolling ashore. Passengers and crew were trapped on board unable to launch boats or to safely make their way to shore.

---

a   Built as Bordeaux; then Vadso

Those who did attempt it were drowned in the process. Rescue vessels were forced by the dangerous coast, tidal currents, waves, and wind to stand offshore unable to provide aid. This drama continued for almost two days with survivors exposed on the deck or up in the rigging on the mast. The ship continued to break up when a huge wave rolled over the ship sweeping everyone into the sea. There were 37 survivors, but 136 persons were lost. Years after the event in 1933, Captain George Alexander MacFarlane, found the Valencia's Lifeboat No. 5 in a farmer's field in the Alberni Canal. There were several stump ranches on the inlet at that time. It was high up on a hillside well above the normal water level. The boat was in good condition and was filled with scrap metal parts so perhaps the boat was salvaged. Being fascinated with nautical history he cut the name board off the boat with an axe and it sat in a cupboard his house for years afterwards. In 1956, when the Maritime Museum of British Columbia opened (then in Esquimalt BC) Mrs MacFarlane donated it and another plate with the number five on it as founding artifacts of the collection.

Valerie K.[a] 130559 Some time after 1983 this tug was hulked and sank alongside at Coal Harbour, Vancouver and was then bulldozed as fill into the site where the Bayshore Hotel tennis court was later located.

Valiant[b] 096988 On August 11, 1966 this tug built in 1891 and owned by Maritime Towing Co. Ltd., Vancouver BC burned and sank near Thrasher Rock BC and was a total loss.

Vampy 312081 On March 18, 1975 this fishboat owned by Sidney T Crosby (MO), Prince Rupert BC foundered north of Reef Island in Hecate Strait on while en route from the Queen Charlotte Islands to Vancouver BC.

Vancouver On March 03, 1834 this schooner ran aground on Rose Spit and was abandoned. She was subsequently wrecked by the sea

---

a   Built as J.W. Dickie; then Comeback; then Valerie K.
b   Built as Kildonan; then Polar King; then Canso Straits; then Volante; then Valiant

after having been looted by local Haida people. (Some reports have her wreck burned by the Haida.)

Vancouver This brigantine arrived on the Pacific coast in May 1853. In August she left Fort Simpson under command of Captain Reed. Reed was dismissed by the HBC being held responsible for the wreck. In August 1853 she was wrecked on Rose Spit QCI BC. She was soaked in oil and burned to prevent her from falling into the hands of local First Nations people who had claimed the wreck.

Vancouver 092775 On March 07, 1895 she went ashore at Mill Bay due to rudder problems but was later salvaged. On February 24, 1897 she ran onto Mary Tod Island and was stuck there for at least a day before being salvaged.

The *Vanlene* (while still relatively intact) from the air. (Image from the collection of the Maritime Museum of British Columbia 000322)

Vanlene 4163-HK (Panama) This vessel, owned by Marlene Shipping Co., c/o Van Shipping Co. Ltd., Hong Kong, was stranded at night on March 14, 1972 while inbound from Japan to Vancouver on a rock 600' southeast of Austin Island. It was said that only her compass, of all her navigational equipment, was in working order when she struck. Then 131 of 300 new Dodge Colt automobiles were lifted off the ship by helicopter before she broke up and sank. The 38–man crew was rescued and taken to Port Alberni. How she ended up on the rocks is still a matter of conjecture, but it appears that the Master simply did not know where he was at the time of impact (it was reported that he thought he was located off the coast of Washington) and that his navigational aids were inoperable. Hopes of salvaging the ship faded quickly when it was discovered she had a major hole in the hull. Concern shifted to the removal of the bunker fuel oil carried in the tanks. Salvagers, (well . . . scavengers really), from nearby towns removed anything movable on the wreck. The winter storms that followed broke the hull up—so that the forward section was all that was visible within a short time.

Varsity[764] (US) On February 09, 1940 this seiner, owned by Joe Cloud in Tacoma WA, went aground 6 miles east of Pachena Point through navigational error. Four crew members were lost and three were saved. Her engines were salvaged and used in the tug *Nitinat Chief*.

Velos[765] On March 22, 1895 she was wrecked near Trial Island while towing the barge Pilot en route to Haddington Island to pick up limestone for the rebuilding of the Point Ellice Bridge. Under the command of Captain Anderson, with a crew of Mate Andrew Christiansen, Chief Engineer Arthur Bloor, Assistant Engineer William Law, Deckhand Frank Duncan, Cook Robert Smith. They were also carrying Frederick Adams the contractor for the construction of the Provincial Parliament buildings. Only Captain Anderson and First Mate Christiansen survived. The 24 men being carried on the barge Pilot also survived the grounding on Trial Island. The *Velos* experienced a steering problem, perhaps the chains fouled or parted in the heavy seas. The *Pilot* overtook the *Velos* and crashed into her with 'terrific force'. She sank next to Trial Island with her mast showing above the water. The tug broke up and only some of the equipment could be salvaged by the hardhat diver Mr McHardie.

Venture 111776 In 1903 this fishboat owned by The Venture Steamship Co. Ltd., Vancouver BC was stranded in Barkley Sound BC. She grounded on Venture Bank in the Queen Charlotte Islands in 1906. On January 23, 1909 she burned at Inverness Cannery, Prince Rupert BC. In 1911 she was wrecked at Vancouver BC.

Venture[766] 129475 She carried 186 passengers on the cannery run to Skeena and Nass Rivers via Prince Rupert BC. On February 24, 1916 she collided while travelling inbound for passage through the First Narrows with the *Wakena*. In 1947 she was destroyed by fire at Hong Kong.

Vera Cruz 198156 On August 18, 1972 this fishboat owned by Charles P Fraser (MO), Victoria BC was stranded and sank in fog in Cox Bay BC northeast of Lennard Island. She was stripped and burned by salvagers.

Vesta[767] (US) In December 1897 this three-masted schooner was in ballast under Captain Humboldt sailing up the coast from Hueneme California to Port Townsend for a cargo of lumber. With continuous stormy weather she was unable to take a navigational sight and the captain presuming his position to be 10 miles south of Cape Flattery carried on his course, but he was 30 miles out in his dead-reckoning. On December 9, 1897 she was overwhelmed by a huge wave and swept over a reef nine miles west of Carmanah Point near Tsusiat Falls. She was washed high up across the beach so far that her masts caught in the trees. The crew disembarked to walk out following the telegraph line. After two days the weather improved, and the captain and four men set out for Carmanah Lighthouse. For many years she sat high and dry used as a cabin by the telegraph lineman. The wreck was later burned to salvage the copper fastenings. One of her anchors and other gear can still be seen in the sand near the Hole-in-the-Wall.

Victorac[768] 153106 On May 16, 1954 this beam trawler owned by Lawrence Doving (MO), Vancouver BC foundered two miles south of Hakai Passage on the west coast of Calvert Island QCI. She was headed for Namu to pick up ice with 21,000 pounds of fish on board when she hit rocks in fog. The crew attempted to make it to Namu after the accident, but she sank about 200 meters offshore. They crew escaped in the ship's launch.

Victory In 1905–1908 she was originally owned by Abraham Reid Bittancourt, Saltspring Island BC. In 1908–1910 she was owned by

Fred MacFarlane and Arthur MacFarlane at Mill Bay BC. She was used for towing logs and scows in the Mill Bay area. She was sold in 1910 and was severely damaged by fire on the beach soon afterwards.

The tug *Victory* showing fire damage to the hull on the beach at Mill Bay BC (Photograph by Captain George A. MacFarlane from the John MacFarlane collection)

Victoria Packet[a] In 1865, while en route from Nanaimo to Victoria this schooner was hijacked by First Nations people at Cowichan Gap. The crew was murdered, and the vessel was later scuttled after being plundered.

Victory Bay 150514 In 1941 she was seized from her Japanese owners by the Canadian Government. In 1942 her ownership transferred to His Majesty the King. On January 8, 1947, this fishpacker was stranded one mile west of Singing Sands on Wickaninnish Bay BC.

---

a   Built as Merlin; then Victoria Packet

Victory V[a] 133884 On September 30, 1938 this tug owned by Ethelbert S Stone and Percy F Stone (JO), Port Alberni BC burned at the Franklin River booming grounds in Alberni Inlet BC.

Victory XII 173743 On April 21. 1979 this tug owned by Hattco Marine Services Ltd., Vancouver BC was abandoned at sea and sank in Georgia Strait.

Vidette On November 18, 1899 this Bark-rigged vessel came ashore on Bonilla Point BC. After several days ashore she managed to free herself when the wind changed direction and she was able to sail on to Redondo California.

Vigilant II 312853 On December 8, 1968 this tug owned by Richmond Tug Boat Co. Ltd., Richmond BC. burned at Halkett Bay in Howe Sound BC.

Viking I[769] 154391 Ken Lund reported that "The Viking I was built in 1927 and was owned and fished by the Erikson family in Prince Rupert for 3 generations. It fished for the Co-op for many years and was often the high boat for halibut landings. I have owned it for the past 15 years and had many good memories. I left it in the hands of a caretaker this summer first time I had ever been away for more than a week. Unfortunately, it sank in Nanaimo Harbour last Wednesday I suspect from complacency on behalf of the caretaker. The Coast Guard jumped right on it and from the start gave no consideration to saving it, just to scrapping it. What should have been a one-day job to raise it dragged into 7 days before the amateur crew decided to tow it to the Brechin Boat ramp in Nanaimo. After a gong show including two popped airbags a crane was brought it to raise the stern enough to start pumping. The crew only managed to get one pump running out of the 6 pumps they had on hand. Coast Guard had seen enough, and that crew was dismissed. Coast Guard was advised to have the ramp clear by the weekend and have a contractor coming

---

a   Built as Marine Express No. 1; then Victory V

from Vancouver with a tug and barge with crane to load the Viking 1 on the barge and haul it to Vancouver. The hull below the waterline still appears sound and divers saw no signs of sprung planks or foul play. There was no insurance."

Viking Mist[770] (US) On March 22, 1975 this gillnetter capsized eight miles east of Comox, in heavy seas, with the loss of Stuart Nelson of Bellingham WA. The overturned hull was in Gillies Bay, Texada Island. Thomas Pomeroy of Ferndale WA was rescued by the US tug *Arapaho*, but his shipmate re-entered the hull in search of a survival suit and disappeared.

Viking Queen[a,771] 153034 She was a tug owned by Mutual Towing Co. Ltd., Vancouver BC. On June 15, 1963 she foundered after striking a submerged object near the northeast point of Texada Island BC and sank slowly.

Vivanna 151132 On December 02, 1950 this tug owned by the Nanaimo Towing Co. Ltd., Nanaimo BC burned in Ladysmith Harbour BC.

Vladimir[772] 103910 On December 29, 1902 this tug owned by James Armstrong, Alberni BC disappeared from her mooring at Port Renfrew BC. She had come from Alberni to assist in some logging operations in Port San Juan. That night a heavy southwest gale blew up and in the morning no trace of the tug could be found. It was though that the tug drifted in the wind into the open sea and became a drifting derelict, foundered, and sank. There was no one on board.

Volunteer 212957 (US) On September 8, 1931 this small sternwheeler was destroyed by fire one and one-half miles east of Pulteney Point, Johnstone Strait BC.

Vreeland[b] She was a classic double-ended wooden Baltic Sea/North Sea fishing vessel. In 1960–1990 she operated/fished out of Roennang,

---

a   Built as A. & L.; then Davis Straits, then Westminster Chief, then Sea Chief, then Viking Queen

b   Built as Loevoen; then Vreeland

Sweden. In 1990 she was sold with her fishing quota to an Urk, Netherlands fisherman. In 1998 in a neglectful state she was sold again to Wiebe Bosma and Patricia Croes who restored the vessel as a yacht. In 2007 they embarked on a voyage from the Netherlands down the west coast of Africa, across the Atlantic to the Caribbean, through the Panama Canal up to Vancouver, BC. On September 12, 2019 she sank at her wharf in Vancouver BC.

Vulcan 107925 On January 28, 1925 this workboat owned by FB Anderson, Vancouver BC burned leaving her keel, boiler, and timbers on the beach at Denman Island opposite Union Bay BC.

W. No. 6[a,773] 141438 On August 30, 1967 this seiner was damaged in a collision with an unidentified tug near Port Hardy BC. She suffered damage to her wheelhouse and the forward part of her hull. On March 19, 1975 she foundered while offshore from Pachena Point with a load of herring at the entrance to Juan de Fuca Strait.

W.G. Mackenzie[b] 310361 The Marwell Equipment Company bought this non-powered suction dredge after their other dredge the *Townsend* was sunk. She was used on was used on the Deas Island Tunnel project. On July 16, 1962 she sank near Egg Island BC.

W.T. 150319 On July 4, 1931 this fishboat owned by Charles M Edwards and John Postgate, Prince Rupert BC burned off Roland Rock, Stephens Island BC.

Wachusett (USS) On July 22, 1881 this US Navy warship struck Ripple Rock suffering damage to her false keel.

Waitemata[c,774] 5384839 On July 3, 1956 this New Zealand freighter was in a collision with the fishboat B.C. *Troller* (Captain Alf Styan), seven miles south southeast of Lennard Island. Captain Alf Styan

---

a   Built as American Girl; then W. No. 6
b   Built as Marshall C. Harris; then W.G. Mackenzie
c   Built as Selsey Bill; then Waitemata

and his son Ken were riding at anchor when the freight hit them with a powerful glancing blow damaging their entire superstructure. She was rolled over on her side but was later righted in a damaged condition. She reached Port Alberni where she was rebuilt and returned to service. The *Waitemata* did not stop.

Wakena[775] (US) On February 24, 1916 she collided with the *Venture* while travelling through the First Narrows. She went aground in fog in Active Pass on Ann Bluff at the north end of the Pass on June 29, 1916. On May 27, 1925 she was destroyed by fire 6–8 miles north of Nanaimo BC.

Walter Earle[a,776] On April 14, 1895 this vessel capsized in Alaskan waters with the loss of her crew of 20 including many Beecher Bay and Sooke First Nations people. A bottle with a note from the crew of the schooner Walter Earl was found on the shore of Prince of Wales Island. The note indicated that two crew members survived and sat on the keel of the capsized vessel composing the note indicating that they did not expect to hold on much longer—it was signed by Henry Butler and Charles Forrest.

Wanderer[777] 064139 On January 29, 1896 this sealing schooner, owned by the Victoria Sealing Co., Victoria BC, was wrecked at San Josef Bay (VI) and was a total loss.

Wanderer[b] 153299 In 1993 this vessel owned by Manning Navigation Ltd.; Vancouver BC collided with the Bowen Island ferry.

Wanderer No. 2 192026 On January 15th, 2017 this fishboat owned by Joseph F Krajc, Victoria BC sank in Lund Harbour and was salvaged after reportedly striking a rock.

---

a   Built as Sylvia Hardy, then Walter Earle
b   Built as Cora May; then RCASC Colonel Ogilvy; then Wanderer

Warlock No. 1[a] 328391 In 1973 this fishboat owned by David R Bruce, Port Alberni BC was reported to have sunk in the Alberni Canal.

Warrimoo[778] 101901 In 1897 this passenger vessel provided service on the All-Red Route travelling between Vancouver and Australia. On August 9, 1895, on her on her maiden voyage to Victoria, she was grounded four miles west of Carmanah Point while inbound from Australia in dense fog. Using kedges, she refloated herself on the next high tide and sailed on to Victoria. She was repaired in Sydney Australia where 65 plates were removed and straightened. In late 1914 the *Warrimoo* was taken up as a troopship. On May 17, 1918 when on a convoy from Bizerta to Marseille she collided with the escorting French destroyer *Catapulte*. In the collision the destroyer's depth-charges were dislodged; they exploded in the water blowing out the bottom plates of both ships, causing them both to sink with some loss of life.

Watson Rock[b] 173615 On August 24, 1976 this troller fishboat owned by Babcock Fisheries Ltd., Vancouver BC was in a collision and sank north of Morning Reef in Grenville Channel BC.

Wawanesa[c] 130915 At one time she served as a tender at the Dominion Cannery. On June 19, 1980, this fishboat owned by Darwin Enterprises Ltd., Vancouver BC exploded and burned at Lasqueti Island BC.

Wa-Yas[779] 153374 On September 29, 1986 this seiner owned by Conrad Plensky, Nanaimo BC sank in Templar Channel off Frank Island BC.

Weaver Lake[780] 158311 On December 7, 1959 this tug, owned by Mission Towing Co. Ltd., Mission BC, sank at Andy's Bay BC when she was crushed between a boom and a Davis raft.

---

a   Built as Daisy G.; then Ohiat Kid; then Warlock No. 1
b   Built as Seven Seas II; then Watson Rock
c   Built as Klatawa; then Wawanesa

Wee Giant[781] 152810 On September 20, 1935 this tug owned by Wilfred G Dolmage, Vancouver BC, burned at Green Point on Harrison Lake BC. The crew beached the tug near the Green Point Logging Camp where the fire burned itself out.

Wee Giant 170765 On January 19, 1970 this tug owned by Lake of the Woods Holding Ltd., Ucluelet BC foundered at the entrance to Pipestem Inlet in 19 fathoms of water.

Wee Polly 197651 On June 02, 1980 this passenger vessel owned by Henry A Watts, Vancouver BC struck an object in Pylades Channel in Georgia Strait BC.

Wee Scott[782] 153177 On December 20, 1930 this tug owned by Ronald Maitland, Vancouver BC burned in the Alberni Canal.

Wellington 090806 She grazed Wellington Rock (Located in Seaforth Channel) on September 19, 1902 while under command of Captain Colin Salmond on a voyage from Ladysmith to Juneau AK with a cargo of coal.

Wempe Bros.[783] (US) This four-masted schooner was registered at San Francisco CA USA. On October 27, 1903 she was stranded and broke up at Bonilla Point BC. She had been en route from San Pedro for Puget Sound. Before she had been driven on to the lee ashore the crew abandoned her and went to Carmanah Lighthouse.

West Coast[a] 156591 In 1929 this vessel is said to have functioned as a rum runner and she formed part of the pre-war Fishermen's Reserve Fleet. She was mobilized September 15, 1939. In 1940 she was commissioned into the Royal Canadian Navy Fisherman's Reserve. She sank on September 28, 1951 at Beaver Pass, BC.

West Vancouver No. 5[784] 134086 On August 12, 1924, at 7:43 am, this ferry was in a collision in dense fog with the fishboat troller *Kikapoo*

---

a   Built as Taiheiyo; then West Coast; then HMCS West Coast; then West Coast

near the Calamity bell buoy in First Narrows, Burrard Inlet BC. In 1935 this ferry, while under command of Captain Darius Smith, collided with the *Princess Alice* near Calamity Shoal at Brockton Point in Vancouver Harbour. The steamer cut a huge hole in the ferry with the loss of a passenger trapped in the wreckage. The ferry sank 8 minutes later. The ferry was raised, repaired, and put back into service.

Western Breeze 192044 On July 12, 2019 this seiner owned by Medanic Fisheries Ltd., Port Moody BC and Govorcin Fisheries Ltd., Vancouver BC sank at her berth in Steveston Harbour BC, was salvaged and moved to Shelter Island Marina, awaiting demolition.

Western Cloud[a,785] 175142 On October 19, 1951 she was returning to Steveston BC with a load of salmon and was swamped by high seas sinking between Cape Mudge and Rebecca Spit in 85 fathoms of water. Her crew were saved by the *Nanceda*: Captain Gordon Baker, E Abrahamson, Bill Garden and Murdock Jackson.

Western Commander 174081 On April 9, 2018 this fishboat owned by Gale Winds Enterprises Ltd., Prince Rupert BC sank after taking on water near Triple Island, in the northern Hecate Strait with the loss of Captain Clyde Dudoward.

Western Crusader[b] 178810 On May 12, 2015 she sank at Shelter Island Marina on the Fraser River.

Western Dispatcher[c,786] 190573 In 1978 this ex-USN submarine catcher converted to a fishpacker was reported to have been broken up and scuttled at Bedwell Bay BC.

Western Express[d] 179082 In 2016 she appeared to be rapidly deteriorating at a float docked in Annieville Slough, in Delta BC. In January

---

a   Built as Pacific Belle; then Western Cloud
b   Built as HMCS Moolock; then Western Crusader
c   Built as USS SC-1272; then Norman Nelson; then Western Dispatcher
d   Built as USATS YMS-297?; then Western Express

2017 she sank at her berth. In August 2017 she was demolished in situ and the remains barged away by the Federal Government.

The smashed bow of the **Western Express** after her collision. (Photograph from University of British Columbia. Library. Rare Books and Special Collections. Fishermen Publishing Society fonds. BC_1532_1249_8)

Western Hemlock[a] 134023 On July 9, 1930 this workboat owned by J McIntosh, Vancouver BC burned at Opposite Arm, Burrard Inlet BC.

Western Maid[b] 158916 In 1940 she was damaged by an explosion and sank. She underwent extensive repairs and was lengthened. In 1942 she was appraised at $10,200. In 1941 she was seized from her Japanese owners by the Canadian Government. In 1942 her ownership transferred to His Majesty the King. In 1942–1944 she was commissioned into the Royal Canadian Navy Fisherman's Reserve as a Canadian Naval Patrol Vessel, (Fishermen's Reserve).

a Built as Ulster; then Western Hemlock
b Built as Westerm Maid; then HMCS Western Maid; then Western Maid

Western Pride[787] 179640 On January 22, 1962 this gillnet fishboat sank in Howe Sound BC on a twelve-mile trip across to Horseshoe Bay. Vessel owner Harold Fearn and his son Timothy were lost. There was a strong wind and rough seas at the time of the incident.

Western Ranger[788] 170947 On June 26, 1977 this fishboat owned by Mervyn F Campbell (MO), Sidney BC struck bottom and sank at Mier Point, in Goletas Channel Vancouver Island BC. Her crew of five evacuated in the dinghy and were rescued by the *Ursa Major* (a volunteer with the Provincial Emergency Program).

Western Shell[a,789] 178797 On October 23, 1949 this tanker ran aground in dense fog a half mile east of the Second Narrows bridge in Vancouver Harbour. She was outbound and ran onto the tidal flats on the north side of the passage. A portion of her cargo was pumped out to lighten ship and she was towed into deeper water by three C.H. Cates & Sons Co. Ltd. tugs. She then proceeded under her own power to the Pacific Salvage Co. for inspection. In May 1977 she sank after explosion near Acajutla, El Salvador.

Westerner 197655 In November 1956 this drum seiner owned by Marian Govorchi was discovered on the rocks on the Gulf side of Saturna Island. The skipper and his three-man crew had died from carbon monoxide poisoning. She was written off as a complete loss but was rebuilt as a fishpacker at North Arm Boat Works for Nerio (Zeke) Zecchel, New Westminster BC.

Westisle[790] 802193 The Transportation Safety Board of Canada reports that "On the morning of March 1, 1999, the herring seiner *Westisle* was experiencing rough seas off the west coast of Vancouver Island. Seawater shipped on deck, down flooded past an improperly secured aluminum fish-loading deck scuttle cover leading to the forward starboard cargo tank, causing a starboard list. Down flooding into the compartment increased when the cover became dislodged.

---

a   Built as USS YO-119; then Western Shell; then Pacific Rae; then Pacific Star; then Layla Express; then Punta Macoris

When the unsecured deck cargo shifted suddenly to starboard, the vessel was reportedly heeled to an angle of about 70 degrees. By ballasting and moving weights, the crew was able to return the vessel to a near upright position. Damage to the vessel was limited to seawater contamination of the main engine fuel injectors and fuel system. No injuries or pollution resulted from this occurrence."

Westport Straits[791] 314875 On February 2, 1968 she was stranded and sank in Kyuquot Sound BC. Under charter to Straits Towing Ltd. to haul logs she had been under tow by the tug Lorne at the time of the incident. A towing socket on the wire line was defective and led to the wreck.

Whiskey Jack[792] "On 11 May 1993, the fishing vessel *Whiskey Jack* was engaged in seafood harvesting and anchored in the shallow waters off Fan Island, Porcher Peninsula, British Columbia. While the heavily laden *Whiskey Jack* was in the process of weighing anchor, a succession of large waves struck on her port quarter. The vessel shipped large quantities of water causing her to rapidly settle by the stern and founder. One of the three crew members succumbed to hypothermia and drowned, and the two others were rescued suffering from hypothermia. The Board determined that the heavily laden *Whiskey Jack* was swamped by successive large waves and foundered. Valuable time was lost because the Search and Rescue (SAR) initiative was prematurely terminated at the communication stage because of confusion regarding the identity of the vessel in distress. This confusion arose from the fact that two vessels had transmitted similar MAYDAY messages almost simultaneously. "

White Cloud[793] On December 08, 1950 this forestry vessel was destroyed by fire while carrying gasoline fuel to First Nations fishermen marooned in three gillnetters in ice-locked Dean Channel. The *White Cloud* was following the RCMP vessel *PWL-17* that was breaking ice at the time of the incident. The three crew members of the *White Cloud* were rescued by a passing vessel owned by the Department of Indian Affairs.

White V 173505 On July 20, 1974 this troller fishboat owned by Danny R Kolnes (MO), Port Alberni BC was stranded and burned in Danvers Inlet east of Fleming Island in Barkley Sound BC.

White Wave 154579 This seiner formed part of the pre-war Fishermen's Reserve Fleet. She participated in the 30 January–25 February 1939 Fishermen's Reserve Training Session. She was however not mobilized for active duty during the Second World War. This seiner owned by British Columbia Packers Ltd., Richmond, BC sank off Tyee Point, Johnstone Strait, BC on July 03, 1978.

Willamette[a,794] (US) On March 15, 1901 while en route to Ladysmith in a dense fog to Oyster Bay this collier, owned by the Pacific Coast Steamship Co., struck Village Point, Denman Island in Baynes Sound. Part of her cargo was removed, and she was salvaged and repaired. The hull was winched out of the water and a repair crew from Moran Bros, Seattle WA replaced plates in situ, and she was refloated and put back in service.

Willapa[b] 81313 (US) In 1889 she ran to Gray's Harbour and Coos Bay Oregon. In 1895 she began to run to southeastern Alaska, every 16 days, from Seattle WA. She was stranded March 19, 1897 on Regatta Reef near Bella Bella while under the command of Captain George Roberts. In 1896 she was stranded at Regatta Reef (near Bella Coola) and salvaged. In 1919 she was laid up. In 1950 she was burned as a spectacle at the Seattle Seafair.

William This may be the first recorded wreck on the southwest coast of Vancouver Island. On January 1, 1854 while she was bound from San Francisco to Victoria while under command of Captain John McIntosh she went ashore about four miles east of Pachena Point. The captain and cook were lost. The rest of the crew were saved by First Nations people who guided the survivors to Sooke.

---

a   Built as Willamette; then Montana
b   Built as General Miles; then Willapa; then Bellingham

William Tell This ship was built for the North Atlantic packet service. She was sailing inbound in ballast from Simonstown South Africa and had reached Dungeness Spit on the US shore when shifting winds forced her back west of Race Rocks. Unfavorable winds prevented her from anchoring, so she spent three days fighting the wind in Juan de Fuca Strait. On December 23, 1865 while under command of Captain Jones she broke up on a reef three miles northwest of Port San Juan. The mainmast was cut so that it formed a bridge to the shore and a crew member was able to take a line ashore at low tide. The whole crew of twenty-two was saved. Captain Spring arrived on the scene with a First Nations crew in a canoe which took them off. The schooner *Surprise* carried the crew to Victoria.

Windsor[795] 225695 (US) On October 3, 1936 this American fishpacker, registered at Ketchikan AK, foundered, and sank northeast side of Grey Rock, off Nanoose BC. Captain HC Timmerman and the crew of 5 rowed ashore in the ship's dinghy. She had been southbound to Anacortes WA at the time of the incident.

Windward 151116 On April 25, 1928 this salvage tug owned by Charles A Widig, Vancouver BC exploded and burned in Secret Cove, Georgia Strait BC. She was a recovered wreck herself that had been rebuilt.

Windy Bay[796] On June 14, 1964 this troller was destroyed by fire and sank in Camano Sound BC. Her crew, Harold Babcock, and Leo Bottolls were rescued by HMCS *Whitethroat*.

Wireless 126783 On September 25, 1930 this tug owned by Pacific (Coyle) Navigation Co. Ltd., Vancouver BC was towing the C.Q.L. No. 4 which became stranded, 8 miles northeast of Entrance Island BC. The *Wireless* sank in Jervis Inlet BC.

Wishing Star No. 1[a] 154677 On September 8, 1967 this seiner owned by Snowcloud Fishing Co. Ltd., Vancouver BC caught fire in the Strait

---

a   Built as Snow Cloud; then Wishing Star; then Wishing Star No. 1; then Wishing Star No. 1

of Juan de Fuca off Sheringham Light and was considered a total loss. On March 25, 1975 she sank at Bull Harbour BC and was declared a total constructive loss.

Wolco VI[a],797 331293 The *Wolco VI* was employed at the Odyssey Camp located in Kwatna Inlet, one of the three helicopter logging camps operated by Helifor, a subsidiary of International Forest Products (Interfor). On February 18. 1996 while engaged in forestry operations off the Odyssey Camp, this small yarding tug took on water, heeled heavily to port, flooded, and sank when the tug operator tried to haul a heavy granite (stone) anchor along the seabed. The operator became trapped inside the tug and lost his life, but the deckhand managed to escape. He radioed for help on his portable radiotelephone and was rescued shortly thereafter by the logging camp helicopter that responded to the call. This vessel was salvaged and put back into service.

Woodside 072680 In 1878 this tug was in Victoria-Sooke service, also towing and jobbing in Victoria BC. On March 12, 1888 while under the command of Captain Colin Cluness she was bound from Victoria for Barkley Sound with three passengers (Mrs Wrede and two children) and six crew members with general cargo when she lost her rudder and went aground near Pachena Point. All were saved, but the vessel was abandoned. During the night, the vessel drifted ashore and became a total loss. The survivors were paddled in a canoe by the First Nations people of Nitinat to Victoria.

Wyrill 130799 On November 26, 1929 this power cruiser owned by Pacific Mills Ltd., Vancouver BC burned at the head of South Bentinck Arm BC in Cousins Inlet BC.

Xihwu Boeing 737-200 This former commercial passenger aircraft is an unusual inclusion in the list. It was sunk on January 14, 2006 as an artificial diving reef.

---

a Built as Wolco VI; then Sea Imp IV

Yachiyo 126541 On December 17, 1928 this fishboat owned by Mrs Reg, Band, Vancouver BC burned and sank at Scotty Bay, Lasqueti Island BC.

YOGN 82 In 1944 she was built by the Concrete Ship Constructors of National City, California. In 1947 she was added to the floating breakwater at Powell River BC. She was anchored with 8–10 concrete 14–16-ton anchors and the hull ballasted with water for stability. In 2019 she was deliberately scuttled at the end of her life.

The crumpled bow of the *Yoho Maru* shortly after the accident (Photograph from the Walter E. Frost fonds in the Vancouver City Archives AM1506-S3-3-: CVA 447-9062.1)

Yoho Maru[798] On May 11, 1968 this Japanese freighter collided with the old Second Narrows Railway Bridge in Vancouver Harbour and bounced off the new one nearing completion to the east. Her bow was pushed back about 35 feet. The center span of the bridge which had been raised to allow the ship through was jammed. After hitting the span, the ship dropped her anchor in mid-channel while water rushed into the gap in her bow. Later the anchor winch jammed, and a derrick barge had to be called to raise the anchor. Pumps were put on board to control the flooding. At the time she was carrying a cargo of 23,000 tons of coal for Japan which had been loaded at Pacific Coast Bulk Terminals in Port Moody BC. She was repaired by Yarrows Ltd. at Esquimalt BC.

Z. Brothers[a] 155202 In 1938 this seiner was proposed as a possible member of the Fishermen's Reserve Fleet but was not taken up by the Royal Canadian Navy. On October 29, 1953 she ran aground on Nelson Island and suffered a hole in her hull. The crew kept her afloat until a salvage tug arrived.

---

a   Z. Brothers; then B.C. Girl I; then B.C. Girl

Zenardi 152725 She was a seiner owned by Mark Lewis, Campbell River BC. On August 10, 1985 she sank in Seymour Narrows after hitting a 'boil' and rolling over on to her side. The crew were all rescued. The boat went down off Brown Bay. Apparently, the boat sank in water too deep to be salvaged.

Zephyr (US) On February 13, 1872 she was a bark that struck a rock on Mayne Island BC while en route from Puget Sound to San Francisco CA. Another account states that the American bark *Zephyr*, from Puget Sound for San Francisco, struck a rock near Mayne Island, February 13, 1870, knocking a big hole in the hull, after which she slid off and sank in ninety fathoms of water. Captain Hipson and seaman James Stewart lost their lives, and First Officer Lusk and the remainder of the crew reached Victoria in a small boat.

Zephyr II[a,799] 157223 In 1931–1932 this vessel was operated as a rum runner shore boat owned by Triangle Freighters, Vancouver BC. On July 15, 1938 she burned in Rocky Passage, Clayoquot Sound BC.

Zip[800] 156898 This Canadian motor vessel, while under command of Captain Pete Jensen, stranded on Bonilla Point reef, early in the morning of October 7, 1936. She was carrying a cargo of salmon bound from Bamfield to New Westminster. The launch was lowered but was quickly swamped and the vessel's master who was trying to bail it out was thrown into the sea. The Mate, Ole Dahl, was drowned (he could not swim) and the other three crew members managed to reach shore. Captain Jensen walked three miles to Carmanah Light to seek help. The *Banfield Lifeboat* started out but broke down and had to be towed back to port. After she went up on the beach her engine was salvaged at low tide by the Baird family. Members of the family also dived underwater from the surface to slowly dismantle the engine. John Quinn loaned a set of wheels to assist in the removal. The base weighed 3 tons and was moved by hand one mile

---

a   Built as Amigo, later Carry Bell, then Zephyr II

to a barge. The engine was salvaged by the owner and installed in the *Nitinat Chief*, then being built.

Zoe Rose[801] (US) On September 6th, 2001, this converted gillnetter owned by Pete and Rachel Feenstra, burned, and sank off the Halibut Banks 10 kilometers east of Gabriola Island. The two owners were rescued by a BC Ferries crew from the *Queen of Cowichan*. The fire was blamed on a propane leak.

Zouie A[802] On October 5, 1958 this salvage vessel sank off Halkett Point, Gambier Island in Howe Sound BC. The owner evacuated to his dinghy and later picked up by the tug *Kerry Ann*.

ZR3[a] (US) In 1942 while loaded with rock ballast this old Alaskan freighter and workboat was deliberately sunk at Oyster Bay (near Vancouver) as a breakwater.

---

a   Built as Muriel; then ZR3;

GLOSSARY

Allision: when a vessel strikes a stationary object, such as a bridge or dock.

Backfire: when ignition happens in a gasoline engine in the combustion chamber and for whatever reason the intake valve is not fully closed, the resultant flame can travel (under force) back up the intake manifold, through the carburetor and out the air intake. If there is no flame arrestor in place, flame exits the engine and is "live" in the engine room—most often just for a second. If a paper air filter is in place—this can catch fire. If there are gas fumes in the engine room, this can cause an explosion. If the engine cover (lid) is close to the top of the carburetor, and is flammable, it can be ignited and If the engineer happens to be in proximity, it can cause flash burns—usually on the face/head.

Collision: when two vessels strike each other

Derelict: a vessel abandoned at sea by its guardian or owner.

Dilapidated vessel: a vessel that meets any prescribed criteria and is significantly degraded or dismantled; or is incapable of being used for safe navigation.

Flotsam: those parts of the wreckage of a ship or its cargo found floating on the sea because of shipwreck.

Founder: when a vessel is overcome by forces of nature so that it is unable to remain afloat.

Hazard: any condition or threat that may reasonably be expected to result in harmful consequences to the environment, coastlines, shorelines, infrastructure or any other interest, including the health, safety, well-being and economic interests of the public. It does not include harmful consequences that are excluded by the regulations.

Jetsam: goods thrown overboard from a vessel that are then left to drift.

Joint Owner (JO): a person who owns part of the shares in a vessel.

Lagan: goods and wreckage lying on the bed of the sea which are thrown overboard to lighten ship with the intent to recover them later. Technically these goods should be marked with a buoy or other marker.

Licence Number: the alphanumeric number issued to vessels by Transport Canada.

Managing Owner (MO): the partner owner who is designated to act on behalf of the overall interests in a vessel.

Registration Number: the unique identification number assigned by the Canada Register of Shipping to vessels.

Scuttle: to deliberately cause a vessel to sink.

Shook: the wooden slats that are used to construct a wooden box.

Wreck: a vessel, or part of a vessel, that is sunk, partially sunk, adrift, stranded or grounded, including on the shore; or, equipment, stores, cargo or any other thing that is or was on board a vessel and that is sunk, partially sunk, adrift, stranded or grounded, including on the shore.

BIBLIOGRAPHY

Bowman, Liza J (2004) *Oceans Apart Over Sunken Ships: Is the Underwater Cultural Heritage Convention Really Wrecking Admiralty Law?* Osgoode Hall Law Journal Vol 42 No. 1 (Spring 2004) Available at: https://digitalcommons.osgoode.yorku.ca/cgi/viewcontent.cgi?article=1388&context=ohlj (website viewed 2020-06-14)

Coates, Ken and Bill Morrison (1990) *The Sinking of the Princess Sophia: Taking the North Down With Her.* Toronto: Oxford University Press.

Crawford, Brian K (2016) *The Wreck of the Steamship Pacific; The Worst Maritime Disaster of the West Coast.* San Anselmo CA: The Crawford Press.

Foster, JG (ed) Archaeology Branch, Ministry of Tourism and Minister Responsible for Culture (1991) *British Columbia Documenting Shipwrecks Shipwreck Recording Guide.* Victoria BC: Province of British Columbia.

Gibbs, "Shipwreck" Jim (1986) *Peril at Sea: A photographic study of shipwrecks in the Pacific.* Atglen PA: Schiffler Publishing Ltd.

Henthorne, Colin (2016) *The Queen of the North Disaster: The Captain's Story.* Madeira Park BC: Harbour Publishing Co. Ltd.

Intergovernmental Oceanographic Commission. *Convention on the Protection of the Underwater Cultural Heritage will enter into force in January 2009* Available at: http://www.ioc-unesco.org/index.php?option=com_content&view=article&id=83&Itemid=112

(website viewed 2020-06-14)

James, Rick (2004) *The Ghost Ships of Royston.* (UASBC: Vancouver BC)

James, Rick (2011) *West Coast Wrecks & Other Maritime Tales.* Madeira Park BC: Harbour Publishing Co. Ltd.

James, Rick and Jacques Marc (2002) *Historic Shipwrecks of the Central Coast of British Columbia*. Victoria BC: Underwater Archaeological Society of British Columbia.

Juvelier, Ben (2018) "Salvaging" History: Underwater Cultural Heritage and Commercial Salvage, "American University International Law Review: Vol. 32: Issue 5, Article 2. Available at: http://digitalcommons.wcl.american.edu/auilr/vol32/iss5/2 (website viewed 2020-06-14)

Keller, Keith (1997) *Dangerous Waters: Wrecks and Rescues off the BC Coast*. Madeira Park BC: Harbour Publishing.

James, Rick and Jacques Marc (2010) *Historic Shipwrecks of the Sunshine Coast*. Victoria BC: Underwater Archaeological Society of British Columbia.

Marc, Jacques (1999) *Historic Shipwrecks of Northeastern Vancouver Island*. Victoria BC: Underwater Archaeological Society of British Columbia.

Mires, Calvin H (April 2014) *The Value of Maritime Archaeological Heritage: An Exploratory Study of the Cultural Capital of Shipwrecks in the Graveyard of the Atlantic*. PhD dissertation presented to the Faculty of Coastal Resources Management PhD Program East Carolina University.

Neitzel, Michael C (1995) *The Valencia Tragedy*. Surrey BC: Heritage House Publishing Co.

Nicholson, George (1965) *Vancouver Island's West Coast 1762–1962*. Victoria BC: George Nicholson.

Norris, Pat Wastell (1999) *High Seas High Risk: the story of the Sudburys*. Madeira Park BC: Harbour Publishing Co. Ltd.

Parks Canada (July 1998, rev. 2000) Guidelines for Evaluating Shipwrecks of National Historic Significance in Canada Available at: https://www.pc.gc.ca/en/docs/pc/guide/epaves-shipwrecks (website viewed 2020-06-14)

Pollack, John, Edward L Affleck, and Wendy Bouliane, (Eds) (2000)

Historic Shipwrecks of the West Kootenay District, British Columbia. Victoria BC: Underwater Archaeological Society of British Columbia.

Rogers, AC (Fred) (1973) *Shipwrecks of British Columbia.* Vancouver: J.J. Douglas Ltd.

Scott, R Bruce (1970) *"Breakers Ahead!"* Sidney BC: Review Publishing House.

Scott, R Bruce (1972) *Barkley Sound: a history of the Pacific Rim National Park area.* Victoria BC: Printed by Fleming-Review Printing Ltd.

Stone, David Leigh, (ed.) (2007) *Historic Shipwrecks of the Lower Mainland of British Columbia.* Victoria BC: Underwater Archaeological Society of British Columbia.

The Ocean Foundation. *Underwater Cultural Heritage.* Available at: https://oceanfdn.org/underwater-cultural-heritage/ (website viewed 2020-06-14)

Tornfelt, Evert E and Michael Burwell (1992) *Shipwrecks of the Alaskan Shelf and Shore* (OCS Report MMS 92-0002). US Department of the Interior Minerals and Management Service Alaska OCS Region.

UNESCO. *Underwater Cultural Heritage* Available at: http://www.unesco.org/new/en/culture/themes/underwater-cultural-heritage/ (website viewed 2020-06-14)

ACKNOWLEDGEMENTS

Special thanks to my colleague Lynn Salmon who reviewed and edited each of the entries in the catalogue of wrecks. Her attention to detail made them more readable and more accurate.

Bill Arnott, Historian, Author, Blogger (The Miramichi Reader)

Lonnie Edward Berrow, Master Mariner

Tom Beasley, Vice-President of the Vancouver Maritime Museum, and the Underwater Archaeology Society of British Columbia

Cliff Craig, Mariner and Marine Entrepreneur

George Duddy, Historian and Engineer

Lea Edgar, Archivist and Librarian, Vancouver Maritime Museum

Robert Hanna, Nautical Researcher

Rick James, Historian, Archaeologist, Marine Historian and Author

Robert Lawson, Marine Historian and Shipwright

Ken Lund, Mariner

Catherine MacFarlane, Heritage Interpreter

Jacques Marc, Explorations Director, Underwater Archaeology Society of British Columbia

Captain Alec Provan, Extra Master Mariner (retired Canadian Coast Guard)

Tad Roberts, Naval Architect and Marine Historian

Judy Thompson, Librarian, Maritime Museum of British Columbia

Brittany Vis, Associate Director, Maritime Museum of British Columbia

Howard White, Publisher Harbour Publishing

Eric Young, Treasurer, the Underwater Archaeology Society of British Columbia

I would also like to acknowledge the encouragement I received during the creative and publishing processes from the members of the Oceanside Writers Group (particularly to Barbara Botham and Gail Madjzoub).

Special thanks to Tom Pope, proprietor of Mulberry Books in Parksville and Qualicum Beach for decades of friendship and book advice which has proven invaluable to this aspiring author. His knowledge of the book trade is unparalleled.

ABOUT THE AUTHOR

JOHN MACFARLANE is a fifth generation Vancouver Islander whose family came there from California in 1859 for the Fraser River Goldrush. He has worked to protect and interpret Canada's natural and historical heritage since 1969 when he joined the Canadian National Parks Service. He is the Curator Emeritus of the Maritime Museum of British Columbia in Victoria BC. The author of 14 books, he was the co-recipient of the prestigious 2020 John Lyman Book Prize of the North American Society of Oceanic History. His book *Around the World in a Dugout Canoe* was on the Best Seller List for 25 weeks. He is a Fellow of the Royal Geographical Society (London) and a recipient of the Sovereign's Medal for Volunteers. He lives on the central east coast of Vancouver Island. His almost full-time avocation is The Nauticapedia (www.nauticapedia.ca), an online nautical history resource which is accessed more than 4 million times yearly.

REFERENCES

1. Daily Colonist (Victoria BC) Tuesday, March 14, 1933 Page 7
2. Heritage Conservation Act [RSBC 1996] Chapter 187
3. https://www.pc.gc.ca/en/docs/pc/guide/epaves-shipwrecks website viewed 05-12-2019
4. https://www.uasbc.com/conservation/overview (Website viewed 13/12/2019);
5. Wrecked, Abandoned or Hazardous Vessels Act (S.C. 2019, c. 1)
6. Adopted by the International Marine Organization (IMO) in 2007 and came into force internationally in 2015
7. The Province (Vancouver BC) November 7, 1950 Page 1
8. Dr John P. Tully presentation to Nanaimo Historical Society March 17, 1970
9. Marc, Jacques. (1999) Historic Shipwrecks of Northeastern Vancouver Island UASBC
10. Times Colonist (Victoria BC) Saturday August 19, 1939 page 1
11. Vancouver Sun (Vancouver BC) Wednesday April 4, 1934 page 1
12. Victoria Daily Times (Victoria BC) Tuesday May 12, 1891 page 1
13. Nanaimo Daily News Monday March 22, 1920 page 1; The Vancouver Sun (Vancouver BC) Tuesday March 23, 1920 page 15
14. Victoria Daily Times Monday, July 28, 1919 page 19; The Province (Vancouver BC) Monday, July 28, 1919 page 7
15. The Province (Vancouver BC) Tuesday September 05, 1972 page 1; Time Colonist (Victoria BC) Thursday September 07, 1972 page 3
16. Nanaimo Daily News (Nanaimo BC) Friday November 19, 1943 page 4
17. Victoria Daily Times (Victoria BC) Friday September 19, 1930 page 11
18. Vancouver Sun (Vancouver BC) Thursday August 31, 1967 page 3
19. Vancouver Sun (Vancouver BC) Tuesday January 12, 1960 page 7
20. The Province (Vancouver BC) Monday August 17, 1898 page 1
21. Times Colonist (Victoria BC) Saturday, September 18, 1937 page 18
22. Times Colonist (Victoria BC) Thursday May 27, 1937 page 18
23. Victoria Daily Times (Victoria BC) Thursday September 10, 1936 page 18
24. The Gazette (Montreal QC) Tuesday August 3, 1858 page 2
25. Vancouver Sun (Vancouver BC) Tuesday March 31, 1959 page 3
26. Vancouver Sun (Vancouver BC) Saturday July 8, 1972 page 2
27. Vancouver Sun (Vancouver BC) Wednesday November 10, 1965 pages 6–7
28. Zachary Dunn (British Columbia Nautical History Facebook Group 02/10/2019)
29. Vancouver Daily World (Vancouver BC) Friday February 22, 1907 page 20
30. The Province (Vancouver BC) Saturday September 29, 1917 page 14
31. Nanaimo Daily News (Nanaimo BC) Saturday August 7, 1886 page 3
32. The Province (Vancouver BC) Thursday April 21, 1966 page 21
33. Marc, Jacques. (1999) Historic Shipwrecks of Northeastern Vancouver Island uasbc
34. Vancouver Daily World (Vancouver BC) Wednesday September 23, 1891 page 8
35. Victoria Daily Times (Victoria BC) Monday March 20, 1916 page 9
36. http://www.tsb.gc.ca/eng/rapports-reports/marine/2014/m14p0150/m14p0150.asp

37 Nanaimo Daily News (Nanaimo BC) Tuesday March 28, 1911 page 1
38 R Bruce Scott (1970);
39 Victoria Daily Times Wednesday March 26, 1902 page 7
40 The Province (Vancouver BC) Monday January 7, 1901 page 7
41 Email (Cliff Craig – Nauticapedia 16/01/2017)
42 Times Colonist (Victoria BC) Wednesday September 4, 1935 page 1
43 Vancouver Sun (Vancouver BC) Saturday August 28, 1937 page 1
44 Rosalind Hildred (British Columbia Nautical History Facebook Group 07/10/2018)
45 http://artificialreefsocietybc.ca/annapolis.html (website viewed 26/01/2020);
46 Email communication (Andrew Clarke- Nauticapedia 13/04/2017)
47 Times Colonist (Victoria BC) Saturday September 19, 1959 page 32
48 Nicholson, George (1962)
49 Transportation Safety Board of Canada
50 Victoria Daily Times (Victoria BC) Saturday July 19, 1930 page 19
51 Courtenay Free Press (Courtenay BC) Thursday February 7, 1929 page 2
52 The Province (Vancouver BC) Thursday March 24, 1910 page 1
53 McLaren, TA & Vickie Jensen (2000); Canada List of Shipping; Times Colonist (Victoria BC) Tuesday October 21, 2014 page 1
54 Interview by John MacFarlane with George Duddy, White Rock BC February 2014
55 Vancouver Sun Friday December 13, 1940 page 21
56 The Province (Vancouver BC) Monday October 8, 1928 page 1
57 Transportation Safety Board of Canada (1993)
58 Transportation Safety Board of Canada (1993)
59 Gordon Newell, Maritime Events of 1969, H. W. McCurdy Marine History of the Pacific Northwest 1966 to 1975, page 71
60 Transportation Safety Board of Canada (1993)
61 The Province (Vancouver BC) Saturday March 29, 1975 page 3
62 http://www.tsb.gc.ca/eng/rapports-reports/marine/2006/m06w0039/m06w0039.asp
63 Times Colonist (Victoria BC) Wednesday July 4, 1956 Page 7
64 Times Colonist (Victoria BC) Wednesday December 7, 1938 page 16
65 The Province Saturday November 13, 1920 Page 1
66 Transportation Safety Board of Canada (1993); The Province (Vancouver BC) Wednesday July 3, 1935 page 1
67 Nanaimo Daily News (Nanaimo BC) Saturday July 26, 1952 page 1
68 Vancouver Daily World (Vancouver BC) Friday September 23, 1898 page 1; The Province (Vancouver BC) October 6, 1904 page 1
69 Al Hoskins (British Columbia Nautical History Facebook Group 21/05/2019)
70 John de Boeck (British Columbia Nautical History Facebook Group 18/06/2018)
71 Vancouver Daily World (Vancouver BC) Wednesday May 4, 1937 page 4
72 Vancouver Sun (Vancouver BC) Tuesday May 15, 1962 page 19
73 Vancouver News-Herald (Vancouver BC) Monday December 10, 1951 page 1
74 Vancouver Sun Friday December 11, 1953 page 1; Times Colonist (Victoria BC) Wednesday September 30, 1953 page 14
75 Victoria Daily Times (Victoria BC) Wednesday July 12, 1911 page 8
76 Vancouver Sun Monday January 23, 1961 page 4
77 The Province (Vancouver BC) Thursday March 29, 1928 Page 1

78 Victoria Daily Times (Victoria BC) Tuesday November 30, 1886 page 4
79 Nanaimo Daily News (Nanaimo BC) Tuesday March 13, 1900 page 1
80 Victoria Daily Times (Victoria BC) Saturday June 7, 1941 page 20
81 Twigg, Arthur M (1997) Union Steamships Remembered 1920–1958 Campbell River: AM Twigg
82 James, Rick (2004) The Ghost Ships of Royston. (UASBC: Vancouver BC)
83 Vancouver Sun Tuesday December 29, 1925 page 1
84 Times Colonist (Vancouver BC) Wednesday June 15, 1960 page 18
85 Vancouver Sun (Vancouver BC) Thursday March 14, 1963 page 64
86 The Province (Vancouver BC) Friday June 23, 1972 page 10
87 The Province (Vancouver BC) Thursday April 18, 1929 page 31
88 John Campbell (British Columbia Nautical History Facebook Group 01/12/2014
89 Nanaimo Daily News (Nanaimo BC) Tuesday May 2, 1950 page 6
90 Tad Roberts (British Columbia Nautical History Facebook Group 25/09/2015)
91 Times Colonist (Victoria BC) Monday, February 27, 1939 page 14
92 The Province (Vancouver BC) Tuesday, June 7, 1977 page 2
93 Drew Clark (Email to John MacFarlane 13/04/2017)
94 Vancouver Sun Tuesday December 29, 1925 page 1; The San Francisco Examiner (San Francisco CA) Sunday May 12, 1929 page 3
95 James, Rick (2004) The Ghost Ships of Royston (UASBC: Vancouver BC)
96 Times Colonist (Victoria BC) Tuesday August 9, 1927 page 1
97 The Province Saturday November 13, 1920 Page 1
98 The Province (Vancouver BC) Saturday March 29, 1975 page 3
99 http://www.tsb.gc.ca/eng/rapports-reports/marine/2002/m02w0089/m02w0089.asp; (website viewed 26/12/2019);
100 The Vancouver Sun (Vancouver BC) Saturday March 13, 1976 page 18
101 Terry Gustafson (BC Nautical History Facebook Group 18/10/2015)
102 Barr, Captain James (1969) Ferry Across the Harbor Vancouver: Mitchell Press
103 Marc, Jacques (1999)
104 Nanaimo Daily News (Nanaimo BC) Wednesday March 9, 1881 page 3
105 Victoria Daily Times (Victoria BC) Thursday November 12, 1903 page 1
106 The Province (Vancouver BC) Tuesday September 05, 1972 page 1; Time Colonist (Victoria BC) Thursday September 07, 1972 page 3
107 Vancouver Sun (Vancouver BC) Friday December 11, 1953 page 1
108 Twigg, Arthur M (1997) Union Steamships Remembered 1920–1958 Campbell River BC
109 Transportation Safety Board of Canada (1993)
110 Jody Louise (British Columbia Nautical History Facebook Group 05/09/2017)
111 The Province (Vancouver BC) Tuesday August 28, 1923 page 22
112 Adam Harding (British Columbia Nautical History Facebook Group 15/10/2019); Charlotte Cooper (British Columbia Nautical History Facebook Group 15/10/2019)
113 The Province (Vancouver BC) Friday March 11, 1938 page 29
114 http://www.tsb.gc.ca/eng/rapports-reports/marine/2002/m02w0147/m02w0147.asp (website viewed 08/12/2019)
115 Transportation Safety Board of Canada (1993)
116 Vancouver Sun (Vancouver BC) Friday December 11, 1953 page 2
117 Vancouver Sun, Thursday December 7, 1961 Page 1

118 The Province (Vancouver BC) Thursday October 8, 1931 page 1

119 Transportation Safety Board of Canada (1993)

120 The Province (Vancouver BC) Thursday June 18, 1964 page 30

121 Vancouver Daily World (Vancouver BC) Monday, October 4, 1915 page 12

122 Times Colonist (Victoria BC) Tuesday October 8, 1991 page 6

123 Email (Ken Gibson – John MacFarlane 2018)

124 The Province (Vancouver BC Saturday July 17, 1948 page 25

125 Vancouver News-Herald (Vancouver BC) Monday August 22, 1955 page 1

126 Vancouver Sun (Vancouver BC) Thursday November 25, 1965 page 10

127 Transportation Safety Board of Canada (1993)

128 The Province (Vancouver BC) Wednesday, June 1, 1910 page 8; Victoria Daily Times (Victoria BC) Thursday February 15, 1912 page 8

129 The Province (Vancouver BC) Friday August 28, 1942 page 15

130 Canada List of Shipping; List of Shipping Casualties Resulting in Total Loss in British Columbia and Coastal Waters Since 1897 (undated manuscript document)

131 Times Colonist (Victoria BC) Friday June 2, 2006 page 3; Vancouver Sun (Vancouver BC) Wednesday, November 9, 1927 page 1

132 Vancouver Sun (Vancouver BC) Friday December 28, 1928 page 4

133 The Province (Vancouver BC) Tuesday, June 7, 1977 page 2

134 Vancouver Sun (Vancouver BC) Saturday December 5, 1931 page 1

135 Times Colonist (Victoria BC) Saturday June 18, 1927 page 1; Times Colonist (Victoria BC) Friday June 24, 1927 page 17; Times Colonist (Victoria BC) Friday November 18, 1927 page 12

136 James, Rick (2004) The Ghost Ships of Royston. (UASBC: Vancouver BC)

137 James, Rick (2004) The Ghost Ships of Royston. (UASBC: Vancouver BC)

138 Daily Province (Vancouver BC) Friday December 4, 1910 page 24

139 The Ottawa Citizen (Ottawa ON) Tuesday July 24, 1906 page 2; Historic Shipwrecks of the Lower Mainland of British Columbia (2007) UASBC, Vancouver BC

140 Times Colonist (Victoria BC) Tuesday July 26, 1932 page 16; Vancouver Daily World (Vancouver BC) Wedne3sday August 29, 1906 page 6

141 Vancouver Sun (Vancouver BC) Wednesday September 1, 1915 page 8; The Province (Vancouver BC) Monday November 7, 1949 page 1; Nanaimo Daily News (Nanaimo BC) Tuesday February 5, 1935 page 1

142 Vancouver Daily World (Vancouver BC) Wednesday January 8, 1913 page 19

143 Vancouver Sun (Vancouver BC) Monday October 21, 1929 page 17

144 Transportation Safety Board of Canada (1993)

145 The Province (Vancouver BC) Friday October 10, 1947 page 1

146 H.W. McCurdy Marine History of the Pacific Northwest 1966 to 1976 (Ed. Gordon Newell) 1977

147 ID Jordan (British Columbia Nautical History Facebook Group 07/05/2016)

148 Times Colonist (Vancouver BC) Saturday September 24, 1949 page 1; Vancouver Sun (Vancouver BC) Monday September 26, 1949 page 32

149 Vancouver Sun (Vancouver BC) Saturday April 7, 1962 page 22

150 Vancouver Sun (Vancouver BC) Thursday November 1, 1934 page 1

151 Vancouver Sun (Vancouver BC) Saturday May 3, 1941 page 19

152 Transportation Safety Board of Canada (1993)

153 Nanaimo Daily News Monday March 22, 1920 page 1; The Vancouver Sun (Vancouver BC) Tuesday March 23, 1920 page 15

154 Victoria Daily Times (Victoria BC) Thursday September 20, 1906 page 1

155 Gordon Newell, Maritime Events of 1947, H. W. McCurdy Marine History of the Pacific Northwest.p.549

156 Victoria Daily Times (Victoria BC) Saturday April 28, 1917 page 8

157 Victoria Daily Times (Victoria BC) Monday January 16, 1922 page 7

158 The Province (Vancouver BC) December 19, 1927 page 20

159 The Province (Vancouver British Columbia) Thursday May 14, 1925 page 7

160 John Mclean reported (British Columbia Nautical History Group 06/10/2014)

161 Dirk Septer (Email to Nauticapedia 22/10/2019)

162 Vancouver Daily World (Vancouver BC) Tuesday December 28, 1897 page 4

163 Victoria Daily times (Victoria BC) Saturday December 23, 1899 page 8

164 Times Colonist (Victoria BC) Monday March 15, 1965 page 8

165 Wilson, Hill (2005) The Marine Pilots of Canada's West Coast

166 James, Rick (2004) The Ghost Ships of Royston. (UASBC: Vancouver BC)

167 Matt Embree (British Columbia Nautical History Facebook Group 24/11/2019)

168 Nanaimo Daily News (Nanaimo BC) Wednesday April 18, 1883 page 2

169 Nanaimo Daily News (Nanaimo BC) Tuesday June 28, 1966 page 1

170 The Province (Vancouver BC) Friday October 22, 1915 page 14

171 Victoria Daily Times (Victoria BC) Wednesday February 14, 1923 page 1

172 LAC RG 12, Vol. 679 Register of Wrecks Atlantic & Pacific Coasts

173 Victoria Daily Times (Victoria BC) Tuesday November 25, 1913 page 6

174 Victoria Daily Colonist January 27, 1911; Victoria Daily Times Wednesday April 29, 1908 Page 7

175 Vancouver Sun (Vancouver BC) Monday December 28, 1925 page 1

176 http://www.tsb.gc.ca/eng/rapports-reports/marine/1995/m95w0021/m95w0021.asp

177 Vancouver Sun (Vancouver BC) Wednesday August 7, 1929 page 10

178 The Province (Vancouver BC) Monday April 7, 1930 page 20

179 Vancouver Sun (Vancouver BC) Tuesday March 31, 1959 page 3

180 Transportation Safety Board of Canada

181 John Campbell (British Columbia Nautical History Facebook Group 22/11/2017)

182 The Province (Vancouver BC) Tuesday January 7, 1958 page 2

183 Transportation Safety Board of Canada (1993)

184 Ken Lund (British Columbia Nautical History Facebook Group 11/01/2019)

185 Victoria Daily Times (Victoria BC) Saturday March 20, 1909 page 8

186 Times Colonist (Victoria BC) Friday August 8, 1980 page 11

187 John McLean (British Columbia Nautical History Facebook Group 23/12/2015)

188 Vancouver Sun (Vancouver BC) Monday September 18, 1972 page 18

189 Victoria Daily Times (Victoria BC) Friday April 19, 1895 page 5

190 Vancouver Sun (Vancouver BC) Tuesday March 23, 1920 page 15; The Victoria Daily Times (Victoria BC) Thursday March 18, 1920 page 12; Marc, Jacques (1999)

191 Vancouver Daily World (Vancouver BC) Saturday June 27, 1908 Page 16; Victoria Daily Times (Victoria BC) Monday June 22, 1908 Page 8; The Province (Vancouver BC) Saturday December 5, 1903 page 11

192 Alberni Valley Times (Port Alberni BC) Tuesday September 26, 1972 page 1

193 Alberni Valley Times (Port Alberni BC) Tuesday July 31, 1973 page 3

194 Victoria Daily Times (Victoria BC) Tuesday, September 9, 1930 page 20

195 Vancouver Sun (Vancouver BC) Friday November 3, 1950 page 1; The Province (Vancouver BC) Friday November 3, 1950 page 2; Nanaimo Daily News (Nanaimo BC) Saturday November 4, 1950 page 1

196 Nanaimo Daily News (Nanaimo BC) Monday November 21, 1977 page 9

197 Vancouver Sun (Vancouver BC) Monday May 20, 1935 page 18

198 Victoria Daily Times (Victoria BC) Wednesday March 15, 1922 Page 8

199 https://en.wikipedia.org/wiki/Vancouver_Island (website viewed 27/01/2020)

200 LAC RG12, A1, Vol 414 Shipping Registers Victoria BC

201 Nanaimo Daily News (Nanaimo BC) Thursday October 29, 1953 page 1

202 Vancouver Sun (Vancouver BC) Saturday August 30, 1952 page 2

203 Vancouver Sun (Vancouver BC) Tuesday February 9, 1932 page 18

204 Nanaimo Daily News (Nanaimo BC) Tuesday March 28, 1911 page 1

205 Victoria Daily Times (Victoria BC) Saturday November 4, 1916 page 8

206 Victoria Daily Times Friday December 24, 1920 page 8; Victoria Daily Times Tuesday December 28, 1920 page 8; Vancouver Sun (Vancouver BC) Friday December 24, 1920 page 7

207 Times Colonist (Victoria BC) Thursday July 12, 1928 page 10

208 The Province (Vancouver BC) Sunday June 21, 1925 page 18

209 Vancouver Sun (Vancouver BC) Wednesday August 31, 1932 page 1

210 Times Colonist (Victoria BC) Friday April 1, 1932 page 19

211 Times Colonist (Victoria BC) Wednesday November 2, 1927 page 8; The Province (Vancouver BC) Monday March 21, 1027 page 18

212 James, Rick (2004) The Ghost Ships of Royston. (UASBC: Vancouver BC)

213 Victoria Daily Times (Victoria BC) Tuesday November 8, 1887 page 4

214 Victoria Daily News (Victoria BC) Wednesday November 18, 1936 page 1

215 James, Rick (2004) The Ghost Ships of Royston. (UASBC: Vancouver BC)

216 Vancouver Sun (Vancouver BC) Thursday November 21, 1912 page 11

217 Vancouver Sun (Vancouver BC) Thursday December 2, 1976 page 1

218 James, Rick (2004) The Ghost Ships of Royston. (UASBC: Vancouver BC)

219 Times Colonist (Victoria BC) Monday December 11, 1939 page 16

220 Brabant, Augustin Joseph (1977); Nanaimo Daily News (Nanaimo BC) Saturday December 26, 1874 page 3

221 Victoria Daily Times (Victoria BC) Thursday October 15, 1925 page 8; Victoria Daily Times (Victoria BC) Monday October 19, 1925 page 9

222 The Province (Vancouver BC) Tuesday December 3, 1935 page 1

223 The Province (Vancouver BC) Friday October 10, 1947 page 1

224 Vancouver Sun (Vancouver BC) Friday October 5, 1962 page 5

225 http://sopf.gc.ca/CMFiles/reports-en/SOPF-Annual-Report-2013–2014-English.pdf; https://www.threesheetsnw.com/tug-of-the-month-elf/

226 Vancouver Sun (Vancouver BC) Saturday April 29, 1939 page 2

227 Nanaimo Daily News (Nanaimo BC) Saturday March 31, 1934, page 1

228 The Province (Vancouver BC) Tuesday May 26, 1931 page 22

229 The Province (Vancouver BC) Monday August 24, 1964 page 2

230 Stephen Barnett. Assistant Administrator, Steveston Harbour Authority (Email to Nauticapedia 27/12/2018)

231 Nanaimo Daily News (Nanaimo BC) Saturday January 30, 1960 page 1

232 Victoria Daily Times (Victoria BC) Saturday June 13, 1931, page 1

233 Mike Pearson (British Columbia Nautical History Facebook Group 24/07/2019); Scott Kristmanson (British Columbia Nautical History Facebook Group 24/07/2019);

234 LAC RG 12, A1A, Vol 414 Shipping Registers Victoria BC

235 The Province (Vancouver BC) Friday February 19, 1904 page 1

236 Times Colonist (Victoria BC) Tuesday August 20, 1946 page 16

237 The Province (Vancouver BC) Monday October 14, 1929 page 1

238 The Province (Vancouver BC) Monday December 3, 1928 page 1; Nanaimo Daily News (Nanaimo BC) Saturday September 25, 1926 page 3; Vancouver Sun (Vancouver BC) Wednesday December 5, 1928 page 22; The Province (Vancouver BC) Friday April 11, 1924 page 30

239 Vancouver Sun (Vancouver BC) Tuesday September 25, 1934 page 16

240 Vancouver Sun (Vancouver BC) Tuesday December 5, 1939 page 18

241 Vancouver Daily World (Vancouver BC) February 9, 1894 page 2

242 The Province (Vancouver BC) Friday October 29, 1920 page 6

243 https://en.wikipedia.org/wiki/Second_Narrows_Bridge (website viewed 07/12/2019)

244 Victoria Daily Times (Victoria BC) Thursday June 14, 1917 page 8

245 Marc, Jacques (1999) Historic Shipwrecks of Northeastern Vancouver Island UASBC; The Daily Colonist (Victoria BC) June 18, 1861

246 http://www.tsb.gc.ca/eng/rapports-reports/marine/2009/m09w0147/m09w0147.asp

247 Vancouver Daily World (Vancouver BC) Wednesday July 8, 1896 Page 3

248 Times Colonist (Victoria BC) Friday December 10, 1949 page 1

249 Historic Shipwrecks of the Lower Mainland of British Columbia (2007) UASBC, Vancouver BC

250 Vancouver Sun (Vancouver BC) Thursday February 7, 1957, page 1

251 Transportation Safety Board of Canada (1993)

252 Chet McArthur (British Columbia Nautical History Facebook Group 01/02/2017)

253 The Province (Vancouver BC) Saturday May 2, 1959 Page 3

254 Vancouver Sun (Vancouver BC) Thursday January 29, 1942 page 24

255 Vancouver Sun (Vancouver BC) Thursday December 23, 1971 page 1

256 http://www.tsb.gc.ca/eng/rapports-reports/marine/2014/m14p0121/m14p0121.asp; (website viewed 13/12/2019)

257 Rogers, A.C. (Jr) Shipwreck Chart No. 3

258 The Province (Vancouver BC) Tuesday October 21, 1947 page 25

259 Coney, Michael (1983); British Columbia Nautical History Facebook Group 26/08/2019)

260 The Province (Vancouver BC) Monday January 31, 1944 page 7

261 The Province (Vancouver BC) Thursday April 30, 1942 page 29

262 http://www.tsb.gc.ca/eng/rapports-reports/marine/1997/m97w0224/m97w0224.asp: (website viewed 26/12/2019)

263 Vancouver Sun (Vancouver BC) Friday August 20, 1965 page 3

264 Vancouver Sun (Vancouver BC) Saturday November 16, 1918 page 15; Victoria Daily Times (Victoria BC) Saturday August 10, 1918 page 10

265 Victoria Daily Times (Victoria BC) Monday December 29, 1913 page 6

266 Times Colonist (Victoria BC) Tuesday August 2, 1977 page 2

267 Vancouver Sun (Vancouver BC) Tuesday October 6, 1953 page 2

268 James, Rick (2004) The Ghost Ships of Royston. (UASBC: Vancouver BC)

269 Nanaimo Daily News (Nanaimo BC) Saturday November 26, 1949 page 1

270 Nanaimo Daily News (Nanaimo BC) Saturday February 17, 1877 page 3

271 Victoria Daily Times (Victoria BC) Friday July 10, 1914 Page 6

272 Nanaimo Daily News (Nanaimo BC) Wednesday April 18, 1883 page 2

273 Vancouver Sun (Vancouver BC) Wednesday April 17, 1963 page 6

274 Nanaimo Daily News (Nanaimo BC) Thursday February 14, 1957 page 13

275 Al Hosking (Facebook British Columbia Nautical History Group 20/09/2015)

276 Vancouver Sun Friday December 11, 1953 page 1

277 Vancouver Daily World (Vancouver BC) Saturday July 10, 1897 page 7

278 The Province (Vancouver BC) Tuesday March 25, 1941 page 6

279 The Forgotten Sisters http://www.evergreenfleet.com/forgottensisters.html website viewed 29/06/2020

280 Nanaimo Daily News (Nanaimo BC) Tuesday March 5, 1929 page 4

281 Vancouver Sun (Vancouver BC) Monday March 31, 1975 page 8

282 Vancouver Sun (Vancouver BC) Monday January 4, 1971 page 4

283 Times Colonist (Victoria BC) Friday December 29, 1911 page 8; The Victoria Daily Times (Victoria BC) Tuesday January 2, 1912 page 8

284 Ottawa Daily Citizen (Ottawa ON) Friday May 4, 1883 page 1

285 The Province (Vancouver BC) Wednesday July 15, 1925 page 11

286 The Province (Vancouver BC) Monday December 27, 1909 page 7

287 Vancouver Sun (Vancouver BC) Friday December 15, 1944 page 1; Nanaimo Daily News (Nanaimo BC) Saturday July 21, 1962 page 2

288 Vancouver Sun (Vancouver BC) Friday November 27, 1942 page 17

289 The Province (Vancouver BC) Sunday July 26, 1931 page 1

290 Times Colonist (Victoria BC) Wednesday September 30, 1953 page 14

291 Vancouver Sun (Vancouver BC) Friday September 12, 1986 page 136

292 Vancouver Sun (Vancouver BC) Tuesday May 25, 1965 page 13

293 Email (Lonnie Berrow—Nauticapedia 2017)

294 Vancouver Sun (Vancouver BC) Tuesday October 14, 1947 page 15; The Province (Vancouver BC) Tuesday October 14, 1947 page 19

295 Vancouver Sun (Vancouver BC) Tuesday December 27, 1932 page 3

296 Times Colonist (Victoria BC) Tuesday April 4, 1978 page 22

297 http://www.tsb.gc.ca/eng/rapports-reports/marine/1994/m94w0010/m94w0010.asp

298 The Province (Vancouver BC) Monday January 7, 1974 page 1

299 The Province (Vancouver BC) Sunday March 6, 1927 page 2

300 The Province (Vancouver BC) Tuesday September 29, 2015 page 3

301 Vancouver Sun (Vancouver BC) Monday November 13, 1972 page 17

302 The Province (Vancouver BC) Friday February 14, 1908 page 15; Times Colonist (Victoria BC) Wednesday February 5, 1908 page 1; Vancouver Daily World (Vancouver BC) Saturday Feb 1, 1908 page 8

303 Nanaimo Daily News (Nanaimo BC) Thursday June 14, 1979 page 8

304 The Province (Vancouver BC) Monday October 2, 1972 page 40

305 Vancouver Sun (Vancouver BC) Thursday January 16, 1919 page 2

306 The Province (Vancouver BC) Thursday September 23, 1926 page 26; Times Colonist (Victoria BC) Thursday October 14, 1926 page 9

307 Transportation Safety Board of Canada (1993)

308 Tad Roberts (August 8, 2015)

309 Email (Ross Holkestad—John MacFarlane 30/08/2016); Transportation Safety Board of Canada (1993)

310 Manitoba Free Press (Winnipeg MB) Monday April 11, 1892 page 2

311 Dave Bartle (British Columbia Nautical History Facebook Group 23/02/2019)
312 Victoria Daily Times (Victoria BC) Monday December 4, 1899 page 3
313 The Province (Vancouver BC) Monday October 7, 1957 page 19
314 Manitoba Free Press (Winnipeg MB) Monday April 11, 1892 page 2
315 The Province (Vancouver BC) Wednesday December 4, 1901 page 1
316 Rogers, AC (Jr) Shipwreck Chart No. 1
317 http://www.tsb.gc.ca/eng/rapports-reports/marine/1995/m95w0013/m95w0013.asp
318 Vancouver Sun (Vancouver BC) Monday February 23, 1959 page 19
319 The Vancouver Sun (Vancouver BC) Tuesday November 7, 1939 page 12
320 The Province (Vancouver BC) Thursday May 23, 1901 page 7; The Province (Vancouver BC) Monday December 2, 1901 page 7
321 Email Communication (Ric Stacey – Nauticapedia 28/05/2017)
322 Nanaimo Daily News (Nanaimo BC) Wednesday November 8, 1967 page 2
323 Victoria Daily Times (Victoria BC) Saturday March 16, 1946 page 3
324 The Province (Vancouver BC) Monday December 27, 1926 page 1; Times Colonist (Victoria BC) Wednesday November 9, 1927 page 5
325 Times Colonist (Victoria BC) Tuesday May 17, 1938 page 1
326 Times Colonist (Victoria BC) Saturday October 13, 1984 page 1
327 Vancouver Sun (Vancouver BC) Thursday June 16, 1938 page 2; Times Colonist (Victoria BC) Wednesday August 12, 1925 page 8
328 Nanaimo Daily Times (Nanaimo BC) Wednesday January 15, 1879 page 3
329 Vancouver Sun (Vancouver BC) Monday March 31,1930 page 1
330 Vancouver Daily World (Vancouver BC) Tuesday, April 15, 1913 page 4
331 Vancouver Sun (Vancouver BC) Saturday September 4, 1937 page 1
332 Victoria Daily Times (Victoria BC) Friday, October 16, 1936 page 20
333 Miles, Fraser (1992)
334 The Province (Vancouver BC) Friday January 2, 1959, Page 1
335 Vancouver Sun (Vancouver BC) Monday February 26, 1951 page 28; Vancouver Sun (Vancouver BC); Vancouver Sun (Vancouver BC) Monday, December 29, 1930 page 14
336 Daily Colonist, Friday, February 9, 1934 Page 11
337 Nanaimo Daily News (Nanaimo BC) Wednesday December 8, 1875 page 3
338 The Province (Vancouver BC) Wednesday October 23, 1963 page 2
339 Vancouver Sun (Vancouver BC) Thursday February 19, 1948 page 3
340 The Province (Vancouver BC) Wednesday October 23, 1963 page 2
341 The Province (Vancouver BC) Saturday January 15, 1955 page 5
342 Cliff Craig (Personal Communication w. John MacFarlane 03/03/2017)
343 Calgary Herald (Calgary AB) Friday September 11, 1964 page 6
344 Transportation Safety Board of Canada (1993); Times Colonist (Victoria BC) Wednesday September 24, 1980 Page 2
345 The Province (Vancouver BC) Thursday, October 12, 1939 page 9
346 The Province (Vancouver BC) Friday August 12, 1932 page 3
347 Times Colonist (Victoria BC) Monday, March 28, 1977 page 1
348 H.W. McCurdy Marine History of the Pacific Northwest page 488
349 Historic Shipwrecks of the Lower Mainland of British Columbia (2007) UASBC, Vancouver BC
350 The Province (Vancouver BC) Saturday October 31, 1914 page 19; Victoria Daily Times (Victoria BC) Monday October 26 page 8
351 Nicholson, George (1965); http://www.nmdl.org/sfs/

352 https://en.wikipedia.org/wiki/Second_Narrows_Bridge (website viewed 07/12/2019)

353 Transportation Safety Board of Canada (1993); The Victoria Daily Times (Victoria BC) Saturday December 20, 1913 page 6

354 The Province (Vancouver BC) Wednesday December 28, 1938 page 18

355 Gibson, Gordon with Carol Renison (1980); Miles, Fraser (1992)

356 The Province (Vancouver BC) Thursday December 2, 1948 page 1

357 Walbran, Captain John T (1909); Victoria Daily Times (Victoria BC) Mon February 22, 1886 page 4; Nanaimo Daily Times (Nanaimo BC) Wednesday November 24, 1886 page 3

358 Victoria Daily Times (Victoria BC) Saturday March 26, 1892 page 7

359 http://www.tsb.gc.ca/eng/rapports-reports/marine/1993/m93w0003/m93w0003.asp; (website viewed 29/12/2019);

360 Vancouver Sun (Vancouver BC) Monday February 3, 1941 page 18

361 Vancouver Sun (Vancouver BC) Monday October 28, 1963 page 1

362 Vancouver Sun (Vancouver BC) Monday July 18, 1966 page 2

363 Vancouver Sun (Vancouver BC) Tuesday May 27, 1952 page 2

364 Vancouver News-Herald (Vancouver BC) Monday August 22, 1955 page 1

365 Vancouver Sun (Vancouver BC) Tuesday, January 4, 1949 page 11

366 Nanaimo Daily News (Nanaimo BC) Tuesday March 28, 1911 page 1

367 http://www.tsb.gc.ca/eng/rapports-reports/marine/2001/m01w0253/m01w0253.asp' (website viewed 08/12/2019)

368 Victoria Daily Times (Victoria BC) Tuesday May 9, 1916 page 8

369 The Province (Vancouver BC) Monday, December 29, 1924 page 1

370 The Province (Vancouver BC) Monday, April 30, 1906 page 1

371 Daily Colonist Tuesday, March 14, 1933 Page 7

372 Vancouver Sun (Vancouver BC) Wednesday August 7, 1929 page 10

373 Vancouver Sun (Vancouver BC) Tuesday March 31, 1992 page 21

374 Alberni Valley Times (Port Alberni BC) Monday April 26, 1993 page 1

375 Nanaimo Daily News (Nanaimo BC) Thursday, August 22, 1963 page 19; The Vancouver Sun (Vancouver BC) Thursday, August 22, 1963 page 10

376 Transportation Safety Board of Canada (1993)

377 Transportation Safety Board of Canada (1993)

378 The Province (Vancouver BC) Saturday August 23, 1975 page 19

379 Transportation Safety Board of Canada (1993)

380 Transportation Safety Board of Canada (1993)

381 The Province (Vancouver BC) Friday April 5, 1946 page 1

382 Nanaimo Daily News (Nanaimo BC) Saturday September 24, 1949 page 1

383 Terry Murphy (British Columbia Nautical History Facebook Group 19/11/2019)

384 Nanaimo Daily News (Nanaimo BC) Saturday February 2, 1957 page 1

385 Vancouver Sun (Vancouver BC) Wednesday December 24, 1947 page 2

386 Vancouver Sun (Vancouver BC) Monday December 28, 1925 page 1

387 The Province (Vancouver BC) Monday November 19, 1928 page 20

388 The Province (Vancouver BC) Monday March 7, 1977 page 1

389 The Province (Vancouver BC) Thursday, November 12, 1942 page 12

390 Vancouver Sun (Vancouver BC) Wednesday April 17, 1963 page 6

391 Times Colonist (Victoria BC) Saturday December 21, 1940 page 18

392 British Columbia Nautical History Facebook Group

393 http://heritage.canadiana.ca/view/oocihm.lac_reel_c3185/125?r=0&s=5 (website viewed 10/01/2020)

394 R Bruce Scott (1970)

395 The Province (Vancouver BC) Friday October 3, 1947 page 1

396 Victoria Daily Times (Victoria BC) Wednesday October 29, 1930 page 22

397 Rick James Letter to the Editor of Western Mariner March 2015

398 http://www.tsb.gc.ca/eng/rapports-reports/marine/1997/m97w0193/m97w0193.asp

399 List of Shipping Casualties Resulting in Total Loss in British Columbia and Coastal Waters Since 1897 (undated manuscript document)

400 Victoria Daily Times (Victoria BC) Tuesday November 30, 1915 page 10

401 Times Colonist (Victoria BC) Tuesday September 13, 1932 page 16

402 Nanaimo Daily News (Nanaimo BC) Wednesday, March 9, 1932 page 1

403 Victoria Daily Times (Victoria BC) Monday December 4, 1899 page 3

404 The Province (Vancouver BC) Monday October 14, 1912 page 25

405 LAC RC12, A1, Vol 414 Shipping Registers, Victoria BC

406 Vancouver Sun (Vancouver BC) Friday April 6, 1945 page 13

407 Vancouver Sun (Vancouver BC) Thursday, April 8, 1915 page 3

408 Mike Wright (24/12/2015 British Columbia Nautical History vFacebook Group)

409 The Province (Vancouver BC) Thursday October 26, 1961 page 19

410 Vancouver Sun (Vancouver BC) Friday, August 19, 1952 page 23

411 Times Colonist (Victoria BC) Wednesday December 7, 1949 page 1

412 Personal Communication (John D.S. Henderson to John M. MacFarlane 14/10/1999)

413 Historic Shipwrecks of the Lower Mainland of British Columbia (2007) UASBC, Vancouver BC

414 Vancouver Sun (Vancouver BC) Thursday January 14, 1932 page 3

415 Vancouver Daily World (Vancouver BC) Wednesday July 12, 1899 page 1

416 Transportation Safety Board of Canada (1993)

417 Vancouver Sun (Vancouver BC) Friday December 15, 1950 page 12

418 The Province (Vancouver BC) Friday October 23, 1931 page 30

419 Dirk Septer (2018) The Disappearance of the RCAF Supply and Salvage Ship M427 B.C. Star in Nauticapedia http://www.nauticapedia.ca/Gallery/BC_Star.php (website viewed 13/01/2020)

420 Lucian Ploias (British Columbia Nautical History Facebook Group 17/12/2016)

421 http://www.tsb.gc.ca/eng/rapports-reports/marine/2004/m04w0235/m04w0235.asp; (website viewed 23/12/2019)

422 Christopher Cole (British Columbia Nautical History Facebook Group 11/02/2018)

423 Russ Warren (British Columbia Nautical History Facebook Group 17/08/2016)

424 The Vancouver Sun (Vancouver BC) Friday December 17, 1915 page 2

425 Rick Howie (BC Nautical History Facebook Group 10/10/2015)

426 Colin Henthorne (Email to Nauticapedia 27/12/2019)

427 Victoria Daily Times (Victoria BC) Wednesday October 12, 1892 page 1

428 The Province (Vancouver BC) Friday February 14, 1908 page 15

429 http://www.tsb.gc.ca/eng/rapports-reports/marine/2004/m04w0235/m04w0235.asp

430 Victoria Daily Times (Victoria BC) October 24, 1936 page 1

431 Miles, Fraser (1992)

432 Alberni Valley Times (Port Alberni BC) Monday September 20, 1976 page 1

433 Kyle Stubbs (British Columbia Nautical History Facebook Group 20/09/2019)

434 Vancouver Sun Wednesday December 5, 1951 page 1

435 The Province (Vancouver BC) Saturday March 18, 1911 page 1; Vancouver Sun Tuesday January 9, 1945 page 7

436 Vancouver Sun (Vancouver BC) Tuesday March 24, 1931 page 14

437 The Province (Vancouver BC) Monday September 10, 1945 page 1

438 Nanaimo Daily News (Nanaimo BC) Monday October 4, 1948 page 2

439 The Province (Vancouver BC) Sunday June 8, 1930 page 47

440 Chilliwack Progress (Chilliwack BC) Wednesday February 19, 1896 page 2

441 Vancouver Sun (Vancouver BC) Saturday February 17, 1934 page 1

442 US National Transportation Safety Board reported (July 26, 2012)

443 Vancouver Sun (Vancouver BC) Thursday August 31, 1967 page 3

444 Mark Simpson (British Columbia Nautical History Facebook Group 21/10/2017)

445 Victoria Daily Times (Victoria BC) Saturday December 30, 1893 page 1

446 Vancouver Sun (Vancouver BC) Thursday October 17, 1933 page 9

447 Victoria Daily Times (Victoria BC) Saturday March 16, 1892 page 7

448 http://heritage.canadiana.ca/view/oocihm.lac_reel_c3185/87?r=0&s=5 (website viewed 10/01/2020);

449 http://heritage.canadiana.ca/view/oocihm.lac_reel_c3185/122?r=0&s=5 (website viewed 10/01/2020); Victoria Daily Times (Victoria BC) Monday May 10, 1897 page 8

450 http://lighthousefriends.com/light.asp?ID=1207 (website viewed in 2016)

451 LAC RG12, A1, Vol 414 Shipping Registers Victoria BC

452 http://www.tsb.gc.ca/eng/rapports-reports/marine/2004/m04w0235/m04w0235.asp

453 The Times (Nanaimo BC) Wednesday, November 25, 1976 page 3

454 Vancouver Sun (Vancouver BC) Friday November 5, 1948 page 1

455 Vancouver Sun (Vancouver BC) Wednesday November 26, 1930 page 1

456 Vancouver Sun (Vancouver BC) Saturday May 31, 1947 page 2

457 Vancouver Sun (Vancouver BC) Tuesday April 28, 1959 page 1

458 Victoria Daily Times (Victoria BC) Friday September 6, 1940 page 1

459 Vancouver Sun (Vancouver BC) Saturday March 21, 1925 page 1

460 Tim Agg (British Columbia Nautical History Facebook Group 05/11/2017)

461 Times Colonist (Victoria BC) Mon June 29, 1936 page 1

462 Victoria Daily Times (Victoria BC) Monday April 17, 1893 page 8

463 Saturday December 11, 1875 page 3

464 Vancouver Sun (Vancouver BC) Monday December 29, 1930 page 14

465 Times Colonist (Victoria BC) Saturday October 13, 1984 page 1

466 http://www.tsb.gc.ca/eng/rapports-reports/marine/2003/m03w0265/m03w0265.asp

467 Gordon Newell, Maritime events of 1921–22, H.W. McCurdy Marine History of the Pacific Northwest, p. 324

468 The Province (Vancouver BC) Saturday October 2, 1915 page 1

469 Nanaimo Daily News (Nanaimo BC) Tuesday March 28, 1911 page 1

470 Vancouver Sun (Vancouver BC) Monday July 14, 1924 page 1; The Province (Vancouver BC) Tuesday July 15, 1924 page 16

471 The Province (Vancouver BC) Friday October 3, 1947 page 1

472 www.tsb.gc.ca/eng/rapports-reports/marine/2005/m05w0110/m05w0110.asp

473 Vancouver Sun (Vancouver BC) Friday, September 12, 1969 Page 73

474 Vancouver Sun (Vancouver BC) Thursday November 15, 1962 page 16

475 Victoria Daily Times (Victoria BC) Monday November 8, 1915 page 8

476 The Province (Vancouver BC) Tuesday September 11, 1945 Page 5

477 The Province (Vancouver BC) Saturday December 5, 1903 page 11

478 Vancouver Daily World (Vancouver BC) Wednesday July 12, 1899 page 1

479 The Province (Vancouver BC) Saturday May 4, 1929 page 1

480 Vancouver Sun (Vancouver BC) Wednesday January 8, 1919 page 9

481 Vancouver Daily World (Vancouver BC) Tuesday December 28, 1897 page 4

482 Nanaimo Daily News Tuesday August 20, 1957 Page 5; Vancouver Sun Friday August 2, 1957 Page 29

483 Times Colonist (Victoria BC) Tuesday April 4, 1978 page 22

484 Time Colonist (Victoria BC) Saturday July 16, 1938 page 28

485 Edmonton Journal (Edmonton AB) Saturday April 5, 1924 page 1

486 Vancouver Sun (Vancouver BC) Monday May 15, 1961 page 2

487 Vancouver Sun (Vancouver BC) Saturday November 3, 1962 page 8

488 The Province (Vancouver BC) Thursday May 7, 1959 page 1

489 The Province (Vancouver BC) Friday February 9, 1906 page 1

490 San Francisco Chronicle Sunday April 13, 1890 Page 15

491 Canada List of Shipping; LAC RG12, A1, Vol 414 Shipping Registers, Victoria BC

492 The Province (Vancouver BC) Monday January 3, 1966 page 6

493 Time Colonist (Victoria BC) Saturday October 28, 1978 page 17

494 Times Colonist (Victoria BC) August 10, 1937 page 2

495 Times Colonist (Victoria BC) Wednesday October 19, 1932 page 1

496 Vancouver Sun (Vancouver BC) Friday December 11, 1953 page 2

497 Nicholson, George (1962)

498 Victoria Daily Times (Victoria BC) Wednesday December 18, 1912, page 6

499 Daily Times (Victoria BC) Thursday February 15, 1923 page 8

500 Vancouver Sun (Vancouver BC) Friday July 19, 1929 page 16

501 Vancouver Daily World Tuesday February 4, 1896 Page 4

502 Vancouver Sun Saturday December 28, 1957 Page 7

503 Times Colonist (Victoria BC) Saturday January 7, 1928 Page 9

504 LAC RG12, A1, Vol 414 Shipping Registers Victoria BC

505 Times Colonist (Victoria BC) Thursday August 13, 1931 page 11

506 The Province (Vancouver BC) Tuesday, June 20, 1950 page 1

507 Alberni Valley Times, Monday, October 21, 1968 page 9

508 Vancouver Sun (Vancouver BC) Thursday November 9, 1950 page 21

509 Vancouver Sun (Vancouver BC) Wednesday, June 21, 1978 page 29

510 Times Colonist (Victoria BC) Monday, November 21, 1960 page 9

511 Vancouver Sun (Vancouver BC) Monday April 5, 1971 page 29

512 Victoria Daily Times (Vancouver BC) Friday July 25, 1924 page 17

513 James, Rick & Jacques Marc (2010); The Province (Vancouver BC) Friday February 14, 1947 page 1

514 Barr, Captain James (1969) Ferry Across the Harbor Vancouver: Mitchell Press

515 The Province (Vancouver BC) Friday August 24, 1928 page 1

516 Vancouver Sun (Vancouver BC) Tuesday February 24, 1959 page 37

517 Vancouver Sun (Vancouver BC) Thursday August 31, 1967 page 3

518 Vancouver Sun (Vancouver BC) Thursday January 21, 1943 page 20

519 Vancouver Sun (Vancouver BC) Friday, February 24, 1961 page 1

520 Times Colonist (Victoria BC) Tuesday May 17, 1938 page 1

521 Vancouver Sun (Vancouver BC) Monday February 26, 1951 page 28

522 Vancouver Sun (Vancouver BC) Wednesday April 25, 1928 page 1
523 The Province (Vancouver BC) Saturday September 30, 1933 page 42
524 Transportation Safety Board of Canada (1993)
525 The Province (Vancouver BC) Tuesday September 29, 2015 page 3
526 The Province (Vancouver BC) Thursday April 6, 1978 page 4
527 The province (Vancouver BC) Friday, September 18, 1936 page 31
528 Times Colonist (Victoria BC) Wednesday November 6, 1974 page 20
529 Vancouver Sun Monday January 31, 1966 page 1
530 Nanaimo Daily News (Nanaimo BC) Wednesday September 18, 1929
531 Times Colonist (Victoria BC) Saturday November 1, 1975 page 1
532 Transportation Safety Board of Canada (1993)
533 Vancouver Daily World (Vancouver BC) Friday September 10, 1909 page 8
534 The Province (Vancouver BC) Saturday August 2, 1930 page 1
535 Vancouver Daily World (Vancouver BC) Saturday May 10, 1913 page 5
536 LAC RG12, A1, Vol 414 Shipping Registers Victoria BC
537 Ottawa Daily Citizen (Ottawa ON) Saturday November 13, 1875 page 3
538 Transportation Safety Board of Canada (1993)
539 The Transportation Safety Board of Canada
540 Times Colonist (Vancouver BC) Tuesday August 27, 1929 page 18
541 The Province (Vancouver BC) Saturday December 21, 1963 page 2; Vancouver Sun (Vancouver BC) Friday August 9, 1964 page 2
542 Calgary Herald (Calgary AB) Friday September 11, 1964 page 6
543 Miles, Fraser (1992)
544 Ottawa Citizen (Ottawa ON) Friday November 12, 1875 page 3
545 Transportation Safety Board of Canada
546 Times Colonist (Victoria BC) Thursday October 5, 1961 page 17
547 Andrew C. Clarke (Email to John MacFarlane 29/04/2017)
548 Transportation Safety Board of Canada (1993)
549 Ed Lien (British Columbia Nautical History Facebook Group 30/11/2019)
550 Edmonton Journal (Edmonton AB) Tuesday January 7, 1958 page 3
551 Times Colonist (Victoria BC) Saturday March 22, 1975 page 2
552 The Province (Vancouver BC) Monday August 29, 1949 page 2
553 Miles, Fraser (1992); The Province (Vancouver BC) Friday, August 28, 1931 page 26
554 http://www.tsb.gc.ca/eng/rapports-reports/marine/2003/m03w0265/m03w0265.asp
555 Vancouver Sun (Vancouver BC) Friday October 9, 1959 page 6
556 Nanaimo Daily News (Nanaimo BC) Saturday November 28, 1874 page 2
557 Vancouver Sun (Vancouver BC) Saturday March 9, 1974 page 1
558 Daily Colonist Tuesday, March 14, 1933 Page 7
559 The Province (Vancouver BC) Thursday, February 10, 1949 page 1
560 Rogers, AC (Jr) Shipwreck Chart No. 3
561 Vancouver Daily World (Vancouver BC) Tuesday September 25, 1923 page 3
562 Nanaimo Daily News (Nanaimo BC) Tuesday March 28, 1911 page 1
563 The Province (Vancouver BC) Friday April 29, 1955 page 1
564 Marc, Jacques. (1999) Historic Shipwrecks of Northeastern Vancouver Island UASBC
565 Bryon Taylor (Email to Nauticapedia 23/01/2019)
566 http://www.tsb.gc.ca/eng/rapports-reports/marine/2009/m09w0193/m09w0193.asp

567 Vancouver Sun (Vancouver BC) Tuesday December 30, 1952 page 1

568 The Province (Vancouver BC) Saturday, September 12, 1925 page 5

569 Vancouver Daily World (Vancouver BC) Monday, November 27, 1893 page 8

570 Nanaimo Daily News (Nanaimo BC) Tuesday March 28, 1911 page 1

571 Mike Wright (British Columbia Nautical History Facebook Group 13/10/2017)

572 The Province (Vancouver BC) Saturday August 13, 1955 page 6

573 The Vancouver Sun (Vancouver BC) Friday, September 12, 1969 Page 73

574 Times Colonist Tuesday February 2, 1954 Page 1

575 Victoria Daily Times (Victoria BC) Saturday April 28, 1917 page 8

576 Victoria Daily Times (Victoria BC) Friday February 10, 1921 page 8

577 The Province (Vancouver BC) Thursday, November 12, 1942 page 12

578 http://www.kodiakmaritimemuseum.org/newsletter/Spring2014.pdf

579 Victoria Daily Times (Victoria BC) Monday January 16, 1922 page 7

580 John Dolmage (British Columbia Nautical History Facebook Group 10/08/2016)

581 Times Colonist (Victoria BC) Wednesday September 23, 1925 page 1

582 http://www.tsb.gc.ca/eng/rapports-reports/marine/2004/m04w0225/m04w0225.asp

583 The Province (Vancouver BC) Thursday, February 8, 1968 page 2

584 The Province (Vancouver BC) Thursday, May 8, 1975 page 12

585 Miles, Fraser (1992)

586 Vancouver Sun (Vancouver BC) Tuesday May 18, 1965 page 33

587 Lonnie Berrow (British Columbia Facebook Group 12/10/2014); John Demosten (British Columbia Nautical History Facebook Group 25/12/2018)

588 The Province (Vancouver BC) Tuesday, September 19, 1922 page 7

589 Transportation Safety Board of Canada (1993)

590 Marc, Jacques. (1999) Historic Shipwrecks of Northeastern Vancouver Island UASBC

591 http://www.tsb.gc.ca/eng/rapports-reports/marine/1992/m92w1022/m92w1022.asp

592 The Province (Vancouver BC) Monday October 20, 1980 page A1

593 Vancouver Sun (Vancouver BC) Thursday August 31, 1967 page 3

594 http://www.tsb.gc.ca/eng/rapports-reports/marine/1992/m92w1012/m92w1012.asp

595 Transportation Safety Board of Canada

596 LAC RG12, A1, Vol 414 Shipping Registers Victoria BC

597 Vancouver Daily World (Vancouver BC) Monday, February 24, 1902 page 5

598 Victoria Daily Times (Victoria BC) Saturday August 8, 1885 page 4

599 Gibbs, Jim A (1968); Transportation Safety Board of Canada (1993); Scott, R.B. (1972); Palm, RS (1978)

600 The Province (Vancouver BC) Thursday April 18, 1901 page 1

601 Vancouver Sun (Vancouver BC) Monday June 28, 1982 page 7

602 Vancouver Sun (Vancouver BC) Tuesday, March 23, 1954 page 33

603 Vancouver Daily World (Vancouver BC) Saturday, June 15, 1918 page 1

604 The Province (Vancouver BC) Sunday June 21, 1925 page 18; Miles, Fraser (1992)

605 Victoria Daily Times (Victoria BC) Wednesday March 17, 1926 page 11

606 Victoria Daily Times (Victoria BC) Thursday November 28, 1918 page 13

607 Rogers, AC (Jr) (1973)

608 Vancouver Daily World (Vancouver BC) Tuesday July 11, 1911 page 10

609 The Province (Vancouver BC) Monday July 31, 1944 page 19

610 Vancouver Sun (Vancouver BC) Thursday August 14, 1947 page 1

611 The Province (Vancouver BC) Friday March 11, 1938 page 29

612 Transportation Safety Board of Canada (1993); The Province (Vancouver BC) Wednesday May 8, 1929 page 31

613 Bob McAuley (British Columbia Nautical History Facebook Group 09/07/2017)

614 Times Colonist (Victoria BC) Thursday August 18, 1965 page 1; Ron Vandergaag (British Columbia Nautical History Facebook Group 02/06/2020)

615 Nanaimo Daily News (Nanaimo BC) Friday November 18, 1949 page 1

616 Nanaimo Daily News (Nanaimo BC) Tuesday September 2, 1952 page 1

617 Vancouver Sun (Vancouver BC) Tuesday December 27, 1932 page 3

618 Vancouver Sun (Vancouver BC) Tuesday May 5, 1959 page 19

619 http://www.tsb.gc.ca/eng/rapports-reports/marine/1994/m94w0010/m94w0010.asp

620 http://www.tsb.gc.ca/eng/rapports-reports/marine/1992/m92w1012/m92w1012.asp

621 Transportation Safety Board of Canada (1993)

622 Time Colonist (Victoria BC) Friday February 10, 1939 page 1

623 Nanaimo Daily News (Nanaimo BC) Tuesday September 27, 1892 page 4

624 Times Colonist (Victoria BC) Thursday December 28, 1944 page 2

625 Transportation Safety Board of Canada (1993)

626 http://alaskashipwreck.com/shipwrecks-a-z/alaska-shipwrecks-s/; The Seattle Times (December 11, 1979) "Hope lingers for 7 on boat" Pg F 8, 3. The Seattle Times (December 12, 1979) "Exposure caused death of 2 on gillnetter" Page E 12

627 Transportation Safety Board of Canada (1993)

628 Victoria Daily Times (Victoria BC) Monday February 9, 1925 page 8

629 H.W. McCurdy Marine History of the Pacific Northwest. Seattle: Superior Publishing Company, 1966., p. 555; Times Colonist (Victoria BC) Monday October 19, 1953 page 2; Times Colonist (Victoria BC) Saturday April 4, 1959 page 4

630 Western Mariner March 2020 Vol 18, Number 1: Samantha J Salvage; Colin Henthorne (Email to Nauticapedia 27/02/2019); William Frankling reported (British Columbia Nautical History Facebook Group 12/10/2014)

631 Mark MacKenzie (British Columbia Nautical History Facebook Group 21/02/1917)

632 Michael Kaehn (British Columbia Nautical History Facebook Group 12/12/2019)

633 The Province (Vancouver BC) Friday February 7, 1958 page 1

634 The Province (Vancouver BC) Wednesday January 25, 1956 page 1; Vancouver Sun (Vancouver BC) Monday July 11, 1955 page 9

635 The Province (Vancouver BC) Wednesday November 19, 1952 page 1

636 Times Colonist (Victoria BC) Sunday June 5, 2005 page 1

637 Victoria Daily Times (Victoria BC) Thursday February 15, 1923 page 1

638 Vancouver Sun (Vancouver BC) Wednesday November 18, 1926 page 3

639 Victoria Daily Times (Victoria BC) Monday April 26, 1897 page 1

640 Victoria Daily Times (Victoria BC) Friday July 18, 1890 page 6

641 Transportation Safety Board of Canada (1993)

642 The Province (Vancouver BC) Friday August 8, 1969 page 2

643 Vancouver Daily World (Vancouver BC) Friday August 3, 1894 page 4; The Province (Vancouver BC) Tuesday January 3, 1911 page 8

644 Times Colonist (Victoria BC) Tuesday October 19, 1965 page 3; The Province (Vancouver BC) Tuesday October 19, 1965 page 23

645 The Province (Vancouver BC) April 28, 1991
646 Les Sharcott (British Columbia Nautical History Facebook Group)
647 Nanaimo Daily News (Nanaimo BC) Friday October 22, 1926 page 5
648 Vancouver Sun (Vancouver BC) Wednesday March 8, 1967 page 29
649 Vancouver Sun (Vancouver BC) Friday December 11, 1953 page 2
650 The Province (Vancouver BC) Tuesday September 29, 2015 page 3
651 The Province (Vancouver BC) Sunday December 20, 1925
652 Vancouver Sun (Vancouver BC) Monday July 18, 1966 page 2; Vancouver Province (Vancouver BC) Thursday September 20, 1984 page 3; Nanaimo Daily News (Nanaimo BC) Thursday September 20, 1984 page 1
653 Transportation Safety Board of Canada (1993)
654 The Transportation Safety Board of Canada
655 Nanaimo Daily News (Nanaimo BC) Saturday November 4, 1950 page 1
656 Victoria Daily Times (Victoria BC) Saturday March 25, 1911
657 Vancouver Sun (Vancouver BC) Thursday August 31, 1967 page 3
658 The Province (Vancouver BC) Monday August 3, 1970 page 2
659 Vancouver Sun (Vancouver BC) Saturday December 11, 1926 page 1
660 Vancouver Sun (Vancouver BC) Thursday June 22, 1961 page 15
661 Victoria Daily Times (Victoria BC) Wednesday November 17, 1909 page 11
662 Vancouver Sun (Vancouver BC) Thursday July 14, 1932 page 1
663 Vancouver Sun (Vancouver BC) Thursday, September 10, 1942 page 17
664 Vancouver News-Herald (Vancouver BC) Thursday October 25, 1956 page 1
665 http://www.tsb.gc.ca/eng/rapports-reports/marine/1992/m92w1022/m92w1022.asp
666 The Province (Vancouver BC) Tuesday, September 2, 1958 page 1
667 Vancouver Sun (Vancouver BC) Monday, July 30, 1923 page 1; Victoria Daily Times (Victoria BC) Tuesday August 14, 1923 page 7
668 Times Colonist (Victoria BC) Friday December 30, 1927 page 15
669 Times Colonist (Victoria BC) Saturday October 13, 1984 page 1
670 The Vancouver Sun (Vancouver BC) Friday December 17, 1915 page 2
671 Historic Shipwrecks of the Lower Mainland of British Columbia (2007) UASBC, Vancouver BC
672 Victoria Daily Times (Victoria BC) Saturday October 27, 1906 page 5
673 William Tauber (Email to Nauticapedia 13/12/2017)
674 Ken Lund (British Columbia Nautical History Facebook Group 25/10/2016)
675 Calgary Herald (Calgary AB) Wednesday November 19, 1913 page 12
676 The Province (Vancouver BC) Monday May 30, 1949 page 6
677 Times Colonist (Victoria BC) Tuesday, May 2, 1961 page 2
678 The Province (Vancouver BC) Tuesday September 26, 1967 page 2
679 Nanaimo Daily News (Nanaimo BC) Thursday September 13, 1934 page 4
680 Vancouver Sun (Vancouver BC) Wednesday June 1, 1932 page 3
681 Vancouver Sun (Vancouver BC) Monday September 19, 1966 page 23
682 The Vancouver Sun (Vancouver BC) Tuesday July 30, 1929 page 14; The Nanaimo Daily News (Nanaimo BC) Wednesday September 18, 1929
683 The H.W. McCurdy Marine History of the Pacific Northwest (Page 167)
684 Nanaimo Daily News (Nanaimo BC) Wednesday April 18, 1883 page 2
685 The Province (Vancouver BC) Saturday October 6, 1956 page 3
686 Miles, Fraser (1992)

687 San Francisco Chronicle Saturday July 1, 1911 page 1

688 Vancouver Sun (Vancouver BC) Monday December 21, 1964 page 1

689 The Province (Vancouver BC) Friday November 7, 1958 page 1

690 Nanaimo Daily News (Nanaimo BC) Saturday October 23, 1943 page 2

691 Vancouver Sun (Vancouver BC) Thursday, November 18, 1948 page 1

692 Victoria Daily Times (Victoria BC) Saturday December 23, 1916 page 10

693 http://heritage.canadiana.ca/view/oocihm.lac_reel_c3185/90?r=0&s=5

694 Vancouver Sun (Vancouver BC) Monday September 27, 1954 page 17; Vancouver News-Herald (Vancouver BC) Monday September 27, 1954 page 1

695 The Vancouver Sun (Vancouver BC) Saturday March 13, 1976 page 18

696 Vancouver Sun (Vancouver BC) Thursday July 11, 1968 page 21

697 The Vancouver Sun (Vancouver BC) Friday June 25, 1971 page 2

698 Times Colonist (Victoria BC) Wednesday, December 17, 1941 page 1

699 Times Colonist (Victoria BC) Wednesday, August 4, 1965 page 3

700 Vancouver Sun (Vancouver BC) Wednesday September 28, 1966 page 57

701 Victoria Daily Times (Victoria BC) Friday, December 3, 1926 page 14

702 Vancouver Sun (Vancouver BC) Thursday November 4, 1982 page 2

703 The Province (Vancouver BC) Saturday January 27, 1951 page 1

704 Vancouver Sun (Vancouver BC) Saturday August 4, 1984 page 2

705 The Province (Vancouver BC) Tuesday July 8, 1902 page 8

706 Historic Shipwrecks of the Lower Mainland of British Columbia (2007) UASBC, Vancouver BC

707 Marc, Jacques. (1999) Historic Shipwrecks of Northeastern Vancouver Island UASBC

708 Vancouver Sun (Vancouver BC) Tuesday June 15, 1954 page 1

709 Fred Wicks (British Columbia Nautical History Facebook Group 25/05/2016); Transportation Safety Board of Canada (1993)

710 Nanaimo Daily News, Tuesday May 5, 1896 page 2

711 Vancouver Sun (Vancouver BC) Saturday July 25, 1964 page 23

712 The Province (Vancouver BC) Wednesday December 4, 1935 page 24

713 The Province (Vancouver BC) Thursday July 30, 1970 page 1–2

714 Nanaimo Daily News, Tuesday May 5, 1896 page 2; The Province (Vancouver BC) Monday February 26, 1968 page 8

715 Transportation Safety Board of Canada (1993)

716 The Province (Vancouver BC) Friday October 18, 1907 page 1

717 Victoria Daily Colonist (Victoria BC) Sunday May 15, 1910 page 13

718 The Province (Vancouver BC) Monday August 8, 1938 page 1

719 The Province (Vancouver BC) Friday May 4, 1962 page 1

720 The Province (Vancouver BC) Monday September 6, 1954 page 25

721 Walbran, Captain John T (1909)

722 Victoria Daily Times (Victoria BC) October 24, 1936 page 1

723 Vancouver Sun (Vancouver BC) Monday June 6, 1966 page 5

724 Vancouver Sun (Vancouver BC) Thursday March 3, 1977 page 19

725 Times Colonist (Victoria BC) Thursday February 13, 1930 page 10

726 Brian Lande (British Columbia Nautical History Facebook Group 28/10/2014)

727 The Leader-Post (Regina SK) Monday, November 17, 1924 page 3

728 The Daily Province (Vancouver BC) Monday December 17, 1906 Page 17

729 Vancouver Daily World (Vancouver BC) Tuesday May 28, 1907 page 1

730 Marc, Jacques. (1999) Historic Shipwrecks of Northeastern Vancouver Island UASBC

731 The Transportation Safety Board of Canada
732 Nanaimo Daily News (Nanaimo BC) Saturday March 5, 1887 page 3
733 Nanaimo Daily News (Nanaimo BC) Wednesday April 18, 1883 page 2
734 Times Colonist (Victoria BC) Monday August 22, 1966 page 3
735 The Province (Vancouver BC) Saturday April 10, 1965 page 2
736 Alberni Valley Times (Port Alberni BC) Thursday March 8, 1973 page 1
737 Vancouver Sun (Vancouver BC) Monday November 29, 1965 page 27
738 Vancouver Sun (Vancouver BC) Wednesday February 17, 1960 page 2
739 Vancouver Sun (Vancouver BC) Thursday August 8, 1929 page 3;
740 Vancouver Sun (Vancouver BC) Thursday August 31, 1967 page 3
741 Victoria Daily Times (Victoria BC) Saturday March 17, 1923 page 8
742 The Province (Vancouver BC) Sunday, March 22, 1924 page 11
743 Shawn Anvelt (British Columbia Nautical History Facebook Group 23/06/2019)
744 The Vancouver Sun (Vancouver BC) Tuesday November 27, 1956 page 16; The Province (Vancouver BC) Saturday October 6, 1956 page 3
745 Nanaimo Daily News (Nanaimo BC) Saturday July 26, 1952 page 1
746 Nanaimo Daily News (Nanaimo BC) Saturday August 30, 1969 page 15; Alberni Valley Times (Port Alberni BC) Monday September 1, 1969 page 1
747 Times Colonist (Victoria BC) Wednesday November 26, 1947v page 1
748 Vancouver Sun (Vancouver BC) Monday January 25, 1943 page 17
749 The Vancouver Sun (Vancouver BC) Thursday November 8, 1928, page 3
750 Transportation Safety Board of Canada (1993)
751 The Province (Victoria BC) Thursday February 15, 1923 page 1; The Victoria Daily Times (Victoria BC) Friday February 16, 1923 page 1
752 The Province (Vancouver BC) Monday June 14, 1937 page 19
753 Vancouver Sun (Vancouver BC) Monday March 31, 1975 page 8
754 Victoria Daily Times (Victoria BC) Monday December 31, 1923 page 5
755 Rolf Leben (British Columbia Nautical History Facebook Group 05/12/2019)
756 Victoria Daily Times (Victoria BC) Monday March 20, 1911 page 14; The Victoria Daily Times (Victoria BC) Friday March 24, 1911 page 11
757 Victoria Daily times (Victoria BC) Tuesday October 10, 1899 page 5; The Victoria Daily times (Victoria BC) Thursday October 12, 1899 page 5
758 Times Colonist (Victoria BC) Saturday July 23, 1960 page 1; The Vancouver Sun (Vancouver BC) Friday August 19, 1960 page 50; Friday November 29, 1963 page 9
759 Vancouver Sun (Vancouver BC) Monday May 17, 1976 page 14
760 Northern Sentinel (Kitimat BC) Wednesday Mar 4, 1970 page 1
761 The Province (Vancouver BC) Tuesday August 28, 1923 page 22
762 Historic Shipwrecks of the Lower Mainland of British Columbia (2007) UASBC, Vancouver BC
763 Victoria Daily Times (Victoria BC) Thursday February 5, 1914 page 6
764 Nanaimo Daily News (Nanaimo BC) Saturday February 10, 1940 page 1
765 Victoria Daily Times Saturday March 23, 1895 Page 1
766 The Province (Vancouver BC) Saturday, February 26, 1916 page 20
767 LAC RG 12, Vol. 679 Register of Wrecks Atlantic & Pacific Coasts
768 The Province (Vancouver BC) Thursday May 20, 1954 page 8
769 Ken Lund reported (British Columbia Nautical History Facebook Group 18/08/2016)
770 The Province (Vancouver BC) Monday March 24, 1975 page 25
771 Transportation Safety Board of Canada (1993)

772 Vancouver Daily World (Vancouver BC) Wednesday December 31, 1902 page 5

773 Vancouver Sun (Vancouver BC) Thursday August 31, 1967 page 3

774 The Province (Vancouver BC) Thursday July 5, 1956 page 8

775 The Province (Vancouver BC) Saturday, February 26, 1916 page 20

776 Vancouver Daily World (Vancouver BC) Saturday, November 2, 1895 page 1

777 LAC RG12, A1, Vol 414 Shipping Registers Victoria BC

778 Vancouver Daily World (Vancouver BC) Saturday August 10, 1895 page 1

779 Transportation Safety Board of Canada (1993)

780 The Province (Vancouver BC) Monday December 8, 1958 page 23

781 The Chilliwack Progress (Chilliwack BC) Thursday September 26, 1935 Page 4

782 Vancouver Sun (Vancouver BC) Monday, December 29, 1930 page 14

783 The Province (Vancouver BC) Wednesday October 28, 1903 page 1

784 The Province (Vancouver BC) Monday, December 29, 1924 page 1

785 The Province (Vancouver BC) Friday October 19, 1951 page 23

786 Historic Shipwrecks of the Lower Mainland of British Columbia (2007) UASBC, Vancouver BC

787 The Province (Vancouver BC) Tuesday January 23, 1962 page 3

788 Times Colonist (Victoria BC) Monday June 27, 1977 page 43

789 The Province (Vancouver BC) Monday October 24, 1949 page 26

790 http://www.tsb.gc.ca/eng/rapports-reports/marine/1999/m99w0033/m99w0033.asp (website viewed 2016)

791 Vancouver Sun (Vancouver BC) Friday March 20, 1981 page 15

792 Transportation Safety Board of Canada (1993)

793 Times Colonist (Victoria BC) Friday December 8, 1950 page 2

794 The Province (Vancouver BC) Thursday, March 21, 1901 page 7

795 Vancouver Sun (Vancouver BC) Monday October 5, 1936 page 5

796 Vancouver Sun (Vancouver BC) Thursday June 18, 1964 page 6

797 http://www.tsb.gc.ca/eng/rapports-reports/marine/1996/m96w0025/m96w0025.asp (website viewed 08/12/2019)

798 Time Colonist (Victoria BC) Wednesday May 15, 1968 page 3

799 Miles, Fraser (1992)

800 Vancouver Sun (Vancouver BC) Tuesday October 13, 1936 page 1

801 Vancouver Sun (Vancouver BC) Friday September 7, 2001 page 2

802 Vancouver Sun (Vancouver BC) Monday October 6, 1958 page 25

www.ingramcontent.com/pod-product-compliance
Lightning Source LLC
Chambersburg PA
CBHW070523010526
44118CB00012B/1056